MW00445630

ASTD Handbook of Measuring and Evaluating Training

Patricia Pulliam Phillips, Editor

ASTD PRESS

Alexandria, VA

© 2010 the American Society for Training & Development

All rights reserved. Printed in the United States of America.

14   13   12   11   10   1   2   3   4   5   6   7   8

No part of this publication may be reproduced, distributed, or transmitted in any form or by any means, including photocopying, recording, or other electronic or mechanical methods, without the prior written permission of the publisher, except in the case of brief quotations embodied in critical reviews and certain other noncommercial uses permitted by copyright law. For permission requests, please go to www.copyright.com, or contact Copyright Clearance Center (CCC), 222 Rosewood Drive, Danvers, MA 01923 (telephone: 978.750.8400, fax: 978.646.8600).

ASTD Press is an internationally renowned source of insightful and practical information on workplace learning and performance topics, including training basics, evaluation and return-on-investment, instructional systems development, e-learning, leadership, and career development.

Ordering information: Books published by ASTD Press can be purchased by visiting ASTD's website at store.astd.org or by calling 800.628.2783 or 703.683.8100.

Library of Congress Control Number: 2009904468

ISBN-10: 1-56286-706-7
ISBN-13: 978-1-56286-706-5

ASTD Press Editorial Staff:

Director: Adam Chesler
Manager, ASTD Press: Jacqueline Edlund-Braun
Senior Associate Editor: Tora Estep
Senior Associate Editor: Justin Brusino
Editorial Assistant: Victoria DeVaux

Copyeditor: Phyllis Jask
Indexing and Proofreading: Abella Publishing Services, LLC
Interior Design and Production: Kathleen Schaner
Cover Design: Ana Ilieva Foreman

Printed by United Book Press, Inc., Baltimore, Maryland

❧ Contents

Foreword vii

Introduction... xi

Acknowledgments xxi

Section I: Evaluation Planning 1

1 Identifying Stakeholder Needs 3
    Lizette Zuniga

2 Developing Powerful Program Objectives............................... 15
    Heather M. Annulis and Cyndi H. Gaudet

3 Planning Your Evaluation Project 29
    Donald J. Ford

Section II: Data Collection 53

4 Using Surveys and Questionnaires.. 55
    Caroline Hubble

5 Designing a Criterion-Referenced Test.................................. 73
    Sharon A. Shrock and William C. Coscarelli

6 Conducting Interviews 85
    Anne F. Marrelli

7 Conducting Focus Groups 97
    Lisa Ann Edwards

8 Action Planning as a Performance Measurement and Transfer Strategy..... 107
    Holly Burkett

**9 The Success Case Method: Using Evaluation to Improve Training
    Value and Impact**... 125
    Robert O. Brinkerhoff and Timothy P. Mooney

10 Using Performance Records.. 135
    Ronald H. Manalu

Section III: Data Analysis **147**

11 Using Statistics in Evaluation 149
George R. Mussoline

12 Analyzing Qualitative Data 165
Keenan (Kenni) Crane

13 Isolating the Effects of the Program 173
Bruce C. Aaron

14 Converting Measures to Monetary Value 189
Patricia Pulliam Phillips

15 Identifying Program Costs 201
Judith F. Cardenas

16 Calculating the Return-on-Investment 213
Patricia Pulliam Phillips

17 Estimating the Future Value of Training Investments 223
Daniel McLinden

Section IV: Measurement and Evaluation at Work **237**

18 Reporting Evaluation Results 239
Tom Broslawsky

19 Giving CEOs the Data They Want 253
Jack J. Phillips

20 Using Evaluation Results 265
James D. Kirkpatrick and Wendy Kayser Kirkpatrick

21 Implementing and Sustaining a Measurement and Evaluation Practice 283
Debi Wallace

22 Selecting Technology to Support Evaluation 295
Kirk Smith

23 Evaluating mLearning 307
Cathy A. Stawarski and Robert Gadd

24 Evaluating Leadership Development 321
Emily Hoole and Jennifer Martineau

25 Evaluating a Global Sales Training Program 337
Frank C. Schirmer

26 Evaluating Technical Training 355
Toni Hodges DeTuncq

27 Evaluating Traditional Training versus Computer Simulation Training for Leader Development 373
Alice C. Stewart and Jacqueline A. Williams

Section V: Voices **385**

    Robert O. Brinkerhoff 387

    Mary L. Broad 392

    Jac Fitz-enz 396

    Roger Kaufman 400

    Donald L. Kirkpatrick 404

    Jack J. Phillips 409

    Dana Gaines Robinson 415

    William J. Rothwell 420

    Epilogue 427

    About the Editor of "Voices" 429

Appendix: Answers to Exercises 431

About the Editor 455

Index 457

❧ Foreword

The term *evaluation* invokes a variety of emotions in people. Some people fear the thought of being held accountable through an evaluation process; others see the prospect of evaluation as challenging and motivating. In either case, measurement and evaluation of training has a place among the critical issues in the learning and development field. It is a concept that is here to stay and a competency all learning professionals should pursue and embrace.

The Measurement and Evaluation Dilemma

The dilemma surrounding the evaluation of training is a source of frustration for many executives. Most executives realize that learning is an organizational necessity. Intuitively we know that providing learning opportunities is valuable to the organization and to employees, as individuals. However, the frustration sets in when there is a lack of evidence to show programs really work. Measurement and evaluation represent the most promising way to account for learning investments and to position learning as a catalyst for organization success. Yet, many organizations are still hesitant to pursue a comprehensive measurement strategy, primarily because they lack the answers to questions such as

- How can we move up the evaluation chain?
- How can we collect data efficiently?
- What data should we collect?
- How can we design a practical evaluation strategy that has credibility with all stakeholders?
- What tools, resources, and technologies are available to us?
- How do we ensure we select the right tools?
- How can we ensure we have the right support throughout the organization?
- How can we integrate data in the management scorecard?
- How do we use evaluation data?

Unanswered questions like these prohibit well-meaning learning professionals and their executives from creating a sound measurement strategy. Thus, they hold themselves back from the benefits of a growing trend in workplace learning.

Measurement and Evaluation Trends

One has only to look at the latest conference agenda to see that the evaluation trend continues. It is not a fad, but a growing topic of continued discussion and debate. Throughout the world, organizations are addressing the measurement and evaluation issue by

- increasing their investment in measurement and evaluation
- moving up the evaluation chain beyond the typical reaction and learning data
- increasing the focus of evaluation based on stakeholder needs
- making evaluation an integral part of the design, development, delivery, and implementation of programs rather than an add-on activity
- shifting from a reactive approach to evaluation to a proactive approach
- enhancing the measurement and evaluation process through the use of technology
- planning for evaluation at the outset of program development and design
- emphasizing the initial needs analysis process
- calculating the return-on-investment for costly, high-profile, and comprehensive programs
- using evaluation data to improve programs and processes.

As these tendencies continue, so do the opportunities for the learning function.

Opportunities for Learning and Development

Leaders of the learning function are challenged by the changing landscape of our industry. Our roles have evolved considerably in the last half-century. In the past, learning leaders were fundamentally charged with ensuring the acquisition of job-related skills; then the role expanded to include developmental efforts including leadership development, management development, and executive development. Today our role takes on broader and more strategic responsibilities.

As the role of learning leaders changes, so does the relationship of the learning and development function to the organization. This requires that learning leaders and fellow organization leaders together view and influence others to see learning and development not as an add-on activity, but as systemic—a critical, integral part of the organization. To be successful in this role, we must embrace the opportunities that measurement and evaluation offer, including

- tools to align programs with the business
- data collection methods that can be integrated into our programs
- data analysis procedures that ensure we tell our success stories in terms that resonate with all stakeholders including senior leaders
- information that can influence decisions being made about our function
- tools to help us show value for investments made in our programs
- information that can help us improve our programs, ensuring the right people are involved for the right reasons.

These along with many other opportunities await us if we are willing to do what it takes to develop the proficiency and the wherewithal to make training measurement and evaluation work.

Call to Action

As a leader of a learning and development function, I challenge all learning professionals and their leaders to take on measurement and evaluation with fervor. No other step in the human performance improvement process provides the mechanism by which we can influence programs and perceptions as does measurement and evaluation. We know that training, development, and performance improvement programs are a necessity to sustain and grow our organizations. But we also know that activity without results is futile. There is no other way to ensure our programs drive results than to apply the measurement and evaluation concepts presented in this publication and others available through organizations such as the American Society for Training & Development. Take on this challenge with baby steps if you must, giant leaps if you dare. But do it! Measuring and evaluating training can be fun and enlightening if we squelch the fears and embrace the opportunities.

Pat Crull, PhD
Vice president and chief learning officer, Time Warner Cable
Former chair, ASTD Board of Directors
May 2010

✎ Introduction to the *ASTD Handbook of Measuring and Evaluating Training*

Learning professionals around the world have a love-hate relationship with measurement and evaluation. On the one hand, they agree that good measurement and evaluation practices can provide useful data; on the other hand, they feel that measurement and evaluation take time and resources. However, no one argues that the need for across-the-board accountability is on the rise. This is especially true with training and development. With this demand comes the need for resources to support learning professionals in their quest to build capacity in measurement and evaluation. The *ASTD Handbook of Measuring and Evaluating Training* and complementary resources are an effort to support learning professionals in this quest.

Measurement and Evaluation: The Challenges and the Benefits

At the most fundamental level, evaluation includes all efforts to place value on events, things, processes, or people (Rossi, Freeman, and Lipsey, 1999). Data are collected and converted into information for measuring the effects of a program. The results help in decision making, program improvement, and in determining the quality of a program (Basarab and Root, 1992).

For decades experts in training evaluation have argued the need for measurement and evaluation. Many organizations have heeded this cry and have applied processes that include quantitative, qualitative, financial, and nonfinancial data. Training functions taking a proactive approach to measurement and evaluation have survived organizational and economic upheaval. Despite the call, however, many training managers and professionals ignore the need for accountability, only to find themselves wondering why the chief financial officer is now taking over training and development. So why is it that many training functions have failed to embrace this critical step in the human performance improvement process?

Measurement and Evaluation Challenges

Barriers to embracing measurement and evaluation can be boiled down to 12 basic challenges.

1. Too Many Theories and Models

Since Kirkpatrick provided his four levels of evaluation in the late 1950s, dozens of evaluation books have been written just for the training community. Add to this the dozens of evaluation books written primarily for the social sciences, education, and government organizations. Then add the 25-plus models and theories for evaluation offered to practitioners to help them measure the contribution of training, each claiming a unique approach and a promise to address evaluation woes and bring about world peace. It's no wonder there is confusion and hesitation when it comes to measurement and evaluation.

2. Models Are Too Complex

Evaluation can be a difficult issue. Because situations and organizations are different, implementing an evaluation process across multiple programs and organizations is complex. The challenge is to develop models that are theoretically sound, yet simple and usable.

3. Lack of Understanding of Evaluation

It hasn't always been easy for training professionals to learn this process. Some books on the topic have more than 600 pages, making it impossible for a practitioner to absorb just through reading. Not only is it essential for the evaluator to understand evaluation processes, but also the entire training staff must learn parts of the process and understand how it fits into their role. To remedy this situation, it is essential for the organization to focus on how expertise is developed and disseminated within the organization.

4. The Search for Statistical Precision

The use of complicated statistical models is confusing and difficult to absorb for many practitioners. Statistical precision is needed when high-stakes decisions are being made and when plenty of time and resources are available. Otherwise, very simple statistics are appropriate.

5. Evaluation Is Considered a Postprogram Activity

Because our instructional systems design models tend to position evaluation at the end, it loses the power to deliver the needed results. The most appropriate way to use evaluation is to consider it early—before program development—at the time of conception. With this simple shift in mindset, evaluations are conducted systematically rather than reactively.

6. Failure to See the Long-Term Payoff of Evaluation

Understanding the long-term payoff of evaluation requires examining multiple rationales for pursuing evaluation. Evaluation can be used to

- determine success in accomplishing program objectives
- prioritize training resources
- enhance training accountability
- identify the strengths and weaknesses of the training process
- compare the costs to the benefits of a training program
- decide who should participate in future training programs
- test the clarity and validity of tests, cases, and exercises
- identify which participants were the most successful in the training program
- reinforce major points made to the participant
- improve the training quality
- assist in marketing future programs
- determine if the program was the appropriate solution for the specific need
- establish a database that can assist management in making decisions.

7. Lack of Support from Key Stakeholders

Important stakeholders who need and use evaluation data sometimes don't provide the support needed to make the process successful. Specific steps must be taken to win support and secure buy-in from key groups, including senior executives and the management team. Executives must see that evaluation produces valuable data to improve programs and validate results. When the stakeholders understand what's involved, they may offer more support.

8. Evaluation Has Not Delivered the Data Senior Managers Want

Today, senior executives no longer accept reaction and learning data as the final say in program contribution. Senior executives need data on the application of new skills on the job and the corresponding impact in the business units. Sometimes they want return-on-investment (ROI) data for major programs. A recent study shows that the number one data point to senior executives responding to the survey (N=96) is impact data; the number two data point is ROI (Phillips and Phillips, 2010).

9. Improper Use of Evaluation Data

Improper use of evaluation data can lead to four major problems:

- Too many organizations do not use evaluation data at all. Data are collected, tabulated, catalogued, filed, and never used by any particular group other than the individual who initially collected the data.

- Data are not provided to the appropriate audiences. Analyzing the target audiences and determining the specific data needed for each group are important steps when communicating results.
- Data are not used to drive improvement. If not part of the feedback cycle, evaluation falls short of what it is intended to accomplish.
- Data are used for the wrong reasons—to take action against an individual or group or to withhold funds rather than improving processes. Sometimes the data are used in political ways to gain power or advantage over another person.

10. Lack of Consistency

For evaluation to add value and be accepted by different stakeholders, it must be consistent in its approach and methodology. Tools and templates need to be developed to support the method of choice to prevent perpetual reinvention of the wheel. Without this consistency, evaluation consumes too many resources and raises too many concerns about the quality and credibility of the process.

11. A Lack of Standards

Closely paralleled with consistency is the issue of standards. Standards are rules for making evaluation consistent, stable, and equitable. Without standards there is little credibility in processes and stability of outcomes.

12. Sustainability

A new model or approach with little theoretical grounding often has a short life. Evaluation must be theoretically sound and integrated into the organization so that it becomes routine and sustainable. To accomplish this, the evaluation process must gain respect of key stakeholders at the outset. Without sustainability, evaluation will be on a roller-coaster ride, where data are collected only when programs are in trouble and less attention is provided when they are not.

Despite these challenges, there are many benefits to implementing comprehensive measurement and evaluation practices.

Measurement and Evaluation Benefits

Organizations embracing measurement and evaluation take on the challenges and reap the benefits. When the training function uses evaluation to its fullest potential, the benefits grow exponentially. Some of the benefits of training measurement and evaluation include

- providing needed responses to senior executives
- justifying budgets

- improving program design
- identifying and improving dysfunctional processes
- enhancing the transfer of learning
- eliminating unnecessary or ineffective projects or programs
- expanding or implementing successful programs
- enhancing the respect and credibility of the training staff
- satisfying client needs
- increasing support from managers
- strengthening relationships with key executives and administrators
- setting priorities for training
- reinventing training
- altering management's perceptions of training
- achieving a monetary payoff for investing in training.

These key benefits, inherent with almost any type of impact evaluation process, make additional measurement and evaluation an attractive challenge for the training function.

Measurement and Evaluation Fundamentals

Regardless of the measurement and evaluation experts you follow, the process to evaluate a training program includes four fundamental steps. As shown in figure A, these steps are evaluation planning, data collection, data analysis, and reporting. When supported by systems, processes, and tools, a sustainable practice of accountability evolves. This is why a focus on strategic implementation is important.

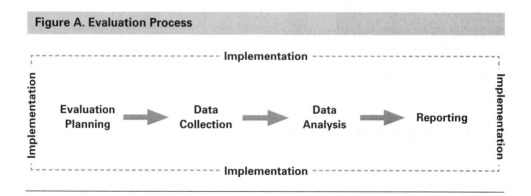

Figure A. Evaluation Process

Evaluation Planning

The first step in any process is planning. The old adage "plan your work, work your plan" has special meaning when it comes to comprehensive evaluation. Done well, an evaluation can come off without a hitch. Done poorly, and evaluators scramble to decide how to go about collecting and analyzing data.

Data Collection

Data collection comes in many forms. It is conducted at different times and involves various data sources. Technique, timing, and sources are selected based on type of data, time requirements, resource constraints, cultural constraints, and convenience. Sometimes surveys and questionnaires are the best technique. If the goal is to assess a specific level of knowledge acquisition, a criterion-referenced test is a good choice. Data gathered from many sources describing how and why a program was successful or not may require the development of case studies. Periodically, the best approach is to build data collection into the program itself through the use of action planning. The key to successful data collection is in knowing what techniques are available and how to use them when necessary.

Data Analysis

Through data analysis the success story unfolds. Depending on program objectives and the measures taken, data analysis can occur in many ways. Basic statistical procedures and content analysis can provide a good description of progress. Sometimes you need to make a clear connection between the program and the results. This requires that you isolate program effects through techniques such as control groups, trend line analysis, and other subjective techniques using estimates. Occasionally, stakeholders want to see the return-on-investment (ROI) in a program. This requires that measures be converted to monetary values and that the fully loaded costs be developed. Forecasting ROI prior to funding a program is an important issue for many organizations.

Reporting

The point of evaluation is to gather relevant information about a program and to report the information to the people who need to know. Without communication, measurement and evaluation are no more than activities. Reporting results may occur through detailed case studies, scorecards, or executive summaries. But to make the results meaningful, action must be taken.

Implementation

Program evaluation is an important part of the training process. But the evaluations themselves are outputs of the processes you use. To make evaluation work and to ensure a sustainable practice, the right information must be developed and put to good use. This requires that the right technologies be put into place at the outset, that a strategy be developed and deployed, and that programs of all types are evaluated in such a way that meaningful, useful information evolves.

The *ASTD Handbook of Measuring and Evaluating Training*

The purpose of this book is to provide learning professionals a tool to which they can refer as they move forward with measurement and evaluation. Each step in the training evaluation process is addressed by experts from corporations, nonprofits, government entities, and academic institutions, as well as those experts who work with a broad range of organizations. Readers will have the opportunity to learn, reflect upon, and practice using key concepts. The handbook will assist readers as they

- plan an evaluation project, beginning with the identification of stakeholder needs
- identify appropriate data collection methods, given the type of data, resources, constraints, and conveniences
- analyze data using basic statistical and qualitative analysis
- communicate results given the audience and their data needs
- use data to improve programs and processes, ensuring the right data are available at the right time.

Scope

This handbook covers various aspects of training measurement and evaluation. Intended to provide readers a broad look at these aspects, the book does not focus on any one particular methodology. Rather, each chapter represents an element of the four steps and implementation of evaluation as described above. The book includes five parts.

Section I, Evaluation Planning, looks at the three steps important to planning an evaluation project. Beginning with identifying stakeholder needs, developing program objectives, then planning the evaluation project, an evaluator is likely to have a successful project implementation.

Section II, Data Collection, covers various ways in which evaluation data can be collected. Although the chapter leads with surveys and questionnaires, other techniques are described. Techniques include using criterion-referenced tests, interviews, focus groups, and action plans. In addition, the Success Case Method is described, as is using performance records in collecting data.

Section III, Data Analysis, looks at key areas involved in analyzing data, including the use of statistics and qualitative methods. Other topics include how to isolate the effects of a program from other influences, convert data to monetary value, and identify program costs to ensure fully loaded costs are considered when assuming the training investment. In addition, a chapter has been included on calculating ROI, an important element given today's need to understand value before investing in a program.

Section IV, Measurement and Evaluation at Work, describes key issues in ensuring a successful, sustainable evaluation implementation. This part begins with estimating the future value of training investment and reporting and communicating results. All too often data are collected and analyzed, only to sit idle. Then the issue of giving CEOs the data they really want is covered as the industry still often misses the mark when it comes to providing data important to the CEO. Of course, even if the data are the right data, if they are not put to use, they serve no real purpose in improving programs. With this issue in mind we've included a chapter on using evaluation data. To ensure a long-term approach to evaluation is integrated in the training function, a strategy for success is a must. In addition, the right technology must be selected to support this strategy. Chapters on implementing and sustaining a measurement practice and selecting technology are included in this section. Section IV wraps up with four case studies describing the evaluation of different types of programs.

Section V, Voices, is a summary of interviews with the experts in training measurement and evaluation. Rebecca Ray spent time with each expert, asking them their views of the status of training measurement and evaluation. This summary section provides readers a flavor of those interviews, which are available as podcasts at www.astd.org/HandbookofMeasuringandEvaluatingTraining.

Contributors

Contributors were selected based on their expertise in each area. Expertise, in this case, is not defined by how many books one has written or how well known one is in the industry. Rather, expertise is defined by what these contributors are actually doing with training evaluation. Readers will hear from external consultants who touch a wide variety of organizations, internal consultants who focus on training evaluation within a single organization, individuals who have experience as both an internal and external experts, and professors who hone and share their expertise through research. Our contributors work in organizations across the United States, Germany, Indonesia, and Dubai, giving the book an international context.

Target Audience

Four groups serve as the target audience for this book. First and foremost, this publication is a tool that all training professionals need to round out their resource library. Managers of training professionals are another target audience. This resource will support them as they support evaluation within their function. Professors who teach training evaluation will find this publication a good resource to address all elements of the evaluation process. The exercises and references will help professors as they develop coursework, challenge their students' thinking, and assign application projects. Finally, students of training evaluation will find this publication valuable as they set off to learn more about evaluation and how it drives excellence in program implementation.

How to Get the Most from the Book

The book is designed to provide a learning experience as well as information. Each chapter begins with key learning objectives. Throughout the text authors have included references to real-life applications, practitioner tips from individuals applying the concepts, additional resources and references, and knowledge checks to assess the reader's understanding of the chapter content. Some knowledge checks have specific correct answers that can be found in the appendix; others offer an opportunity for the reader to reflect and discuss with their colleagues. To get the most out of the book readers should

1. review the table of contents to see what areas are of most interest
2. read the objectives of the chapter of interest and upon completion of the chapter, work through the knowledge check
3. follow up on prescribed action steps, references, and resources presented in the chapter
4. participate in the ASTD Evaluation & ROI blog (www1.astd.org/Blog/category/Evaluation-and-ROI.aspx), where additional content is presented and discussed among your colleagues.

We hope you find the *ASTD Handbook of Measuring and Evaluating Training* a useful resource full of relevant and timely content. Over time we will add to this content through our Evaluation & ROI blog, the Measuring and Evaluating Training website, and other channels of delivery. As you read the content and have suggestions for additional information, workshops in content areas, and supporting material, please let us know. You can reach me at patti@roiinstitute.net, and I will work with ASTD to ensure learning professionals get the information they need for successful training measurement and evaluation.

References

Basarab, D. J. and D. K. Root. (1992). *The Training Evaluation Process*. Boston: Kluwer Academic Publications.

Phillips, J. J. and P. P. Phillips. (2010). *Measuring for Success. What CEOs Really Think About Learning Investments*. Alexandria: ASTD.

Rossi, P. H., H. E. Freeman, and M. W. Lipsey. (1999). *Evaluation: A Systematic Approach* 6th ed. Thousand Oaks, CA: Sage.

✌ Acknowledgments

No work is solely the result of individual effort. A team of motivated people, excited about the topic of measurement and evaluation, created this publication.

Many thanks go first to Cat Russo who had the original idea and asked for my involvement. I was thrilled to be a part of such a project. Of course Tora Estep, Jacqueline Edlund-Braun, Dean Smith, and the rest of the ASTD publishing team were more than instrumental in making this happen. Their guidance and support are the foundation for this much-needed publication and the supporting elements that will make this product useful to learning professionals for years to come.

To say thank you isn't enough for the willingness of Rebecca Ray to develop the podcast series, *Voices*. Rebecca's enthusiasm for the project was contagious. Her willingness to interview world-renowned experts and develop the summaries found in the book is representative of the fervor with which Rebecca tackles a project. Her idea to "tweet" about the interviews and continue supporting the book for perpetuity goes well beyond the call of duty—and is much appreciated!

Speaking of *Voices*, many thanks go to the world-renowned experts. These people cleared the path for the rest of us interested in showing the value of training and development. They took time out of their busy schedules to participate. To have Don Kirkpatrick, Jack Phillips, Robert Brinkerhoff, Dana Robinson, Jac Fitz-enz, Bill Rothwell, Mary Broad, and Roger Kaufman share their views on the past, present, and future states of measurement and evaluation is a prize for us all.

Of course, there would be no book without the contributors. What a group of professionals! Every one of them was immediately willing to take a part in this project. I have known many of the contributors for a period of time and am familiar with their work in measurement and evaluation. Others, I only met during this project, and I am grateful for the opportunity to have done so. The good work going on in training measurement and evaluation is worldwide. Saying thank you is not enough for what each person contributed not only to this book, but for what they contribute to our profession.

Acknowledgments

To the staff at the ROI Institute: Thank you. Without you very little would be accomplished. Special thanks go to our in-house editors, Alison Frenzel and Beth Phillips. Their tireless support is unprecedented.

Finally—my most heartfelt thanks go to Jack. Yes, you are a leader in the industry, you have written a lot of books, you're considered a guru in many circles, and you're world renowned. You are also the inspiration that drove me to embrace training measurement and evaluation. But more than any of that, you are the person who challenges and encourages me, brings me coffee every morning, and keeps me laughing. Thank you!

Patricia Pulliam Phillips
April 2010

✍ Section I

Evaluation Planning

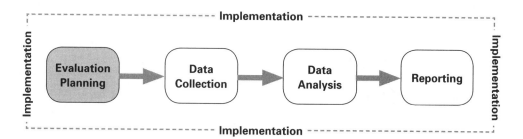

It is a well-established fact that planning evaluation up front yields superior results. For one thing, evaluators know which measures they need to look at to identify whether a program has actually made a difference. Evaluations are thus systemic, rather than reactive.

And yet, most instructional design models typically place the emphasis on evaluation at the end of the model. Take for example ADDIE: assess, design, develop, implement, and *evaluate*. Note that the model indicates that evaluation occurs after the program has been implemented.

Successful measurement and evaluation processes begin when stakeholder needs are identified and can inform the overall program design by identifying measures that are important to the organization. Asking the following questions clarifies expectations about business impact, job performance, knowledge acquisition, and the preferred approach to delivering content:

- ▪ What is the opportunity for the organization?
- ▪ Is the opportunity worth pursuing?
- ▪ What are the specific business measures that need to improve so that we are successful with this opportunity?

- What is or is not happening on the job (or in a system) that if changed would contribute to the improvement in the business measures?
- What do people need to know to improve the business measures?
- How best can the knowledge, skill, or information be delivered?

When the needs and expectations for a program or process are defined, developing specific, measurable objectives that will achieve these expectations becomes easier and increases the likelihood of program success. In addition, program objectives set the stage for evaluation, by leading evaluators toward the key questions they will ask during the evaluation, the timing at which the data will be collected, and the criteria for success.

With defined expectations and objectives in hand, the next step in the evaluation process is to plan the evaluation project. The more detailed the planning, the easier the execution.

In Section I, Evaluation Planning, you will learn to

- identify stakeholder needs
- develop powerful objectives
- plan the evaluation project.

Chapter 1

Identifying Stakeholder Needs

Lizette Zuniga

In This Chapter

This chapter explores critical factors and methods to conduct needs assessment. Upon reading this chapter, you will be able to

- explain the importance of conducting a needs assessment
- identify the four steps of the needs assessment process
- identify four methods to conduct a needs assessment.

The Importance of Conducting a Needs Assessment

Measurement and evaluation begin with conducting a needs assessment. If the needs important to all stakeholders are not clarified in the beginning, then measures taken during the evaluation are based on guesswork. Although needs assessments are often used to help the learning and development department plan and budget for the training calendar, they are also critical to addressing isolated issues. Needs, opportunities, and deficiencies are identified on an organizational level, as well as at a job task level. The key is to ensure that needs important to all stakeholders are addressed so that when a program rolls out, it does so with results in mind. Regardless of the scope of the needs assessment, a variety of issues should be considered if training programs are to be successful.

The Order Taker Versus the Consultant

The traditional approach to conducting needs assessment has been to merely fulfill the customer's order. Similar to going through a fast-food drive-through, the order taker simply notes the customer's request and then passes it on for fulfillment. There may be an additional question or two such as "do you want fries with that?"; however, questioning is kept to a minimum.

In the context of learning, the client may request specific training. For example, a customer requests leadership development for all of middle management. The order taker may already know what's available on the market or may research the available leadership development programs targeting middle management. Senior management chooses and launches a program. What kind of data points can be reported on a process such as this? More than likely, utilization numbers may be reported, such as how many managers have completed the program, cost of program per manager, or number of training hours. In addition, satisfaction or reaction data (Level 1) may also be reported, such as the percentage of managers who found the program to be useful on the job. Maybe this is a program that even has built-in learning measures, such as the percentage of managers who used effective communication skills in a role-play exercise during class.

But a problem arises when a learning group wants to report outcomes on job performance and business levels (Levels 3 and 4). To determine whether the program addressed performance deficiencies or affected business measures, a guessing game ensues in the absence of proper needs assessment. This is one of the key differences between the traditional order taker and the consultant. The consultant acts as a guide for the customer in understanding thoroughly the situation at hand. The consultant carefully listens for the stated as well as the sometimes unstated. The consultant asks key questions to help identify the solution(s) needed, including

- What is the reason for requesting leadership development?
- What is or is not happening on the job with middle managers?
- What are the middle managers not doing on the job that they should be doing?
- How is their performance affecting the business?
- What data sources are available for further analysis and review?

Table 1-1 lists several key questions to ask when conducting a needs assessment.

Needs assessment is an important step because the goal for training is for it to "stick." Without understanding the needs, it's hit or miss whether the intervention was the correct one. See figure 1-1 for an illustration of the importance of needs assessment.

Table 1-1. Key Questions to Ask About the Proposed Program

- Why is this an issue?
- Are there multiple solutions?
- Who will support the program?
- What happens if we do nothing?
- Who will not support the program?
- How much will the solution cost?
- Are there important intangible benefits?
- Is a forecast needed?
- How can we fund the program?
- Is there a potential payoff?
- Is this issue critical?
- Is this issue linked to strategy?
- Is it possible to correct it?
- Is it feasible to improve it?
- How much is the problem costing us?
- Can we find a solution?

Figure 1-1. Case Application: Customer Service Representatives

In one organization, the operational manager noted that customer satisfaction scores had decreased by 10 percent and decided to implement a customer service refresher course for the customer service representatives. After the launch, the operational manager noticed no difference in the customer satisfaction scores. Without conducting a proper needs assessment, it was nearly impossible to determine what intervention was needed to affect the customer satisfaction scores favorably. A needs assessment would have helped to determine what was causing the decrease in customer satisfaction and thus identify the correct intervention.

In this same case, after the customer service refresher training failed, the operations manager conducted a needs assessment and analyzed operational data. The operations manager partnered with the learning department and conducted phone interviews with a random sample of the customer base. By collecting and analyzing these sets of data, they discovered that the average call handle time had increased and customers reported that they were passed around. In fact, a single representative seldom handled a customer call to completion. The learning department also conducted focus groups with the call center representatives and found two problems. First, customer service representatives were not well informed about new product releases and were therefore unable to thoroughly answer customers' questions. Second, the technology that was supposed to help them perform their jobs was, instead, a hindrance. To navigate pages and find customer-specific data while handling phone calls became a source of frustration because the web pages were slow to load.

Gap Analysis

Gap analysis is a tool used to answer two primary questions: Where are we? Where do we want to be? In the formal use of gap analysis, a variance is established between current capabilities and business requirements. Often, in business settings, market research or historical performance data are used to determine the desired benchmark within a given industry. Once this is determined, then a company can determine the gap between actual or current performance and the industry benchmark or desired performance. In non-business settings, a similar process occurs. Current performance or baseline data on specific measures are determined; then desired performance is determined based on benchmarking data, stakeholder needs, or other means. The difference between the desired and the current performance is the gap or the target for performance improvement. Figure 1-2 depicts the relationship between desired performance, current performance, and the gap in performance.

Four Steps to Needs Assessment

Following are four broad steps to conducting needs assessment:

1. Define the business requirement.
2. Understand the current state.
3. Determine the gap between current state and business requirement.
4. Identify needed solution or intervention to close the gap.

Step 1: Define the Business Requirement

Step 1 identifies the desired or required standards for optimal organizational success. This analysis focuses on industry standards or strategic initiatives that outline organizational goals or performance standards. Sometimes, this type of analysis includes key performance indicators, as well as the skills, knowledge, and abilities needed to accomplish these successfully. Competencies may also be used to establish levels of abilities needed in a given job. It is important to identify the goals or standards and not just observe current practices.

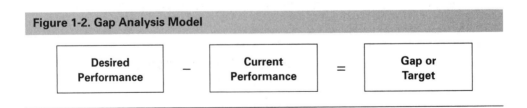

Figure 1-2. Gap Analysis Model

| Desired Performance | − | Current Performance | = | Gap or Target |

Step 2: Understand the Current State

This step identifies the current level of performance and the existent issues or problems. It is absolutely critical to determine the underlying causes for not achieving the level of business requirement. In this step, the cost of the problem is also calculated or estimated. This will guide the decision-making process for determining whether the cost of the problem is more or less than the cost of the solution.

✦ **Practitioner Tip** ✦

When conducting needs analysis, it is imperative to remain objective. Avoid the urge to jump to conclusions prematurely or to make assumptions about what the real issues or solutions are. Maintain a neutral disposition, and let the data speak for themselves.

The Cost of a Problem

Problems often are expensive, and resolution can have a tremendous impact. To determine the cost of a problem, its consequences must be analyzed and converted to monetary values. Table 1-2 shows a list of potential problems. Some can easily be converted to money, whereas others are more challenging to convert. Those that cannot be converted within given project constraints are left as intangibles. Time can easily be converted into money by calculating the fully loaded cost of the individual's time performing unproductive tasks. Errors, wastes, and delays can also be calculated based on the monetary effect of such problems. Measures such as customer satisfaction, employee engagement, and teamwork are often more challenging to convert to money, but can be if resources are available.

Step 3: Determine the Gap between Current State and Business Requirement

This step pinpoints the specific difference between step one and two. If the industry average for call center absenteeism is 5.4 percent and the current state is 12.3 percent, the gap is defined as the difference between these two points, or 6.9 percent. This now becomes the target for performance.

Step 4: Identify Needed Solution or Intervention to Close the Gap

Once the business requirements are identified and the current level of performance is thoroughly understood, including the causes for the deficiencies that resulted in a specific gap, a solution can now be identified. When the preceding steps are followed, step four

Table 1-2. Potentially Costly Problems

- inventory shortages
- excessive employee turnover
- errors/mistakes
- employee withdrawal
- waste
- accidents
- delays
- excessive staffing
- bottlenecks
- employee dissatisfaction
- productivity problems
- customer dissatisfaction
- inefficiencies
- excessive conflicts
- excessive direct costs
- equipment damage
- equipment underusage
- excessive stress
- excessive program time

generally follows with much greater ease, eliminating guesswork because it is focused, on-the-mark, and a practice of good stewardship.

Sometimes this process will result in more than one solution and may require seeking help from more than one department. Although human resources or learning groups may be the ones to uncover what is needed to close the gap, the solution may require assistance from information technology or operations.

Figure 1-3 explains the outcome of these four steps when applied in a case study.

To Train or Not to Train...That Is the Question

Sometimes organizations get into the trap of applying training to most or all problems. Although a noble effort to address gaps, this eventually leads to problems going unaddressed and training becoming undervalued. The purpose of training—to improve

Figure 1-3. Case Application: Leadership Development

A large financial company discovered a substantial increase in turnover among its frontline employees. To understand the causes of turnover, management examined several data sources, including exit interview data, departmental turnover analysis, and an employee satisfaction survey. They also created a customized questionnaire targeting frontline employees. Management applied the four steps of needs assessment and concluded the following:

1. The average turnover rate for the financial industry is 13.3 percent.
2. Several data points describe the current state:
    - The current turnover rate* for this company's frontline employees is 32.4 percent.
    - The cost of current turnover (annualized) is $323,500, based on internally established turnover calculations.
    - The causes of turnover were identified as 77 percent communication problems between manager and employee, 11 percent better opportunity elsewhere, 8 percent lack of recognition, and 4 percent other.
3. The gap is 9.1 percent.
4. The solution applied was a leadership development program with an emphasis on leadership communication and rewards/recognition.

The four steps described above helped identify the need and prescribe a solution that directly addressed the problem.

*Source: *Workforce Management* (2007).

skills, knowledge, and/or attitudes that affect performance on the job—needs to be clearly understood to answer this question. Performance deficiencies that will not be changed as a result of training should be further analyzed to determine the correct solution(s). Solutions can be grouped in three broad categories: people, process, and technology. Training interfaces with all three of these groupings. Questions in the different categories, outlined in table 1-3, will help guide the process of understanding the needed solution.

Training Affects People, Process, and Technology

Below are some examples of people, process, and technology indicators that may require training:

- new employee
- new job role
- performance deficiencies
- safety issues
- new technology or upgrades
- strategic initiatives
- job prospect/career development

Table 1-3. People, Process, and Technology

People	Process	Technology
Do the employees have the talent, competence, and/or skills to support optimal organizational performance?	Do the business processes facilitate optimal organizational performance?	Do the tools and technology improve organizational performance?

- new or improved business process
- new product
- new or changed policy or procedure.

Methods of Conducting Needs Assessment

An important step in conducting needs assessment is determining the method of collecting data. Four methods are useful in collecting needs assessment data—questionnaires, interviews, focus groups, and competency skill assessments—each with its own benefits and pitfalls. These methods for collecting needs assessment have proven to be very useful.

Regardless of the method, defining the overall purpose for the needs assessment is imperative. For example, if company X is implementing a strategic plan and has identified a strategic initiative to build business acumen among middle management, then the needs assessment should examine the current business acumen of the middle management group, as well as determine the desired level of business acumen. What are the specific domains of deficiency for this group? What is not happening on the job and in business as a result of business acumen deficiency? In this case, once the purpose has been defined, questions can be designed that correlate with the purpose.

Questionnaire

Questionnaires are often used in needs assessment, enabling the person gathering the data to collect from a large, representative sample of the population and also provide consistency in amassing the data. Generally, questionnaires are easy to analyze, particularly with the available Internet survey websites or survey software that automates the analysis process. It is important to design easy-to-read questionnaires that are well organized and quick to complete. Table 1-4 presents some benefits and pitfalls of questionnaires.

Interviews

Conducting structured interviews is a common method of needs assessment. It allows a skilled interviewer to collect data on a planned set of questions in the respondents' own

Table 1-4. Benefits and Pitfalls of Questionnaires

Benefits	Pitfalls
Generally questionnaires require less time from the respondent.	Variables may affect response rates, but sometimes people do not want to respond to electronic or written questionnaires.
Questionnaires collect information from a large group of people.	Spend time determining the purpose of the questionnaire to avoid collecting data that are not useful. Without understanding how the data will be used, questionnaires become fragmented and useless.
Determining statistically significant results from quantitative data helps decision making be more accurate.	Ensure that someone with the know-how conducts survey design, implementation, and analysis. Without this, data may not be useful.

words. Generally, open-ended questions are used, and, sometimes, the interviewer probes further to understand key insights of the business needs. Interviews may be particularly helpful in understanding performance needs. Table 1-5 presents the benefits and pitfalls of using interviews.

Table 1-5. Benefits and Pitfalls of Interviews

Benefits	Pitfalls
The interviewer collects qualitative information from individuals who are informed on the topic.	There is no anonymity, which may be an issue in the workplace.
Interviewers can probe deeper to further understand issues, allowing interviewees to expand on their answers.	Interviews generally require more time and expense.
Interviewees can say what they want to say in their own words and are not forced to choose from available options.	Interviewees may not represent the larger group.
The face-to-face interview allows for the full gamut of communication: nonverbal aspects, tone of voice, and body language.	Interviewers may be biased and may present questions and analyze results in a skewed manner.
Interviews often provide a richer data set.	Interviewees may be reticent to disclose work-related information due to the sensitivity of the data.

Focus Groups

Focus groups can be an excellent way to delve deeper into needs assessment. They are similar to interviews in that an interviewer or facilitator is present and questions are prepared, but different in that the focus group is usually conducted with eight to12 individuals at the same time. Focus groups also have the added benefit of probing deeper, depending upon the responses of the participants. Table 1-6 presents benefits and pitfalls of focus groups.

Competency Skill Assessment

This type of assessment focuses on the skills, knowledge, and attitudes required for a given job that contribute to organizational success. Skill gaps can be quickly ascertained given a competency model that outlines levels of competency within each competency area. Often, competency skill assessments are distributed in a multirater or 360° fashion, collecting perspectives from the individual, his or her immediate manager, and sometimes even direct reports and colleagues. Some competency assessments are self-reports, allowing an individual to rate his or her own proficiency levels for each of the competencies within his or her job. Table 1-7 presents the benefits and pitfalls of competency skill asessments.

Determining the Right Method

When determining the best method for conducting a needs assessment, consider the following questions:

- How have the needs been assessed in the past and to what degree were these methods effective?
- What is the budget for needs assessment?

Table 1-6. Benefits and Pitfalls of Focus Groups

Benefits	Pitfalls
The facilitator can interview 8–12 individuals at the same time.	Avoid the "group think" mentality, where individual expression is minimized in effort to reach consensus.
The interviewer can probe deeper and go beyond the planned questions depending upon the answer.	The group may not be representative of the entire population.
Focus groups have the added benefit of the possibility of one individual's answer triggering thoughts or memories in another.	Sensitive topics may be difficult to discuss in a workplace setting, especially with an internal facilitator.
Group answers can provide further insights into key problem areas.	It is very important for the facilitator to be skilled to avoid detours.

Table 1-7. Benefits and Pitfalls of Competency Skill Assessments

Benefits	Pitfalls
It can be hosted via Internet/intranet, thereby automating data analysis.	Questions may focus on specific competencies, not on collecting data about other issues affecting work.
Specific areas are flagged for further development on an individual basis.	Competency skills assessment measures ability rather than performance.
It groups development areas together to understand group or departmental gaps.	Disagreement may surface about level of competence between respondents who fill out an assessment of the same person.
By using 360° evaluation, data are collected from more than one source.	To protect the anonymity of the direct reports, a minimum of 3–5 direct reports should participate.

- How much time do the respondents have for needs assessment?
- What is the deadline for completing the needs assessment?
- What is the preferred mode of communication for the respondents?
- What is the nature of data collected? Are the data sensitive in nature?

Summary

Needs assessment is a critical step in determining the learning and performance deficiencies that affect a business. By clarifying needs, a program can be better positioned for results important to all stakeholders. Those who conduct needs assessment serve their clients by acting in a consultant capacity, avoiding the order taker role. Needs assessment can be achieved by understanding the business requirements, identifying the current state, quantifying the gap, and selecting the needed solution(s). By carefully selecting the appropriate method, needs assessment can be performed in a way that is nonintrusive and yet thorough. All of this, of course, is with the end result in mind: to implement solutions that will yield favorable returns for the organization.

Discussion Questions: Conducting Needs Assessment

Now that you have read this chapter, respond to the following discussion questions.

1. Why is it important to conduct needs assessment?
2. Describe the four steps in needs assessment.

3. Think of a current project on which you are working. Describe how you can apply these four steps to your project.
4. Given the same project, which method(s) will you use to collect data? Why?

Knowledge Check: Needs Assessment for Customer Service Representatives

Referring back to the case presented in figure 1-1, respond to the following questions. Check your answers in the appendix.

1. State in your own words the importance of conducting needs assessment as it applies to this case. What are the consequences of not conducting a needs assessment?
2. What solutions would you recommend?
3. What outcomes would you report after the solutions were implemented?

About the Author

Lizette Zuniga, PhD, is a consulting associate with the ROI Institute. With more than 15 years' professional experience, Zuniga has expertise in strategic planning, leadership, and team development; program evaluation; ROI; survey design; and needs assessment. She facilitates certification courses on behalf of ASTD in Measuring and Evaluating Learning and ROI. Zuniga has conducted various impact studies and holds an MS in psychology, with a concentration in cross-cultural psychology and psychometry from Georgia State University, and a PhD in leadership and human resource development from Barry University. She is certified in ROI evaluation and Myers-Briggs inventory. She co-authored *Costs and ROI: Evaluating at the Ultimate Level* (2008) with Jack Phillips and also published several articles and case studies in books on management development, ROI, and organizational culture. Her email address is zunigalizette@gmail.com.

References

Brown, J. (Winter 2002). "Training Needs Assessment: A Must for Developing an Effective Training Program." *Public Personnel Management* 31(4): 569–78.

Morgan, J. M. and J. K. Liker. (2006). *The Toyota Product Development System.* New York: Productivity Press.

Phillips, J. J. and E. F. Holton. (1995). *In Action: Conducting Needs Assessment.* Alexandria, VA: ASTD.

Phillips, J. J. and P. P. Phillips. (2008). *Beyond Learning Objectives: Developing Measurable Objectives That Link to the Bottom Line.* Alexandria, VA: ASTD Press.

Workforce Management. (2007). *2007 Voluntary Turnover Rates by Industry,* available at http://compforce.typepad.com/compensation_force/2008/02/2007-turnover-r.html.

Chapter 2

Developing Powerful Program Objectives

Heather M. Annulis and Cyndi H. Gaudet

··· **In This Chapter** ···

This chapter explores the levels of objectives essential to designing and measuring programs that make a difference in organizations. Upon reading this chapter, you will be able to

- describe reasons to link objectives to organizational needs and priorities
- identify levels of objectives
- write a powerful objective.

The Importance of Developing Powerful Objectives

Powerful objectives drive powerful results. Linking program objectives to organizational objectives allows top-level executives to recognize the value of learning initiatives to the bottom line of the organization. Asking three simple questions will create a roadmap to powerful program outcomes that link to the organization's bottom line.

- What will the training accomplish for the organization?
- What will the training accomplish for the participants?
- How will the accomplishments be measured?

The Meaning and Value of Objectives

Objectives provide direction, focus, and guidance as well as create interest, commitment, expectations, and satisfaction. An objective is a statement describing an intended outcome rather than a "how to" statement. It describes the intent of the program and allows the reader to visualize final results. Objectives are linked to organizational needs and should reflect measures of value important to all stakeholders. These statements help determine if programs are tightly linked to the business and if the work is relevant to the business. If it's not measured, is it a necessary activity? Objectives help determine if efforts are exerted in the correct places. They are "necessity not luxury" (Phillips and Phillips, 2008).

Objectives drive everything that happens in a program, including teaching strategies, assignments, and assessments. Therefore, it's hard to believe that many programs are delivered without formal statements. The effort to formalize objectives at the onset of the program design and communicate them to participants enhances the ability to plan the course and the participants' ability to achieve program goals. These statements are essential in communicating to participants and stakeholders expectations before, during, and after the program. Objectives clearly define the purpose and expected outcome of the program and drive an organization's results.

Levels of Objectives

It is helpful to link objectives to evaluation strategies. This linkage provides a systematic, results-based process. Six levels of objectives position programs for success from multiple stakeholder perspectives. Some stakeholders will only be interested in data collected at the higher levels; however, the levels create a chain of impact. Table 2-1 describes the six levels of objectives. Level 0 describes inputs and indicators. Level 1 focuses on reaction and planned action of the program participants. Level 2 assesses the participants' learning during the program. Level 3 determines if the participants can use the information learned during the program. Level 4 captures how the participants' use of the information affects the business. Finally, Level 5 compares the cost to the benefits of the program. This data categorization is the foundation for developing powerful program objectives. The levels of objectives take the learning leader from needs assessment to final stages of evaluation, thereby establishing the chain of impact of performance improvement programs.

Constructing Powerful Objectives

Objectives should have SMART characteristics: They should be specific, measurable, achievable, realistic, and time bound. SMART characteristics ensure powerful objectives are set. Table 2-2 details the characteristics of SMART objectives.

Table 2-1. Levels of Objectives

Level of Objective	Measurement Focus	Typical Measures
0—Inputs and Indicators	Scope, volume, efficiencies, and costs of the project	• Participants • Hours • Costs • Timing
1—Reaction and Perceived Value	Reaction to the project or program, including the perceived value	• Relevance • Importance • Usefulness • Appropriateness • Intent to use motivation to take action
2—Learning and Confidence	Learning to use the content and materials, including the confidence to use what was learned	• Skills • Knowledge • Capacity • Competencies • Confidence • Contacts
3—Application and Implementation	Using content and materials in the work environment, including progress with actual items and implementation	• Extent of use • Task completion • Frequency of use • Actions completed • Success with use • Barriers to use • Enablers to use
4—Impact and Consequences	The consequences of using the content and materials expressed as business impact measures	• Productivity • Revenue • Quality • Time • Efficiency • Customer satisfaction • Employee engagement
5—ROI	Comparing monetary benefits from program to program costs	• Benefit-Cost Ratio (BCR) • ROI (%) • Payback period

Source: Phillips and Phillips (2008).

Table 2-2. Characteristics of SMART Objectives

	Description
Specific	Objectives must represent the specific desired outcomes from the standpoint of all critical stakeholders.
Measurable	Objectives must be developed so that measures of success are evident. Measurable indicators make it possible to assess whether the objectives are achieved or not. Program owners must be able to measure the objective, considering the type of measure and resource constraints.
Achievable	Objectives must stretch participants, designers, and developers toward improvement but remain reasonable in doing so.
Realistic	Objectives must be realistic given the conditions, resources, time period, and support available to achieve the objectives.
Time bound	Objectives must represent the achievement of results within a certain period.

Note: For variations of SMART objectives, visit http://rapidbicom/created/WriteSMARTobjectives.html.

✎ Practitioner Tip ✐

Effectively written learning objectives are one of the greatest success tools for achieving my exact learning, change, or performance initiatives. They provide a critical direction and essential structure that grounds the whole learning experience. I am convinced that with clear objectives, I will reach my desired outcome.

Sandra Dugas
Author, *The Savvy Manager*

Objectives should be specific, not vague. They should be measurable so that success is immediately evident. They should also be achievable while remaining challenging. Always set objectives higher than achieved previously, but not so high that they can never be achieved. For instance, a 99-percent uptime is more achievable than 100 percent. The closer to a near perfect score, the more difficult it becomes. Objectives should be realistic. Conditions and resources must support the opportunity to achieve the objectives. Finally, objectives must be time bound. In the example, "achieve annual sales figure of 30,000 machines," the "annual" criteria makes it time bound. Otherwise, the team would not have a deadline for achieving the target.

To construct powerful objectives, three Cs should be included: conduct, condition, and criterion.

Conduct. Conduct is also known as performance or behavior of the participant and is the most observable part of the learning objective. If the learning leader can observe the conduct, then it can be measured. Once the designer determines which objective should be included, then he or she can determine which verb best describes the behavior.

Condition. Conditions ensure that learners understand what is expected of them. For example, managers may be tasked with creating department purpose statements. A condition could include incorporating the companies' core competencies from the mission statement. This level of specificity communicates not just what to do but also identifies the requirements associated with the expectation.

Criterion. Criterion states *how well* the participant should perform. Criterion is the measure of success. Accuracy, speed, and quality are associated with criterion of learning objectives. These variables suggest the importance of how well a task is completed. The explanation expressed in the criterion helps the learning leader better assess the conduct of the participant. Accuracy communicates how close to perfect one must complete the task. For example, the participant must connect the life support tubes using the checklist 100 percent of the time. Failure to meet the accuracy clause could result in death. Sometimes the speed with which a task is completed is critical to the situation. For example, the participant must connect the life support tubes in less than one minute. In this example, the speed with which the objective is completed could save the life of the patient. When speed and accuracy are not critical, quality emerges as an essential measurement. Quality suggests that a standard is expected from the learner. For example, the learner will hook up the life support unit in less than one minute with system-ready displays.

Levels of Objectives

As presented in table 2-1, there are six levels of objectives. These levels follow the scheme of the levels of evaluation. The levels of objectives represent the chain of impact that occurs as people become involved in a project.

Level 0: Input Objectives

Input objectives relate to the resources and conditions required to accomplish a project. As programs begin, some issues arise: How much will it cost? What resources are required? What expertise should be included? How many employees are needed? How much time is required? When will the program occur? How long will it last? Input objectives are based on input needs. This level of objective is referred to as Level 0 because it includes items that all programs must consider. Reviewing analysis data that support program appropriateness is considered at this level. Is this a compliance issue or is it a program that fills a need for profit making or cost avoidance?

Input objectives are often overlooked as critical success factors of programs. Table 2-3 lists a few examples of input objectives. The planning phase of a program requires appropriate input objectives. People involved in the program should be determined from the onset of the program. Scope provides information about the program so that stakeholders understand what *will* and *will not* be included in the program. The audience of a program helps focus appropriateness of content and delivery methods.

Level 1: Reaction Objectives

Reaction objectives are a first indication of success. Although some argue that reaction objectives are implied or understood, they should be communicated specifically to help participants identify what they will do differently as a result of the program. Helping participants focus on desired planned action(s) after the program keeps the learning centered around results. Defining desired participant reaction helps create powerful programs that help participants *purposefully* plan to use the knowledge from the program. The chain of impact in measurement and evaluation begins with constructing reaction objectives. Table 2-4 details several reaction objectives.

Reaction, or Level 1, objectives can be used to improve program design to achieve positive reactions. If people do not figure out the WIIFM (what's in it for me?) early in the program, they may lack the motivation to participate, disrupt learning, or sabotage project success. Engaging participants from the beginning of the program will ensure they are more likely to learn new knowledge and skills, transfer learning to their jobs, and affect the success of the organization.

Level 2: Learning Objectives

The most common objective is the learning objective, otherwise known as an instructional objective. Compared with the previous two levels of objectives, this level is more complex.

Table 2-3. Examples of Input Objectives

- The program will be conducted with at least 20 participants per session.
- For sales staff only.
- Begins in February and concludes in May.
- Keeps within a budget of $50,000.
- Uses in-house e-learning modules.

⨕ **Practitioner Tip** ⨖

Create powerful objectives and frame them in a way so you can adjust and expand them to meet the new realities. And remember, powerful objectives drive powerful outcomes.

Wayne R. Davis
Author, *Game Plan for Change: A Tabletop Simulation*
for Igniting Growth Through Transformation

The learning objective refers to the performance of the participant and assesses the participants' learning during the program. The knowledge the participant gains to implement a particular skill or apply information on the job drives business results. Learning objectives begin to illustrate the chain of impact of powerful objectives. Constructing the learning objective appropriately ensures program success. Table 2-5 provides several examples of learning objectives.

Table 2-4. Examples of Reaction Objectives

At the end of the conference, participants should rate each of the following statements four out of five on a five-point scale:

- The facilitator responded to questions effectively.
- The materials were well organized.
- Exercises demonstrated the connection between theory and reality.
- The course provided me with new information.
- The course content is relevant to my job.
- The course content is important to my job success.
- I intend to apply the content.

Table 2-5. Examples of Learning Objectives

The participant will be able to

- identify three labels located on the cable while operating the handheld device
- demonstrate three mission-critical customer service skills over the telephone
- discuss the signs of potential safety issues on the platform
- complete change leadership simulation with assigned team members during the training session
- match cables to proper locations using company color codes while wearing protective gear.

❧ **Practitioner Tip** ❧

Start by understanding the organization's objectives and then align learning to those objectives. Talk with your CEO, senior leaders, and members of your governing body to obtain the specific, measurable objectives for the organization and a sense of their priority. Next talk with the owner or sponsor of each objective and determine if learning can play a role in achieving it. If training can make a contribution and if it is a high-priority goal, agree on specific, measurable goals. Also discuss and agree on the expected impact of this training in achieving the organization's objectives and agree on the reinforcement and other actions required for application and effect.

David Vance
Founding and former president, Caterpillar University (2001–2007)
President, Manage Learning LLC (2007–present)

Level 3: Application Objectives

Powerful reaction and learning objectives set the stage for participants to transfer knowledge and skills gained to the workplace. Application objectives, referred to as Level 3 objectives, determine if the participant can use information learned during the program. Participants focus on achieving reaction and learning objectives at the onset of a program. Application objectives are a necessary link between what was learned (Level 2) and determining the impact (Level 4) participant learning will deliver. Application objectives answer the following questions:

- What new or improved *knowledge* was applied to the job?
- What is the *frequency* of skill application?
- What new *tasks* will be performed?
- What new *steps* will be implemented?

See table 2-6 for examples of application objectives.

Level 4: Impact Objectives

Impact objectives are often the level of objective that gets the most attention at the executive level of the organization. Level 4 objectives capture how participants' use of the information affects the business. A change in conduct will have some effect on the organization, even if it is a negative one. Impact objectives allow the learning leader to create statements clearly derived from the needs and goals of the organization. See table 2-7 for several examples of impact objectives.

Impact objectives include hard data, soft data, or a combination of both. Often, the combination of the two data types creates the most powerful impact objective (Phillips and others, 2007).

Table 2-6. Examples of Application Objectives

- At least 90 percent of participants will be using WIMBA in their online instruction within 90 days of the training session.
- Sexual harassment activity will cease within two months after the zero tolerance policy is implemented.
- Within one year, 50 percent of participants will submit a prospectus demonstrating saving costs to their manager.

Hard Data. Hard data are the primary measurements of improvement presented in terms of black and white facts. Hard data are traditionally used to make decisions in organizations and are typically categorized as output, quality, cost, and time.

Soft Data. The preference of hard data over soft data should not minimize the importance of soft data. Soft data focused on customer service, work climate, and job satisfaction can provide much needed clarification of harder data.

When impact objectives show the consequence of the application, expressed in meaningful measures that include data that are understandable and desirable by top executives, the chain of impact of program objectives is realized. Impact objectives are essential to measuring business results. They link business performance-to-performance issues identified as gaps in the organization.

Level 5: ROI Objectives

The term return-on-investment (ROI) represents a precise and actual value calculated by comparing program costs to benefits. Phillips and Phillips (2008) recommend that ROI objectives (Level 5) be reserved for key strategic programs—important, expensive, and

Table 2-7. Examples of Impact Objectives

- Inventory shrinkage fell by 20 percent at the Northern Region stores, within one month.
- After three months, customer service complaints decreased by 10 percent in the Slots department.
- Customer interactions increased to 10 per day for 50 percent of the shipping staff.
- Product defects decreased from 250 to 200 by yearend.
- Department-wide engagement score increased by one point on annual index.

high-profile initiatives. Not all programs should have an ROI objective, but when used correctly, ROI objectives can answer accountability concerns for your program sponsor.

Four strategies can help set appropriate ROI objectives (Phillips and Phillips, 2008).

- Use the same values used to invest in capital expenditures such as equipment and facilities costs. Usually this figure ranges from 15 to 20 percent. Using this strategy, organizations would expect the ROI at the same expected value from other investments.
- Estimate an ROI at a higher standard than the value required for other investments. This usually means the value is set at 25 percent. The rationale for this strategy accounts for the subjectivity surrounding estimations and the new nature of an ROI process for performance improvement projects.
- Determine a break-even point for the ROI target. A 0-percent ROI indicates program costs were recaptured and the value is captured in intangible items that are not converted to monetary value, such as morale or behavior change.
- Allow the program sponsor to set the ROI target based on expectations of the return of the program. The sponsor is sometimes the responsible party that has the most information regarding what the return "should" yield.

Developing ROI objectives that are unrealistic only detracts from the value. What matters most is how the target audience perceives the value of the data and that the data communicate the value of the program. Table 2-8 outlines what the levels of objectives for a software implementation project might look like.

Summary: Connecting Needs, Objectives, and Evaluation

Hopefully, training programs are not dreamed up in a vacuum. They are well-thought-out efforts designed and developed based on driving forces of business needs. By basing program objectives on stakeholder needs, programs are aligned with business outcomes in mind. Objectives are the result of careful analysis that links learning leader efforts to strategic goals of the organization. The actions of program audiences help drive the most effective results. These results can be designed, linked, and subsequently communicated using six levels of objectives. Powerful objectives representing the six levels position the program for ultimate success. In addition, it positions the evaluator so that relevant measures of program success can be taken. Program objectives are the foundation for good measurement and evaluation. Clear alignment between stakeholder needs, program objectives, and measurement and evaluation ensure not only successful programs, but successful evaluation. Figure 2-1 shows a V-model of connection among levels of objectives.

Table 2-8. Levels 1–5 Objectives for a Software Implementation Project

Level 1—Reaction Objectives

After reviewing the software, the participants will

- provide a rating of four out of five on the relevance for specific job applications
- indicate an intention to use the software within two weeks of the workshop (90-percent target).

Level 2—Learning Objectives

After participating in the workshop, participants will

- score 75 or better on a software test (80-percent target)
- demonstrate four of the five key features of ACT! with zero errors:
  —enter a new account
  —create a mail-merge account
  —create a query
  —send an email
  —create a call report.

Level 3—Application Objectives

Following the workshop, the participants will

- enter data for 80 percent of new customer prospects within 10 days of workshop completion
- increase the number of planned follow-up contacts with customers within three months of workshop completion
- use the software daily as reflected by an 80-percent score on an unscheduled audit of use after one month of workshop completion.

Level 4—Impact Objectives

Three months after implementation, there should be

- fewer customer complaints regarding missed deadlines, late responses, and failure to complete transactions
- reduced time to respond to customer inquiries and requests
- increased sales for existing customers
- increased customer satisfaction composite survey index by 20 percent on the next survey.

Level 5—ROI Objective

Implementing new software should achieve a 25-percent return-on-investment using first-year benefits.

Source: Phillips and Phillips (2008).

Figure 2-1. V-Model: The Objective Connection

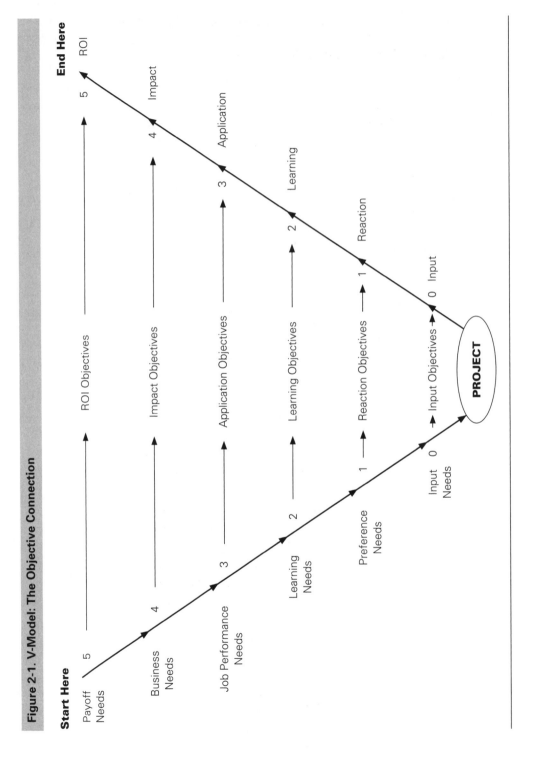

Knowledge Check: Identify the Level of Objective

In the table, indicate the level of evaluation that matches the objective. Check your answers in the appendix.

Objective	Evaluation Level
1. Decrease time spent on completing scheduled machinery maintenance from two days to one.	
2. Complete all 10 steps on the teller checklist before noon each day.	
3. Calculate a 1:4 cost-benefit ratio for the leadership development program two years after implementation.	
4. Increase posttest scores by 10 points over pretest scores.	
5. Increase customer satisfaction scores on annual stakeholder survey.	

About the Authors

Heather M. Annulis, PhD, CPLP, is assistant director of the Jack and Patti Phillips Workplace Learning and Performance Institute (WLPI) and associate professor of Workforce Training and Development at the University of Southern Mississippi. She is the director of the Workforce Training and Development master's degree program and WLPI's Training and Development Certificate Program. In 2006, she was named to the *Mississippi Business Journal's* prestigious list of *Mississippi's Top 40 Under 40*. She holds a PhD from the University of Southern Mississippi, is a Certified Professional in Learning and Performance (CPLP) from ASTD, and recently earned the honor of Distinguished e-Learning Professor at USM. She can be reached at heather.annulis@usm.edu.

Cyndi H. Gaudet, PhD, is director of the Jack and Patti Phillips Workplace Learning and Performance Institute (WLPI) at the University of Southern Mississippi, a full-time professor in the Department of Economic and Workforce Development, and director of the Human Capital Development doctoral program. Her cutting-edge workforce development research received awards from NASA, the Southern Growth Policies Board, and ASTD. She has presented at more than 100 regional, national, and international conferences, and her research has been published in journals such as the *HRD Quarterly, International Journal of Instructional Media, NABTE Review, URISA Journal,* and the *Delta Pi Epsilon Journal,* with the most recent acceptance in the *Performance Improvement Quarterly* focusing on post-Katrina workforce development for the Gulf coast region. She can be reached at cyndi .gaudet@usm.edu.

References

Phillips, J. J. and P. P. Phillips. (2008). *Beyond Learning Objectives.* Alexandria, VA: ASTD.

Phillips, J. J., P. P. Phillips, R. Stone, and H. Burkett. (2007). *The ROI Fieldbook: Strategies for Implementing ROI in HR and Training.* Burlington, MA: Butterworth-Heinemann.

Additional Reading

Carliner, S. (2003). *Training Design Basics.* Alexandria, VA: ASTD.

Gagné, R. M. (1985). *The Conditions of Learning and Theory of Instruction.* New York: CBS College Publishing.

Mager, R. F. (1997). *Preparing Instructional Objectives: A Critical Look in the Development of Effective Instruction,* 3rd ed. Atlanta: CEP Press.

McArdle, G. E. (2007). *Training Design and Delivery,* 2nd ed. Alexandria, VA: ASTD.

Phillips, J. J. and P. P. Phillips. (2002). *Measuring ROI in the Public Sector.* Alexandria, VA: ASTD.

Phillips, P. P. and J. J. Phillips. (2005). *Return on Investment Basics.* Alexandria, VA: ASTD.

Chapter 3

Planning Your Evaluation Project

Donald J. Ford

In This Chapter

This chapter explores the techniques for planning a comprehensive evaluation, including planning data collection, data analysis, and project management. Upon reading this chapter, you will be able to

- ▨ describe the importance of planning for effective evaluation
- ▨ align stakeholder needs, program objectives, and evaluation outcomes
- ▨ identify different techniques to collect and analyze evaluation data
- ▨ use a comprehensive evaluation-planning tool to manage evaluation projects.

The Importance of Planning for Effective Evaluation

Evaluation, like everything else in life, takes careful planning to reap what one sows. The need to plan an evaluation before conducting it has always been recognized, but the scope and complexity of evaluation projects today demand even better planning than in the past. Without proper planning, evaluations often run into trouble. Data may become contaminated and conclusions drawn may be invalid. Evaluations may also fall behind schedule, go over budget, and be abandoned altogether. Thus, launching an evaluation without a plan is similar to taking a trip without an itinerary.

Project Alignment

Vital to planning evaluation is to decide who will use evaluation findings and for what purposes. This is critical to establishing the scope of the evaluation and the kinds of data that will need to be collected. Also essential to planning evaluation is encouraging stakeholders to base their decision making on facts. It is important to define the kinds of decisions that stakeholders are likely to make and determine the types of data and information that would be most useful to the decision-making process.

A second key purpose of evaluation is to determine the effectiveness of performance improvement solutions and hold accountable those responsible for designing and implementing human resource development programs. To determine program effectiveness and accountability, the right kinds of data must be collected and analyzed, and the effect of the solution must be isolated from other influences that may affect program outcomes.

Both of these key purposes—decision making and accountability—are driven by the objectives of the program being evaluated. Powerful objectives that are clearly measurable position programs for success, whereas weak objectives without measures set up a program evaluation for difficulty, if not failure.

Data Collection Planning

Evaluation data may consist of many kinds of information, from the numerical to the attitudinal. Because the types of evaluation data vary with the nature of programs and the needs of stakeholders, it is important to have a variety of data collection methods available to address a wide range of learning and performance improvement solutions.

❧ **Practitioner Tip** ❧

In planning evaluation design, I identify the outcomes of the job and make sure they are measurable. This allows for a baseline measurement of how well job performers are doing and can be compared to end-of-program outcomes to measure the impact. This gives a more reliable and accurate measure than job behavior because it is tied directly to the business goals.

Dennis Mankin, CPT
Principal Consultant, Beacon Performance Group

Techniques to Collect Evaluation Data

This section will briefly introduce the major techniques used for data collection, describe their uses, and summarize the advantages and disadvantages of each collection method. In Section II of this book, you will learn in more detail how to design and use each data collection method.

Surveys and Questionnaires

One of the most widely used data collection techniques, surveys and questionnaires, allows evaluators to collect data from large numbers of people with relative ease and can be summarized and analyzed quickly.

Tests and Assessments

Tests are the oldest form of educational evaluation and still considered to be the best gauge of learning. Though we typically think of paper-and-pencil tests, assessments for evaluation may include any of the following: written tests and quizzes, hands-on performance tests, or project/portfolio assessments.

Interviews

Probably the most widely used data collection method, the individual interview is the most flexible data collection tool available and also the easiest to deploy. All it takes is an interviewer armed with a list of questions and a subject willing to answer them. In evaluation, interview subjects are often drawn from project sponsor or client, senior managers responsible for business decisions related to the evaluation, participants in training, managers of training participants, instructors, and instructional designers responsible for training.

Focus Groups

Long a staple of market researchers, focus groups, or group interviews, also have become an important tool for evaluators. Although more widely used in needs analysis, focus groups of training participants and key stakeholders conducted after training programs can yield rich data to help understand how training affects learners and their organizations.

Action Plans

An action plan is a great tool to get learners to apply new skills on the job. It is usually created at the end of training and is meant to guide learners in applying new skills once they return to work. It may also involve their supervisors and become a more formal performance contract. For evaluation, action plans can be audited to determine if learners applied new skills and to what effect.

Case Studies

Case studies are one of the oldest methods known to evaluators. For many years, evaluators have studied individuals and organizations that have gone through training or performance improvement and written of their experiences in a case study format. This method is still widely used and forms the basis of entire evaluation systems, such as Robert Brinkerhoff's Success Case Method (2003).

Performance Records

This category includes any existing performance data the organization already collects, often in computer databases or personnel files. Organizations now measure a massive amount of employee activity that is often relevant to training evaluators, including the following kinds of performance records: performance appraisals, individual development plans, safety, absenteeism and tardiness, turnover, output data (quantity and time), quality data (acceptance, error, and scrap rates), customer satisfaction, labor costs, and sales and revenues.

Advantages and Disadvantages of Data Collection Methods

No single data collection method can cover all the needs of evaluation and none are perfect. Table 3-1 compares the relative advantages and disadvantages of the methods described above and is a job aid in selecting data collection methods.

Data Collection Planning Tool

To put together an effective data collection plan, the following questions are key:

- What objectives are being evaluated?
- What measures are being used to evaluate the objectives?
- Where are the sources of data?
- How should data be collected?
- When should data be collected?
- Who should be responsible for collecting the data?

The answers to these six questions can then be assembled into a worksheet that will become the final work plan driving the data collection phase of evaluation. Table 3-2 is a tool to record planning decisions about data collection.

Table 3-3 is an example of how the data collection planning tool has been applied to evaluating a new hire orientation and on-boarding program that included initial training, facilities tour, follow-up training 30 days later, and supervisor and peer mentoring.

Table 3-1. Comparison of Data Collection Methods

Collection Method	Advantages	Disadvantages
Surveys and Questionnaires	• Flexible data collection tool that can be custom designed to cover a wide range of issues • Easy to administer and analyze • Provide a level of precision that other data collection tools lack • Allow for large-scale participation in evaluation studies that otherwise would be cost prohibitive	• Often misused and overused in situations where they yield little valid information • Response rates for non-mandatory surveys tend to be low, causing problems in generalizing conclusions • Difficulty of designing good survey questions that are unambiguous and yield data that are valid and reliable • Asking questions that are beyond the knowledge level of respondents, creating problems with inaccurate or missing data items
Tests and Assessments	• Well-developed body of science in the construction, administration, and analysis of tests • Can verify individual competencies acquired through training • Can judge the effectiveness of training design and implementation • Can demonstrate the contribution of training to the development of human capital	• Time required to create tests must be justified by the need to verify acquisition of new knowledge and skill • Unpleasant experience for learners; participant resentment and anxiety increases when personnel decisions may result from test scores • In high-stakes testing (when a test is used to make a decision about a person's job or career), must comply with complex legal requirements governing the use of tests in the workplace
Interviews	• Highly flexible tool that allows for in-depth exploration of issues related to evaluation • Allow for probing of attitudes and emotions that underlie people's behavior • Enable evaluators to build rapport with interview subjects and "get inside their heads" to explore issues from the subject's point of view	• Take a great deal of time, both for the evaluator and the interviewee • Without the proper preparation, interviews provide data of limited usefulness • Tendency for respondents to tell evaluators what they think they want to hear, rather than the unvarnished truth

(continued on next page)

Table 3-1. Comparison of Data Collection Methods (continued)

Collection Method	Advantages	Disadvantages
Interviews (continued)		• Difficulty in data analysis and drawing conclusions, due to the time-consuming task of transcribing and reviewing interview data and their subjective nature
Focus Groups	• More efficient than individual interviews • Encourage synergy and interaction among participants that can yield higher-quality data than individuals might report in isolation • Encourage stakeholder participation in the evaluation process, thus building support for training evaluation work • Identify intangible issues that might not otherwise surface through other data collection efforts	• Require careful planning and design and a skillful facilitator • Unplanned focus groups can degenerate into gripe sessions or get off topic easily • If participants do not represent the target population, findings cannot be generalized to the larger group • Individual participants may create problems by either over participating (monopolizing speaking time) or under participating (remaining silent)
Action Plans	• A flexible tool that can be customized for individual use • Allow each participant to chart his or her own course in applying new skills • Easily yields evaluation data supplied by participants themselves, in conjunction with their supervisors • Increase the amount of skill transfer, a key goal of any training program	• Require a firm commitment from learners that is often lacking • If supervisors are not on board, the action plan is unlikely to stick • Some learners never get a chance to apply new skills, because their job or their manager does not allow it • Data are often anecdotal and idiosyncratic, making them difficult to analyze and draw valid conclusions about training effectiveness
Case Studies	• Capture stories of people's life experiences • Long history in education and a well-developed body of literature exists to guide case study evaluation research • Allow in-depth study of the effect of training and highlight individual differences that may be central to understanding the effectiveness of an intervention	• Require the active participation of stakeholders and their commitment to follow through and tell their stories • Highly dependent on situational variables that cannot easily be replicated, so generalizing evaluation findings is problematic

Collection Method	Advantages	Disadvantages
Case Studies (continued)	• Often yield insights that other methods may gloss over	• Subjective and narrative nature of case studies makes them susceptible to charges of manipulation. Evaluators may be tempted to highlight cases that prove their point while ignoring or suppressing other evidence
Performance Records	• Existing data source can save time and money • Sometimes more valid and reliable than newly collected data because the organization may have already vetted the information and established quality standards for its collection and reporting • Immediately relevant to the business and capture key business factors that stakeholders are interested in tracking • Historical archives may be available to allow for extended longitudinal studies tracking key variables	• Most organizations do not track or report performance data in a way that is useful to evaluators. May have to substantially rework data to get them in the appropriate format • Validity and reliability of company-collected performance records may be suspect, depending on the quality of the data collection and storage systems • Getting access to performance data can be difficult. Many organizations closely guard data about performance as proprietary; individual employees also have some control over the release of information about their personal work history

Data Analysis Planning

Once data have been collected, it is critical to analyze these properly to draw the correct conclusions. Many techniques exist, depending on the type of data collected. This section reviews the three most common data analysis techniques used in evaluation.

✎ **Practitioner Tip** ✎

In planning data collection for classroom settings where the participant has access to a computer, an online survey is used. At the end of the class, data are automatically tabulated and provided to trainers and instructional designers so they can make immediate adjustments based on participant feedback.

Nishika de Rosairo
Human Capital, Deloitte Consulting LLP

Table 3-2. Data Collection Plan Template

DATA COLLECTION PLAN

Purpose of This Evaluation: _____

Responsibility: _____   Date: _____

Program/Project: _____

Level	Broad Program Objective(s)	Measures	Data Collection Method/Instruments	Data Sources	Timing	Responsibilities
1	Reaction and Planned Action					
2	Learning and Confidence					
3	Application and Implementation					
4	Business Impact					
5	ROI					

© The ROI Institute, 2004. Used with permission.

Table 3-3. Application of Data Collection Plan

Level	Objective	Measures	Data Collection Method	Data Sources	Timing	Responsibilities
1	Satisfied with learning experience	% satisfied	Survey	Learners	End of class	Instructor
2	Identify company's business model and HR policies	% items correct	Test	Learners	End of class	Instructor
3	Comply with company's HR policies	% in compliance	Performance records	HR Supervisors	First 6 months employment	Employee relations/ supervisors
4	Increase retention of new hires	% turnover rate	Performance records	HR	Track for 12 months	HR
5	Payback from new hire orientation	• Cost of training • Benefit of lower turnover	• Training budget • Performance records	• Training • HR	After 1 year	• Training manager • Employment manager

Techniques to Analyze Data

Statistical Analysis

Statistical analysis is appropriate whenever data are in numeric form. This is most common with performance records, surveys, and tests.

Statistics has three primary uses in evaluation:

- summarize large amounts of numeric data, including frequencies, averages, and variances
- determine the relationship among variables, including correlations
- determine differences among groups and isolate effects, including t-test, analysis of variance (ANOVA), and regression analysis.

Qualitative Analysis

Qualitative analysis examines people's perceptions, opinions, attitudes, and values—all things that are not easily reduced to a number. It addresses the subjective and the intangible, such as interviews, focus groups, observations, and case studies. Although difficult to master, this form of analysis gives a more complete in-depth understanding about how stakeholders think and feel about training and performance improvement. The data, once summarized in some form, are then analyzed to discover the following:

- **Themes:** common, recurring facts and ideas that are widely expressed and agreed upon
- **Differences:** disparate views and ideas expressed by different individuals and groups of people under study and the reasons for these differences
- **Deconstructed Meaning:** the underlying values, beliefs, and mental models that form the cultural foundation of organizations and groups.

Isolating Program Effects

Just because we measure a result does not mean that training caused it. Organizations are complex systems subject to the influences of many variables, and isolating the effects of an individual program can be confusing and difficult. Yet, it is essential to identify the causes of increased knowledge and performance if we intend to properly evaluate training outcomes.

Financial Analysis

When evaluation is taken to the fifth level—ROI—financial analysis becomes important. This includes assembling and calculating all the costs for the program and converting the benefits to monetary values wherever possible. The primary use of financial analysis in evaluation is to calculate a return-on-investment at the end of the program. Secondary uses include forecasting potential paybacks on proposed training and determining if business goals related to financials have been achieved.

Program Cost Calculation

When an ROI study is conducted, costs have to be considered. It's important that all stakeholders agree on the costs at the outset. Generally, costs must be fully loaded, including both direct and indirect costs, to be acceptable in financial calculations. Table 3-4 highlights common direct and indirect evaluation costs that need to be captured.

Advantages and Disadvantages of Data Analysis Methods

Like data collection methods, no single data analysis method works in all cases. Table 3-5 highlights the advantages and disadvantages of each technique to assist in making decisions about when to use each data analysis method.

Data Analysis Planning Tool

Data must be analyzed appropriately to draw the correct conclusions about the program being evaluated. Answer the following questions to help plan this crucial phase:

- What are the needs of key stakeholders who will receive the final report?
- What data items have been collected?
- What data types are there?
- How can you isolate the effects of the program/solution?

Table 3-4. Common Direct and Indirect Costs for a Program

Direct Costs	Indirect Costs
• Needs assessment • Design and development • Delivery and implementation • Evaluation of labor, equipment, and materials	• Participant salaries while in training • Management time devoted to program • Travel expenses for participants • Administrative and overhead costs • Cost of benefits and perks of participants and management

Table 3-5. Comparison of Data Analysis Methods

Analysis Method	Advantages	Disadvantages
Statistical Analysis	• Well-established with a long track record of success • Offers a variety of techniques to treat any numerical data type • The level of precision is unmatched by other analytical techniques • Many tools to automate the analysis and reduce the time and cost of conducting statistical analysis	• Statistics often frighten the uninitiated. The learning curve is steep, once one goes beyond the rudimentary • The many techniques available may result in inappropriate methods being used • Statistical techniques in the wrong hands can be deliberately misused, leading to deception and erroneous conclusions
Qualitative Analysis	• Brings out the richness of detail and human side of evaluation • Allows stakeholders to construct their own judgments about the effectiveness of programs and gives them a vehicle to participate in the process • Captures the intangible benefits of training • Useful in troubleshooting problems and documenting lessons learned	• Labor intensive • Requires considerable skill, if done correctly; if done poorly, it produces invalid results • Open to multiple interpretations, leading to questions of objectivity • May be considered less reliable than hard numbers • More difficult to convert to ROI
Isolating Program Effects	• Essential to isolate program effects from other variables • Several techniques exist to help isolate effects • Increases credibility of ROI	• Difficult to prove cause and effect • Some techniques rely on subjective opinion and may be challenged
Financial Analysis	• Standard part of corporate finance that has a long history and established standards and procedures • Puts human resource development programs on a par with other business functions that have always had to justify their expenses by showing the monetary benefits that accrue to organizations	• Arriving at the monetary value of the costs and benefits can be challenging • When the benefits are intangible, it's nearly impossible to calculate monetary benefits • Considerable effort required to analyze monetary information must be weighed against the value of doing so • ROI attempted on only a small percentage of high-value programs

Analysis Method	Advantages	Disadvantages
Program Cost Calculation	• Must accurately capture costs to calculate ROI • Provides greater financial visibility and control over training costs	• Cost data may not be readily available • Deciding what to include in costs can be difficult

- How can you best summarize and describe the data?
- How can you best find relationships and differences among the data?
- What data can be converted to monetary value?
- What data should be reported as intangible benefits?
- Who will be responsible for conducting the data analysis and reporting the results?

Using the data analysis plan worksheet in table 3-6, you can organize and plan the analysis phase down to each data item being collected. This tool also helps plan later phases, including ROI, if so desired.

Table 3-7 provides an example of how the data analysis planning tool could be applied.

In the example, based on the same new hire orientation and on-boarding program used in the data collection planning example, you can see how evaluation data items are linked to stakeholder needs and categorized by data item and type. The analysis includes methods to isolate the effect of the program from other variables, methods to describe and summarize the data, methods to draw inferences and conclusions about the data, and whether the data can be converted to monetary value or will be reported as an intangible benefit.

✍ Practitioner Tip ✍

In planning evaluation analysis, I ask stakeholders, "What would success look like?" This provides the organizational target we want to evaluate. We always have to remember to ask ourselves, "Why are we evaluating?" The answer tells us if we should focus on qualitative formative data or quantitative summative data and what kinds of measures and analysis we need to conduct. For instance, are we trying to decide which solution to choose among several options, justifying the training budget to the chief financial officer, or determining if we have met the expectations of key stakeholders?

Joe Willmore
Principal, Willmore Consulting Group LLC

Table 3-6. Data Analysis Plan

Program: _____   Responsibility: _____   Date: _____

Stakeholder Need	Data Items	Data Type (Quantitative/ Qualitative)	Methods to Isolate Effects	Descriptive Analysis Methods	Inferential Analysis Methods	Monetary Value (Y/N)	Intangible (Y/N)

Table 3-7. Application of Data Analysis Plan

Program: New Hire Orientation and On-Boarding program   Responsibility: _____ (Name) Evaluator   Date: _____   Now

Stakeholder Need	Data Items	Data Type (Quantitative/ Qualitative)	Methods to Isolate Effects	Descriptive Analysis Methods	Inferential Analysis Methods	Monetary Value (Y/N)	Intangible (Y/N)
Verify satisfaction with learning experience	Reaction survey questions	Quantitative	Survey design	• Mean • Standard deviation	Correlate satisfaction with learning	N	Y
Verify knowledge of company's business model and HR policies	Quiz—multiple choice	Quantitative	• Text design • Validity study	• Mean • Standard deviation	• Item analysis • Reliability study	N	N
Verify compliance with company's HR policies	Initial performance appraisal	Quantitative and qualitative	• Control group • Expert opinion	Frequency distribution	t-test (control vs. new hires)	N	N
Determine effect on retention of new hires	Turnover rate	Quantitative	Expert opinion	Turnover ratio	• Cost of turnover • Causes of turnover	Y	N
Calculate payback from program	• Program costs • Program benefits	Quantitative	Expert opinion	ROI	Estimated value of benefits	Y	Y

A Comprehensive Evaluation Planning Tool

To manage the many details of evaluation planning, a comprehensive tool is a must. The planning tool is broken into four phases so that it can be used throughout the program evaluation process to plan and capture key evaluation data.

Phase 1: Establish the Evaluation Baseline

During the needs analysis phase, begin planning the evaluation and collecting baseline information that will establish measures for the program's objectives and allow comparison with the final results.

Phase 2: Create the Evaluation Design

During the design of the training program, create a detailed evaluation design, including the evaluation questions to be answered, the evaluation model to be used, and the methods and tools for data collection. At this time, also decide what kinds of data analysis will be conducted, based on the types of data to be collected and the nature of the evaluation questions to be answered.

Phase 3: Create the Evaluation Schedule

During the evaluation design process, create or incorporate a separate schedule for evaluation into the overall training plan. This will ensure that evaluation tasks are scheduled and milestones are met.

Phase 4: Create the Evaluation Budget

During the evaluation design process, develop a separate budget or at least separate line items for evaluation. This will ensure that evaluation work has the necessary resources to achieve its goals. Figure 3-1 is a sample of a comprehensive evaluation planning worksheet that can be used to plan out an evaluation of training or performance improvement solutions.

With this plan as a guide, evaluation becomes more manageable. It is also a great communication vehicle to share with key stakeholders so they can see the proposed scope and cost of the evaluation, along with its likely benefits and the potential payback if implementation occurs as planned. To illustrate this, figure 3-2 shows the comprehensive evaluation plan for the new hire orientation and on-boarding program described earlier.

Figure 3-1. Comprehensive Evaluation Planning Tool

Project: _____

Client: _____

Selected solution(s): _____

_____

1. **Establish the evaluation baseline.**

   Business goals: _____

   _____

   Business measures: _____

   _____

   Data sources: _____

   ☐ Existing measure   ☐ New measure

   Performance goals: _____

   _____

   Performance measures: _____

   _____

   Data sources: _____

   ☐ Existing measure   ☐ New measure

   Learning goals: _____

   _____

   Learning measures: _____

   _____

   Data sources: _____

   ☐ Existing measure   ☐ New measure

2. **Create the evaluation design.**

   Evaluation question(s) for business goal(s): _____

   _____

   Evaluation question(s) for performance goal(s): _____

   _____

   Evaluation question(s) for learning goal(s): _____

   _____

   Evaluation design model(s): _____

   _____

   Data collection methods: _____

   _____

(continued on next page)

Figure 3-1. Comprehensive Evaluation Planning Tool (continued)

Evaluation tools

☐ Survey _____

☐ Focus group _____

☐ Interview _____

☐ Case study_____

☐ Performance record_____

☐ Action plan_____

☐ Test_____

Quantitative analysis methods (central tendency, dispersion, association, differences):_____

_____

Qualitative analysis methods (thematic, comparative, deconstruction): _____

_____

Monetary analysis methods (ROI, cost-benefit):_____

3. Create project evaluation schedule.

Project Name: _____

Action Step	Target Date	Responsibility	Information Source or Comments
PLANNING			
1. Determine purpose and evaluation level of this project.			
2. Review program/intervention, objectives, and content.			
3. Identify key stakeholder expectations.			
4. Identify data sets for Levels 5, 4, and 3 measurements (hard and soft) and determine current availability of performance data for these measures.			
5. Identify or develop specific objectives and baseline data for each level of follow-up evaluation.			

Action Step	Target Date	Responsibility	Information Source or Comments
6. Determine responsibility for Level 1 and Level 2 evaluation (course designer, facilitator/instructor, vendor, or internal) and how these data will be provided.			
7. Determine methods and instruments to be used and the timing of data collection.			
8. Finalize data collection plan.			
9. Draft data collection instruments (interviews, focus groups, questionnaires).			
10. Review options for scannable or electronic format.			
11. Select strategy for isolating the effects of training.			
12. Select strategy for converting data to monetary value.			
13. Identify costs to include in analysis.			
14. Finalize ROI analysis plan.			
15. Field test questionnaire and other instruments and revise as necessary.			
16. Finalize instruments in scannable/electronic format.			
17. Finalize letter to accompany questionnaires and get appropriate executive signature/approval.			
18. Collect data and tabulate data per data collection plan and ROI analysis plan.			
• Questionnaire			
• Organization performance records			
• Other			
19. Tabulate costs of intervention.			

(continued on next page)

Figure 3-1. Comprehensive Evaluation Planning Tool (continued)

Action Step	Target Date	Responsibility	Information Source or Comments
20. Analyze data, isolate, and convert.			
21. Develop conclusions and recommendations.			
22. Develop report(s) for target audience(s).			
23. Review draft report(s) with project team.			
24. Present results to target groups.			
FOLLOW-UP REQUIREMENTS			
25. Project critique and lessons learned.			
26. Storage/filing of documentation.			
27. Potential use of data reported.			

4. Create evaluation budget.

Budget Category	Budget Item	Rate	Amount	Total
Direct labor	Evaluator's time	$ daily, fully burdened	# of days	Rate X amount
Indirect labor	Participants' and managers' time	$ hourly, fully burdened	# of total hours	Rate X amount
Consultant labor	Consultants' time (if outsourcing)	$ daily	# of days	Rate X amount
Materials	Purchase, printing, shipping, distribution, and collection of evaluation materials	$/item produced	# of total items	Rate X amount
Equipment	Computers, printers, scanners, flip charts, projectors, etc.	$/item	Total of all items	Add all items purchased/ rented
TOTAL				(sum above)

© The ROI Institute, 2004. Used with permission.

Figure 3-2. Application of Evaluation Planning Tool

Comprehensive Evaluation Planning Tool

Project: _New Hire Orientation and On-Boarding program_

Client: _VP, HR_

Selected solution(s): _Initial training, facilities tour, follow-up training 30 days later, and supervisor and peer mentoring_

1. **Establish the evaluation baseline.**

   Business goals: _Increase retention of new hires_

   Business measures: _Turnover rate (as percentage of total employees annualized)_

   Data sources: _HR Employment Dept._

   ☒ Existing measure   ☐ New measure

   Performance goals: _Comply with company's HR policies_

   Performance measures: _Initial performance appraisal after six months_

   Data sources: _HR Employee Relations Dept._

   ☒ Existing measure   ☐ New measure

   Learning goals: _Identify company's business model and HR policies_

   Learning measures: _Multiple-choice test at end of class_

   Data sources: _Learning objectives and content of class_

   ☐ Existing measure   ☒ New measure

2. **Create the evaluation design.**

   Evaluation question(s) for business goal(s): _Will the new on-boarding program reduce turnover to below the industry average as measured by the HR Turnover Ratio and Industry Trade Associations?_

   Evaluation question(s) for performance goal(s): _Will the new on-boarding program help 100 percent of new hires to comply with the company's HR policies as measured by their supervisor's initial performance appraisal?_

   Evaluation question(s) for learning goal(s): _Will the new on-boarding program help new hires identify key facts about the company's business model and HR policies as measured by an end-of-class test with a 75-percent passing score?_

   Evaluation design model(s): _Phillips' ROI Model, quasi-experimental design with control group (recently hired employees who did not participate in the on-boarding program)_

   Data collection methods: _survey, test, performance records_

(continued on next page)

Figure 3-2. Application of Evaluation Planning Tool (continued)

Evaluation tools

☒ Survey *Participant reaction survey* _____

☐ Focus group _____

☐ Interview _____

☐ Case study _____

☒ Performance record *Initial performance appraisal* _____

☐ Action plan _____

☒ Test *Postclass multiple-choice knowledge check* _____

Quantitative analysis methods (central tendency, dispersion, association, differences): _____
Means, standard deviation, t-test, test item analysis, turnover trending _____

Qualitative analysis methods (thematic, comparative, deconstruction): *Open-ended survey*
responses: thematic and comparative analysis _____

Monetary analysis methods (ROI, cost-benefit): *ROI* _____

Knowledge Check: Planning Evaluation

Directions: Answer the questions below about evaluation planning, based on the content of the chapter. Check your answers in the appendix.

1. Why has evaluation planning become so important to effective evaluation?
2. What is a technique to ensure alignment among stakeholder needs, program objectives, and evaluation outcomes?
3. List seven ways to collect data.
4. What are the key questions to ask when planning data collection?
5. List three ways to analyze data.
6. What are the key questions to ask in planning data analysis?
7. What are the four phases of evaluation planning?

About the Author

Donald J. Ford, PhD, CPT, is a training and performance improvement consultant specializing in instructional design and human resource management. He has worked in human resources for more than 20 years, including internal training management positions and also as president of Training Education Management LLC, a consulting firm. For his clients, he has developed custom classroom, self-study, and web-based training;

conducted performance and needs analyses; facilitated groups; managed improvement projects; taught courses; and evaluated results. Ford holds a BA and an MA in history and a PhD in education, all from UCLA. He has published 35 articles and four books on topics in training, education, and management, including his latest work, *Bottom-Line Training: Performance-Based Results* (2005). Ford has presented at numerous conferences and has worked overseas in Asia, Latin America, and the Middle East. He speaks Spanish and Mandarin Chinese. He may be reached at donaldjford@verizon.net or at www .TrainingEducationManagement.com.

References

Brinkerhoff, R. (2003). *Success Case Method.* San Francisco: Berrett-Koehler.

Additional Reading

Ford, D. (Jan. 2004). "Evaluating Performance Improvement," *Performance Improvement.* 43(1): 36–41.

Geis, G. and M. Smith. (1999). "The Function of Evaluation," *Handbook of Human Performance Technology.* 2nd Ed. Stolovitch and Keeps, eds. Pfeiffer, 130–150.

Guba, E. G. and Y. Lincoln. (1992). *Effective Evaluation: Improving the Usefulness of Evaluation Results Through Responsive and Naturalistic Approaches.* San Francisco: Jossey-Bass.

Kirkpatrick, D. (1996). *Evaluating Training Programs: The Four Levels.* San Francisco: Berrett-Koehler.

Phillips, J. J. (2003). *Return on Investment in Training and Performance Improvement Programs,* 2nd ed. Boston: Butterworth Heinemann.

Phillips, J. J., P. P. Phillips, and T. Hodges-DeTuncq. (2004). *Make Training Evaluation Work.* Alexandria, VA: ASTD.

Stake, R. ed. (1967). *Curriculum Evaluation.* Skokie, IL: Rand McNally.

✎ Section II

Data Collection

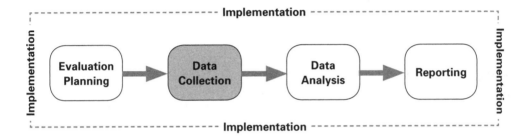

Istorians' Fallacies by David Hackett Fischer (1970) provides an entertaining, yet important look at the problem-solving discipline of history. A historian is a person who asks questions about past events and explains the findings through statistical generalization, narrative, models, or analogy. One simple quote from the book sums up the importance of historians asking relevant questions:

…..we can hardly blame science just because we've asked the wrong questions.

—Ernst Cassirer (1874-1944)
Jewish German historian and philosopher

Much like historians, evaluators must ask the right questions the right way. All too often we report what we believe to be true based on our evaluation, but in the end, the questions asked (or measures taken) weren't the right ones. Or, if they were the right questions, they were asked in such a way that an objective (not to mention accurate) response could not be offered.

Data collection is nothing more than asking questions so that we can get the answers we need to measure the progress of and success with our programs. Just what those questions are, how we ask them, whom we ask, and when we ask depend on the objectives set during the planning phase (see Section I). There is no one best way to collect evaluation data. There is, however, a *better* way after you consider

- type of data
- time requirements
- resource constraints
- cultural constraints
- convenience.

In Section II, you will learn how to

- collect quantitative data
- collect qualitative data
- access data that are already available
- build data collection into the program.

References

Hackett Fischer, D. (1970). *Historian's Fallacies.* New York: HarperPerennial.

Chapter 4

Using Surveys and Questionnaires

Caroline Hubble

In This Chapter

This chapter discusses questionnaires, which are one of the most common data collection instruments used in capturing evaluation data. A planned, structured questionnaire that asks the right questions the right way ensures the needed data are collected. In this chapter you will learn to

- ▨ secure a plan
- ▨ create the content
- ▨ optimize the effectiveness
- ▨ prepare for distribution
- ▨ execute the tool.

Steps in Developing Surveys and Questionnaires

Once evaluation planning is complete, the plans are put into motion, thereby initiating data collection. Collecting the data is a critical activity in the evaluation process, and using effective and efficient data collection instruments is essential. Developing and implementing the questionnaire or survey evolves by completing the following five phases:

- **S**ecuring a plan
- **C**reating the content
- **O**ptimizing the effectiveness
- **P**reparing for distribution
- **E**xecuting the tool.

By completing these phases and maintaining the scope of the data collection instrument, the foundation is set to collect the data needed to answer the study's questions.

Securing a Plan for the Questionnaire

By definition, a questionnaire is an instrument designed to ask questions to capture a wide range of data from attitudes and specific improvement data. A survey, which is a type of questionnaire, is more limited and focuses on capturing attitudes, beliefs, and opinions of the respondents (Phillips and Stawarski, 2008). Because questionnaires can be customized to meet specific evaluation needs, they are one of the more frequently used data collection instruments. Don't assume, however, that they require minimal effort to implement. As with all projects, successful questionnaires require a carefully thought out plan.

A Clearly Defined Purpose Is Critical to Success

Successful questionnaires are built on sound design and are linked to the evaluation study's research questions. To be successful in using a questionnaire, consider the following:

- Why is the questionnaire needed?
- What research questions will the collected data answer?
- Is the questionnaire the right instrument to collect the needed data?
- Based on the organization's needs, culture, and data sources, will the questionnaire work for gathering the data?

Answering these questions helps define the feasibility and purpose of the questionnaire. The data collection plan is a critical tool in determining the practicality of using a questionnaire. The objectives, specific measures, and data sources provided in the data collection plan help formulate the purpose of the questionnaire.

Maintaining the Scope Keeps the Data Collection Focused

Once you decide that the questionnaire is feasible and you define the purpose, the next step is documenting the questionnaire's scope. As mentioned above, questionnaires are flexible tools able to collect a wide variety of data. While this is a valuable asset, it can present a challenge. The questionnaire has the potential to evolve beyond its intended purpose because of its ability to collect a wide range of data. When this happens, content not related to the study can be incorporated, and the tool loses focus. To ensure this doesn't occur, it is essential to adhere to the scope of the questionnaire. The purpose and goals of the questionnaire define the scope. Once the scope is documented, it should be maintained throughout the life cycle of the questionnaire.

Detailed Plans Ensure Critical Activities Are Completed

Once you identify the purpose and scope of the questionnaire, create a detailed plan for the design, development, and implementation of the tool. In addition to the data collection plan (see table 4-1), develop a portion of the evaluation project plan to identify the design, testing, and implementation steps. Once identified, incorporate the timeline and resources to complete the work (see table 4-2). When developing the timeline, it is vital to factor in sufficient time for development and testing of the questionnaire. Although these activities are time consuming, they are important. It is extremely challenging to make any changes to an implemented questionnaire without compromising the study's credibility.

Creating the Questionnaire's Content

After you define the purpose and outline the plan, the next task is to develop the questionnaire's content. This process is probably the most labor-intensive part of developing the questionnaire and involves two primary activities. First, determine the structure of the questionnaire. Once identified, you can then develop the actual questions. These steps ensure the questionnaire has the required elements to gather the needed data to answer the study's research questions.

The Structure of the Questionnaire Identifies Where to Put the Content

Developing an outline of what and where the content should be placed within the questionnaire is the first step in successfully creating the content. Placing all the relevant information, instructions, and questions in the appropriate place and in an organized manner ensures the respondents are able to provide accurate and valuable data. There are three main areas of the structure: the introduction, body, and conclusion.

The Introduction Sets the Tone

The introduction is the first section of the questionnaire that the respondent reads, and it sets the tone for the remainder of the instrument. Because of this, it is important to include all the relevant information to engage the reader. The primary content includes informing

Table 4-1. Sample Data Collection Plan

Level	Broad Program Objective(s)	Measures	Data Collection Method	Data Sources	Timing	Responsibilities
1	**Satisfaction/ Planned Action** • Relevance to job • Recommend to others • Overall satisfaction with course • Learned new information • Intent to use material	At the end of program, 90% of participants will rate the applicable questions a 4.00 out of 5.00 (strongly agree/ agree indicating satisfaction)	End of course evaluation	Participants	End of course	• Participants Data in LMS • Facilitator (introduce/ remind)
2	**Learning** Increase in knowledge, skills, and attitudes regarding selling	• 100% participants are able to demon-strate use of the 5 selling steps • 100% of participants achieve a passing score (85%) in one attempt at end-of-program assessment	• Role play • End of program assessment	Participants	End of course	• Facilitator • Data in LMS

Level	Broad Program Objective(s)	Measures	Data Collection Method	Data Sources	Timing	Responsibilities
3	**Application/ Implementation** • Ability to use selling steps (including extent able to use) • Frequency of using selling steps • Enablers / barriers to applying selling steps	• 100% of participants are able to successfully use the selling steps (4.00 out of 5.00 on success scale) • 100% of participants achieve a passing score (85%) in one attempt at end-of-program assessment	Questionnaire	Participants	60 days postcourse	Evaluation team/lead
4	**Business Impact** N/A	N/A	N/A	N/A	N/A	N/A
5	**ROI** N/A					

Comments: Evaluating program to Level 3—Application/Implementation

Table 4-2. Sample Evaluation Project Plan—Data Collection

ID	Task	Start	Finish	Resource(s)	Done
2.1	**Data Collection**				
2.1.1	Identify data utility	05.01.08	06.01.08	CH	X
2.1.2	Develop data collection instrument(s)				
2.1.2.1	Create draft questionnaire	06.01.08	06.12.08	CH	X
2.1.2.2	Review	06.12.08	06.30.08	CH, team	X
2.1.2.2.1	Review with evaluation team	06.13.08	06.20.08	CH	X
2.1.2.2.2	Review with stakeholder team	06.21.08	06.22.08	Team	X
2.1.2.3	Update based on results	06.23.08	06.28.08	CH	X
2.1.2.4	Finalize/test questionnaire	06.29.08	07.06.08	CH, team	X
2.1.2.5	Develop high-response strategy	06.01.08	07.06.08	CH, team	X
2.1.2.6	Finalize questionnaire communication	06.15.08	07.06.08	CH, team	X
2.1.3	Collect data during program				
2.1.3.1	Level 1 and Level 2 data	05.17.08	05.17.08	SH	X
2.1.4	Collect data postprogram				
2.1.4.1	Level 3 data	07.15.08	07.29.08	CH, team	X
2.1.4.1.1	Implement questionnaire admin/communications plan	07.10.08	07.31.08	CH, team	X
2.1.4.1.2	Implement questionnaire	07.15.08	07.15.08	CH, team	X
2.1.4.1.3	Close questionnaire	07.29.08	07.29.08	CH	X

the respondent of the purpose of the questionnaire and evaluation study, why he or she was chosen to participate, what will be done with the data he or she provides, the timeline for completing the questionnaire, and a point of contact if questions arise. Finally, incorporate any specific details into this section, such as whether responses will remain anonymous and the estimated time it will take to answer the questions.

The Body Drives Successful Data Collection

The body is where the questions are incorporated. Use different sections to identify the focus of the questions. A best practice is to divide the questions into sections based on the levels of evaluation. This format provides a flow that supports successful data collection.

The Conclusion Thanks the Respondent

Finalizing the questionnaire with a short conclusion section acknowledges the end of the questionnaire and provides an opportunity to thank the respondent for his or her time and contributions. This section can include any final instructions and reminders. If using a paper-based questionnaire, provide critical information to remind the respondent what to do with the completed document. Finally, repeat the point-of-contact information in case the respondent would like to follow-up after completing the questionnaire.

Developing the Perfect Question Involves a Few Critical Steps

Of all the activities involved in developing a questionnaire, creating the questions is the most important and time-consuming task. Asking the right question the right way drives the data collection and supports efficient data analysis. By following the three key steps below, you increase your likelihood of collecting the data you require.

Step 1: Identify the question's intent. The intent of the question derives from the specific objectives identified on the data collection plan. For each level of evaluation targeted for collecting data, the specific measure defines the exact data needed to determine if the program's objective was achieved or not. This information forms the intent of the questions.

Step 2: Determine the type of question. Various question types are available, and selecting the right one ensures you're asking the question the right way. Becoming familiar with the different question types (see table 4-3) facilitates the selection of the best one for the need. When selecting the question type, consider the consequences of the question format. For example, open-ended questions enable the respondent to freely provide information but may lead to extensive analysis. For rating-scale questions, using odd- or even-numbered scales depends on the need of the questionnaire, because there is no conclusive right or wrong way (Fink, 2003). Ultimately, the goal is to ensure you select the best question type to support the intent of the question.

Step 3: Finalize the question. Content that is well written further guarantees that the right question is being asked the right way. As each question is formulated, keep the point of view (first or second person), tone, and tense consistent. The question should not contain unfamiliar words, acronyms, or make assumptions about what the respondent knows. When working with rating-type questions, confirm that the question's statements align to the actual options available. For ratings scales that involve terminology that may

Table 4-3. Sample Question Types

Close-ended question

Multiple-choice:

While applying the skills and knowledge acquired from the Leadership Development program, I was supported /enabled by the following *(select all that apply)*:

- ☐ Management
- ☐ Support from colleagues and peers
- ☐ Confidence to apply
- ☐ Networking
- ☐ Other (please specify below)

One answer:

Of the measures provided below, which one measure is most directly affected by your application of the collaborative problem-solving process?

- ☐ Personal productivity
- ☐ Cost savings
- ☐ Sales/revenue
- ☐ Quality
- ☐ Time savings
- ☐ Other (please specify below)

Open-ended question

Free text:

In addition to the above, what other benefits have been realized by the Leadership Development Program? Use the text box below to provide your answer.

```

```

Numeric:

Approximately how many new sales leads did you identify as a result of your participation in the Sales Marketing Retreat? _____

Rank or order question

For there to be successful virtual networking within the Virtual Learning Community, rank the following items in order of importance where 1 is the most important and 5 is the least important:

- ___ Discussion groups
- ___ Professional place to meet with program peers and faculty (for example, chat rooms)
- ___ Student, alumni, and professor contact information
- ___ Student expertise captured, shared, and valued
- ___ Student personal/professional profiles (for example, interests, success stories, etc.)

Rating-scale question

Likert:

Since attending the Leadership Development Program, you have confidence in your ability to meet with individuals to discuss performance concerns.

Strongly Agree	Agree	Neither Agree nor Disagree	Disagree	Strongly Disagree

Semantic differential:

Based on your participation in the Brand Awareness Seminar, please indicate the extent to which your attitude has improved regarding the company's brand message.

No Improvement	1	2	3	4	5	Significant Improvement

not be commonly known (for example, very successful to not successful), provide definitions for each choice. This will not only help the respondent select the most accurate choice for his or her situation but ensure the question's intent is understood by all respondents. Last, review the questions to validate that they do not contain leading or loaded statements that could potentially influence the respondent into answering a certain way.

✍ Practitioner Tip: ✍

Before building your questionnaire, confirm the objectives (at each level) with key stakeholders and be knowledgeable of the survey tool's capabilities and limitations.

—Clifton Pierre
Certified ROI Professional

Optimizing the Effectiveness of the Questionnaire

Two final steps occur before launching the questionnaire. First, draft and review the completed questionnaire to ensure the needed information is incorporated. Second, test the instrument. When these steps are completed, the questionnaire's effectiveness is stronger and there is greater data collection success.

Draft Questionnaires Validate That the Elements Are Incorporated

Drafting the questionnaire ties the content together to develop the completed draft data collection instrument. This is the opportunity to review the introduction, body, and conclusion of the questionnaire to confirm the needed information is included. A thorough review also verifies the flow of the questionnaire is acceptable, the reading level is appropriate, and overall appearance is professional and appealing. While reviewing the draft questionnaire, consider how the questionnaire will be administered. Does the survey tool support the type of questions and functionality (for instance, skip logic) needed to administer the questionnaire?

Review the specific content to validate that the needed questions are integrated. Compare the questions included in the questionnaire against the data needed to complete the analysis. Finally, review the entire document for typos and other editing elements. Remember, the final draft should be an accurate, complete representation of the questionnaire so it can be tested to confirm it is ready for distribution.

Questionnaire Tests Confirm Content and Functionality

Completing a thorough test of the tool is one consistent activity that occurs with successful questionnaires. The four main areas to focus on during testing are the functionality, experience, accuracy, and alignment of the tool. The feedback regarding these areas either confirms the soundness of the tool or provides insight into improvements that need to occur before it is administered. When completing the test, have a sample group of the actual respondent population complete a test run. If this is not possible, have individuals participate who are similar to the respondent group. Developing a specific document to capture the required feedback from the test group is a best practice.

Focus Area 1: Functionality. Whether the questionnaire is administered electronically or is paper-based, the functionality of the tool needs to be tested. If it is an electronic questionnaire, check to make sure the links work, the question features are functioning correctly (for example, drop-down boxes, rankings, and so on), and other specific elements are performing as desired (for instance, moving between pages, skip logic, and so on). For a paper-based questionnaire, review the layout to ensure there is space to provide responses and the respondent can see the questions.

Focus Area 2: Experience. Another valuable area to enlist feedback involves the experience when completing the questionnaire. Ask the test group to provide feedback regarding the questionnaire's appearance, flow, layout, and ease to complete. This information, along with identifying how long it took to complete, further supports a successful launch.

Focus Area 3: Accuracy. Accuracy of the questionnaire involves confirming that needed content and instructions are included, and the right questions are asked the right way. Also review the validity and reliability of the instrument during the test. To be an effective data collection instrument, the questionnaire needs to provide consistent results over time (reliability) and measure what it is intended to measure (validity) (Phillips and Phillips, 2007).

Focus Area 4: Alignment. One area that is frequently overlooked during the development of a questionnaire involves how the collected data will be used and analyzed. After the results of the test are back, they should be reviewed to confirm their utility. Can the results be analyzed to answer the research questions? Is there the ability to compare the results with the baseline data? Addressing these types of questions allows for adjustments to be made, which ultimately supports efficient data analysis.

Preparing for the Questionnaire's Distribution

With the questionnaire completed, there are final activities to complete to successfully collect the data. The first step is to finalize the respondent population. After the group of respondents is determined, perform various administrative tasks before the questionnaire is ready for distribution.

The Right Respondent Group Reinforces Credibility

Determining the respondent population is a key step that you must complete before you launch the questionnaire. This information is captured on the data collection plan. The sources represent individuals who can provide relevant and accurate information from their experiences related to the evaluated program. Once the population has been verified as a credible source, the next step is to determine the sample size.

Determining the sample size involves identifying the number in the population, the confidence interval and level, the degree of variability, and the organization's normal response rate (see figure 4-1). These factors, and using a sample size table, determine the sample size.

The final consideration is determining whether or not the responses will be anonymous. The best practice is to maintain respondent confidentiality because it encourages open, candid responses. There is a link between respondents remaining anonymous and their honesty (Phillips and Stawarski, 2008). If it is challenging, however, to collect anonymous responses, have a third-party resource collect the results.

Administrative Tasks Clear the Path for a Seamless Launch

Obtaining a 100-percent response rate is the ultimate goal. Although this may not always be feasible, there are strategies that support achieving high response rates. Guiding Principle #6 of the ROI Methodology states if no improvement data are available for a population or

Figure 4-1. How to Determine the Sample Size

Determining the sample size can be completed using sample size tables and the five steps below.

Step	Example
1. Determine the population size	350
2. Determine the confidence interval (margin of error or results accuracy)	±5
3. Determine the confidence level (risk willing to accept that sample is within the average)	95% confidence
4. Determine the degree of variability (degree to which concepts measured are distributed within population)	• Estimate divided more or less 50%–50% on the concepts • Using a sample size table, base sample size needed is 187
5. Estimate the response rate to determine final sample size needed	Based on the organization's normal 85% response rate, the final sample size needed is 220 (187/.85)

Key Take-Away: Various sites on the Internet provide useful tools (for example, sample size tables, calculators) for determining the sample size.

Source: Watson (2001).

from a specific source, it is assumed that little or no improvement has occurred (Phillips and Phillips, 2005). Following this principle, if individuals do not provide data, no assumptions about the improvements experienced will be made. Therefore, it is critical to obtain as many responses as possible to ensure the data are collected to answer the research questions.

Incorporating applicable strategies identified in table 4-4 greatly improves the chances of reaching the desired response rate. Additionally, you should follow a comprehensive communication strategy that includes four key components.

Component 1: Content. The communication's content provides relevant information so respondents are fully aware of the questionnaire and its purpose. The details describe the action needed, the process for successfully providing the information, and the expected use of their responses. Other information to incorporate includes point of contact for questions, completion due date, and approximate time it will take to complete the questionnaire. Last, identify information relevant to reminders and thank you communications.

Component 2: Delivery Method. Use a variety of methods to deliver the needed communications. Although written communications are the most common method, using various delivery methods (for example, reminder phone call, in-person dialogue) can positively influence the response rate.

Component 3: Resources. Using a variety of resources (for example, executives, managers) to communicate the information about the questionnaire increases the awareness and potential response rate.

Component 4: Timeline. The timeline is the last piece of the communication strategy. As needed, adjust the timeline to prevent distraction with other initiatives. To further support achieving the desired response rate, build in extra time in the event the questionnaire's response time needs to be extended.

Executing the Questionnaire to Collect the Data

With all the elements in place, it is finally time to launch the questionnaire (see the sample in figure 4-2). On the day the questionnaire is to be implemented, prepare the

Table 4-4. Examples of Strategies for Improving Response Rates

The following strategies can improve the response rate of the questionnaire:

- ☐ Have the introduction letter signed by a top executive, administrator, or stakeholder
- ☐ Indicate who will see the results of the questionnaire
- ☐ Inform the participants what action will be taken with the data
- ☐ Keep the questionnaire simple and as brief as possible
- ☐ Make it easy to respond to; include a self-addressed, stamped envelope or email
- ☐ If appropriate, let the target audience know that it is part of a carefully selected sample
- ☐ Send a summary of results to the target audience
- ☐ Review the questionnaire at the end of the formal session
- ☐ Add emotional appeal
- ☐ Allow completion of the survey during work hours
- ☐ Design the questionnaire to attract attention, with a professional format
- ☐ Use the local point of contact to distribute the questionnaires
- ☐ Identify champions who will show support and encourage responses
- ☐ Provide an incentive (or chance for incentive) for quick response
- ☐ Consider paying for the time it takes to complete the questionnaire

Source: Phillips and Phillips (2005).

Figure 4-2. Sample Follow-Up Questionnaire

Our records indicate that you participated in the Leadership Program (LP). Your participation in this follow-up questionnaire is important to the program's continuous improvement and the effect the program is having on the organization. Completing this questionnaire will take approximately 30 minutes, and we request your responses by January 31, 2010. Should you have any questions, please contact caroline@roiinstitute.net. Thank you in advance for your contributions!

APPLICATION

	Yes	No
1. I applied the knowledge/skills I learned during the Leadership Program.	○	○

2. I spend the following percent of my total work time on tasks that require the knowledge/skills covered in the Leadership Program (circle the applicable answer).

   0%   10%   20%   30%   40%   50%   60%   70%   80%   90%   100%

	Strongly Agree	Agree	Neutral	Disagree	Strongly Disagree
3. I used at least one technique learned from the Leadership Program to improve my leadership capabilities.	○	○	○	○	○
4. I completed at least one step in my action plan for becoming a better leader.	○	○	○	○	○

5. While applying the knowledge and skills from the Leadership Program, I was supported by the following:

   (check all that apply)

   ☐ tools and templates provided

   ☐ my management

   ☐ support from colleagues and peers

   ☐ confidence to apply the materials

   ☐ networking

   ☐ other

   If "other" selected above, please describe: _____

6. The following deterred or prevented me from applying the Leadership Program's knowledge and skills:

   (check all that apply)

   ☐ no opportunity to use the material

   ☐ lack of support from management

   ☐ not enough time

   ☐ lack of confidence to do it

   ☐ lack of resources

   ☐ other

   If "other" selected above, please describe: _____

RESULTS

7. As a result of applying skills I attained from participating in the Leadership Program, the below measures have improved as follows

Note: When answering these questions please use the following scale:

(5) Significant improvement = the measure has improved by at least 90% in the past three months

(4) Strong improvement = the measure has improved by at least 75% in the past three months

(3) Some improvement = the measure has improved by at least 50% in the past three months

(2) Limited improvement = the measure has improved by at least 25% in the past three months

(1) No improvement = the measure has improved by 0% in the past three months

(0) N/A = this measure is not applicable to my work

	Significant Improvement 5	Strong Improvement 4	Some Improvement 3	Limited Improvement 2	No Improvement 1	N/A 0
Productivity	O	O	O	O	O	O
Sales / revenue	O	O	O	O	O	O
Quality of work	O	O	O	O	O	O
Cost savings	O	O	O	O	O	O
Efficiency	O	O	O	O	O	O
Time savings	O	O	O	O	O	O
Teamwork	O	O	O	O	O	O
Innovation	O	O	O	O	O	O
My job satisfaction	O	O	O	O	O	O
My employees' job satisfaction	O	O	O	O	O	O
Customer satisfaction	O	O	O	O	O	O
Other	O	O	O	O	O	O

If "other" selected, please describe the other measures that were positively influenced by the program:

_____

8. Recognizing that other factors could have influenced the above improvements, I estimate the percent of improvement that is attributable (i.e., isolated) to the Leadership Program is (express as a percentage where 100% represents fully attributable)

_____ %

9. My confidence in the estimation provided in the above question is (0% is no confidence; 100% is certainty)

_____ %

10. I have the following suggestions for improving the Leadership Program:

Thank you again for your time and valuable contributions!

_____

communication and if applicable, verify the electronic questionnaire is ready to accept responses. A best practice is to check the responses shortly after launching the questionnaire. If responses have been received, it is confirmation that the process is working. However, if there are no responses, double check to confirm the questionnaire request was received. When sending the reminders, providing the response rate further encourages individuals to complete the questionnaire. Finally, once all the responses are collected, officially close the questionnaire and begin analyzing data.

‰ Practitioner Tip ‰

When using a questionnaire, think ahead and have an administrative plan that includes effective strategies, timelines, and resources that support data collection. Be creative—consider including healthy competition across departments or facilities to motivate responses.

—Melissa Scherwinski
Measurement Coordinator

Knowledge Check

For each practice exercise below, select the option that you think represents the best formatted and written question. After you are done, check your answers in the appendix.

Practice 1:

Option A:
Following your participation in the program, did you receive the right quantity and quality of resource material?

Option B:
Following your participation in the program, did you receive

1. Quantity of resource material? (yes, no, other—please specify)
2. Quality of resource material? (yes, no, other—please specify)

Practice 2:

Option A:
I think the new call-tracking database is effective (strongly agree to strongly disagree).

Option B:
I think the new, top-of-the-line call-tracking database is effective (strongly agree to strongly disagree).

Practice 3:

Option A:

The facilitator was effective (strongly agree to strongly disagree).

Option B:

The facilitator encouraged participation in discussions during the course (strongly agree to strongly disagree).

Practice 4:

Option A:

As a result of participating in the Process X program, to what extent were you able to use the five processing steps? (completely successful—guidance not needed; somewhat successful—some guidance needed; limited success—guidance needed; no success—not able to do even with guidance; N/A—no opportunity to use)

Option B:

Were you able to successfully use the five process steps? (yes, no)

Practice 5:

Option A:

As a result of the Team-Building Conference, there has been a reduction in silo thinking in the departments (strongly agree to strongly disagree).

Option B:

As a result of the Team-Building Conference, the departments are exchanging ideas and best practices (strongly agree to strongly disagree).

About the Author

As director of consulting services with the ROI Institute, **Caroline Hubble, CPLP, CRP,** facilitates various courses on the ROI Methodology and provides expert coaching to individuals working toward ROI certification. Hubble's professional background includes financial industry experience, where she managed training evaluation, analytics, and operations for business line and enterprise-wide training departments. She has successfully designed and implemented evaluation and reporting strategies for various complex programs. Her operational, project, and relationship management expertise is noted for significantly contributing to improved business practices.

Hubble holds a BA in psychology from Rollins College and is a Certified ROI Practitioner. She received her ASTD Certified Professional in Learning and Performance (CPLP) credentials in 2006. She can be reached at caroline@roiinstitute.net.

References

Fink, A. (2003). *How to Ask Survey Questions*. Thousand Oaks, CA: Sage Publications.

Phillips, P. P. and J. J. Phillips. (2005). *Return on Investment Basics*. Alexandria, VA: ASTD.

Phillips, P. P. and J. J. Phillips. (2007). *Show Me the Money*. San Francisco: Berrett-Koehler.

Phillips, P. P. and C. A. Stawarski. (2008). *Measurement and Evaluation Series, Book 2 Data Collection*. San Francisco: Pfeiffer.

Watson, J. (2001). *How to Determine a Sample Size: Tipsheet 60*. University Park, PA: Penn State Cooperative Extension.

Additional Reading

Alreck, P. L., and R. B. Settle. (1995). *The Survey Research Handbook: Guidelines and Strategies for Conducting a Survey*, 2nd ed. New York: McGraw-Hill.

Fink, A. (2003). *The Survey Handbook*, 2nd ed. Thousand Oaks, CA: Sage Publications.

Walonick, D. S. (2004). *Survival Statistics*. Bloomington, MN: StatPac, Inc.

 **Chapter 5**

Designing a Criterion-Referenced Test

Sharon A. Shrock and William C. Coscarelli

In This Chapter

This chapter describes the process of creating valid and defensible criterion-referenced tests—tests that measure the performance of an individual against a standard of competency. This chapter will enable you to

- distinguish between norm-referenced and criterion-referenced tests

- describe the basic steps in designing a criterion-referenced test

- use the decision table to estimate the number of items to include on a criterion-referenced test

- use the Angoff technique to set the cut-off score for a criterion-referenced test.

A Rationale and Model for Designing a Criterion-Referenced Test

Two types of tests are in common use today—norm-referenced tests (NRTs) and criterion-referenced tests (CRTs). These tests are constructed to provide two very different types of information. Norm-referenced tests are created to compare test takers against one another, whereas criterion-referenced tests are designed to measure a test taker's performance against a performance standard. NRTs are appropriately used to make selection decisions. For example, one might use an NRT to select the strongest applicants for admission to veterinary school; a valid NRT would be helpful in making those decisions, because there are typically many more applicants to vet schools than there are available openings. These tests are commonly given in schools, but are also used within personnel departments to improve hiring decisions. CRTs, however, are widely used in professional certification exams and are typically more appropriate in a training and performance improvement environment, when an organization needs to verify that workers can accomplish important job tasks. In terms of Kirkpatrick's (1994) four evaluation levels, CRTs are appropriately administered following training to see if trainees have met the objectives of instruction—Level 2 evaluation.

A Criterion-Referenced Test Development Model

Even though CRTs are informative and useful to organizations, the procedures for constructing these tests have only recently been disseminated beyond professional psychometricians to training and performance improvement specialists. Figure 5-1 displays the model written by Shrock and Coscarelli (2000, 2007), which overviews the steps of creating CRTs that are both valid and defensible.

Because most training professionals, even those with graduate school degrees in instructional design, have not been schooled in measurement theory and practice, they typically write tests similar to the teacher-made tests they took so frequently during their own educational experiences. The majority of those tests will have been "topic-based" tests, neither designed to reliably separate test-taker scores from one another, nor grounded in specific competencies that would support a criterion-referenced interpretation of scores (Shrock and Coscarelli, 2007). Such invalid assessments are poor, even dangerous, examples to follow in today's high-stakes world of competition and litigation.

The Value of Criterion-Referenced Testing

This chapter introduces some of the most essential guidelines to follow to make testing work for you and your organization. In particular, this chapter provides guidance for establishing content validity, determining test length, and setting the passing score for CRTs. Indeed, valid and defensible testing is doable in most organizations and the rewards are many: employees made more productive through improved knowledge and skill; a training and development staff guided by data to maximum effectiveness; a performance improvement function armed with the solid knowledge required to pinpoint problems through evaluation at Levels 3, 4, and 5—transfer, results, and ROI (Phillips, 1996); and an organization that succeeds for both its employees and its customers.

Figure 5-1. Model for Criterion-Referenced Test Development

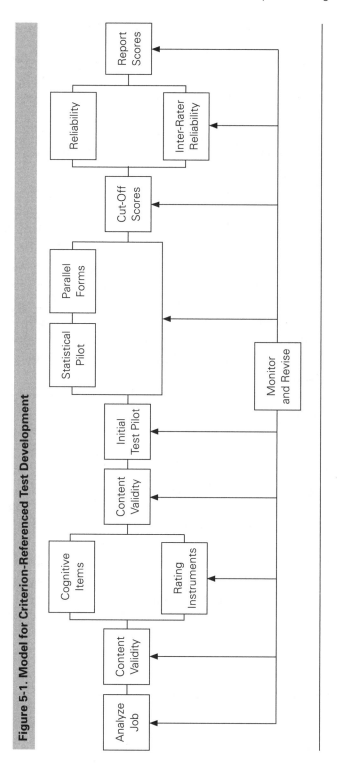

Ensuring That Tests Provide Valid and Defensible Information

Test validity and test defensibility both have roots in a single concept: job relatedness. In fact, the term *job relatedness* is a technical and legal phrase. Simply put, a test that does not measure what people actually know and do to perform a job successfully cannot be expected to produce valid information about who can do that job. Furthermore, administering tests that are not verifiably job related to make substantive decisions about test takers (for example, hiring or promotion decisions) is likely to be found illegal if challenged.

Content Validity

Although there are many different kinds of test validity (for example, face validity, predictive validity, concurrent validity, as well as others), the most important one for CRTs to possess is content validity. In the context of testing employees, the content of the test is valid if it asks test takers to demonstrate that they have job-related knowledge or can perform job-related tasks. One must understand an important legal qualification at this point. The test cannot demand that the employee demonstrate greater knowledge or more proficient performance of tasks than that required to do the job successfully. It is the role of an NRT to determine whom among the test takers has the greatest knowledge and/or performs the job tasks the best. The goal of the CRT is to distinguish between those who are competent to perform the job and those who are not. Notice how the CRT development process will require the organization to engage in a very healthy examination of what employees actually must do on their jobs and how well they must do it.

Procedure for Establishing Content Validity. The process of formally establishing content validity is straightforward and conceptually simple. Job analysis performed by subject matter experts (SMEs) is the basis of the competency statements upon which the test items are written. Following item creation, SMEs must then examine the items and verify that they match important job knowledge and/or tasks. SMEs performing this review should also report any items that are unclear, have implausible incorrect answers among multiple-choice options, require a knowledge of vocabulary or terminology greater than that required by the job, or contain other suspected flaws. Because SMEs are often new to test creation, it is a good idea for the test designer to have some other knowledgeable colleague read over the test, looking for item flaws, such as cues to the correct answers.

Importance of Test Documentation. Legal defensibility of the test is likely to be important if performance on the test has substantial consequences for test takers, if the test measures mastery of competencies that protect health and safety, or if the test fulfills compliance obligations in a regulated field. To maintain legal defensibility of the test, it is critical to document the test-creation process. Because of content validation's centrality among legal criteria, documentation of the content-validation procedure and reviewers is essential. Not only are the names of those SMEs who validated the content of the exam important elements of the test documentation, but also their credentials to serve in that role. Be certain to complete contemporaneously all test documentation as the steps in creating the test are taken. Trying to reconstruct test documentation after the test has been challenged is not likely to be successful.

Test Length

Determining how many items to include on a test is one of the most challenging decisions in creating the test. There is no simple guideline or rule that easily answers this question. We know that test length is positively related to test reliability—the consistency of test scores over repeated administrations or across different forms of the test. A longer test allows more accurate assessment than a shorter test, assuming all of the items are of equal quality. (This is another way of saying a bigger collection of invalid items doesn't help.) However, longer tests are more expensive to create and, obviously, more expensive to administer, assuming that test-taking time is time lost to instruction or lost on the job.

Problems with Uniform Test Length. Some decision makers, especially those in senior management, seek to simplify the test length decision by dictating a uniform test length throughout an organization, that is, mandating that all tests administered will have a specific number of items, usually 50 or 60. This practice is generally not wise. Organizations that use tests strategically will determine carefully the business consequences of testing errors when deciding on the necessary quality of the test—one component of which is test length. Remember there are two types of CRT errors—erroneously classifying someone who has not acquired the competencies assessed by the test as a "master" of them or judging as a "nonmaster" someone who is truly a master performer of the competencies. Therefore, tests that measure critical competencies and/or have serious consequences for test takers should be the longest tests the organization administers.

Content Domain Size and Test Length. Another important factor in determining test length is what psychometricians often call content domain size. The objective from which the items have been written describes the content domain, and theoretically, its size refers to the total number of possible items that could be written from that objective. Obviously, for most objectives, that could be a very large number. An actual count of the possible items, however, is not the intent of considering domain size. Rather, most test writers can imagine that the possible sizes of different objective content domains vary considerably. For example, compare the content domain sizes of the following objectives:

- From memory, state the number of elements represented in the periodic table.
- Without reference material, multiply any two-digit number by any two-digit number.
- Given an instrument panel with all values represented, determine the cause of loss of altitude of the Boeing 747.

Without attempting to count the possibilities that could be written to measure any of these objectives, most test writers can see that the first objective represents an extremely small content domain; the second one represents a much larger, but finite domain; and the third one represents a large domain with less certain boundaries. Extending this comparison to item numbers, objective one can be measured with one item, whereas, objectives two and three are going to require considerably more items. In addition, objective three will require creating multiple items to assess the most common and the most dangerous causes of an airliner dropping in altitude. Criticality of the objective is a key governor of how thoroughly mastery of a large domain should be explored by test items.

Relatedness of Objectives and Test Length. An additional factor that affects test length is how closely related the objectives that the test assesses are to one another. For example, if one objective represents a competency that is a prerequisite to performance of another objective, test items that measure the latter objective will simultaneously measure the former. For example, items that measure competency in long division also measure competencies in multiplication and subtraction. The point for test length is that if the responses for items that measure a given objective are likely to be the same as responses to items that measure a second objective (responses are positively correlated), fewer items will likely suffice to assess these two objectives than would be required to assess two unrelated objectives (responses to which are likely uncorrelated). Essentially, the test writer can take advantage of the dual assessment properties of some items.

Problems with "Weighting" Test Items. Research on the relationship between test length and test reliability indicates that for each objective measured, the gain in reliability attributed to each item that is added to the test starts to decline after the fourth item (Hambleton, Mills, and Simon, 1983). Reliability continues to increase as items are added, but the rate of improvement starts to decline after the fourth item. Even though this finding is useful, most test writers think that, among the objectives assessed by a test, some objectives are likely to be more critical than others. The more critical objectives warrant more test items included to measure them. In fact, this practice is the legitimate way to "weight" test scores; rather than weighting important items by multiplying the points awarded for correct answers to them, it is far better to weight important competencies by including more test items that measure them. The additional items improve the test's quality, whereas multiplying item scores simply multiplies the effect on total test scores of any error associated with the multiplied item.

A Decision Table for Test Length Determination. Table 5-1 was created to help test writers decide how many items for each objective assessed by the test should be included on the completed test (Shrock and Coscarelli, 2007). Read from left to right, the table indicates in the last column an estimated number of test items per objective following decisions about criticality of the objective, content domain size, and relatedness to other objectives. Notice that estimated total test length would then be the sum of the numbers of items included for each objective measured by the test.

It should be noted that table 5-1 provides only estimates based on the factors discussed above that impinge on the test length decision. The final decision regarding test length is always a matter of professional judgment, and the opinions of SMEs can be essential in making the criticality, content domain size, and objectives relatedness decisions.

Setting the Test's Mastery Cut-Off Score

Unlike NRTs, where the meaning of a test score is a statement (typically a percentile) reflecting where that score falls in relation to the scores obtained by others in a given comparison group, the score on a CRT has meaning only in relation to (above or below)

Table 5-1. Decision Table for Test Length Determination

	Criticality of Objective	Content Domain Size	Relatedness to Other Objectives	Number of Test Items
If the Objective Is:	Critical	From Large Domain	Unrelated	10–20
			Related	10
		From Small Domain	Unrelated	5–10
			Related	5
	Not Critical	From Large Domain	Unrelated	6
			Related	4
		From Small Domain	Unrelated	2
			Related	1

a predetermined cut-off, that is, "passing" score. Typically, a test taker's raw score on a CRT is not reported; instead the test taker is reported as either a master or a nonmaster based on his or her CRT performance. Therefore, CRTs require that this cut-off score be established.

It is not uncommon for an organization to establish the cut-off score centrally, that is, to create a single cut-off score for all tests administered within the organization. Such cut-off scores might even be determined by a single manager and communicated as a directive to all test developers and administrators (not to mention test takers) affected. Too often, these singular cut-off scores reflect the school experiences of a handful of managers, that is, 80 percent was a B grade in high school, so 80 percent becomes the mandated passing score throughout an organization. CRT cut-off scores determined in this manner are likely to be indefensible if challenged through the courts.

The Angoff Method of Cut-Off Score Determination

There are several different recognized, defensible ways to set the CRT cut-off score. The technique presented here is one that belongs to a class of techniques called conjectural methods. The Angoff method (named for the psychometrician who devised it) is probably the technique used most often to set the passing scores for professional certification exams. Its popularity is no doubt largely due to its logistical feasibility, and its wide application probably strengthens its defensibility in the face of a challenge.

Steps in Using the Angoff Method. The Angoff technique relies on SME ability to estimate for each item the likelihood that a "minimally competent" test taker (one who is just competent enough to do the assessed job tasks) will answer correctly. The list of steps in implementing the Angoff method follows.

1. Begin by carefully selecting SMEs who are totally familiar with the competencies that the test assesses and who are also knowledgeable about the skill sets of persons who succeed and those who do not succeed in performing those competencies on the job.
2. If at all possible, bring the SMEs together at a common location where they can work both independently and together without interruptions.
3. Give each SME the items proposed for the test (or for inclusion in the item bank for the test), including the proposed correct answer to each item.
4. Separate the SMEs and ask them to read each item and for each item individually estimate the probability (from 0 to 100) of the "minimally competent" performer answering that item correctly. Clarify that their estimates can be any value from 0, (indicating that virtually no minimally competent performer will get the item correct) to 100 (indicating that virtually any minimally competent performer will answer correctly); estimates

need not be in 10- or 25-percent increments, that is, they can be .67 or .43—whatever probability best reflects the SME's judgment. You will have to stress that the "minimally competent" performer is not an incompetent performer; rather, the minimally competent person is a just-passing master of the competencies reflected in the items.

5. Bring the SMEs back together and examine their estimates for each item. Ask them to discuss and reconcile any estimates that deviate by more than 10 percentage points.

6. Add up the probability estimates for each SME.

7. Add all of the totals and divide by the number of SMEs—average the total estimates across all SMEs.

8. The average estimate is the proposed cut-off score for the test. This cut-off score can be adjusted higher or lower depending on whether the organization is especially concerned about preventing nonmasters from assuming the assessed job position or whether the greater concern is failing to recognize true masters.

Knowledge Check: A Microtest to Practice Setting a Cut-Off Score

For this practice exercise, assume that you are an SME trying to establish a cut-off score for a test composed of the following five items. The test has been created to measure competence in creating CRTs using some of the information from this chapter. Read each item, choose the best answer, and note the correct answer appearing below the last choice. Then estimate the probability that the minimally competent test designer will answer the item correctly. (A real test to measure this competency would require far more items than appear here; this microtest is just for practice with setting a cut-off score.) Check your answers in the appendix.

Probability

_____ 1. Nearly every high-school graduating class selects a valedictorian and salutatorian. What kind of decision do these choices represent?
   a. Norm-referenced
   b. Criterion-referenced
   c. Domain-referenced
   d. None of the above

(Answer is a.)

_____ 2. Ann goes bowling. Every time she rolls the ball, it goes into the gutter. In testing terms, Ann's performance might best be described as
   a. both reliable and valid
   b. neither reliable nor valid
   c. valid, but not reliable
   d. reliable, but not valid

(Answer is d.)

_____ 3. According to the research on the relationship between test length and test reliability, a test that measures seven objectives should have a total of how many items?
   a. 7
   b. 14
   c. 21
   d. 28

(Answer is <u>d</u>.)

_____ 4. Which of the following is most likely a criterion-referenced test?
   a. A fourth-grade teacher-made geography test
   b. A state driver's license test
   c. A spelling bee contest
   d. A standardized college admission exam

(Answer is <u>b</u>.)

_____ 5. Which of the following objectives would probably be represented by the largest number of questions on a test?
   a. Given the relevant numerical values, calculate gross national product for the United States in 2008.
   b. Given a decade from history and a choice among national political leaders, identify the most influential leaders of the specified time period.
   c. Given access to survey data regarding food preferences, religious beliefs, national origin, age, and gender, generate strategies for weight loss among those who responded.

(Answer is <u>c</u>.)

_____ Cut-Off Score (sum of estimates)

Guidelines for Creating Criterion-Referenced Tests

As you might imagine from looking at the 13 steps in the Model for Criterion-Referenced Test Development (figure 5.1), there are quite a few decisions and processes you will have to attend to for creating a valid CRT. However, in this section we have tried to distill the most pressing CRT issues into eight guidelines that should serve as important mileposts for your efforts.

1. Clarify the purpose of any test you are asked to create. If the purpose is to rank order test takers or choose the best performers, use a norm-referenced test. Use a criterion-referenced test when you want to make a master/nonmaster decision about individual test takers based upon their performances of specific competencies.
2. Be certain that your CRT assesses only job-related competencies; its content validity and defensibility rely on a careful job analysis.

3. Document the content validation process and all subsequent steps taken in creating the test; the defensibility of the test relies heavily on contemporaneous documentation.

4. Because test reliability is related to test length, make strategic decisions regarding the criticality of testing consequences before determining test length; the more critical the competencies assessed, the longer the test should be.

5. Consider the content domain size implied by the competencies assessed as well as the relatedness of the assessed competencies to one another in determining test length. Include more items on the test for critical competencies, those that require mastery of a large content domain, and those that are unrelated to other competencies assessed by the test.

6. Use a defensible, recognized technique to set the cut-off score that separates masters from nonmasters; the Angoff technique is perhaps the easiest one logistically for most organizations to use.

7. Be certain that the SMEs chosen to participate in the Angoff cut-off score determination understand the concept of "minimal competence." Allow the SMEs to practice estimating probabilities for several items and share their opinions to help them reach consensus about the concept of "minimal competence" for the assessed job competencies. Remind SMEs that the estimated probability for any item should not be below the chance probability of answering the item correctly. For example, the minimum probability estimate for a four-choice multiple-choice item should be .25.

8. Adjust the cut-off score up or down depending on which error in test results—false positives or false negatives—the organization most wants to minimize.

About the Authors

Sharon A. Shrock, PhD, graduated from Indiana University in 1979 with a PhD in instructional systems technology. She joined the faculty at Virginia Tech before moving to Southern Illinois University Carbondale, where she is currently professor and coordinator for the instructional design and technology programs within the Department of Curriculum and Instruction. She specializes in instructional design and program evaluation and has been an evaluation consultant to international corporations, school districts, and federal instructional programs. She is the former co-director of the Hewlett-Packard World Wide Test Development Center. Shrock is first author (with William C. Coscarelli) of *Criterion-Referenced Test Development: Technical and Legal Guidelines for Corporate Training* (2007), now in its third edition, and has written extensively in the field of testing and evaluation. In 1991, she won the Outstanding Book Award for *Criterion-Referenced Test Development* from both AECT's Division of Instructional Development and from the National Society for Performance and Instruction. She can be reached at sashrock@siu.edu.

William C. Coscarelli, PhD, graduated from Indiana University in 1977 with a PhD in instructional systems. He joined the faculty at Southern Illinois University Carbondale, where he is professor emeritus in the instructional design program of the Department of Curriculum and Instruction. He also served as the co-director of the Hewlett-Packard World Wide Test Development Center. Coscarelli is a former president of the International Society for Performance Improvement (ISPI), an international association dedicated to improving performance in the workplace. He was ISPI's first vice president of publications and is the recipient of ISPI's Distinguished Service Award. He is author of the *Decision-Making Style Inventory* (2007), coauthor (with Gregory White) of *The Guided Design Guidebook* (1986), and second author (with Sharon Shrock) of *Criterion-Referenced Test Development: Technical and Legal Guidelines for Corporate Training* (2007). He has made more than one hundred presentations in his career and written more than 60 articles. He can be reached at coscarel@siu.edu.

References

Hambleton, R. K., C. N. Mills, and R. Simon. (1983). Determining the Lengths for Criterion-Referenced Tests. *Journal of Educational Measurement* 20(1): 27–38.

Kirkpatrick, D. L. (1994). *Evaluating Training Programs: The Four Levels*. San Francisco: Berrett-Koehler.

Phillips, J. J. (1996, April). Measuring ROI: The Fifth Level of Evaluation. Technical and Skills Training. www.astd.org/virtual_community/comm_evaluation/phillips/pdf. Retrieved November 9, 2009.

Shrock, S. A. and W. C. Coscarelli. (2000). *Criterion-Referenced Test Development: Technical and Legal Guidelines for Corporate Training and Certification*. Washington, DC: International Society for Performance Improvement.

Shrock, S. A. and W. C. Coscarelli. (2007). *Criterion-Referenced Test Development: Technical and Legal Guidelines for Corporate Training*. San Francisco: Pfeiffer.

Additional Reading

Cizek, G. J. and M. B. Bunch. (2007). *Standard Setting: A Guide to Establishing and Evaluating Performance Standards on Tests*. Thousand Oaks, CA: Sage Publications.

Downing, S. M. and T. M. Haladyna, eds. (2006). *Handbook of Test Development*. Mahwah, NJ: Lawrence Earlbaum.

Hambleton, R. K. (1999). Criterion-Referenced Testing Principles, Technical Advances, and Evaluation Guidelines. In Gutkin, Terry and Cecil Reynolds eds., *The Handbook of School Psychology* 3rd ed. New York, NY: Wiley and Sons, 409–433.

 **Chapter 6**

Conducting Interviews

Anne F. Marrelli

·························· **In This Chapter** ··························

In interviews, an individual responds orally to questions asked orally by one or more persons. Interviews may be conducted face-to-face or via telephone or video conferencing. This chapter provides basic guidelines for developing and applying interviews to collect data for evaluating training and other development programs. By reading this chapter, you will learn to

- ▓ identify situations in which interviews are an effective data collection method
- ▓ develop interview questions
- ▓ plan and conduct interviews
- ▓ identify appropriate analysis techniques for the data you collect in interviews.

Types of Interviews

There are two basic types of interviews: structured and unstructured. Descriptions of each are listed below.

Structured Interviews

In a structured interview, the interviewer asks a series of preplanned questions to all interviewees. The interviewee may be asked to select one of several choices provided (close-ended questions) or may be asked to respond in his or her own words (open-ended questions).

Tables 6-1 and 6-2 are examples of close-ended and open-ended questions.

Unstructured Interviews

In unstructured interviews, each interviewee may be asked different questions, and no response choices are provided. The interviewers are free to develop their own questions based on the interviewees' particular characteristics or experiences or their responses to previous questions.

Structured interviews are usually more efficient and accurate for collecting factual information. For this type of information, consider using close-end questions with a list of response choices for each question; however, allow for other responses. Using a response scale makes

Table 6-1. Example of Close-Ended Question

How often do you think you will apply what you learned in class to your work?

  a. Every day
  b. Once a week
  c. Once a month
  d. Every few months
  e. Less than every few months

Table 6-2. Example of Open-Ended Question

How do you plan to apply what you learned in class to your work?

_____

_____

_____

_____

_____

_____

analyzing data much easier and faster. Open-ended questions can provide the most in-depth information for complex issues and topics related to people's personal experiences and ideas. Many interviews combine both structured and unstructured techniques. For example, an interviewer may begin with a series of standard, preplanned questions about an employee's overall reactions to a training program and then tailor subsequent questions to better understand the employee's responses.

Using Interviews for Evaluating Training

Interviews are a useful tool for assessing participants' and other stakeholders' perceptions of a training or development program and the extent to which participants have applied their learning to the job (that is, how their work behaviors have changed). Interviews capture a range of perspectives and can be easily modified for different stakeholders, both within and outside an organization. For example, when I was working at a large aerospace firm, a colleague and I conducted an evaluation of a pilot 360-degree feedback process. We interviewed the engineers, their raters, their managers, and the top executive. Although the topics of the interviews were the same, we worded the questions differently for each group. Each group provided a different perspective on the usefulness of the process and how it could be improved.

Employees, their coworkers and managers, and other stakeholders can be interviewed to determine how a training or performance improvement program has changed the work performance of employees. For example, managers can be questioned about the quality of their employees' work in the targeted area before and after a training program. For employees who have direct client contact, the clients could also be interviewed about the service provided to them.

Interviews can be used to collect anecdotal data about the value of the training, both through success stories in which the training program played an important role in preparing an employee to successfully resolve a problem and through incidents in which the training did not provide adequate preparation. Anecdotal data provide dramatic demonstrations of the effect of a training or development program. They spark interest in an evaluation report or presentation because they give real-life examples and provide the human story behind the research.

Interviews are also an effective approach to identifying obstacles to the success of the training program. For example, using carefully crafted questions, the interviewer can guide interviewees to candidly discuss the problems they faced in applying their classroom learning to the job. This information can then be used to plan how to better support transfer of learning to the job.

Advantages and Disadvantages of Interviews

As with any other data collection method, interviews have distinct advantages and disadvantages. Several are summarized below.

Advantages

- The primary advantage of interviews is the in-depth information they can provide. Typically, people are reluctant to provide similarly detailed responses in a written questionnaire or focus group.
- Through the personal interaction with the interviewee, the interviewer can build rapport and trust, and thus promote sharing candid information that the interviewee would not provide in a survey or focus group.
- Questions can be tailored to the characteristics and circumstances of individual interviewees.
- The interviewer can probe for more detail, clarity, and context of the information the interviewee offers or expand the scope of the interview to include topics that arise.
- In face-to-face interviews, the interviewer can observe body language, gestures, and tone of voice that reveal feelings and attitudes toward both the interview itself and the topic of discussion.
- The personal connection inherent in interviews helps to build buy-in for supporting or revising training programs.

Disadvantages

- Interviews are expensive and time consuming.
- Skilled interviewers are required to obtain high-quality data.
- It can be difficult to accurately and fully record the interviewee's responses.
- The qualitative data obtained may be difficult and laborious to analyze.
- Interviews are potentially biased, both in how the interview is conducted and how the interviewee responds from the perspective of the interviewer, the interviewee, situational variables, and the interaction of these. For example, a female interviewee may respond differently to a female interviewer than she would to a male interviewer on some topics.
- Some people find interviews threatening and will not provide candid information.
- It can be difficult or impossible to determine the accuracy of the information provided by the interviewee.

Use Multiple Methods of Data Collection

To ensure that the evaluation data you collect are accurate and reliable, use more than one method of collecting information. All research methods have weaknesses and strengths. When you use interviews to collect data, also use a method with complementary strengths and weaknesses. Multiple methods provide a sounder basis for your conclusions. The data collected with different instruments also illuminate multiple facets of the issue and, therefore, provide deeper and broader insights. The data, and therefore the evaluation, will have more credibility with your internal or external clients. For example, because interview administration and data analysis are time consuming, interviews are usually not practical for large groups. However, they can be used to collect initial information to develop questions for surveys or focus groups that will allow for input from much larger populations to verify the interview data collected. Interviews also can be used to follow up surveys or focus groups to collect more in-depth information from a subset of the survey or focus group respondents.

Guidelines for Planning and Conducting Interviews

The eight steps of planning and conducting an effective interview are presented below.

Step 1: Identify the Specific Objectives and Respondents for the Interview

The first step in planning an interview is to clearly define the information you want to collect and identify the people who can best provide that information. Do you want to know how employees feel about a program, what they learned, or if they applied what they learned to the job? Who can most accurately answer your questions: the employees themselves, their managers, their customers, or their coworkers?

For example, we want to know if the 30 managers who completed the "Giving Employees Useful Feedback" course are applying what they learned on the job. Because employees are the recipients of the feedback, we will ask them about the feedback provided by their managers. We do not have the resources to interview all 240 employees of the managers, so we will draw a random sample of one employee per manager to interview.

Step 2: Plan How to Record and Analyze Data

Because the methods used to collect and analyze the data are interdependent, it is important to plan how you will analyze the data before making a final decision to use interviews for evaluation data collection. You need to determine if the resources and skills required for summarizing and interpreting the data collected will be available to you. Close-ended interview questions typically produce quantitative data, while open-ended questions result in qualitative data. Usual methods of summarizing quantitative data obtained from interviews are frequencies, percentages, and cross-tabulations; these may then be used with more advanced statistical methods, such as correlations or tests of significant differences, for example, chi-square and t-tests, and analysis of variance. Content analysis techniques are typically used for qualitative interview data.

Step 3: Develop the Interview Protocol

Interviewers should develop an interview protocol or script to ensure all needed information is collected and the interviews are consistent for all interviewees. The protocol should include

- instructions to the interviewers
- space to record demographic information about the interviewee that is relevant to the evaluation (This information should be completed before the protocol is given to the interviewer.)
- an introductory statement for interviewees to explain the purpose of the interview, the procedure to be followed, the length of the interview, and an explanation of confidentiality
- the questions that will be asked
- a closing statement thanking the interviewees for their time and explaining next steps
- space for the interviewer to record the interviewee's responses.

Figure 6-1 is an example of an interview protocol.

When preparing the interview questions, do not ask for information that can be easily obtained elsewhere, such as in personnel records. Organize questions by topic and arrange them from general to specific within each topic. At the conclusion, allow time to ask the interviewees if there is anything they would like to add.

❧ Practitioner Tip ❧

- Include only one idea in each question
- Use simple, familiar language
- Use complete sentences
- Do not use words or terms that have multiple meanings
- Use positive rather than negative inquiries whenever possible
- Screen the content, wording, and tone for potential offensiveness

---

Figure 6-1. Sample Interview Protocol

Interview for the "Giving Employees Useful Feedback" Course Evaluation

Interviewer Name: _____

Interviewee Name:_____ Phone Number: _____

Work Unit: _____ Years of Work Experience: _____

Interview Date and Time:

_____

Instructions to Interviewer are in italics.

Opening Statement

Read the following statement to the interviewee:

Hello, [name]. My name is .... *[Take a moment here for small talk to build rapport.]* We are talking to a sample of the employees of the managers who recently participated in the "Giving Employees Useful Feedback" course to find out if they are applying what they learned in class on the job. The information you provide will be kept confidential. It will only be seen by the evaluation analysts who will summarize the data for all employees. This information will help us improve the training course.

I will ask you several questions about the feedback your manager has given you in the last month. Depending on your responses, the interview will take from five to 30 minutes. We are defining feedback as information about your performance that explains what you did well or how you could improve. Feedback can range from a few words as your manager passes you in the hall to a long discussion in his or her office.

Questions

Ask the interviewee the following questions and note the responses below each question.

1. In the last month, has your manager given you feedback?

    Circle employee's response: Yes   No

2. Did you request feedback from your manager in the last month?

    Circle employee's response: Yes   No

If the employee responded no to both Questions 1 and 2, skip to the Closing Statement.
If the employee responds yes to Question 2, ask:

   2a: Approximately how many times did you ask the manager for feedback?
   2b: Please describe the situations in which you asked for feedback.

Proceed with Question 3 if the employee responded yes to Question 1. Otherwise, skip to the Closing Statement.

3. How would you rate the helpfulness of the feedback your manager has given you in the past month?

    _____ Very helpful
    _____ Helpful
    _____ Somewhat helpful
    _____ Not helpful
    _____ Harmful

(continued on next page)

Figure 6-1. Sample Interview Protocol (continued)

4. Please describe the most helpful feedback your manager has given you in the past month. As best as you can remember, tell me about the situation and what the manager said.

5. Why did you find this feedback especially helpful?

(Note: Additional questions would appear here.)

Closing Statement

Read the following statement to the interviewee:

This concludes the interview. Thank you for taking the time to help us improve managerial training. Your input is valuable. We will present the results of the interviews to the executive team next month.

Step 4: Pilot Test and Revise the Interview

Pilot testing is a vital component of interview development. In a pilot test, interviews are conducted with a small group of participants to identify revisions needed to the questions, instructions, and data-recording procedures. You should also try out the data analysis techniques and preview the potential difficulty and time requirements for the full analysis.

Step 5: Plan the Interview Schedule

In most cases, limit each interview to 45 minutes or less. Many people find it difficult to focus fully for longer periods. Schedule sufficient time between interviews to allow time for the interviewers to refine their notes on the open-ended questions. Immediately after each interview, the interviewers should type up and expand their notes while their memory is fresh.

Plan to conduct the interviews in a private, quiet place, preferably in a neutral location, such as a conference room rather than the interviewee's or interviewer's office. Invite the selected employees to participate in the interviews at least two weeks in advance. Inform them of the purpose of the interviews and the time, location, and expected duration of the interview. Send interviewees a reminder a few days before their scheduled interview, restating the purpose and benefits of the interview; providing the date, time, and location; and expressing appreciation for their participation.

Step 6: Select and Train the Interviewers

Select interviewers who have strong listening, analytical, and writing skills and are also personable and friendly. The interviewers should not be in the employee's chain of command

and should be perceived as objective. The accuracy and completeness of the interview re-cord can be increased by having two interviewers conduct each interview.

Provide training for the interviewers one or two days before the interviews begin. During the training, explain the purpose of the interviews and how the collected data will be used. Review the interview protocol and have each interviewer conduct at least two practice interviews, fol-lowed by feedback on their performance. Also include the following points in the training:

- The interviewers should dress as the interviewees typically do.
- Interviewers should spend a moment chatting with the interviewee to build rap-port and ease anxiety before beginning to ask questions.
- The interviewer should check their understanding of the interviewee's responses to open-ended questions by restating and paraphrasing them.
- Probe the interviewee's responses to open-ended questions to obtain more detail and clarity by asking follow-up questions such as, "What do you mean by…?" or "What happened next?"
- Interviewers should not lead or shape the interviewee's responses with comments or judgments such as, "That must have been very difficult," or "Why would you do such a thing?" They must remain neutral.
- Record the interviewees' responses in their own words as much as possible.
- Whenever possible, record the exact language of the interviewees so that the flavor and meaning of their responses is captured. Nonverbal forms of communication such as fidgeting, frowns, or shrugs, should also be recorded and reported.
- Interviewers need to remember that the interviewee should do 90 percent of the talking. Give the respondent time to think, respect silence, and do not interrupt him or her.

Step 7: Conduct the Interviews

A coordinator should be assigned to monitor the interview process to ensure everyone is in the right place at the right time, confirm that the interviewers have the materials they need, answer questions, follow up if interviewees do not appear as scheduled, and alert the evaluation project manager of any issues. The project manager should be readily available so that any problems can be quickly resolved. Following the interview, send each intervie-wee a thank you note.

Step 8: Summarize and Analyze the Data

As soon as the interviewers have prepared their interview notes for submission, the co-ordinator should review the notes and check that the interview was fully and accurately documented. If responses are missing or unclear, the notes should be returned to the interviewer for prompt clarification.

The selected analysis techniques should be used by an individual who is well trained in data analysis. It is important to check and recheck calculations and summaries of qualitative responses to be sure they are correct.

Knowledge Check: Developing an Interview Protocol

You have been asked to create an interview protocol for an evaluation of a year-long new employee on-boarding program. The objective of the interviews is to determine if employees who completed the program in the previous six months found it useful and, if so, how. Develop a sample protocol that includes at least three questions. Check your answer in the appendix.

About the Author

Anne F. Marrelli, PhD, is a senior organizational psychologist in the Organizational Effectiveness group in Air Traffic Operations in the Federal Aviation Administration. She has more than 25 years of experience in organizational performance improvement. Former employers include the U.S. Merit Systems Protection Board, American Express, Hughes Electronics, Educational Testing Service, and the County of Los Angeles. Marrelli earned a doctoral degree in learning and development from the University of Southern California and has published numerous journal articles and book chapters. She may be reached at anne.marrelli@faa.gov.

References

Fowler, F. J. (2002). *Survey Research Methods,* 3rd ed. Thousand Oaks, CA: Sage Publications.

Marrelli, A. F. (1998). "Ten Evaluation Instruments for Technical Training." In *Another Look at Evaluating Training Programs,* D. L. Kirkpatrick ed. Alexandria, VA: American Society for Training and Development, 58–65.

Pershing, J. L. (2006). "Interviewing to Analyze and Evaluate Human Performance Technology." In *Handbook of Human Performance Technology: Principles, Practices, Potential,* J. A. Pershing ed. San Francisco: Pfeiffer, 780–94.

Phillips, J. J. (1991). *Handbook of Training Evaluation and Measurement Methods,* 2nd ed. Houston, TX: Gulf.

Rubin, H. J. and I. S. Rubin. (1995). *Qualitative Interviewing: The Art of Hearing Data.* Thousand Oaks, CA: Sage Publications.

Webb, E. J., D. T. Campbell, R. D. Schwartz, and L. Sechrest. (2000). *Unobtrusive Measures* rev. ed. Thousand Oaks, CA: Sage Publications.

Additional Reading

Kvale, S. and S. Brinkmann. (2009). *InterViews: Learning the Craft of Qualitative Research Interviewing.* Thousand Oaks, CA: Sage Publications.

Patton, M. Q. (2002). *Qualitative Research and Evaluation Methods,* 3rd ed. Thousand Oaks, CA: Sage Publications.

Rubin, H. J. and I. S. Rubin (2005). *Qualitative Interviewing: The Art of Hearing Data,* 2nd ed. Thousand Oaks, CA: Sage Publications.

Chapter 7

Conducting Focus Groups

Lisa Ann Edwards

In This Chapter

This chapter explores techniques for gathering data about the causes of performance problems so that appropriate solutions such as skills training and learning and development activities can be created. After reading this chapter, you will be able to

- ▪ select participants and ensure participation
- ▪ identify three techniques for conducting focus groups
- ▪ summarize qualitative data that lead to solutions.

The Importance of Using Focus Groups

A focus group is a small group discussion conducted by an experienced facilitator. A focus group is designed to solicit qualitative data on a specific topic. The benefit of using focus groups to collect data is that focus groups allow the learning and development professional to gather data from multiple sources and probe for more detail than what can be provided through a questionnaire. The challenge of managing focus groups is that they can easily become unfocused and produce interesting, but not useful data. Focus groups require careful planning to ensure that the sessions are facilitated consistently across multiple groups and result in useful data. With careful planning and facilitation, focus groups can be an excellent source of information that can be acted upon.

Selecting Participants

The first step to ensure successful focus groups that result in useful data is to identify, select, and invite the appropriate participants to the focus groups. Identify and select individuals for the focus groups who best reflect the group of individuals for whom a problem exists, and create a solution. For example, if the identified problem is that new sales associates are struggling to meet their sales goals, then new sales associates should be represented in the focus groups. In another example, if the identified problem is that technology employees leave the organization prior to their second-year anniversary, then technology employees who are approaching their second-year anniversary should be represented in the focus groups.

Include 10 percent of the total researched population in the focus group. For example, if there are 1,000 employees who represent the target audience, plan to include 100 individuals in the focus groups. Invite 10 to 15 participants to ensure attendance of six to 12 participants in each focus group, the ideal focus group size.

Selecting a Facilitator

Select a facilitator who has experience running focus groups to ensure success. Even experienced facilitators will need to coordinate their approach if multiple facilitators will be used in different geographic locations. Several advantages and disadvantages exist when using a facilitator from inside the organization, as well as when using one from outside the organization. These advantages and disadvantages are outlined in table 7-1.

Format of the Focus Group Session

Focus groups can be facilitated in several different formats, and three of them are described below. In selecting a format, be sure to prepare well in advance of the focus group sessions,

---

✌ **Practitioner Tip** ✆

An effective way to gain commitment and ensure participation is to send an invitation from the CEO to participate in the focus group. The invitation must clearly define the purpose of the focus group, the importance of the focus group, time involvement, and how the data will be used, and must also ensure the confidentiality and anonymity of all responses.

Table 7-1. Advantages and Disadvantages of Using Internal and External Facilitators

	Experienced Internal Facilitator	Experienced External Facilitator
Advantages	• No additional direct costs • Able to get started faster • May be better able to influence participation if he or she has a positive reputation inside the organization • May be better able to manage difficult conversations because he or she understands the context better and can anticipate likely challenges	• May be more appealing to participants knowing that an objective, outside facilitator will run the focus group • May be better able to create trust with participants, resulting in an open and honest discussion • May be better able to manage difficult conversations because he or she is not a company spokesperson and does not need to defend the company's actions
Disadvantages	• May be harder to remain objective and refrain from becoming the company spokesperson • May hinder participation from participants who are not comfortable being honest • May create distrust that the information will remain confidential and have no effect on the participants' career within the company	• Additional direct costs • May take longer to get the project started

and consider running a test session to ensure that the format provides useable data that can be acted upon. Below are three recommended formats: group interview, Ishikawa (fishbone diagram), and the nominal group technique.

Group Interview. The first way to conduct a focus group is to use a carefully crafted set of interview questions to ask the group. The set of questions can include

- behavior-based questions that uncover the current behaviors of an individual (for example, How do you learn how to effectively prospect for new clients?)
- attitudes, opinions, and beliefs questions that reveal what someone thinks about a particular topic (for example, What do you think is the biggest challenge facing emerging leaders in our company?)

✌ **Practitioner Tip** ✍

If commitment to participating in the focus group is likely to be low, consider offering an incentive, such as a gift card to a coffee shop, a t-shirt, or mug. If protecting the identity of the participants is important, use an incentive that does not later serve as an indicator to others that the individual was a participant in the focus group.

- personal characteristics that help identify a particular group and potentially segment their responses (for example, How many years have you worked at our company?)
- participant expectations (for example, How do you think you should learn the new skills of a sales representative?)
- self-classification or self-perceptions that participants have about themselves (for example, How do you define your level of expertise at managing teams?)
- knowledge that participants currently posses or are lacking (for example, What are the steps to enter new invoices into the financial system?) (Neuman, 2005).

Identify the series of questions to ask the focus groups and organize these into an interview guide. Organize all questions around common themes and ideas so that question topics are not scattered and unfocused. Ideally, broader conceptual questions, such as questions about specific behaviors, habits, and beliefs, should be asked at the start of the group interview, followed by more specific questions about challenges faced in the participant's current role. Questions to get input on possible solutions should be asked at the end of the focus group. Include set-up discussion or explanations in the interview guide, in addition to the questions, so that the facilitators conduct the sessions in the same manner.

Ishikawa Diagram. A second way to conduct a focus group is by using an Ishikawa diagram to brainstorm ideas related to the root cause of a problem. After all ideas about the root causes have been identified, the group narrows the list of causes down to a few through

---

✌ **Practitioner Tip** ✍

To better understand an individual's perceptions of possible training solutions while minimizing the amount of group influence, first present the solution. Then, ask participants to record their thoughts about the solution on a printed survey, prior to expressing their ideas aloud. This activity can be integrated into the session and provides a good way for participants to carefully consider what they think before hearing anyone else's ideas, therefore minimizing the amount of influence another participant might have on the group input.

---

voting. The Ishikawa diagram, also known as a fishbone diagram, was named after Kaoru Ishikawa, who used the diagram to help teams identify cause and effect. There are three main steps to this process:

1. Identify the problem prior to the sessions. Before conducting the focus group, carefully articulate the problem that needs to be solved. For example, "Sales people need to close sales faster in the client relationship" or "Emerging leaders need to be ready for leadership roles within 12 months."

2. Brainstorm as many ideas as possible during the session. At the start of the focus group, the facilitator explains that they will use the fishbone diagram as way to think about the cause categories that affect the problem that needs to be solved. Any cause categories can be used; the most common cause categories are people, machines, materials, methods, and environment. The facilitator explains that the group will brainstorm, in round robin fashion, one cause per turn, until all ideas are exhausted. All ideas are welcome, and the purpose of this part of the exercise is to brainstorm as many ideas as possible. Figure 7-1 illustrates an example of a fishbone diagram for solving a sales problem.

3. Narrow the causes down to a few choices. After all ideas are exhausted, organize all of the causes by ease of implementation and cost, if matching solutions were implemented, within a four-block diagram. Figure 7-2 illustrates an example. Finally, the group votes on the causes it believes are most instrumental to resolving the identified problem and thus identifies the top priorities. Participants vote five to 10 times on the most important causes. If the number of causes is small, such as what is illustrated in the example, use fewer votes; more votes can be assigned if there are more causes from which to choose. After voting, the most important causes will become apparent (Scholtes, Joiner, and Streibel, 2003).

Nominal Group Technique. The third format for conducting focus groups is the nominal group technique. This approach allows unbiased input to be collected efficiently and accurately, and input is solicited from participants in a carefully structured format.

❧ Practitioner Tip ❧

To get participants to think of as many ideas as possible on their own before hearing other's ideas, consider asking all participants to write as many causes as they can think of before asking for everyone's input. Participants can write their ideas on sticky notes, writing one cause idea per note. After everyone is finished, they can then place their notes under the appropriate cause categories. Then, the facilitator can review each of the cause ideas with the group, prior to beginning another round of idea generation with the group.

Figure 7-1. Sample Ishikawa or Fishbone Diagram

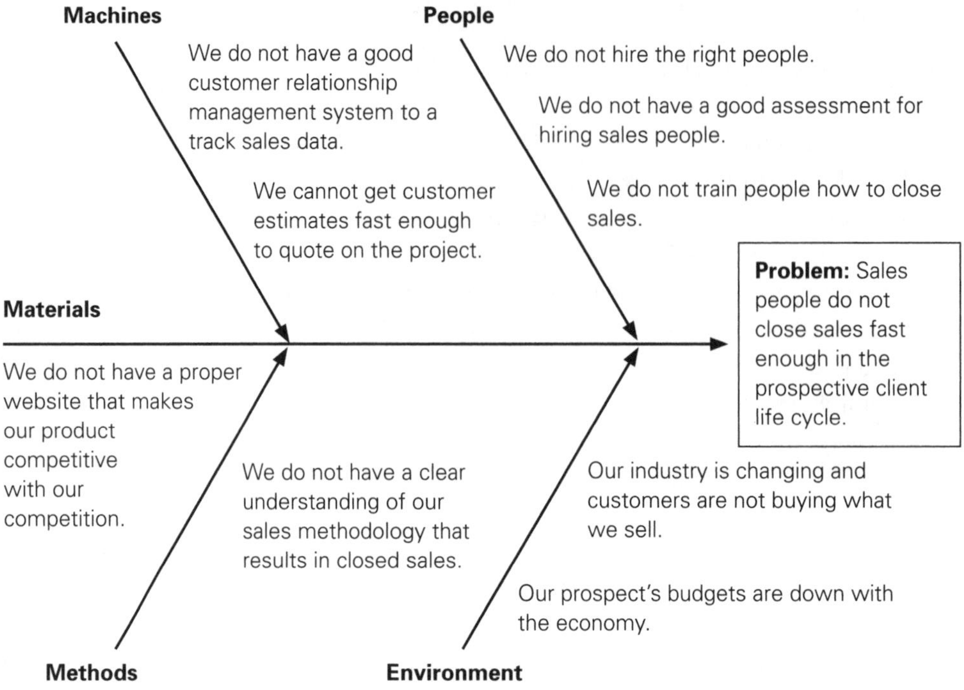

Machines — We do not have a good customer relationship management system to a track sales data.

We cannot get customer estimates fast enough to quote on the project.

People — We do not hire the right people.

We do not have a good assessment for hiring sales people.

We do not train people how to close sales.

Materials — We do not have a proper website that makes our product competitive with our competition.

Problem: Sales people do not close sales fast enough in the prospective client life cycle.

We do not have a clear understanding of our sales methodology that results in closed sales.

Our industry is changing and customers are not buying what we sell.

Our prospect's budgets are down with the economy.

Methods   **Environment**

The nominal group technique unfolds quickly in 10 easy steps.

1. Briefly describe the process along with a statement of confidentiality. Underscore the importance of participant input and explain what participants must do and what their input means to the organization. Clarify the performance issue that the focus group will be discussing. For example, "Today, we'd like to hear from you—why you believe some of your colleagues fail to make the transition from a management role to a leadership role in our organization."

2. Ask participants to make a list of specific reasons why they believe their colleagues have the specific performance issues and record their ideas on a piece of paper. It is very important for the question to reflect the actions or potential actions of others, although their comments will probably reflect their own views (and that is what is actually needed).

3. In a round robin format, each person reveals one reason at a time, recording each cause on flip chart paper. Do not attempt to integrate the issues; just record the data on paper.

Figure 7-2. Sample Four-Block Diagram

Inexpensive	We do not have a good customer relationship management system to track sales data.	We do not train people how to close sales. We do not hire the right people. We do not have a good assessment for hiring sales people. We do not have a clear understanding of our sales methodology that results in closed sales.
Costly	Our prospect's budgets are down with the economy. Our industry is changing and customers are not buying what we sell. We do not have a proper website that makes our product competitive with our competition.	We cannot get customer estimates fast enough to quote on the project.

Difficult to implement ⟵⟶ Easy to implement

Seek to understand the issue and fully describe it on paper. Place the lists on the walls so that when this step is complete, as many as 50 or 60 items are listed and visible.

4. Next, consolidate and integrate the lists. Some of the integration is easy because the items may contain the same words and meanings. For others, ensure the meanings of the causes are the same before consolidating. When integrated, the remaining list may contain 30 or 40 different reasons for the performance issue at hand.

✺ Practitioner Tip ✺

Use the four-block criteria that are most important in your organization. For example, if the two criteria are cost and ease of implementation, use those criteria as illustrated in figure 7-2. If degree of impact and ease of implementation are more important, then use those two criteria.

5. Ask participants to review all of the items, carefully select which 10 items they consider to be the most important causes, and then list them individually on index cards. At first, participants will not be concerned about which cause is number one, but instruct them to simply list the 10 most important ones on the cards. Participants usually realize that their original list was not complete or accurate, and they will pick up other issues for this list.

6. Participants sort the 10 items by order of importance, the number one item being the most important and number 10, the least important.

7. In a round robin format, each participant reveals a cause, starting from the top. Each participant reveals his or her number one item, and 10 points are recorded on the flip chart paper next to the item. The next participant reveals the number one issue and so on, until the entire group offers the top cause for the performance issue. Next, the number two reason is identified, and nine points are recorded on the flip chart paper next to the item. This process continues until all cards have been revealed and points recorded.

8. The numbers next to each item are totaled. The item with the most points becomes the number one cause of the performance issue. The one with the second most points becomes the second cause, and so on. The top 15 causes are then captured from the group and reported as the weighted average cause of the performance issue from that group.

9. This process is now completed for all groups. Trends begin to emerge quickly from one group to the other. The actual raw scores from each group are combined for the integration of the focus groups.

10. The top 15 scores are the top 15 reasons for the performance issue (Phillips and Edwards, 2009).

Concluding the Session

At the conclusion of the session, remind participants that their feedback will remain anonymous and explain how their input will be used. Clarify the next steps, including what you will be doing next, how the results will be communicated to senior management, and how and when you will communicate the results with the group. Finally, provide your contact information to participants in case they have any questions later.

❧ **Practitioner Tip** ❧

If geography and costs are an issue, consider running the focus group by teleconference and in a webinar format. Although conducting a focus group in person is ideal, a skilled facilitator who is experienced in running interactive webinars can effectively run the focus group in this format and produce useable data.

Getting to the Results

Chapter 12 clarifies how to analyze qualitative data so that the information is meaningful and productive. To ensure that the qualitative data analysis goes smoothly, make certain that the conclusion of each session produces clear results. This is especially important when conducting multiple focus group sessions, because all of the data resulting from each of the groups is combined. Tabulating the top priorities produced by each focus group is an effective way to make the final step in the qualitative data analysis process go smoothly. The combined qualitative data analysis will point to specific training solutions.

Matching Solutions to Needs

Finally, after the data from all of the groups have been combined, the next step is to identify appropriate solutions. In selecting the right solution, consider long-term versus short-term costs as well as effect and time needed to implement a solution. If possible, forecast return-on-investment prior to implementation. Finally, before implementing any solution, present the focus groups' combined data results and proposed solutions back to the focus groups for their input on the solutions. This last step ensures that the solution matches the needs identified by the groups, and that the needs identified at the time of the focus groups are still relevant by the time the solution is developed (Phillips and Edwards, 2009).

Knowledge Check: Focus Groups

Now that you have read this chapter, check your learning by taking the quiz below. Check your answers in the appendix.

1. The best candidates for a focus group are the people who are performing well at the performance issue at hand. True or False?
2. How many participants should be selected to represent a sample of the population under consideration?
3. An internal facilitator is the best person to conduct a focus group. True or False?
4. What focus group format is the best method to obtain accurate results?
5. After organizing all the data and identifying a solution, it is not necessary to review the solution with the focus group. True or False?

About the Author

Lisa Ann Edwards is a talent development professional whose expertise is based on more than 20 years of experience in the media, technology, printing, and publishing industries. As senior director of talent management for Corbis, a Bill Gates-owned global media company, Edwards is responsible for talent management solutions that ensure talent engagement and retention and serve to feed the talent pipeline.

Edwards has co-authored *Managing Talent Retention: An ROI Approach* (2009) and *Measuring ROI in Coaching for New Hire Employee Retention: A Global Media Company*, published in *ROI in Action Casebook* (2008). She is working on her next book on self-leadership.

Edwards speaks at conferences and works with audiences across the world covering Asia-Pacific, Europe, and North America. She has worked with *Fortune* 500 organizations ranging from technology to health care to media to the public sector on talent development.

References

Neuman, L. W. (2005). *Social Research Methods: Quantitative and Qualitative Approaches,* 6th ed. White Plains, NY: Allyn and Bacon.

Phillips, J. J. and L. Edwards. (2009). *Managing Talent Retention: An ROI Approach*. San Francisco: Pfeiffer.

Scholtes, P., B. Joiner, and B. Streibel. (2003). *The Team Handbook,* 3rd ed. Madison, WI: Joiner/Oriel Inc.

Additional Reading

Krueger, R. (2000). *Focus Groups: A Practical Guide for Applied Research*, 3rd ed. Thousand Oaks, CA: Sage Publications.

Morgan, D. and R. Krueger. (1997). *Focus Group Kit*. Thousand Oaks, CA: Sage Publications.

Bystedt, J. and G. Fraley. (2003). *Moderating to the Max: A Full-Tilt Guide to Creative Insightful Focus Groups and Depth Interviews*. Ithaca, NY: Paramount Market Publishing.

ॐ Chapter 8

Action Planning as a Performance Measurement and Transfer Strategy

Holly Burkett

In This Chapter

This chapter explores techniques for implementing action planning as a performance measurement and transfer strategy. Upon completion of this chapter you will be able to

- describe the importance of action planning as a performance measurement tool
- apply techniques for implementing action planning as a transfer strategy
- analyze action plan data to determine a solution's value.

Why Action Planning?

Consider the following workplace scenarios. A dynamic manufacturing environment seeks to increase labor efficiency through continuous process improvement and work redesign. A state agency determines that management skill gaps in coaching and development have adversely affected attraction and retention of key personnel and that a competency-based management development program is the key to closing gaps. A call center begins a training initiative designed to reduce call escalations through improved on-the-job training among call center staff.

What do these scenarios have in common? Each initiative addresses a critical business need; each represents a substantial investment of time and resources; each commands high visibility and management interest; and each requires accomplishing specific, measurable performance objectives. In addition, each solution lends itself to the use of action planning as a performance measurement strategy to achieve desired application and impact outcomes.

What Is Action Planning?

Action planning is a powerful and flexible process for managing and measuring the performance objectives of a training solution and ensuring that objectives are effectively aligned with desired business results. A key output of the process is an action plan document in which project or program participants outline detailed actions to accomplish specific goals connected to program objectives. The action plan answers questions such as

- What steps or action items will be taken as a result of learning?
- What on-the-job improvements or accomplishments will be realized with participants' applied skills/knowledge?
- How much improvement can be linked to the program?

In cases where action planning is used to measure business impact measures and return-on-investment (ROI), an action plan can also provide data about participants' estimations of the

- monetary value of improvement
- intangible benefits of a program
- enablers and barriers to applying learned skills and knowledge
- other influences related to performance improvement.

✌ Practitioner Tip ✌

Using a customized action plan as a performance tool focuses attention on relevant skills and behavior…and provides good quality, substantial information when determining application and performance improvement in the job setting…In addition to the action plan process, use a follow-up questionnaire to track the extent to which participants used the training and achieved on-the-job success. The action plan documentation and completed questionnaire should both be analyzed for results.

Source: Stone (2008).

In short, action planning is the process of planning what needs to be done and by whom, when it needs to be done, and what resources or inputs are needed to do it. It is the process of operationalizing your strategic objectives.

How Does it Work?

Figure 8-1 shows the sequence of steps involved with implementing an action planning process.

Before the Program

All learning projects should begin with a clear focus on the end in mind. This includes defining initial business needs and aligning project or program objectives to those needs. In the action planning process, the up-front "before" steps help to assess the potential value and feasibility of the action planning approach. For example, can participants' on-the-job actions influence targeted business measures? Are the right resources available to assist participants with planned actions? Is there a commitment from participants and their managers to support action planning follow-up? This preliminary assessment ensures that action planning is linked to a strategic framework, that it is positioned as an integral part of implementation, and that it does not take place in a vacuum as an add-on, hit-or-miss activity. For these reasons, the following sequence of steps is important to consider before you initiate the action planning process.

Identify Objectives of the Solution

For programs or solutions targeting ROI measurement, broad objectives are first established across five levels of evaluation during the evaluation planning process. The example provided in table 8-1 shows how the action planning process was aligned with high-level reaction, learning, application, and impact objectives for a strategic career development initiative intended to increase organizational capacity and efficiency. In this example, the business need (increased operational capacity) was the starting point for determining program objectives and corresponding evaluation targets across multiple levels.

Integrate Action Planning into the ADDIE (Assessment, Design, Development, Implementation, and Evaluation) Cycle

Although action planning is a common data collection method for capturing measures of program effectiveness, the action plan requirement must be properly integrated with the entire assessment, design, development, implementation, and evaluation cycle of training or solution development. By planning early and defining linkages, learning professionals can give clear direction to the stakeholders about the schedule, scope, and resource requirements of an action planning process.

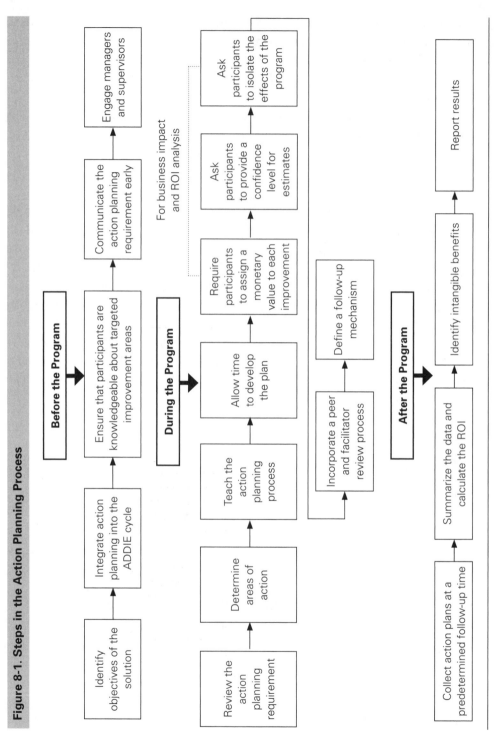

Figure 8-1. Steps in the Action Planning Process

Source: Burkett (2008). Adapted from Phillips and Phillips (2003).

Proper linkage also ensures that action plans are used to support specific objectives identified through the evaluation planning and needs analysis process. For example, table 8-1 shows the objectives outlined for a career development initiative. In this case, defined business needs drove impact objectives (Level 4, increased operational capacity) and impact measures (increased labor efficiencies, increased productivity). Application (Level 3) objectives (employees will complete development discussion action plan with their managers within 60 days of completing program) were based upon needs analysis data showing gaps between current and desired job-task, coaching behaviors.

Table 8-1. Case Example: The Linking Process for Career Development Initiative

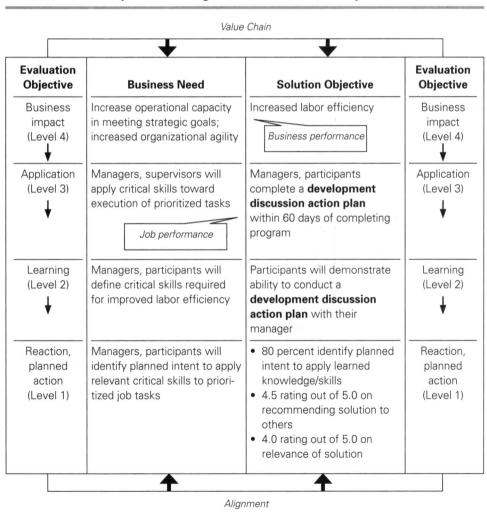

Evaluation Objective	Business Need	Solution Objective	Evaluation Objective
Business impact (Level 4)	Increase operational capacity in meeting strategic goals; increased organizational agility	Increased labor efficiency *Business performance*	Business impact (Level 4)
Application (Level 3)	Managers, supervisors will apply critical skills toward execution of prioritized tasks *Job performance*	Managers, participants complete a **development discussion action plan** within 60 days of completing program	Application (Level 3)
Learning (Level 2)	Managers, participants will define critical skills required for improved labor efficiency	Participants will demonstrate ability to conduct a **development discussion action plan** with their manager	Learning (Level 2)
Reaction, planned action (Level 1)	Managers, participants will identify planned intent to apply relevant critical skills to prioritized job tasks	• 80 percent identify planned intent to apply learned knowledge/skills • 4.5 rating out of 5.0 on recommending solution to others • 4.0 rating out of 5.0 on relevance of solution	Reaction, planned action (Level 1)

Value Chain

Alignment

Identified skill/knowledge gaps determined specific learning needs, which were reflected in Level 2 learning objectives for the program. Finally, learning preferences appeared as Level 1 reaction objectives (achieve 4.0 out of 5.0 on overall satisfaction). With this approach, the action planning process was positioned as a value-added strategy that supported desired performance goals and business results.

Ensure That Participants Are Knowledgeable about Targeted Improvement Areas

Participants are often the individuals closest to the workplace areas needing improvement and are a reliable source of data for identifying how improved actions affect specific business improvement measures. However, when using the action planning process, it is important to confirm that participants are capable of providing estimates of the cost or value of the business units of measure being monitored and that they have the power to take action themselves or to be relatively assured that their actions will be supported in the workplace.

Communicate the Action Plan Requirement Early

An important prerequisite to successful action planning is to provide an understanding of how it works, how specific action items are developed, and how action planning data will be used. Communicate the action planning requirement to participants and their managers *prior* to the program. Communication can be conducted via email announcements, program descriptions that include action planning requirements, brown bag informational sessions, staff meeting attendance, and/or preprogram briefings with participants and their managers. Include available support tools, such as examples of key measures, charts, graphs, or completed action plans, in these briefings. Advance communication helps participants and stakeholders take the program more seriously and assume more ownership of the transfer of learning back to the workplace.

Engage Managers and Supervisors

A well-designed action planning process will include provisions for management support and review (Burkett, 2004). For example, management and stakeholder input is needed to ensure that action plans address specific business measures. Managers and supervisors are also a key resource in defining and eliminating potential barriers to on-the-job application of participants' planned actions. Many organizations have effectively leveraged management support to convey the importance and value of action planning during early communications or program briefings as well during the opening segments of a program in which action planning is required (Burkett, 2005).

During the Program

The sequence of steps in the action planning process during the program are to review the action planning requirement, determine areas for action, teach the action planning process, allow time to develop a plan, require participants to estimate the monetary value of each improvement and ask them to rate their confidence of those estimates, isolate the effects of the program, incorporate a peer review process, and define a follow-up mechanism.

Review the Action Planning Requirement

During the opening of the program, it is important to remind participants that they will be encouraged and expected to apply learned skills and knowledge back on the job and that the action plan is intended as a performance support tool. It is also important to make sure that participants understand the "line of sight" linkage between their applied actions on the job and the consequence of those actions upon desired impact objectives or business results.

Determine Areas for Action

Identifying potential areas for action is one of the first tasks for action planning participants. Areas or measures of action should originate from the objectives and needs of the program or project and should focus on on-the-job application of acquired skills and knowledge. Participants can develop a list of potential action areas on their own, or generate a list of action items during a group discussion. The list may include a business measure needing improvement or represent an opportunity for increased operational or job performance. Typical categories of measures include

- productivity
- sales, revenue
- customer service
- quality, process improvement
- efficiency
- work habits
- time savings
- cost savings.

Common questions to be considered when developing action plan items include

- How long will this action take?
- Are resources available to achieve this action?
- What barriers, if any, could interfere with accomplishing this action?

Teach the Action Planning Process

Participants need clear instructions and examples when being asked for performance improvement data. Action items that support desired business measures should be written so that targeted actions are *observable* and obvious to everyone involved when they occur. Providing specific examples is an important step in this process. Examples include

- identify and secure a new customer account, by (date)
- analyze job tasks using the "difficulty, importance, frequency" scale when creating assemblers' training plans, weekly
- apply the "schedule, scope, and resource matrix" to an IT project, by (date)
- apply the five-step call escalation process with customer calls, daily
- initiate three cost-reduction projects, within 60 days of training.

For maximum effectiveness, each action item should be written with active verbs, include a completion date, and state what resources or individuals are needed for successful completion. Figure 8-2 shows an example of a completed action plan for a career development initiative. In the sample action plan, participants complete the left column where they list one to three actions they will take as a result of the program. Identified actions are consistent with targeted business improvement measures (efficiency) and performance goals targeted in the program.

Allow Time to Develop the Plan

Giving participants ample time to develop and complete a plan outlining their intended actions and projected results during the session is critical. Plans can be completed individually or in teams. Facilitators can monitor the progress of individuals or small groups to keep the process on track and to answer questions.

Require Participants to Assign a Monetary Value to Each Improvement

For impact and ROI analysis, ask participants to determine, calculate, or estimate the projected monetary value for each improvement outlined in the plan. For this step to be effective, it may be helpful to provide examples of typical ways in which values can be assigned to the actual data (Phillips, 2003).

As shown in figure 8-3, suggested questions for helping participants identify potential improvement (Level 3 and Level 4) data *during the program* include

- What specific actions will you apply based upon what you have learned?
- What specific unit of measure will change as a result of your actions?
- As a result of these work improvements, please estimate the monetary benefits to your line or department over a one-month period.
- What is the basis for your estimate?

Figure 8-2. Sample Action Plan for Career Development Initiative

Name _____ **Instructor Signature** _____ **Follow-Up Date** _____

Objective To apply skills and knowledge gained from career development program **Evaluation Period** _____ **to** _____

Improvement Measures: _____ Efficiency

Action Steps	Analysis
As a result of this program, what specific actions will you apply based upon what you have learned?	What specific unit of measure will change as a result of your actions? (see above)
1. Conduct development discussion with manager, within 30 days of program completion.	1. What is the unit of measure? _____ Efficiency
2. Enlist support from my manager to apply skills and talents toward cross-functional job rotation or project assignment with engineering group, within 60 days.	2. As a result of the anticipated changes, please *estimate* the monetary benefits to your line or department **over a one month period.** _____ $768
3. Initiate follow-up with development discussions and recommended actions to close skill gaps, biweekly, or as determined.	3. What is the basis of this estimate? (How did you arrive at this value?)
	$32 per hour x 6 hours a week x 4 weeks a month = $768 month
	Based on salary and average time spent on project, rework per
	week due to issues with product change-overs, material supply
	4. What level of confidence do you place on the above information? (100%=Certainty and 0%=No confidence) _____ 85%
	5. What percentage of the change above was the *direct result* of applying skills learned in the career development program? (0%–100%) _____ 60%
	6. What other influences, besides training, might have influenced these improvements? _____ Project management software
Intangible benefits:	**What barriers, if any, may prevent you from applying what you have learned?**
Improved cooperation with manager. Better focus on performance priorities and the "big picture." Improved visibility to upper management—allows me to be more strategic in promoting my skills and talents for career mobility and job satisfaction.	Lack of follow-up due to work volume, conflicting priorities from corporate, moving targets

Source: Burkett (2008).

Figure 8-3. Action Plan Template

Name _____ Instructor Signature _____ Follow-Up Date _____

Objective _____ **Evaluation Period** _____ **to** _____

Improvement Measures: _____

Action Steps

As a result of this program, what specific actions will you apply based upon what you have learned?

1. _____
   _____
2. _____
   _____
3. _____
   _____
4. _____
   _____

Intangible benefits:

_____
_____
_____

Analysis

What specific unit of measure will change as a result of your actions? (see above)

1. _____
2. _____
3. As a result of the anticipated changes, please **estimate** the monetary benefits to your line or department over a one-month period. _____
4. What is the basis of your estimate? _____
5. What level of confidence, expressed as a percentage, do you place on the above estimate? (100% = Certainty and 0% = No confidence) _____ %
6. What other factors, besides training, may contribute to process improvements or changes you make? _____
7. What barriers, if any, may prevent you from using skills or knowledge gained from this program? _____
   _____

Source: Phillips (2003).

Ask Participants to Provide a Confidence Level for Estimates

Because the process of converting performance improvement data to monetary value may not be exact and the amount may not be precise, participants are asked to indicate their level of confidence in values defined in the action plan.

Figure 8-3 illustrates a suggested question for capturing this information and allowing participants a mechanism for expressing potential discomfort with their ability to be precise. Specifically, what level of confidence, expressed as a percentage, do you place on the above estimate? (100% = Certainty and 0% = No confidence)

Ask Participants to Isolate the Effects of the Program

Although the action plan is initiated to support achievement of performance and impact objectives, actual performance improvement, or lack of it, may be influenced by other factors. For example, in the career development initiative, action plans generated to improve labor efficiency could only take partial credit for improved efficiency measures 60 days later because other variables like new product cycles and change-over processes influenced the desired result (Burkett, 2001).

While at least nine methods can be used to isolate the effects of a training or performance improvement solution, participant estimations are typically an appropriate source for providing data about the effect of learning gains and on-the-job application of learning. The individuals who have actually learned new skills and applied them to daily operations are a credible source of input about the real-world effect of a training program, because they know how much they have applied new skills and how many other influences may have influenced job or operational performance. They are the ones closest to the business areas of improvement being targeted and are generally very effective at providing cost data and program isolation and data conversion input (Phillips and Burkett, 2008).

Incorporate a Peer and Facilitator Review Process

Facilitator and peer reviews of plans are highly recommended to promote action learning and ensure that action items are related to defined objectives. In some cases, space is included on an action plan for the facilitator's signature to indicate that the plan is approved and appropriate. Considerations for facilitator and peer review include the following:

- Do planned actions relate to the skills and knowledge contained in the program objectives?
- Do planned actions answer the "So what?" question? "So what?" is the consequence of participants' applied actions to the business or business unit.

- Do planned actions meet SMART (specific, measurable, achievable, relevant, time-bound) criteria?
- Do plans describe measures that can be easily collected?
- Does the time to complete actions seem reasonable or manageable?
- What degree of work disruption, if any, is involved with task completion?
- What enablers/barriers may enhance or impede planned actions?

Peer group input on action planning sparks greater energy, creativity, and commitment. Reflecting on planned actions provides the best impetus for learning and performance change to occur.

Define a Follow-Up Mechanism

Participants need to leave the session with a clear understanding of the timing of the action-plan implementation and the planned follow-up. There should be open discussion of when the data and forecasted, planned improvements will be collected, analyzed, and compared to *actual* actions and improvements. Options for follow-up include

- The group reconvenes to review whether planned actions and targeted improvements were achieved. When feasible, this is the most effective way to reinforce progress and accurately assess enablers/barriers to participants' implementation of planned actions. Many organizations build the action plan follow-up session into the program schedule (that is, 30 days after the last session) to reinforce action planning as an integral part of the program, to promote application of learned knowledge/skills, and to ensure that participants and/or managers plan their schedule accordingly.
- Participants review the action plan with their immediate manager and forward a copy to the evaluator.
- A meeting is held with the participant, his or her immediate manager, and the evaluator to review the plan and success with intended objectives.
- Participants send the action plan directly to the evaluator and review it during a conference call.
- Participants send the action plan directly to the evaluator with no meeting or discussion. This approach is most common.

After the Program

After completion of the program, the final sequence of steps in the action planning process are to collect action plans, summarize the data and calculate ROI, identify intangible benefits, and report the results. For maximum effectiveness, use evaluation data gathered from completed action plans for continuous improvement purposes. This includes uncovering data about enablers and barriers to action plan application so that needed adjustments can be made for future implementations that lend themselves to an action planning process.

Collect Action Plans at a Predetermined Follow-up Time

Because it is critical to have an excellent response rate, several activities may be needed to make sure that action plans are completed and returned for analysis in a timely manner. Some organizations use reminder emails or phone calls. Others offer assistance to participants who are developing or refining their final plan. Using a follow-up questionnaire to track the extent to which participants were able to use action plans is also helpful. Integrating planned follow-up approaches into the action planning process can lead to a 60- to 90-percent response rate (Phillips and Phillips, 2005).

Summarize the Data and Calculate the ROI

When using action plans to capture business impact and ROI results, each action plan should have annualized monetary values associated with improvements. Also, each individual will have indicated the percentage of improvement directly related to the program, along with a confidence level reflecting any degree of uncertainty with the subjective nature of the data. Because subjectivity of participant estimates may be a concern to stakeholders, there are several guiding principles for making adjustments to increase the credibility of the performance improvement data (Phillips and others, 2006):

- If no improvement data are available for a population or from a specific source on an action plan, evaluators assume that no improvement has occurred.
- Discard and omit extreme data items and unsupported claims on an action plan when calculating the cost benefits of an improvement.
- To be conservative, have participants estimate only annual improvements.
- Adjust values by the estimated percentage of improvement *directly* related to the program using a multiplication process. This helps isolate the effects of the program or solution.
- Adjust the improvement from the previous step by multiplying it by a confidence percent, which reflects participants' level of confidence in their estimate. The confidence level is actually an error suggested by the participant and is used to be conservative. The confidence factor is then multiplied by the amount of improvement.

The monetary values determined in these five steps are totaled to arrive at a total benefit for the program. Because these values are annualized, the total of these benefits becomes the annual benefits from the program.

Table 8-2 provides an example of how the above techniques were applied to action plans collected from the career development initiative. These values were then used as cost benefit data and compared to program costs in the final ROI analysis and calculation.

Identify Intangible Benefits

Other important outcomes of interest to senior management include intangible benefits. As shown in figure 8-2, action plans can provide important input about intangible benefits linked directly to the program but not converted to monetary values.

Report Results

Results data are meaningless if they are not used properly and communicated to the sponsors, executives, managers, and participants who have a strong interest in the project. Communicating action planning results helps position the workplace learning function as a viable business partner with a focus on helping stakeholders define results-based, value-added solutions. Communication can take many forms, including full case study or impact reports, streamlined executive summaries, postings on internal websites, or articles submitted to a company newsletter, to name a few.

Summary

Integrating a results-based action planning process into your learning and development "tool kit" can add credibility to the workplace learning function from multiple perspectives. Specifically, an action planning process helps to

- organize and document the link between learning and on-the-job performance
- facilitate transfer of learned knowledge/skills through an action learning and peer feedback process
- deepen participants' personal commitment to achieving performance outcomes
- show the contribution of select programs
- provide a quick method to evaluate at Levels 3 and beyond
- demonstrate to stakeholder groups that programs and services are designed to add value and deliver results.

The key to success with this approach is to build it into the learning and development process during the early planning stages and to allow sufficient time to teach the action planning process. In general, the job aid in figure 8-4 will help you decide if your organization or your targeted program is ready to implement and support an action planning strategy.

Table 8-2. Case Example: Using Action Plan Estimates to Measure Business Impact and ROI

Calculation: A × B × C × D = E (Total adjusted monthly benefit)
E × 12 = F (Annualized benefit)

Action Plan # N = 35	Business Unit of Measure	Monthly Improvement Value (A) x	Percent Confidence Estimate (B) x	Percent Change Due to Program (C) x	Total *Adjusted* Monthly Benefit (D) =	Annualized Program Benefit (E) x 12
1	Efficiency	$3,000	80%	60%	$1,440	$17,280
2	Productivity	$1,875	60%	45%	$506.25	$6,075
3	Productivity	$2,500	35%	50%	$437.50	$5,250

Total annualized benefit *directly* attributable to program from action plans 1–3 (above) $28,605

Total annualized benefit *directly* attributable to program from other action plans collected   + $250,395

Total annualized benefit *directly* attributable to program from all action plans collected   = $279,000

ROI calculation:

Net benefits attributable to training ($279,000) – Program costs ($83,300) = ($195,700)   235% ROI

Program costs ($83,300) × 100 = ROI %

Source: Burkett (2008).

121

Figure 8-4. Job Aid: Readiness Checklist

Readiness Checklist for Action Planning Implementation

The following areas will help you assess organizational readiness for action planning as a performance measurement and transfer strategy.

Readiness Factors	Yes	No
Clear business objectives have been established for the program	☐	☐
Clear performance objectives have been defined for the program	☐	☐
Clear learning objectives have been defined for the program	☐	☐
The program requires data about success with application objectives	☐	☐
Participants are knowledgeable about targeted improvement areas	☐	☐
Participants have sufficient workplace support to implement planned actions	☐	☐
Barriers and enablers to successful application of the action plan have been defined	☐	☐
Managers are available for communication about action planning progress	☐	☐
Program staff are capable and competent to teach the action planning process	☐	☐
Sufficient time has been allotted in the program design for participants to develop and complete the action plan	☐	☐
Sufficient time has been allotted in the program design for facilitators to review and approve participant action plans	☐	☐
Sufficient time has been allotted in the program design for peers to review and approve individual action plans	☐	☐
Follow-up mechanisms have been defined	☐	☐
Management review mechanisms have been defined	☐	☐
Methods and resources for summarizing action planning data have been defined	☐	☐
Action planning results will be used for continuous improvement activities	☐	☐

Knowledge Check: Using Action Plans to Calculate ROI

Now that you have read this chapter, try your hand at using action plan data to identify impact (Level 4) results and calculate ROI (Level 5). Check your answers in the appendix.

Scenario: Coaching Program

- results obtained from 20 of 30 participants
- 20 completed action plans

- 10 participants did not provide data and/or data were incomplete
- data from 18 participants' action plans have been analyzed, isolated, and annualized
- total monetary benefit influenced by the coaching initiative is $84,109
- two additional action plans remain to be analyzed.

1. **Instructions:** Using the formula provided, calculate the total adjusted monthly benefit (Column E) and the annualized program benefit (Column F) for the remaining two action plans collected from the coaching program.

Calculation: A x B x C x D = E (Total adjusted monthly benefit)
E x 12 = F (Annualized benefit)

Action Plan #	Unit of Measure	Monthly Improvement Value (A) x	Confidence Level (B) x	Percent Change Due to Program (C) x	Percent Time Applied to Productive Tasks* (D)	Total *Adjusted* Monthly Benefit = (E)	Annualized Program Benefit (use 12) (F)
19	Productivity	$12,000	50%	70%	60%	$	$
20	Time	$8,500	40%	60%	70%	$	$

*Note: In this example, Column D was added to further estimate the extent to which time savings benefits actually affected business measures of productivity. Time savings benefits represent an improved business measure only when the time saved is applied to business tasks.

2. **Instructions:** Now that the performance improvement data have been analyzed from all available action plans, calculate the ROI of the coaching program.

Coaching Program	Your Answer	Actual Answer
Action plan #19	$	$
Action plan #20	$	$
Data from 18 other action plans, isolated and annualized	$84,109	$84,109
10 other participants who did not supply data	-0-	-0-
Total annualized benefits from the coaching program	$	$
Total costs of the program	$65,000	$65,000
Your ROI calculation: $\dfrac{\text{Net benefits attributable to training (\$) - Program costs (\$) = (\$)}}{\text{Program costs (\$)}} \times 100 = \text{ROI \%}$	ROI = ____ %	ROI = ____ %

About the Author

Holly Burkett, SPHR, CPT, is principal of Evaluation Works in Davis, California. A certified ROI professional since 1997, she has more than 20 years' experience assisting public and private sector clients develop evaluation processes and tools to define the business value of diverse WLP programs. Sample clients include Apple Computer, the National Security Agency (NSA), Premera Blue Cross, and the California Department of Transportation. Recognized as an evaluation expert with the U.S. Office of Performance Review (OPR), she also serves as editor of ISPI's *Performance Improvement* journal and a select item writer for the Human Resource Certification Institute (HRCI). Publications include coauthoring *Data Conversion* (2008) and *The ROI Fieldbook* (2006), as well as an award-winning case study in *ROI in Action* (2008). She earned her master's degree in human resources and organization development from the University of San Francisco and is currently pursuing doctoral studies in Human Capital Development. She can be reached at burketth@earthlink.net.

References

Burkett, H. (2001). Program Process Improvement Team. In P. Phillips ed. *In Action: Return on Investment Volume 3*. Alexandria, VA: ASTD.

Burkett, H. (April 2004). Using Action Plans to Measure Job Performance, Business Impact, and ROI. *ASTD Links*. Alexandria, VA: ASTD.

Burkett, H. (2005). Evaluating a Career Development Initiative. In D. Kirkpatrick ed. *Evaluating Training Programs: The Four Levels*, 3rd ed. San Francisco: Berrett-Koehler.

Burkett, H. (2008). Measuring ROI in a Career Development Initiative: A Global Computer Company. In P. P. Phillips and J. J. Phillips eds. *ROI in Action Casebook*. San Francisco: Jossey-Bass/Pfeiffer.

Burkett, H. (April 2008). Using Action Plans to Align Performance with Desired Results. Preconference workshop, 46th Annual ISPI International Conference. San Francisco, CA.

Phillips, J. J. 2003. *Return on Investment in Training and Performance Improvement Programs,* 2nd ed. Boston: Butterworth-Heinemann.

Phillips, P. P. and H. Burkett. (2008). *Data Conversion: Calculating the Monetary Benefits*. San Francisco: Pfeiffer.

Phillips, J. J. and P. P. Phillips. (January 2003). Using Action Plans to Measure ROI: A Case Study. *Performance Improvement Journal* 42(1): 22–31.

Phillips, P. P. and J. J. Phillips. (2005). *Return on Investment Basics*. Alexandria, VA: ASTD.

Phillips, J. J., P. P. Phillips, R. Stone, and H. Burkett. (2006). *The ROI Fieldbook: Strategies for Implementing ROI in HR and Training*. St. Louis, MO: Elsevier/Butterworth-Heinemann.

Chapter 9

The Success Case Method

Using Evaluation to Improve Training Value and Impact

Robert O. Brinkerhoff and Timothy P. Mooney

In This Chapter

The Success Case Method (SCM) evaluation method measures and evaluates training accurately, simply, and quickly, in a way that is both extremely credible and compelling. Upon reading this chapter, you will

- acquire a strategic, future-directed perspective on training evaluation

- learn the practical steps in a Success Case Method study

- understand the factors that should be addressed in helping an organization improve the business impact from training.

The Success Case Method

Results derived through applying the SCM are actionable. We can make strategic and constructive use of evaluation findings that actually helps training clients be more effective and successful.

There is an additional strategic outcome that the SCM helps achieve. For decades training and development professionals have recognized that manager support for training is absolutely vital to success. When managers support training and learners, it works. When they don't, it does not. As a result, we have begged and cajoled managers to support our efforts. But despite our pleas, most managers find other things more important to do. With the Success Case Method, we are able to give them a clear and data-based business case for supporting training. We can show them specific actions they can take to reinforce learning and performance, and tie these directly to bottom-line results and economic payoff to them and their organization. Then, rather than trying to make all sorts of mandatory prescriptions for support actions, we can simply show managers the data and let them do what they are paid to do: look at the facts and make a business decision.

The SCM uncovers and pinpoints the factors that make or break training success. Then, it shows how these factors can be more effectively managed so that more learning turns into worthwhile performance in the future. It is aimed directly at helping leaders in an organization discover their organization's "learning disabilities" then figure out what needs to be done to overcome these problems. Over time, the SCM helps an organization become better and better at turning an ounce of training investment into a pound of effective performance.

Defining Success

Most kinds of training conducted in organizations currently are based on the belief that some employees need certain knowledge or skills to perform their jobs correctly or improve their current job performance, and thus training is provided. Trainees are then supposed to return to their jobs and correctly use the training-acquired skills to perform in their jobs. Eventually, so goes this rationale, the company will benefit from the application of these skills in increased revenues, higher-quality products, more productive employees, increased output, decreased scrap rates, and so forth. Note that the benefit to the organization derives not from what was learned but from what actually gets used—that is, value doesn't come from exposure to the training or the acquisition of new capability. Instead, value comes from the changes in performance that the training eventually leads to.

There are other reasons that training is conducted, such as to promote advancement and career fulfillment, to avoid legal exposure, to meet regulatory requirements to provide certain training, or simply to offer training because it is perceived as a staff benefit, and this may help recruitment and personnel retention. These sorts of training do not necessarily require applying skills to produce value, and thus they are not the focus of typical SCM applications.

So for most training, impact and value are achieved only when the training actually gets used to improve or sustain job performance. Thus training success is defined as application of training-acquired capabilities in improved performance and job results.

Training Evaluation Realities

Two realities about training programs must be recognized and effectively dealt with because they dramatically influence the way we should think about and conduct evaluation of training. The first reality is predictable results, which we will discuss before moving on to the second reality.

Reality One: Predictable Results

Training programs typically produce reliable—and unfortunately marginal—results. The results that some trainees achieve may not be at all marginal, but over a large group of trainees, overall results are typically mediocre at best. Some people use their learning in ways that get great results for their organizations. Others do not use their learning at all. Most others may try some parts of it, notice little if any changes or results, and eventually go back to the ways they were doing things before. The good news is that the few who actually use their training in effective on-the-job applications often achieve highly valuable results; we have seen, for example, where just one manager used her training to help land a $500 million sale, a result that would not have been achieved had she not participated in the training. In another instance, a senior leader used his training to increase operating income for his business division by more than $1.87 million. These are dramatic and exceptionally valuable results; we have documented many more less dramatic outcomes that were nonetheless significant and worthy.

So, the problem is not that training does not work at all; it is just that it does not work frequently enough with enough trainees. In most cases, a typical training program produces only a few quite successful trainees who achieve these great results. Similarly, there is typically a small (but sometimes not so small) percentage of people who, for one reason or another, just were not able to use their training at all, or didn't even try to. The bulk of trainees are distributed between these extremes.

Making a business case to "grow" impact. A key principle of the SCM is that we can learn a lot from inquiring into the experience of these extreme groups. A SCM study can tell us for example, how much good a training initiative produces when the learning it produces is used in on-the-job performance. If the good that it produces is a great deal of good, such as when some trainees use their learning in a way that leads to highly valuable business results, then we know that the training had great potential for a high return-on-investment. When we find that the training produces really worthwhile results, but that it worked this well with only a small number of trainees, then we can construct a defensible business case for investing time and resources to extend the good results to more people.

Tyranny of the mean. Typical quantitative evaluation approaches are based on reductionist statistical procedures, such as calculating a mean or "average" effect. But, because training typically only helps achieve worthwhile results for a small proportion of the trainees, on average training will always be calculated to be mediocre. When we have a range of effects, those at the high end will be offset by those at the low end when we calculate a mean score. Assume for purposes of illustration that we have two different training programs: program A and program B. In training program A, assume further that we had an evenly split distribution of impact such that one half of the trainees did extremely well with their training, using it in improved performance to get worthy results. The other half did not use their learning at all. If we added these two halves of the distribution together and divided by the total number of trainees, as we would do in determining a mean score, then the training would look to have, overall, mediocre results. Assume that program B worked equally well with virtually all of the trainees, but was mediocre in that none of the trainees used their learning in useful ways, although none failed to use their learning either. That is, they all used it, but all in a mediocre way.

When we calculate the mean impact of program B, it will appear to have had exactly the same results as program A. In reality, however, these two programs represent two different strategic scenarios. In the case of program A, it has great potential because it produced excellent results, although for only half of the trainees. It is clearly a powerful intervention, although for some reason only half of the participants were able to get these results. Program B, however, has little to no promise, as it works well with virtually no one. It is probably not worth keeping.

This "tyranny of the mean" effect is very powerful and at the same time very dangerous. It probably explains why, on average, most training programs have over the years been assessed as having only mediocre effects. On average, it is true that most training does not work well. But some programs work well with some of the people, and this represents their great potential for being leveraged for even greater results.

The SCM avoids this tyranny of the mean effect by intentionally separating out the trainees that used their training, then aiming to discover what value those applications of the training produced. So, the SCM does not ask: "On average, how well is the training working?" (we already know the answer to that question: not very well). Instead, the SCM asks, "When the training works (is used), what good does it do?"

Reality Two: Training Alone Never Works

Training and performance improvement practitioners wanting to evaluate their success have struggled for decades with the seemingly intractable issue that "other factors" are always at work with training. In a sales training program, for example, we might see an increase in sales, or we might not. How do we know it was the training that led to increased sales or the failure to get increases? Maybe it was some other factor, such as a change in the market, a new incentive to sell more, or something else. Training alone does not produce results. There are always a number of nontraining factors that enable or impede successful results from the training. Supervisory support, incentives, opportunities to try out learning, and the timing of the training, to name a few, are examples of the sorts of nontraining or *performance system* factors that determine whether and how well training works to improve performance.

A corollary of this reality is the fact that, when training works or does not work, it is most often the case that the nontraining factors account for more of the success than features and elements of the training intervention or program itself.

This second reality of training evaluation strongly suggests that most—potentially 80 percent or more—of the failures of training to achieve results are *not* caused by flawed training interventions, they are caused by contextual and performance system factors that were not aligned with and were otherwise at odds with the intended performance outcomes of the training. Thus, when we evaluate "training" impact, we are most often in reality evaluating an organization's performance management system.

This fact is nothing new. We have known for years that the major reasons for failures of training to achieve impact are that training readiness and performance support factors were never adequately developed or implemented. Most evaluation models and methods have attempted to cope with this reality by attempting to isolate the training related causes.

In common practice, the way that this reality is often dealt with is to avoid it and evaluate only the training itself, asking whether it appeared to be useful in the eyes of participants, and sometimes going so far as to measure whether people actually learned anything. But going beyond this to measure application of learning has typically not been very productive. First, surveys of learning application produce discouraging results, showing quite predictably that most trainees have not applied or sustained use of their learning. Second, when we discover that most trainees are not using their learning in sustained performance, there is little to do with this information, because trying to improve the rate of application by improving the training program itself will not yield concomitant improvements in applying learning on the job.

The Success Case Method, on the other hand, makes no attempt to "parcel out" or otherwise isolate the training-related causes or to make any training-specific causal claims.

Instead, we leverage the fact that training never works alone or in a vacuum. We seek in an SCM study to identify all of the major factors that helped or hindered achieving worthwhile performance results from training so that we can build on and leverage this knowledge into recommendations for increasing performance in later iterations of training efforts. We discovered in an evaluation of a training prgoram for financial advisors, for instance, that almost all new advisors who were successful in applying their learning and getting good financial results had also made use of additional resources that helped them practice new emotional competence skills on the job. We also discovered that nearly all of the successful advisors sought and received feedback from a manager or peer. We concluded that the training was very unlikely to get any positive results without such additional interactions. This led in turn to recommendations to future trainees and their managers to be sure to provide time and opportunity for such assistance, as without it, the training was likely to be ineffective and wasted.

Leveraging the Two Realities

The Success Case Method begins with a survey to determine the general distribution of those training graduates who are using their learning to get worthwhile results and those who are most likely not having such success. In the second stage of an SCM study, we conduct in-depth interviews with a few of these successes and nonsuccesses—just enough of them to be sure we have valid and trustworthy data. The purpose of the interviews is two-fold. First, we seek to understand, analyze, and document the actual scope and value of the good results that the apparently successful people have claimed from the survey phase. This allows us to verify the actual rate of success, and also gauge its value. In an SCM study of sales representatives, for example, we were able to determine that the actual rate of success was about 17 percent; that is, 17 percent of the trainees who completed the training used their new learning in sustained and improved performance. Further, we could determine that the results they achieved were of a known value, in this example the typical results were worth about $25,000 per quarter in increased profits from sales of products with more favorable margins.

This first part of the SCM, identifying the quantitative distribution of extremes of success, is typically accomplished with a brief survey. That is, we usually conduct a simple survey of all the participants in a training program and ask them, through a few carefully constructed items, the extent to which they have used their learning to get any worthwhile results. Although a survey is often used, it is not always necessary. It may be possible to identify potential success cases by reviewing usage records and reports, accessing performance data, or simply by asking people—tapping into the "information grapevine" of the organization.

A survey is most often used, however, because it provides the additional advantage of being able to extrapolate results to get quantitative estimates of the proportions of people who report using, or not using their training. Also, when careful sampling methods are used, then probability estimates of the nature and scope of success can also be determined.

Second, in the interview phase we probe deeply to identify and understand the training related factors (using certain parts of the training or particular tools taught in the training, for instance) and performance system factors (supervisory assistance, incentives, feedback, and so forth) that differentiated nonsuccesses from successes. We know that when the training works, it is likely that is has been supported by and interacted with certain replicable contextual factors. Knowing what these factors are enables us to make recommendations for helping subsequent trainees and later versions of the training initiative achieve better results.

Putting information from both of these SCM phases together creates highly powerful and useful information. First, we know what rate of success the training had, and the value of that rate in terms of the nature of the results that successful trainees were able to achieve using their learning. This lets us extrapolate the *unrealized* value of the training initiative—the value that was "left on the table" by the program due to its rate of nonsuccess instances.

Figure 9.1 represents a typical distribution of training results, showing a relative small proportion of trainees who used their learning and achieved positive results, and the larger percentage of those who did not achieve worthwhile results. Added to this figure is a notation of that proportion of the distribution that represents a positive return on the training investment (ROI), and that proportion of it that had a negative return. The area above the darker and solid-line arrow shows that the trainees in this portion of the distribution achieved a positive ROI; we assume for purposes of this illustration that the value of the positive results in this portion of the distribution is indeed greater than the cost of providing and supporting the training for these people depicted in this portion. That is, whatever was spent to train the people who are represented in the solid-line area of the distribution was exceeded by the value of the results they achieved. However, everything to the left of this dividing line represents a loss or negative ROI. These people in the area above the dotted line were trained, but did not use their learning in ways that led to positive results.

Given this, the larger the area of the distribution above the solid-line arrow, then the greater the ROI. If we doubled, for example, the number of people who used their learning and got positive results, then we have clearly dramatically increased the overall ROI of the training, because the costs for training all of the people in the distribution are roughly the same for each individual. Or, looked at another way, the distribution to the left of the solid-line

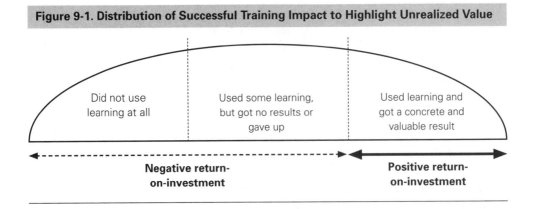

Figure 9-1. Distribution of Successful Training Impact to Highlight Unrealized Value

arrow area represents the unrealized value of the training. If we could take actions needed to "move" more people from the left portions of this distribution to the far right portion, then we would be increasing ROI and impact. And this is exactly the principal aim of the Success Case Method—to "grow" ROI and increasingly leverage more results from training.

We know from the interview phase of the study both what the value of success is, and also the factors that enable success. This lets us make a business case for growing the far right side of the distribution in figure 9-1. We can ask, for instance, what the value would be if we could grow the number of successful application instances by 10 percent. Then, we can ask what it might take to attempt this, for example, getting more managers to support the training, or getting more trainees to use the same job aid as their successful counterparts did.

We should also point out that it is not always necessary to make conclusions about impact in terms of dollar values. We used such values in the preceding example only to make the case simple and clear. In SCM practice, we encounter many instances where programs that do not entail such simply translated results can likewise benefit greatly from SCM methods.

This, in a nutshell, is how the SCM works. First, a survey (or sometimes another information harvesting method) is used to gauge the overall distribution of reported success and nonsuccess. This is followed by an in-depth interview phase where we sample cases from each extreme of the distribution and dig deep to understand, analyze, and document the specific nature of exactly how the training was used and exactly what verifiable results it led to. Our aim is to discover, in clear and inarguable terms, exactly how the training was used (if it was) and exactly what value (if any) it led to. The standard of evidence is the same as we would use in a court of law: it must be provable beyond a reasonable doubt, documentable, verifiable, and compelling.

From this, we are able to conclude the following:

- When training works, what value does it help achieve?
- How frequently and at what rate does it work this well?
- When it works, why? What factors help or hinder results?
- What is the value lost when training does not work?
- What is the case for making it work better?
- What would it take to make it work better; would such efforts be worthwhile?

Knowledge Check: Questions to Assess Understanding of Content

Answer the questions to assess your knowledge of the content. Check your answers in the appendix.

1. According to the Success Case Method, why is it often misleading to try to isolate the impact of the training program in an evaluation study?
   a. often it is too difficult to do
   b. other contextual factors are always operating and affect the business impact
   c. employee motivation is the biggest determinant of business impact, so it will make the training look ineffective
   d. only some training is expected to produce measurable business results
2. The Success Case Method looks at both the *value* obtained from the training and the *unrealized value*. Why are both concepts important? What fundamental questions do each of these two concepts address?
3. What is the best way to significantly increase the ROI of training?
   a. turn classroom training into e-learning programs, which will significantly reduce the costs per training hour
   b. shorten the length of time of any training program to make it more efficient
   c. improve the amount of information/skill people acquire in the training; the more they learn they better they will be able to produce results
   d. get more people to use the training in ways that make a difference to the business

About the Authors

Robert O. Brinkerhoff, PhD, is an internationally recognized expert in training effectiveness and evaluation and the principal architect of The Advantage Way. His next-generation ideas have been heralded by thought leaders ranging from Donald L. Kirkpatrick to Dana Gaines Robinson and adopted by dozens of top-tier organizations, including Bank of America, Children's Healthcare of Atlanta, Motorola, and Toyota.

A keynote speaker and presenter at hundreds of industry conferences and institutes world-wide, Brinkerhoff is a recent ISPI Award of Excellence recipient.

Brinkerhoff is the author of *Telling Training's Story* (2006), *The Success Case Method* (2003), and *High Impact Learning* (2001). He is coauthor with Timothy P. Mooney of *Courageous Training: Bold Actions for Business Results,* which was released in June 2008.

A professor emeritus at Western Michigan University where he was responsible for graduate programs in human resource management, Brinkerhoff originally earned his doctorate in program evaluation at the University of Virginia. Brinkerhoff can be reached at robert.brinkerhoff@wmich.edu.

Timothy P. Mooney is a partner with the Advantage Performance Group, a wholly owned subsidiary of BTS Group AB. He works directly with clients on consulting projects and is the practice leader for The Advantage Way. Prior to joining Advantage in 2000, he served in a senior management capacity for DDI, working closely with leading global organizations. In addition, he has more than 25 years of corporate sales management and consulting experience.

Mooney holds a BA in psychology from Butler University in Indianapolis and an MA in industrial/organizational psychology from the University of Akron. He is a frequent speaker and writer on the topic of achieving measurable business impact from training. He recently coauthored a book with Robert O. Brinkerhoff, *Courageous Training,* which was released in June 2008. Other publications include "Level 3 Evaluation" in the *ASTD Handbook for Workplace Learning Professionals* (2008); "Creating Credibility with Senior Management" and "Taking a Strategic Approach to Evaluation" in *The Trainer's Portable Mentor* (2008); and "Success Case Methodology in Measurement and Evaluation" in *ISPI Handbook: Improving Performance in the Workplace,* vol. 3. (2009). Mooney can be reached at tmooney@advantageperformance.com.

Additional Reading

Brinkerhoff, R. O. (2006). *Telling Training's Story.* San Francisco: Berrett-Koehler.

Brinkerhoff, R. O. (2002). *The Success Case Method.* San Francisco: Berrett-Koehler.

Mooney, T. and R. O. Brinkerhoff. (2008). *Courageous Training.* San Francisco: Berrett-Koehler.

Chapter 10

Using Performance Records

Ronald H. Manalu

······························ **In This Chapter** ······························

This chapter explores how to use performance records as the source of evaluation. Upon completion of this chapter, you will be able to

- ▧ explain the value of performance records as one of the most important data sources for measuring and evaluating performance improvement programs

- ▧ identify steps to arrive at performance records given the program is not designed to drive business measures

- ▧ list key factors to consider when developing a new record-keeping system.

Collecting data using performance records is important in evaluating and measuring any training program. Performance records and reports of the organization are often regarded as the most useful and credible data source for return-on-investment (ROI) analysis (Phillips, 2003). Performance records include the documents and reports that reflect performance in a work unit, department, division, region, or overall organization and include all types of measures, which are usually available in abundance throughout an organization.

Collecting data from the performance records is the heart of business impact evaluation because they usually reflect data needed. Most senior managers are interested in business impact data and value the information developed in reports they routinely monitor. Most organizations have had their performance records systems in place and are able to manage and track progress in achieving business objectives. Although performance records are available to provide data specific to employee behavior and job performance, the role of the training evaluator is to focus on measures relevant to the organization, not the individual.

Some improvement programs are designed to improve specific business measures. For this kind of program, the measures have been predetermined. In this situation the evaluator must assess the availability of the specific measures, select which performance records to use, process or convert existing data into more usable data, and decide whether or not to create a new reporting system.

Program evaluators may also face situations to measure and evaluate a training or improvement program that had no direct link to business measures when it was designed and delivered. In this case, the situation becomes more complex. Program evaluators have to acceptably link the existing program objectives to business measures. After establishing the link, then the process of assessing availability of measures begins. Figure 10-1 describes the process of collecting the data using performance records.

Linking Programs to Specific Measures

The first step in the model is to link the program to business measures. If a needs assessment was conducted, the linkage is already evident. If the linkage does not already exist, the program evaluator has to deliberately link the program objectives and the expected business impact measures. The challenge here is to understand how the program influences specific business measures. The link between capability building, behavioral applications, and business results must be carefully understood to justifiably argue that the specific program affects specific result areas. For example, a leadership development program may have an effect on a wide range of results, such as cost or time savings, employee satisfaction

---

ᨒ Practitioner Tip ᨒ

Many existing performance records can be adapted to the program's evaluation needs. Create a new system only when none exists or the existing ones do not provide the data you need.

Figure 10-1. Collecting Data Using Performance Records

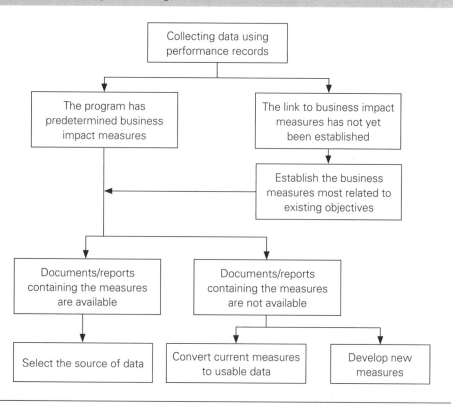

and engagement, enhanced productivity, or improved quality, whereas a compensation plan presentation may have an effect on costs, job satisfaction, productivity, and quality. Table 10-1 illustrates the typical impact measures for projects and programs. This table helps program evaluators identify measures that could be potentially linked to their programs. After establishing the link, the next step is to find the performance records containing the specific measures.

Sometimes, collateral measures move in harmony with the program. For example, efforts to improve safety may also improve productivity and increase job satisfaction. Thinking about the adverse affect on certain measures may also help. For example, when cycle times are reduced, quality may suffer, or when sales increase, customer satisfaction may deteriorate. Finally, program team members must prepare for unintended consequences and capture them as other data items that might be connected to or influenced by the program.

Table 10-1. Typical Impact Measures for Projects and Programs

Program	Key Impact Measurement
Absenteeism control/reduction	Absenteeism, customer satisfaction, delays, job satisfaction, productivity, stress
Association meetings	Absenteeism, costs, customer service, job satisfaction, productivity, quality, sales, time, turnover
Business coaching	Costs, customer satisfaction, efficiency, employee satisfaction, productivity/output, quality, time savings
Career development/ career management	Job satisfaction, promotions, recruiting, expenses, turnover
Communications programs	Conflicts, errors, job satisfaction, productivity, stress
Compensation plans	Costs, job satisfaction, productivity, quality
Compliance programs	Charges, losses, penalties/fines, settlements
Diversity	Absenteeism, charges, complaints, losses settlements, turnover
Employee retention programs	Engagement, job satisfaction, promotions, turnover
Engineering/technical/training conferences	Costs, customer satisfaction, cycle times, downtime, job satisfaction, process time, productivity/output, quality, waste
Ethics programs	Fines, fraud, incidents, penalties, theft
E-learning	Cost savings, cycle times, error reductions, job satisfaction, productivity improvement, quality improvement
Executive education	Absenteeism, costs, customer service, job satisfaction, productivity, quality, sales, time, turnover
Franchise/dealer meetings	Cost of sales, customer loyalty, efficiency, market share, quality, sales
Golfing events	Customer loyalty, market share, new accounts, sales, upselling
Labor-management cooperation programs	Absenteeism, grievances, job satisfaction, work stoppages

Program	Key Impact Measurement
Leadership development	Cost/time savings, development, efficiency, employee satisfaction, engagement, productivity/output, quality
Management development	Absenteeism, costs, customer service, job satisfaction, productivity, quality, sales, time, turnover
Marketing programs	Brand awareness, churn rate, cross-selling, customer loyalty, customer satisfaction, market share, new accounts, sales, upselling
Medical meetings	Compliance, efficiency, medical costs, patient satisfaction, quality
Orientation, on-boarding	Early turnover, performance, productivity, quality of work, training time
Personal productivity/time management	Job satisfaction, productivity, stress reduction, time savings
Project management	Budgets, quality improvement, time savings
Quality programs	Costs, cycle times, defects, response times, rework
Retention management	Engagement, job satisfaction, turnover
Safety programs	Accident frequency rates, accident severity rates, first aid treatments
Sales training/meetings	Customer loyalty, market share, new accounts, sales
Self-directed teams	Absenteeism, customer satisfaction, job satisfaction, productivity/output, quality, turnover
Sexual harassment prevention	Absenteeism, complaints, employee satisfaction, turnover
Six Sigma/lean projects	Cost, cycle times, defects, response times, rework, waste
Software projects	Absenteeism, costs, customer service, job satisfaction, productivity, quality, sales, time, turnover

(continued on next page)

Table 10-1. Typical Impact Measures for Projects and Programs (continued)

Program	Key Impact Measurement
Stress Management	Absenteeism, job satisfaction, medical costs, turnover
Supervisor/team leader program	Absenteeism, complaints, costs, job satisfaction, productivity, quality, sales, time, turnover
Team building	Absenteeism, costs, customer service, job satisfaction, productivity, quality, sales, time, turnover
Wellness/fitness programs	Absenteeism, accidents, medical costs, turnover

Source: Phillips and Phillips (2008).

Identifying Appropriate Records

In most organizations, business impact data that can be used to show the improvement resulting from a program are available (Mondschein, 1999). In most situations, program evaluators do not need to create a new reporting system to arrive at the specific measures. Using existing performance records makes data collection easy and cost-effective. The question is, where do the records exist? Figure 10-2 shows a sampling of the vast array of possible documents, systems, databases, and reports that can be used to select the specific impact measures.

In a situation where the same impact measures are available by more than one record, ask some key questions to help evaluators select the most appropriate data sources.

Which Document/Report Shows Credible Measures of the Program Effect?

For example, measuring customer satisfaction after implementing a service improvement program could use different sources of data. The data can be obtained from the survey conducted by the customer service department or from an external independent institution. The data obtained from the survey conducted by the customer service department could be as objective as the other survey, but sometimes the result of the survey is questioned due to the potential of bias of the department conducting the survey. The potential of bias might happen because the evaluators are measuring their own performance. In this case, some organizations prefer using an external independent survey widely known throughout the industry. For them, this source of data is more credible.

Figure 10-2. Sources of Data

Department records	Work unit reports
Human capital databases	Payroll records
Quality reports	Design documents
Manufacturing reports	Test data
Compliance reports	Marketing data
Sales records	Service records
Annual reports	Safety and health reports
Benchmarking data	Industry/trade association data
R&D status reports	Suggestion system data
Customer satisfaction data	Project management data
Cost data statements	Financial records
Scorecards	Dashboards
Productivity records	Employee engagement data

Source: Phillips and Phillips (2007).

Are the Data Widely Accepted Throughout the Organization?

For example, in measuring the success of a training program aimed at addressing retention, several sources of data could be monitored to measure the program's success. Some practitioners would use engagement and satisfaction data. In these surveys, employees are asked about their satisfaction or dissatisfaction related to their current job. The survey also reveals whether the employees were planning to leave the company in the near future. Most line managers would favor looking into the turnover rate after the program was implemented rather than the satisfaction survey. For them, the turnover rate is more directly linked to the profit or loss of the company.

Which Data Sources Are the Timeliest Measures of the Program Effect?

This question addresses the period between interventions to performance. For example, a leadership development program is expected to give feedback on the improvement in accuracy of numbers in financial reports produced by the accounting department. The issue is to determine how much time is required for the participants to apply the leadership behaviors that lead to improvement in accuracy of numbers in financial reports. The concern regarding time to performance would be affected by which financial report period was the source of data to track participants' impact progress.

Converting Current Measures to Usable Data

Occasionally, existing performance measures are integrated with other data. Keeping them isolated from unrelated data can be difficult. In this situation, all existing measures should be extracted and recalculated as necessary to render them more appropriate for comparison in an evaluation. At times, conversion factors may be necessary. For example, in one retail company, the average weekly sales increase may be presented as a measure of impact of a sales training program. However, part of the improvement in the sales numbers is also influenced by the increase in quantity of goods sold—not just effective behaviors applied. Therefore, it will be more acceptable if the performance measure is converted to profit contribution (percentage) of units sold. The conversion can be done by multiplying the average weekly sales increase with the percentage of profit contribution of store sales.

Developing New Measures

In some cases, data needed to measure the effectiveness of a program may not be readily available. Program evaluators must work collaboratively with other unit managers to develop new record-keeping systems. At this stage, program evaluators must thoroughly consider the expected return of this additional record-keeping system against the cost of obtaining such measures. If the effort to develop this additional record-keeping system is much higher than the expected benefit, it is meaningless to do this.

In one organization, an induction training program was implemented for every new employee corporate wide. This program was designed along with an initiative to socialize corporate core values to new employees. At the design phase of the program, the measurement only focused on using knowledge and skills. After three groups of participants attended the program, the top management began questioning the business contribution of the program. Several measures of the effect of this program were set, including early turnover—represented by the percentage of employees who left the company during the first six months of their employment. The management wanted to know whether the program had an influence on reducing new employee turnover. At that time, there was no record system to track the new employee turnover rate. Because the data are important and the benefit of knowing the result of the program is much more valuable than its cost, a new record system was implemented.

The following are factors to consider when creating new record-keeping systems:

- Which department will be in charge of developing this new system?
- Who will be responsible for collecting and monitoring the data?
- Who will be responsible for analyzing the data and reporting the findings?

- Will input forms be used for data input?
- Where will the data be recorded and stored?

Answering these questions usually involves other departments or management decisions beyond the scope of program administrator or evaluator.

Final Thoughts

The process of collecting data using performance records can occur in different ways. Usually the data are available in abundance within the organization, but there are steps required to obtain such data. The essential issue underlying the process is understanding the link between the program and the business measures. Having a clear line of sight between the program and business measures enables the program evaluator to do the next processes: selecting the most appropriate source of data to use, converting current measures into more usable measures, and finally building additional record keeping system to get new measures.

Knowledge Check: Case Study

Situation

Retail Merchandise Company (RMC) is a national chain of 420 stores, located in most major U.S. markets. RMC sells small household items, gifts, electronics, and jewelry, as well as personal accessories. The executives at RMC were concerned about the slow sales growth and were experimenting with several programs to boost sales. One of the concerns focused on the interaction with customers. Sales associates were not actively involved in the sales process; they usually waited for a customer to make a purchasing decision and then proceeded with processing the sale. Store managers analyzed the situation to determine if more communication with the customer would boost sales. Their analysis revealed that using simple techniques to probe and guide the customer to a purchase should boost sales in each store.

The senior executives asked the training and development function to experiment with a simple customer interactive skills program for a small group of sales associates.

A program produced by an external supplier was preferred to avoid the cost of development, particularly if the program proved to be ineffective. The specific charge from the management team was to implement the program in three stores, monitor the results, and make recommendations. If the program increased sales and presented a significant payoff for RMC, it would be implemented in other stores.

The sales associates were typical of the retail store employee profile. Most were not college graduates but had a few months of retail sales experience. Turnover was high and formal training had not been a major part of previous sales development efforts.

The Solution

The training and development staff conducted a brief initial needs assessment and identified five skills that would need to be covered in the program. Their analysis revealed that sales associates did not have these skills or were uncomfortable with using them. They selected a program called "Interactive Selling Skills," which significantly focused on skill practices. The program, an existing product from an external training supplier, would be tried in the electronics area and 16 people would be trained in each store. It would be taught by the staff of the training supplier for a predetermined facilitation fee. The program involved two days of training where participants practiced each skill with a fellow classmate, followed by three weeks of on-the-job application. Then, a final day of training would be conducted that included a discussion of problems, issues, barriers, and concerns about using the skills. Additional practice and fine-tuning of skills was a part of that final session.

Questions for Discussion

1. Which type of data do the senior management team desire?
2. What performance records should be used to look for business impact measurement?
3. If the performance record available to measure the effect of the training program is the average weekly sales per employee, do you find the need to convert these numbers into a more usable data?

Source: Phillips (1997).

Check your answers in the appendix.

About the Author

Ronald H. Manalu is a senior consultant of Learning Resources, a UK-based human capital consulting firm providing solutions in the areas of leadership, sales, customer service, team building, and communications. For more than a decade, he has been helping organizations growing their business through human capital development. He holds certifications from world-renowned human resources consulting institutions; among them are Development Dimensions International (DDI), as master trainer to conduct Targeted Selection Administrator Certification Workshops, and as master trainer to conduct Facilitating Skills Certification Workshops. Manalu is also certified to deliver HRDQ's Leadership and Negotiation Workshops. Recently, he collaborated with ROI Institute to measure and evaluate learning for organizations in Indonesia.

Based in Jakarta, Indonesia, Manalu facilitates training programs for executives and staff of organizations from various industries. His clients include, among others, Bank Indonesia, Coca-Cola Bottling Indonesia, Indonesian Attorney General's Office, Toyota Motor

Manufacturing Indonesia, UNICEF, Ford Motor Indonesia, Circle K, Hewlett-Packard, Indonesia Family Planning Coordinating Board, and L'Oreal Indonesia. He also serves as adjunct faculty member in Faculty of Economics University of Indonesia, where he teaches business communications.

Manalu holds a master's degree in strategic management from Prasetiya Mulya Business School, Jakarta, Indonesia. He may be reached at ronald@lresources.co.id.

References

Mondschein, M. (1999). *Measurit: Achieving Profitable Training*. Leawood, KS: Leathers.

Phillips, J. J. (1997). *BCR/ROI Case Application: Retail Merchandise Company (RMC); Return on Investment in Training and Performance Improvement Programs*. Houston, TX: Gulf Publishing Company, 154–155.

Phillips, J. J. (2003). *Return on Investment in Training and Performance Improvement Programs,* 2nd ed. Burlington, MA: Butterworth-Heinemann.

Phillips, P. P. and J. J. Phillips. (2007). *The Value of Learning: How Organizations Capture Value and ROI and Translate Them into Support, Improvement and Funds*. San Francisco: Pfeiffer.

Phillips, J. J., and P. P. Phillips. (2008). *Beyond Learning Objectives: Develop Measurable Objectives That Link to the Bottom Line*. Alexandria, VA: ASTD.

Additional Reading

Phillips, P. P. and C. A. Stawarski. (2008). *Data Collection: Planning for and Collecting All Types of Data*. San Francisco: Pfeiffer.

✄ Section III

Data Analysis

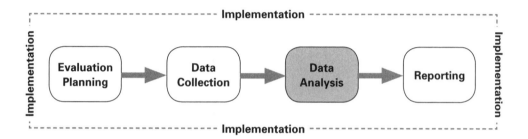

W hile the evaluation model shows data analysis following data collection, analysis actually occurs during the planning phase, the data collection phase, and even carries on through reporting and implementation. Throughout the evaluation process data are analyzed and considered. Appropriate data analysis is imperative if stakeholders are to make good decisions from the information evolving through the evaluation process. But what is appropriate data analysis? Well, it depends.

The type of analysis that takes place depends on

- type of data
- size of population
- acceptable error
- type of measures
- time requirements
- resource constraints
- cultural constraints
- convenience.

Good analysis balances the experimental context with the organizational context. Program participants and their supervisors, peers, and direct reports do not function in a lab. They work in dynamic organizations where decisions are swiftly made, in some cases with minimal information. So conducting the best data analysis possible given the constraints is a must. To be successful, however, evaluators must know the "right" way to analyze data and then be able to balance accuracy with costs, ensuring the results are reported in the right context.

In Section III you will learn basic analysis techniques to

- describe evaluation results
- isolate program effects from other influences
- convert data to monetary value
- calculate return-on-investment (ROI).

Chapter 11

Using Statistics in Evaluation

George R. Mussoline

·· **In This Chapter** ··

This chapter explores the basic statistical analysis that can be conducted to interpret the data collected from the evaluation program. Upon completion of this chapter, you will be able to

- ▧ explain the importance of using statistics in analyzing data

- ▧ identify the appropriate statistics to analyze the data

- ▧ interpret the statistics to have a better understanding of the data set

- ▧ apply the steps to calculate the statistics to interpret the evaluation program data

The Importance of Using Statistics in Analyzing Data

Typically, data collected from an evaluation program are the result of a survey, exam, or assessment. There are other methods to collect the data; however, the end result is usually the compilation of responses to questions. These responses could be the result of the participants' reaction to how much they agree (for example, on a scale of 1 [completely disagree] to 5 [completely agree]) with a survey question; the number of times an answer choice was selected on a multiple-choice test question; or the result of an evaluator's observation of how well a specific task was performed (for example, on a scale of 1 [incomplete/incorrect] to 5 [complete/correct]). No matter what the collection method, the end result is data that can be organized, characterized, summarized, and presented. The following sections of this chapter give methods to interpret the evaluation data so that the data can be converted into actionable information. This actionable information can then be used to support decisions or inform the end user of areas where additional data are needed to support the final decision. This information comes from the application of descriptive and inferential statistics.

Descriptive Statistics

Descriptive statistics clarify the various features of a data set. Descriptive statistics are the end result of the methods to collect, present, organize, and characterize the data set. These statistics describe the various features of a data set so the end user can draw conclusions and compare one data set to another. Some common descriptive statistics are the measures of central tendency, which include the mean, median, and mode, and measures of variability including the standard deviation, sample variance, and range. These statistics will be discussed further in the following sections of this chapter.

Inferential Statistics

Inferential statistics are used to make a decision or an inference from a small set of data (a sample) to a larger group (the population). Inferential statistics can be defined as the methods used that make it possible to associate the characteristics of a population or the ability to make a decision concerning a population based only on the results of a sample.

Measures of Central Tendency

Some of the most common descriptive statistics are the mean, median, and mode. The mean (arithmetic mean, sometimes referred to as the average) is a commonly used measure that describes the data set's tendency around a specific value. The mean is calculated by

---

❧ Practitioner Tip ❧

When looking at data, it is important to analyze them in a way that allows the quantitative data to provide you direction on what your audience is trying to tell you and context for examining qualitative data. Both quantitative and qualitative data create synergies and are much more powerful together than they are apart.

—Jennifer Iannetta
Merck & Co.

✍ **Practitioner Tip** ✍

People tend to want to use descriptive statistics—incorrectly—to make generalizations and predictions. So I'm always careful to include an explanation that descriptive statistics are not in and of themselves representative of any population—other than the test respondents, and therefore shouldn't be used to predict opinions or behaviors.

—Ira Greenberg
PDG

---

summing all the values in the data set and dividing that sum by the total number of values. Table 11-1 is an example series of values that represent the grades that were recorded for a midterm exam.

The mean grade from this data set is calculated by summing all the grades and dividing that sum by 8 (the number of grades). This calculation is expressed below:

$$(98 + 96 + 95 + 92 + 90 + 88 + 88 + 85)/8$$

$$732/8 = 91.5$$

The median is another measure of central tendency. It is the middle value in the ordered sequence of the data. When the data set contains an odd number of values, the median is represented by value that is in the mid-point of the sequenced data set. When the sample size is an even number, then the median lies between the two middle values in the

Table 11-1. Midterm Exam Grades

Student	Grade
A	98
B	96
C	95
D	92
E	90
F	88
G	88
H	85

sequenced data set. The median, in this situation, is then found by calculating the average of the numerical values representing the two middle values. The median from the data set in table 11-1 is 91. This is because the data set contains an even number of values; the middle values are 90 and 92, thus, (90 + 92)/2 = 91.

A third measure of central tendency is called the mode. The mode is the value in the data set that occurs the most. The mode is calculated by tallying the number of times each value occurs in the data set. Looking to table 11-1, all values occur only once except 88, which occurs twice. Therefore, 88 is the mode for the data in table 11-1. If no value is present more than one time, then the data set has no mode. Note that there is a difference between a data set having no mode and a mode of zero. If zero is the most frequently observed value in the data set, then zero is the mode for those data. Additionally, one data set can have more than one mode. In the circumstance where more than one value occurs in the data set with the same frequency, then the data set is described as bimodal. Because of these circumstances, the mode is not used for anything more than describing the data set.

In general, the mean is a more precise measure than the median and the mode, while the mode is a more precise measure than the median. Table 11-2 is a set of general guidelines that may give additional clarity about when to use these measures of central tendency.

Measures of Variation

The measures presented in the previous section (mean, median, and mode) describe the central tendencies for the data set. Additional measures (range, standard deviation, and sample variance) describe the variability of the data set. These measures of variation describe the dispersion or "spread" in the data set.

Table 11-2. Guidelines for Using Measures of Central Tendency

Measure	When to Use
Mode	When analyzing categorical data (for example, baseball team affiliation, religious affiliation, political party affiliation, etc.) or when values fit into a category and these categories are mutually exclusive
Median	When analyzing data that contain extreme values (for example, a data set that contains extremely high and low exam scores)
Mean	When analyzing a normal data set that is not categorical in nature and does not contain extreme values (for example, a set of exam scores, the number of seconds it takes an individual to run the 100 yard dash during a track season, the number of hits a baseball player has over a baseball season, etc.)

The range describes the total spread in the data set. It is the difference between the highest and lowest values in the data set. The range for the data in table 11-1 is 13 (98 − 85 = 13). The range is only one measure of variability, and it gives an indication of the dispersion of the data; however, it should not be the only measure of variability reported. The standard deviation and the sample variance are additional measures of variability that add to the description of the data set's variability.

The sample variance and standard deviation represent the average amount of variability in the data set or the average distance the data points are from the mean. The larger the sample variance or standard deviation, the larger the average distance each data point is from the mean of the data set. The computation of a standard deviation is accomplished by

1. subtracting the mean of the data set from each value in the data set
2. squaring each individual difference
3. summing all these squared deviations
4. dividing this sum by the total number of values minus one
5. calculating the square root of this value.

The sample variance is simply the square of the standard deviation. Sample variance and standard deviation will always be positive values because, as indicated in step 2 above, the differences in the sample value and the mean are squared in each computation. Sample variance and standard deviation values can be zero, but never negative. The only time when the sample variance can be zero is when there is no variation in the data set (for example, all values in the data set are exactly the same). In this case, the range would be zero, and the mean, median, and mode would all be the same value.

Many computer software packages including Microsoft Excel, SPSS, and Minitab compute the descriptive statistics listed above, so *it is not necessary to know how to compute these values*. What is important is that the end user *knows how to interpret and use these statistics to understand the data set*. The statistical analysis of the data in the following section is the output of the software packages Excel and Minitab. The descriptive statistics data can be obtained from Excel by going to the Tools Menu, selecting Data Analysis, and then Descriptive Statistics. The descriptive statistics menu is presented in figure 11-1.

Interpreting and Understanding the Data

An example data set is presented in table 11-3. These data will be used to calculate the descriptive statistics referenced above and enable additional interpretations of the results. The data presented in table 11-3 are a typical data set that might be received from a survey or evaluation conducted immediately following a training session. Table 11-3 shows two

Figure 11-1. Descriptive Statistics Menu in MS Excel

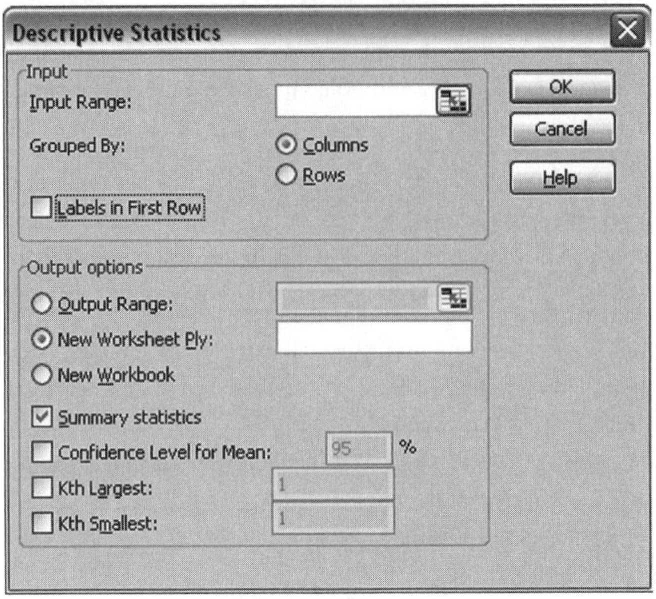

potential sets of the responses for one specific question asked on the training program evaluation, namely "How likely are you to recommend this course to a friend or colleague?" (1 = not at all; 5 = definitely).

To get an appropriate understanding of the data set, represent the data visually so the end user can see any interesting trends in the data. Figures 11-2 and 11-3 are histograms of the data presented in table 11-3. A histogram is one way of visually representing the data set; it is a vertical bar representation of the frequency distribution where the frequencies are represented by bars. The frequencies can be presented as counts or percentages. Histograms allow the end user to view how the data are distributed. This visual representation allows the end user to quickly observe any trends in the data: Are the data clustered around one end of the scale? Are the data trending toward the middle of the scale? Are the data evenly dispersed over the entire range of the scale? This is important so that the end user can have a quick understanding of the data and any general trends that are present in the data set. Additional statistical interpretation of the data will further define the data set; however, this visual representation gives a first pass, general look at the data and any trends that may exist.

Table 11-3. Example Data

How likely are you to recommend this course to a friend or colleague?
(1 = not at all; 5 = definitely)

Respondent	Data Set 1	Data Set 2
1	3	1
2	3	1
3	3	1
4	3	2
5	3	2
6	3	2
7	3	3
8	3	4
9	4	5
10	4	5
11	4	5
12	4	5
13	4	5
14	4	5
15	4	5
16	5	5
17	5	5
18	5	5
19	5	5
20	5	5
21	5	5
22	5	5
23	5	5
24	5	5
25	5	5
26	5	5
27	5	5
28	5	5
29	5	5
30	5	5

Figure 11-2. Histogram of Data Set 1

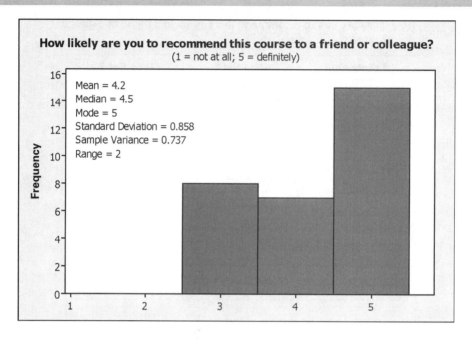

How likely are you to recommend this course to a friend or colleague?
(1 = not at all; 5 = definitely)

Mean = 4.2
Median = 4.5
Mode = 5
Standard Deviation = 0.858
Sample Variance = 0.737
Range = 2

Figure 11-3. Histogram of Data Set 2

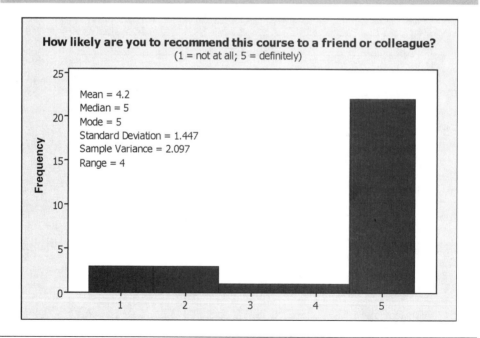

How likely are you to recommend this course to a friend or colleague?
(1 = not at all; 5 = definitely)

Mean = 4.2
Median = 5
Mode = 5
Standard Deviation = 1.447
Sample Variance = 2.097
Range = 4

Table 11-4 is the descriptive statistics output from Excel of the data presented in table 11-3. As seen from figures 11-2 and 11-3, the two data sets are visually quite different (data set 1 has no responses of 1 or 2 whereas data set 2 has six values or 20 percent of the sample responding 1 or 2). However, the mean and the mode presented in table 11-4 for each data set is the same. The visual representation of the data enables the end user to see that even though two measures of central tendency (that is, the mean and the mode) are the same for each data set, the data sets are actually quite different. The differences in the data sets come to light visually in the respective histograms and when the measures of variability (standard deviation, sample variance, and range) are evaluated.

The standard deviation and sample variance for data set 1 are 0.858 and 0.737, respectively. The standard deviation and sample variance for data set 2 are 1.447 and 2.097, respectively. How does the end user of the data interpret these results? An interpretation of the standard deviations for each data set will be discussed; however, the same general interpretation can also be applied to the sample variance because the standard deviation is simply the square root of the sample variance.

✑ Practitioner Tip ✎

Ideally, instructional designers will want to clearly understand during their course planning whether they will be following up with Level 1, 2, or 3 evaluations. And those tests should be developed at the same time as the course. In that way, the assessment will be meaningful and useful.

—Ira Greenberg
PDG

Table 11-4. Microsoft Excel Descriptive Statistics Summary

Data Set 1 Output

Mean	4.2	4.2
Median	4.5	5
Mode	5	5
Standard Deviation	0.858	1.447
Sample Variance	0.737	2.097
Range	2	4

The standard deviation for data set 1 is 0.858, which indicates that the "average" scatter of the data points around the mean value in data set 1 is 0.858 units around the mean. In other words, data set 1 has a standard deviation of 0.858 units, which indicates that *most* responses in this sample are clustered within 0.858 units around the mean value of 4.2 (for example, between 3.3 [4.2 – .858] and 5.0 [4.2 + .858]). The standard deviation for data set 2 is 1.447, which indicates that the "average" scatter of the data points around the mean value in data set 2 is 1.447 units around the mean. Therefore, the *most* responses in data set 2 are clustered within 1.447 units around the mean value of 4.2 (for example, between 2.8 and 5.0 because the upper end of the scale is 5). The interpretation of these data is that data set 1 is more closely clustered around the mean value whereas data set 2 is more dispersed across the response scale. This can be visually observed in figure 11-4, where the two data sets are fitted to a standard curve and presented on the same graph. The standard curve in figure 11-4 was created using Minitab Statistical Software package. Minitab enables the end user to fit a normal curve to the data sets.

Additional Statistics

The descriptive statistics in the previous sections of this chapter enable the end user to have a good general understanding of the data set and its properties. However, additional basic

Figure 11-4. Standard Curve Comparison of Data Sets 1 and 2

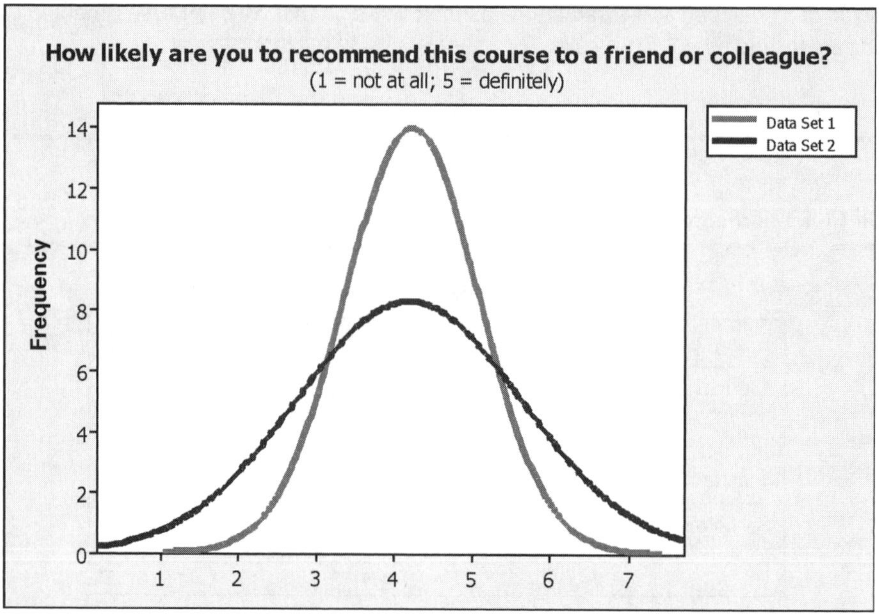

✎ **Practitioner Tip** ✎

Culture can have a definite impact on survey scores and their analytic results. Typically, the value of 3.5 on a 5.0 scale in the United States translates to a lower score in Japan. Organizations need to be mindful of cross-cultural differences to ensure measurements are interpreted accurately.

—Jean Grabowski
Merck & Co.

---

statistics further describe the data set and enable the end user to have an even better understanding of the data. Again, many computer software packages (Excel, SPSS, Minitab, and so forth) compute these additional statistics, so *it is not necessary to know how to compute these values*. What is important is that the end user *knows how to interpret and use these statistics to understand the data set*.

The additional statistics presented in this section further describe the shape of the data set. It is important to understand the data set's shape because the shape is a visual representation of the way the data are distributed. Once the shape of the data is visualized (for example, through a histogram as in figures 11-2 and 11-3 or through a fitted curve as in figure 11-4), then additional descriptions that define the data's symmetry can be evaluated. The distribution of the data could be relatively flat or peaked. This measure is the kurtosis of the data. Additionally, the distribution of the data set can either be symmetrical or not. If the distribution is not symmetrical, then it is asymmetrical or skewed.

The kurtosis of the data set is one method to measure the shape of the data. Kurtosis is a measurement that has to do with how flat or peaked a distribution appears. The kurtosis of data set 1 is −1.484 and the kurtosis of data set 2 is 0.484. Why is this important? How would one use this information? Kurtosis is a useful statistic to evaluate because it is another indication of how tightly the data points are centered around the mean. In data set 1, the curve is more peaked than that of data set 2. Normally distributed data establish the baseline for kurtosis: not too flat, not too sharply peaked. Data that followed a normal distribution perfectly would have a kurtosis value of 0. Because significant kurtosis indicates that the data are not normal, you may think of the statistic as a first check for normality. Another method to evaluate the shape of the data is to review the mean and median. If these two values are the same, then the data set can be considered symmetrical or not skewed. If the value of the mean is greater than that of the median, then the data are generally considered to be positively skewed (or right skewed). If, on the other hand, the mean is less than the median, then the data are considered to be negatively skewed (or left skewed).

Positive skewed or right-skewed data are so named because the "tail" of the distribution points to the right, and because its skewness value will be greater than 0 (or positive). Salary data are often skewed in this manner: many employees in a company make relatively little, while increasingly few people make very high salaries. Left-skewed data are also called negatively skewed data (the distribution's tail points to the left, and it produces a negative skewness value). Failure rate data are often left skewed. An example of left-skewed data is month ending accounting transaction activity. A lot of businesses "close" their accounting books at month's end, and this transaction activity is typically left skewed. When a data set is skewed, then the more accurate measure of central tendency is the median, not the mean, because very few values in the data set are extreme values and cause the mean to be a mis-representation of the data set's central value.

When plotting data from an evaluation plan, it may be desirable to end up with data that are right or left skewed. The desired skewness depends upon the type of question that is posed to the survey participant. For example, a left-skewed data set may be observed from a survey question when most respondents "agree" with the proposed statement. Additionally, a set of exam scores may be left skewed when most individuals performed well on the exam. A quick and simple way to compute the skewness of the data set is to subtract the value of the median from the mean. If value of this difference is positive, then the distribution is positively skewed. If value of this difference is negative, then the

Figure 11-5. Right- or Positively Skewed Data Distribution

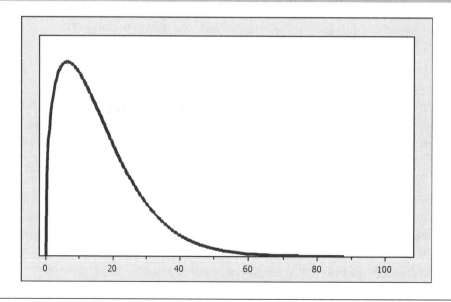

Figure 11-6. Left- or Negatively Skewed Data Distribution

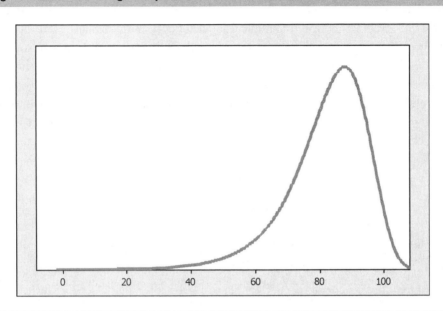

distribution is negatively skewed. Table 11-5 is the same output from Excel as presented in table 11-4 with the addition of the skewness and kurtosis values. The skewness values are calculated using a formula different than the one presented above. The formula used to calculate the skewness from Excel takes into consideration the standard deviation of the distribution to allow different data sets to be compared to one another.

Table 11-5. Additional Microsoft Excel Statistics Summary

	Data Set 1 Output	Data Set 2 Output
Mean	4.2	4.2
Median	4.5	5
Mode	5	5
Standard Deviation	0.858	1.447
Sample Variance	0.737	2.097
Range	2	4
Skewness	−0.487	−1.469
Kurtosis	−1.484	0.484

Chi-Square

Another useful statistic is called a Chi-square ($\chi2$) distribution. Chi-square is a common distribution used to test how well a sample fits a theoretical distribution or to test the independence between categorical variables. For example, a Chi-square distribution would be a useful statistic if a manufacturer wants to know if the occurrence of three types of defects (small particle size, broken pellets, and high moisture content) is related to shift (day, evening, night). A Chi-square distribution describes the likelihood of obtaining each possible value of a statistic from a random sample of a population; in other words, what proportion of all random samples of that size will give that value.

T-Test

An important property of the t-test is its robustness against assumptions of population normality—in other words, t-tests are often valid even when the samples come from non-normal populations. This property makes them one of the most useful procedures for making inferences about population means. A t-test could be used to evaluate the hypothesis test of the mean of one or two normally distributed populations. Several types of t-tests exist for different situations, but they all use a test statistic that follows a t-distribution under the null hypothesis.

Sample t-test 1. Tests whether the mean of a single population is equal to a target value. For example, is the mean height of female college students greater than 5.5 feet?

Sample t-test 2. Tests whether the difference between the means of two independent populations is equal to a target value. For example, does the mean height of female college students significantly differ from the mean height of male college students?

Paired t-test. Tests whether the mean of the differences between dependant or paired observations is equal to a target value. For example, if you measure the weight of male college students before and after each subject takes a weight-loss pill, is the mean weight loss significant enough to conclude that the pill works?

T-test in regression output. Tests whether the values of coefficients in the regression equation differ significantly from zero. For example, are high school SAT test scores significant predictors of college GPA?

Summary

The proper use of statistics will enable the end user to better understand the data collected as part of an evaluation program. Statistics that measure the data set's central tendencies and those that measure the data set's variance help give a good overall description of the data. Additionally, visual representations of the data set will enable the end user to quickly observe any trends in the data and get a better understanding of the data collected as part of the evaluation program. As discussed, it is important for the end user to understand how to interpret the data in order to make better decisions (it is not necessary for the end user to fully understand how to calculate the statistics). This chapter discussed basic statistics to help interpret the data set; additional statistics can be used to further understand the data and additional information on these statistics can be found in the suggested readings at the end of this chapter.

Knowledge Check: Statistical Analysis

Now that you have read this chapter, try your hand at calculating and interpreting the data in the following data set.

On a scale of 1 (no knowledge at all) to 10 (complete understanding), please rate your level of comprehension of the subject matter discussed in the training session.

Respondent	Data Set 1—Knowledge before attending training	Data Set 2—Knowledge after attending training
1	5	9
2	6	8
3	4	9
4	5	8
5	7	9
6	3	8
7	3	9
8	8	9
9	6	8
10	5	8
11	5	9
12	5	9
13	3	8
14	7	9
15	3	8
16	6	7
17	3	7
18	5	9
19	2	9
20	5	8

Following the steps described in this chapter, what are the general statistics and the interpretation of the statistics?

1. Using Microsoft Excel, calculate the mean, median, mode, standard deviation, sample variance, kurtosis, skewness, and range.
2. Create a histogram of the data.
3. Fit a curve to the data.
4. Determine if the data are symmetrical or skewed (if they are skewed, are the data left or right skewed?).

Check your answers in the appendix.

About the Author

George R. Mussoline is the manager of evaluation and assessment within Merck & Co.'s Global Human Health Learning & Development department. He is responsible for designing, implementing, and reporting the results of the evaluation strategies associated with the various learning interventions within the department. He is a coauthor of the article entitled "Level 3 Evaluation Data: A Visual Interpretation" (Proven-Human Integration, 2009). He can be reached at George_Mussoline@Merck.com.

Additional Reading

Berenson, Mark L., and D. M. Levine. (1996). *Basic Business Statistics—Concepts and Applications,* 6th ed. Englewood Cliffs, NY: Prentice Hall.

Gladwell, M. (2008). *Outliers—The Story of Success.* New York: Little, Brown.

Levitt, S. D., and S. J. Dubner. (2005). *Freakonomics.* New York: HarperCollins.

Lewis, M. (2003). *Moneyball: The Art of Winning an Unfair Game.* New York: W. W. Norton.

Mager, R. F. (1997). *Measuring Instructional Results,* 3rd ed. Atlanta: The Center for Effective Performance, Inc.

Reichheld, F. F. (2006). *The Ultimate Question: Driving Good Profits and True Growth.* Boston: Harvard Business School.

Salkind, N. J. (2006). *Tests & Measurement for People Who (Think They) Hate Tests & Measurement.* Thousand Oaks, CA: Sage.

Salkind, N. J. (2008). *Statistics for People Who (Think They) Hate Statistics,* 3rd ed. Thousand Oaks, CA: Sage.

Williams, M. A., and S. Pautz. (2004). *Guide to Minitab: Minitab Release 14.* Lexington, MA: Rath & Strong.

✎ Chapter 12

Analyzing Qualitative Data

Keenan (Kenni) Crane

--------------------------------- **In This Chapter** ---------------------------------

This chapter explores various ways to analyze data from interviews, focus groups, case studies, and other qualitative data collection methods without having to be a qualitative researcher. Upon completion of this chapter, you will be able to

■ describe the importance of qualitative data to support and give credibility to the monetary data

■ describe three types of validity in qualitative data

■ apply a four-step approach to organize your descriptive data.

The Importance of Using Qualitative Data

Qualitative data are typically defined as information that can be captured that is non-numerical. These data are obtained through interviews, focus groups, observations, case studies, and document reviews. They can be captured through pictures, videos, emails, text messages, and social networking sites. By their very nature qualitative data are subjective with a potential for researcher's bias. Although argument about which is better—

qualitative or quantitative—often ensues, the fact is that both types of data are important in describing the success of training programs.

Unfortunately for evaluators, good analysis of qualitative data often requires more time and effort than do most quantitative research analyses. One reason for this is that to get greater insight into the significance of qualitative data, codes, themes, and even numerical values are often assigned to these data. Once the assignment is made, then the data are manipulated to achieve a better of meaning of the data. Too often, however, evaluators do not want to go these lengths to analyze their qualitative data, and thereby, threaten the reliability of their story of program success and force a greater reliance on more believable data that are quantitative in nature.

However, without qualitative data, quantitative data are limited in what they reveal about program success. Quantitative data are known to "show" the results of an evaluation, whereas qualitative data are known to "tell" the story. Table 12-1 presents a comparison of quantitative and qualitative analysis objectives as described by Mach and others (2005).

Without strong qualitative analysis, the evaluation researcher provides a skewed look at results—either by lack of balance (quantitative and qualitative) or by weak analysis. What is required after gathering case studies, interviews, and focus group data is a creative yet structured way of observing the data, sorting and coding the data, noticing patterns in the data, and reobserving and revisiting the data. In the final presentation and analysis, this synthesized information can help explain quantitative data and return-on-investment (ROI) findings to the customer or client.

Table 12-1. Comparison of Quantitative and Qualitative Objectives of Analysis

Quantitative	Qualitative
Seek to confirm hypotheses about phenomena	Seek to explore phenomena
Instruments use rigid style of eliciting and categorizing response to questions	Instruments use more flexible, iterative style of eliciting and categorizing responses to questions
Use highly structured methods such as questionnaires, surveys, and structured observation	Use semi-structured methods such as in-depth interviews, focus groups, and participant observation

Source: Mach and others (2005).

A Word About Validity in Qualitative Research

Because of their inherent subjectivity, it is important to consider the perceived validity of qualitative data. In reporting evaluation findings and linking data points with less tangible qualitative data, we need to concern ourselves with being plausible, credible, trustworthy, and therefore defensible to our customers and clients. Our ultimate goal is to explain our quantitative findings and contribute to the theory on which we base future evaluation projects.

Types of Validity

Researcher bias, or finding what you want to find, can be a criticism of quantitative as well as qualitative findings. And although some qualitative researchers reject the framework of validity that is found in quantitative research (Trochim, 2006), we want to do everything possible to avoid this kind of criticism and to know that we have taken as many precautions as necessary to report the clearest and most valid picture to our clients.

Three types of validity are important to think about when working with qualitative data. The first type of validity is descriptive, which answers the question, "How accurate is the information—for example, behaviors, settings, and times—that is reported?" The second type of validity is called interpretive validity and answers the question, "Has this information—thoughts and viewpoints, for instance—been accurately understood and reported?" The third type of validity is theoretical validity, which answers the question, "Have we adequately considered all possible explanations for the results we are reporting and not just fit the data to our bias?"

Approaches to Managing Validity

We can promote credibility in reporting qualitative data by taking a few common sense approaches with each of the three types of validity. Johnson (1999) suggests the approaches described in table 12-2.

Techniques to Analyze Qualitative Data

There are various ways to analyze qualitative data. Donald Ratcliff's compilation provides a description of the following techniques:

- typology
- taxonomy
- constant comparison/grounded theory
- analytic induction
- logical analysis/matrix analysis

Table 12-2. Approaches to Managing Validity

Type of Validity	Approach
Descriptive	Use multiple observers or researchers to interpret, cross-check, and explain the data.
Interpretive	Ask for participants' feedback about the interpretations being made to clear up any misunderstandings. Use actual words and phrases in direct quotations in the report.
Theoretical	Search for alternative explanations that do not fit your predictions and discuss with colleagues and peers.

- quasi-statistics
- event analysis/microanalysis
- metaphorical analysis
- domain analysis
- hermeneutical analysis
- discourse analysis
- semiotics
- content analysis
- heuristic analysis
- narrative analysis.

Although this long list is impressive, there are still other ways in which qualitative data can be analyzed, ranging anywhere from nominal group technique (Phillips and Phillips, 2007) to card sorting and affinity diagrams (Straker, 1997). The key is to recognize that analyzing qualitative data is an iterative process, not a linear process. Good analysis requires evaluators to review, reflect, code, and then review, reflect, and code again, until ultimately a story emerges. By following the four steps that follow, a relatively structured approach to analyzing qualitative data can be used, thereby saving evaluators time while still providing a reliable story of program success.

Four Steps to Qualitative Analysis

Whether data are collected using interviews, transcribed notes, case studies, or questionnaires, the best place to begin your analysis is to organize the data. Once organized, read and read multiple times. Begin to identify common ideas and patterns through a process of coding or finding words and phrases to represent consistent themes. Remember, while preset codes are a starting point, the fun in qualitative analysis is watching the themes emerge through the data. So be ready to add to your predetermined codes or change them as the story unfolds. The following four steps may help bring some structure to a by-design unstructured process.

Step 1: Observing and Searching

- Read through all the qualitative data—case studies, questionnaires, and comments—without judgment.
- Search and be objective in your observations (have others do the same).
- Keep in a "discovery" mindset rather than prejudging the data.

Step 2: Sorting and Coding

- Use condensed words or phrases to identify key categories.
- Be consistent throughout.
- Underline and highlight.

Step 3: Discovering and Coding

- Step back and notice patterns in how you sorted the information.
- Find similarities.
- Find differences.

Step 4: Reobserve and Reread

- Notice if you have a linear map or a three-dimensional map.
- Rethink: if you have found parts and have a linear map, now look at the whole picture and find a three-dimensional picture.
- Look at data again for new insights.
- Finally, involve others in discussion and brainstorm for alternative insights.

Analysis comes within the process and as a result of the process. It is impossible to remove all subjectivity. Having multiple people, however, go through the data in the same way can improve reliability. Common threads will emerge.

Final Thoughts

Evaluation results need to inform, not just with important facts about quantitative data, but also describe other findings that emerge through the analysis. Qualitative analysis is an iterative process and the results that come out of it help evaluators describe what people say, what they mean or need, what they do, and the culture in which they work. How qualitative results are presented both in written report and verbal report form is important. The key to success is to be clear about what you are trying to achieve through your communication. Chapter 18, Reporting Evaluation Results, describes the importance of communicating evaluation results in detail.

Qualitative results can place emphasis on areas of importance. They can describe scenarios and situations that demonstrate a point. They can explain how the quantitative data presented were derived and how to improve a program's overall success. The argument should not be about which is better, quantitative versus qualitative, but rather how best to use them both to demonstrate the success of training.

Knowledge Check: Analyzing Qualitative Data

Now that you have read this chapter, let's see what you learned about analyzing qualitative data. Check your answers in the appendix.

1. Why are qualitative data important to training measurement and evaluation?
2. List three types of validity you need to be concerned with in qualitative analysis. What does each type of validity address?
3. List four steps for analyzing qualitative data.

About the Author

Keenan (Kenni) Crane, PhD, is an internationally experienced consultant in individual, group, and organization development using a systems approach to help managers improve performance and strengthen business relationships. For 20 years, Crane has coached leaders in *Fortune* 500 corporations, family businesses, and not-for-profit organizations to develop leadership and interpersonal and social skills while facilitating a smooth transition during corporate and cultural changes.

In addition to her doctorate in organization and group development, she holds a master's degree in experimental psychology, a master's degree in counseling/ human relations, and a BA in psychology and pre-med (magna cum laude). She is presently a full-time faculty member in the e-Business School at Hamdan Bin Mohammed e-University in Dubai, United Arab Emirates. She can be reached at K.Crane@HBMeU.ac.ae or kennicrane@kennicranephd.com.

References

Johnson, R. B. (1999). *Examining the Validity Structure of Qualitative Research.* In A. K. Milinki ed. *Cases in Qualitative Research: Research Reports for Discussion and Evaluation.* Los Angeles: Pyrczak Publishing, 160–65.

Mach, N., C. Woodsong, K. M. MacQueen, G. Guest, and E. Namey. (2005). *Qualitative Research Methods: A Data Collector's Field Guide.* Research Triangle, NC: Family Health International.

Phillips, P. P. and J. J. Phillips. (2007). *A Strategic Approach to Retention Improvement: Southeast Corridor Bank.* In *Proving the Value of HR.* Birmingham, AL: ROI Institute.

Ratcliff, D. (undated). *15 Methods of Data Analysis in Qualitative Research,* available at http://qualitativeresearch.ratcliffs.net/15methods.pdf.

Straker, D. (1997). *Rapid Problem Solving with Post-It Notes.* Cambridge, MA: Da Capo Press.

Trochim, W. M. (2006). *The Research Methods Knowledge Base,* 2nd ed., available at www.socialresearchmethods.net/kb/.

Additional Reading

Creswell, J. W. (2008). *Educational Research: Planning, Conducting, and Evaluating Quantitative and Qualitative Research.* Upper Saddle River, NJ: Pearson/Merrill Prentice.

Denzin, N. K. and Y. S. Lincoln. eds. (2005). *The Sage Handbook of Qualitative Research.* Thousand Oaks, CA: Sage, available at http://www.loc.gov/catdir/toc/ecip053/2004026085.html.

Miles, M. B., and A. M. Huberman. (1994). *Qualitative Data Analysis: An Expanded Sourcebook.* Thousand Oaks, CA: Sage.

Patton, M. Q. (1990). *Qualitative Evaluation and Research Methods.* Thousand Oaks, CA: Sage.

Rossi, P. H., M. W. Lipsey, and H. E. Freeman. (2007). *Evaluation: A Systematic Approach.* Thousand Oaks, CA: Sage.

Shadish, W. R., T. D. Cook, and L. C. Leviton. (1992). *Foundations of Program Evaluation: Theories of Practice.* Newbury Park, CA: Sage.

Spencer, L. M. and S. M. Spencer. (1993). *Competence at Work: Models for Superior Performance.* New York: Wiley.

Isolating the Effects of the Program

Bruce C. Aaron

In This Chapter

This chapter explores techniques that can be used to isolate the effects of programs from the effects of other factors when evaluating business performance measures. Upon completion of this chapter, you will be able to

- explain the importance of isolating the unique contribution of a program to business outcomes
- identify techniques available to isolate the effects of a program
- select the appropriate isolation technique for any situation and level of evaluation.

The Importance of Isolating the Effect of a Program

Two particularly important challenges face consultants conducting training evaluations: collecting accurate data to describe program effects and isolating the effects of the program. Isolating program effects is a critical component of measurement and evaluation and is essential for ensuring credibility because factors other than the program can influence business results (see figure 13-1).

Figure 13-1. The Importance of Isolating Program Effects

Bill was excited. He was presenting for the first time to the new CEO. She had been running the company for a year now and had begun several initiatives that had an effect on programs in the human resources department. One of these had led to the establishment of the Leadership Institute, which Bill had designed and developed. Now Bill was meeting with her to present his first report on the impact of the Institute. Bill presented data showing significant increases in several important metrics, such as employees' satisfaction with work, supervisors' job satisfaction ratings, and increased production. Then he summarized by indicating how successful the Leadership Institute had been to date. The CEO, however, reminded Bill of several other initiatives, such as the new performance management system, the improved employee benefits package, and the organizational realignment she had led. "How do you know what effect the Leadership Institute has had on the results you're showing here, apart from the impact of these other initiatives?" she asked. Bill's stomach churned a bit as he began to respond; he didn't have a credible answer to the question. The CEO was about to realize the same thing.

In organizations, programs are implemented within complex systems of people, processes, and events. The only way to know the connection between a particular program or project and measured business impact is to deliberately isolate the effects of the program on the specific business outcomes of interest. This ensures that the data analysis allocates to the program only that part of the performance improvement that is connected to the program. Without this important step, the conclusions of the study will lack credibility because other important influences might affect results as the program is conducted. Many other factors (job redesign, incentives, rewards, compensation, technology, operational systems, and other internal processes) can influence improvement in business results. Similarly, factors external to the department or function area, or to the organization, can influence performance. Giving full credit for performance results to a single program without accounting for other factors that clearly have a similar potential effect on results is questionable. Credible evaluation requires an effort to ensure that only the results that are directly attributable to the program should be reported to stakeholders.

Fortunately, a variety of techniques can be used to isolate the effects of the program from other influences. These include using control groups, trend and forecast analyses, and using

---

✑ Practitioner Tip ✑

Identify the isolation technique during evaluation planning. This allows the best technique to be identified for the specific context, and to associate this important part of the evaluation plan with key stakeholders.

---

expert input from a various sources. Each technique has different advantages and drawbacks, and the choice of which to apply depends on the situation.

Techniques for Isolating the Effects of a Program

Table 13-1 shows a list of these techniques.

These approaches can reasonably be condensed into a smaller number of manageable categories: control groups, trend and forecast analysis, and estimates. Exploring these in greater technical detail and with statistical sophistication, however, is beyond the scope of this chapter.

Chain of Impact: The Initial Evidence

Before presenting the techniques, examine the "chain of impact" implied in the different levels of evaluation (see figure 13-2). The chain of impact must be in place for the program to drive business results. It models the results and the process by which we intend to achieve those results. Isolation of program effects, although not itself a link in this chain, must be applied to the business results data to determine the change that can be attributed uniquely to the program.

The chain of impact assumes that measurable business impact achieved from a training program should be derived from applying skills and knowledge on the job over a specified time after one completes the program (training programs serve as a common example; other types of programs might result in slightly different models). Logically, then, successfully applying program material on the job should stem from new knowledge, skills, and/or attitudes learned in the program, which are measured at Level 2. Therefore, for business results to improve (Level 4), this chain of impact implies that measurable on-the-job applications are realized (Level 3) when new knowledge and skills are learned (Level 2).

Table 13-1. Techniques for Isolating the Efffects of Programs and Projects

- Control group arrangement
- Trend line analysis of performance data
- Forecasting performance data
- Participant's estimate of impact
- Supervisor's estimate of impact
- Management's estimate of impact
- Estimates based on expert opinion or previous studies
- Calculation or estimation of the impact of factors other than the program
- Customer estimate of impact

Figure 13-2. The Chain of Impact

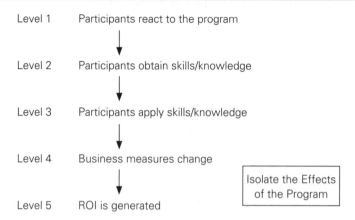

Attributing business impact to the program is difficult without evidence of the chain of impact. Concluding that the program caused any performance improvements is illogical if there is no learning or application of the material on the job. Literature and practice support this approach of modeling a chain of impact based on the different levels of evaluation (Alliger and Janak, 1989). A practical requirement, therefore, is to collect data across all levels of evaluation when conducting an ROI evaluation. Data must be collected at lower levels when a higher-level evaluation is conducted.

Despite its importance, the chain of impact does not prove a direct connection between the program and business impact. Isolation is necessary to make this direct connection and determine the amount of improvement attributable to the program.

Using Control Groups

The classic approach to isolate the impact of a program is using control groups in an experimental research design (Wang, 2002). This approach involves using an experimental group that participates and a control group that does not. Compose both groups as similarly as possible and, if feasible, randomly select participants for each experimental or control group. When this is possible, both groups are subjected to the same environmental influences, with the program itself as the difference in the performance of the two groups. Differences in outcomes can be then be attributed to the program, because it remains as the only systematic influence that explains observed differences in performance between the groups—the magnitude of the effect on business results indicates the unique contribution of the program. The basic control group design is presented here, but variations of the design are relevant to different situations and various threats to validity. These topics are addressed in more detail in *Isolation of Results: Defining the Impact of the Program* (Phillips and Aaron, 2008).

Basic control group design. The basic control group design has an experimental group and a control group, as illustrated in figure 13-3. The experimental group participates in the program, whereas the control group does not. Data are gathered on both groups before and after the program. The results for the experimental group, when compared to the control group, reveal the impact of the program.

There should be no significant differences between groups in characteristics that can influence the final outcome data, independent of the outcome of the program. The participants in each group should be at approximately the same job level, experience, ability, working conditions, and possibly even location.

Practically speaking, control group designs often are not feasible in organizational settings; one must explore other approaches of isolating the effects of the program on performance. Organizations face tradeoffs between research principles and feasibility: higher costs are often associated with measurement and evaluation, and the very nature of a control group assumes that some will receive the potential benefits and others will not. A control group evaluation design also implies a longer evaluation timeline. Consider the following questions to determine if a control group is the best isolation technique for your program:

- Is the population large enough to divide into groups?
- Is the population homogeneous—representing similar jobs and similar environments?

Figure 13-3. Control Group Design

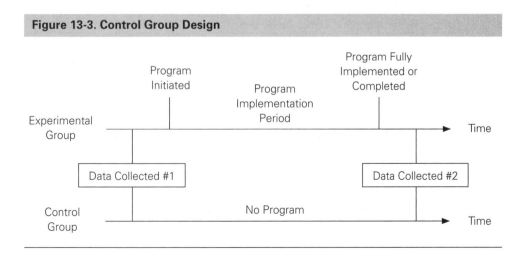

- What is the particular measure that matters to the organization?
- What variables may be affecting the measure? These variables are used to select the comparison groups for the control group arrangement.
- Using the Pareto Principle, which of the variables most strongly influences the output measure(s)?
- Can the program be withheld from a particular group? Sometimes, this occurs naturally because it might take a long time to roll out a program. Employees who receive the program last may be as many as three to six months behind those who participate in the program first, creating an opportunity to compare the last group with the first group.
- Is a pilot offering planned, and could the pilot group be matched with other groups for comparison?

Several rules are helpful when a control group arrangement is feasible:

- Keep the groups separated by different locations, different buildings, different shifts, or different floors.
- Minimize communication between the groups.
- If possible, do not let the control or experimental group know that they are part of an experiment and being compared with others.
- Monitor data on a short-term basis to check for improvements in both groups.
- Watch out for the Hawthorne effect (a change in behavior caused not by the program but by the special attention of the study itself) from the experimental group. Attend to the group as required by the program design, but try to minimize other interactions.
- Do not create expectations beyond the norm that may influence the results (for example, do not tell people that they are a special group and top performance is expected).

Because control groups are a powerful and credible method for isolating the impact of an intervention, consider using one to determine whether the support and opportunity are available to allow their use in evaluating important programs.

Using Trend Lines and Forecasts

When a control group analysis is not feasible for isolating the impact of a program, the next logical choices are two specific, closely related techniques. The first is trend line analysis, a simple process of forecasting the measure in question using preprogram data. The second method, the forecast technique, is more general and can be used when other influences have entered the process. A mathematical relationship or model is developed so that the data can be forecasted, not just projected on a trend line.

Trend line analysis. With this approach a trend line is drawn, using previous performance on the outcome measure as a baseline, extended into the future. When the program is conducted, actual performance is compared with the projected value shown by the trend line. Any improvement in performance over that predicted by the trend line can then be reasonably attributed to the program, if two conditions are met:

- The trend established prior to the program would be expected to continue in the absence of the program. The process owner(s) should be able to provide input to reach this conclusion. If the answer is no (indicating other factors would affect the outcome trend), the trend line analysis should not be used. If the answer is yes, the second condition must be met.
- No other *new* variables or influences entered the process *after* the program was conducted (that is, no additional influences entered the process beyond the program). If the answer is yes, another method must be used. If the answer is no, the trend line analysis will develop a reasonable and credible estimate of the impact of the program.

Figure 13-4 shows an example of this trend line analysis taken from sales revenue in a retail store chain. The vertical axis reflects the level of sales in millions. Data are shown before and after a sales incentive program was introduced in July. As shown in the figure, there was an upward trend in the data prior to implementing the incentive program. Although the program had a dramatic effect on sales, the trend line shows that improvement would have

Figure 13-4. Sample Trend Line of Retail Product Sales

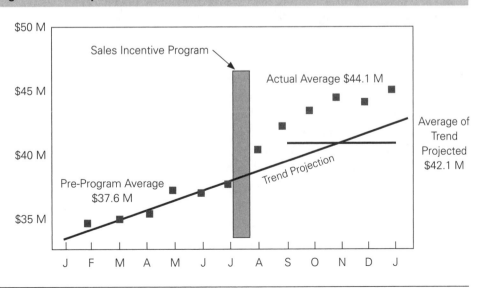

continued anyway, based on the previously established trend. The temptation is to measure the improvement by comparing the average six months of sales prior to the program ($37.6 million) to the average of six months after the program ($44.1 million) yielding a $6.5 million difference. However, a more accurate comparison is the six-month average after the program compared to the trend line average ($42.1 million). In this example, the difference is $2 million. Using this more conservative measure increases the accuracy and credibility of the isolation process. In this case, the two conditions outlined above were met (yes on the first; no on the second).

Preprogram data must be available before this technique can be used, and the data should have some reasonable degree of stability. If the variability in the data is high, the stability of the trend line becomes an issue. If the stability of the data cannot be assessed from a direct plot, use more detailed statistical analyses to determine if the data are stable enough to make the projection (Salkind, 2000). A trend line can be projected with a simple analytical function available in many calculators and software packages, such as Microsoft Excel. The primary advantage of this approach is that it is simple and inexpensive. If historical data are available, draw a trend line and estimate the differences. Although not exact, it does provide a quick assessment of a program's potential impact.

Using trend line analysis can be straightforward and credible. To use trend lines effectively, a yes answer is necessary for these four questions:

- Are historical data available for the measure at hand?
- Are at least six data points available?
- Do the historical data appear to be stable when they are plotted over time?
- Is it anticipated that there will be no other influences, factors, or processes implemented at the same time of the program?

Forecasts. A more analytical approach to trend line analysis is using forecasting methods that predict a change in performance variables. This approach is a mathematical variation of trend line analysis in which other variables are accounted for at the time a program is implemented. The actual performance of the outcome measure is compared with a forecasted value of that measure. The forecasted value is derived by taking the additional influence into account. A linear model, in the form of $y = ax + b$, is appropriate when only one other variable influences the output performance and that relationship is characterized by a straight line. Instead of drawing the straight line, a linear equation is developed, which calculates a value of the anticipated performance improvement. Figure 13-5 provides an example of how this technique works.

Figure 13-5. Example of the Application of Forecasting Methods

A large retail store chain with a strong sales culture implemented a sales training program for sales associates. Applying the new skills should increase the sales volume for each associate. An important measure of the program's success was the sales per employee, collected six months after the program and compared with the same measure prior to the program. The average daily sales per employee prior to training, using a one-month average, were $1,100 (rounded to the nearest $100). Six months after the program, the average daily sales per employee were $1,500.

After reviewing potential influencing factors with several store executives, only one factor—the level of advertising—appeared to have changed significantly during the period under consideration. The advertising staff had developed a mathematical relationship between advertising and sales. Using the historical values, a simple linear model yielded the following relationship: $y = 140 + 40x$, where y is the daily sales per employee and x is the level of advertising expenditures per week (divided by 1,000). This least squares function used to derive this equation is a routine option on some calculators and is included in many software packages. The level of weekly average advertising expenditures in the month preceding the program was $24,000, and the level of expenditures during the six months after the program was $30,000. Assuming that the other factors that might influence sales were insignificant, store executives determined the impact of the advertising by plugging in the new advertising expenditure amount (30) for x and calculating the average daily sales, which yielded $1,340. Therefore, the new sales level caused by the increase in advertising was $1,340. Because the new actual sales value was $1,500, then $160 ($1,500 − $1,340) could be attributed to the program.

A challenge with this predictive approach is presented if additional influences need to be accounted for, which requires more sophisticated statistical techniques and software for multiple variable analyses. Even then, a good fit of the data to the model may not be possible.

The primary advantage of this process is that it can predict business performance measures without the program, if appropriate data and models are available. Using more complex models can be a helpful option for practitioners familiar with the assumptions and requirements of general linear model techniques. Presenting more complex specific methods is beyond the scope of this chapter and is contained in other publications (Armstrong, 2001). However, you do not need complex approaches to unearth the value of using straightforward approaches described here.

Using Estimates

If the previously discussed techniques are not feasible, consider using estimates to isolate program effects. Estimates are by nature subjective and should be considered only after the other approaches have been exhausted, but they can provide powerful and credible evidence connecting the program to the observed business results. In businesses and other organizations with dynamic environments and time constraints, decisions will be made with the best available data. Ultimately, these decisions will be more subjective, not less, to the extent that all reasonable and credible data are not brought to bear.

Essentially, this approach involves using estimates from a variety of experts, with the participants of the programs often being the most credible source. Take a conservative approach to estimation with some accounting for the error or reliability of the estimates. Obtain estimates from participants, their managers, or sometimes, senior managers.

Participant, manager, and senior manager estimates. The effectiveness of this approach assumes that the sources of data can be used to determine or estimate how much of a performance improvement is related to the program. When using this technique, assume that the program is focused on improving performance, that one or more business measures have been identified prior to program implementation and have shown improvement, and that there is a need to link the program to the specific amount of performance improvement to determine the monetary impact of the improvement. This information can be gathered using a focus group, an interview, or a questionnaire. Detailed guidelines for collecting estimate data using each of these approaches can be found in other sources (Phillips and Aaron, 2008).

However, the process has some disadvantages. As an estimate, it lacks the objective accuracy desired by some professionals. Also, the input data may be unreliable from participants who are incapable of providing these types of estimates, either because they might not be aware of exactly which factors contributed to the results, or because they may be reluctant to provide data. If the questions come as a surprise, the data will be scarce.

Several advantages make this technique attractive. It is a simple process, easily understood by most participants and by others who review evaluation data. It is inexpensive, takes little time and analysis, making the results an efficient addition to the evaluation process. Participant estimates originate from a credible source—the individuals who actually produced the improvement. Sometimes, the participants' immediate manager may be the more credible source. When this is the case, this is the ideal source. Periodically, senior managers are the ideal source. In any case, the process to develop the estimates is easy. The relative ease with which these data can be collected, however, should not entice evaluators into an over-reliance on this approach; always consider more rigorous approaches (such as controlled research designs, trend and forecast analyses) first. If time and resources permit, estimates can be a corroborating and enlightening source of data even when other methods are also feasible.

The advantages of estimating offset the disadvantages in cases where the more rigorous research designs discussed previously cannot be used. As with the very act of measurement, isolating the effects of a program will never be completely precise and error free, and estimates can be sufficiently accurate for clients and management groups. These key audiences tend to readily accept the approach. Living in an ambiguous world, they understand that estimates have to be made and often are the only way to approach an issue. They understand the challenge and appreciate the conservative approach to estimation, often commenting that the actual value is probably greater than the value presented. This process is particularly appropriate when the participants are managers, supervisors, team leaders, sales associates, engineers, and other professional and technical employees.

The steps to estimating the contribution of a program include

- identifying the factors that contribute to improving a business measure
- estimating the contribution of the improvement specifically due to the program under evaluation given the variety of factors (typically reported as a percentage)
- describing the basis for the estimate
- adjusting for error in the estimate by identifying the level of confidence associated with the estimated contribution (typically reported as a percentage).

Figure 13-6 presents an example of how the estimation process works.

Customer estimates of program impact. One helpful approach in some narrowly focused situations is to solicit input on the impact directly from customers. In these situations, customers are asked why they chose a particular product or service or to explain how individuals applying skills and abilities have influenced their reaction to the product or service. This technique focuses directly on what the program is designed to improve. For example, after a teller training program was conducted following a bank merger, market research data showed that the percentage of customers who were dissatisfied with teller knowledge was reduced by 5 percent when compared with market survey data before the training program. Because the training program was the only factor during this time to affect teller knowledge, the 5 percent reduction in dissatisfied customers was directly attributable to the program.

Of course, customer estimates can be used only in situations where customer input can be obtained. Even then, customers may not be able to provide accurate data. They must be able to see the influencing factors to isolate them. However, because customer input is usually credible, the approach is helpful in the situations in which it can be used.

Figure 13-6. Example of the Estimation Process

A large financial institution had implemented various initiatives to increase opportunities for branch staff to cross-sell several products. The initiatives included

- sales training
- incentive systems
- goal setting/management emphasis
- marketing
- other.

Six months after the sales training, one measure being tracked showed improvement. Credit card accounts had increased by 175 per month on average. The training team wanted to know how much of the increase was due to the sales training. The training team mailed branch managers a questionnaire asking them various questions regarding the program. A series of questions focused specifically on the contribution of the sales training.

The manager for a branch located in the Southern Division brought her team together to identify the causes of the increase in credit card accounts. Together they identified the contribution of each factor and adjusted for error in their estimates by reporting their confidence in their estimation. The result was the lowest possible estimate given a range of estimates.

Monthly Increase in Credit Card Accounts: 175		
Contributing Factors	**Percent of Average Impact on Results**	**Percent of Average Confidence Level**
Sales Training Program	32%	83%
Incentive Systems	41%	87%
Goal Setting / Management Emphasis	14%	62%
Marketing	11%	75%
Other _____	2%	91%
TOTAL	100%	

The contribution of the sales training program was calculated at 175 credit card accounts x 32% contribution factor x 83% confident in estimate = 46.48% new credit card accounts per month due to the sales training program.

Summary

Isolating the effects of a program is a critical step when making the connection between results and the program. Various techniques are available, including control groups, trend lines and forecasting, and using estimates, which may come from a variety of sources.

Knowledge Check: Isolating Program Effects Using Trend Line Analysis

As part of a quality improvement program, Micro Electronics, an electronics components manufacturer, conducted a series of training programs to improve quality. One measure of quality is reject rate, which is the percent of items returned for rework. Because of the overall emphasis in quality for the last year, there has been a downward movement in the reject rate. The business conducted a continuous improvement program (CPI) to improve the reject rate in one work unit. All employees of this work unit were involved in the program, conducted in July. After the program was completed, the training staff measured the impact of the program on the reduction of rejects. The chart below shows the reject rate six months before and after the program was implemented. The trend lines show the relative trends and midpoint values both before and after the program.

Using the figure below as your guide, what is improvement in reject rates due to the program? Check your answers in the appendix.

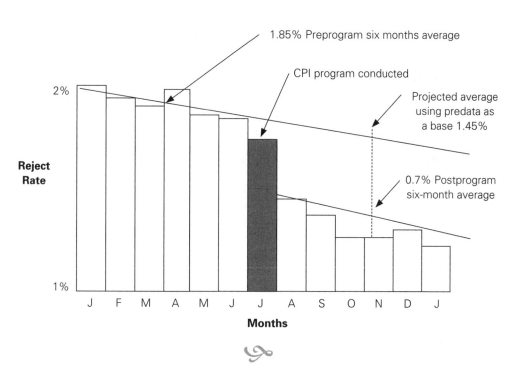

About the Author

Bruce C. Aaron, PhD, CPLP, is a capability strategy manager for Accenture, a global management consulting, technology services, and outsourcing company (www.accenture .com). He has authored or co-authored dozens of publications on topics in statistics, measurement, evaluation, instructional technology, and group decision-making systems. His most recent publication is *Isolation of Results: Defining the Impact of the Program* (2008). Aaron presents at a variety of international conferences such as AERA, AEA, ASTD, ISPI, SALT, and The Psychometric Society. Aaron received a master's degree in School Psychology and a PhD in Educational Measurement and Evaluation from the University of South Florida, and he is a Certified Professional in Learning and Performance (CPLP). Aaron can be reached at bruce.aaron@accenture.com.

References

Alliger, G. M. and E. A. Janak. (1989). "Kirkpatrick's Levels of Training Criteria: Thirty Years Later." *Personnel Psychology* 42: 331–342.

Armstrong, J. ed. (2001). *Principles of Forecasting: A Handbook for Researchers and Practitioners.* Boston: Kluwer Academic Publishers.

Phillips, J. P. and B. C. Aaron. (2008). *Isolation of Results: Defining the Impact of the Programs.* San Francisco: Pfeiffer.

Salkind, N. (2000). *Statistics for People Who (Think They) Hate Statistics.* Thousand Oaks, CA: Sage.

Wang, G., Z. Dou, and N. Lee. (2002). "A Systems Approach to Measuring Return on Investment (ROI) for HRD Interventions." *Human Resource Development Quarterly* 13(2): 203–24.

Additional Reading

Aiken, L. (1991). *Psychological Testing and Assessment,* 7th ed. Boston: Allyn and Bacon.

Brinkerhoff, R. O. and D. Dressler. (July 2002). "Using Evaluation to Build Organizational Performance and Learning Capability: A Strategy and a Method." *Performance Improvement.*

Kaufman, R. (July 2002). "Resolving the (Often-Deserved) Attacks on Training." *Performances Impermanency* 41(6).

Keuler, D. (2001). "Measuring ROI for Telephonic Customer Service Skills," *In Action: Measuring Return on Investment* vol. 3. P. Phillips ed. Alexandria, VA: ASTD, 131–58.

Phillips, P. P. and J. J. Phillips. (2002). "Evaluating the Impact of a Graduate Program in a Federal Agency," *In Action: Measuring ROI in the Public Sector.* P. Phillips ed. Alexandria, VA: ASTD, 149–72.

Phillips, P. P. and J. J. Phillips. (2007). *Proving the Value of HR: ROI Case Studies*. Birmingham, AL: ROI Institute.

Phillips, P. P. and J. J. Phillips. (2007). *Proving the Value of HR: ROI Case Studies*. Birmingham, AL: ROI Institute.

Russ-Eft, D. and H. Preskill. (2001). *Evaluation in Organizations: A Systematic Approach to Enhancing Learning, Performance, and Change*. Cambridge, MA: Perseus Books.

Surowiecki, J. (2004). *The Wisdom of Crowds: Why the Many Are Smarter than the Few and How Collective Wisdom Shapes Business, Economies, Societies, and Nations.* New York: Doubleday.

Chapter 14

Converting Measures to Monetary Value

Patricia Pulliam Phillips

In This Chapter

This chapter explores techniques for converting measures to monetary value. Upon completion of this chapter, you will be able to

- ■ explain the importance of converting a measure to money
- ■ identify techniques available to convert a measure to money
- ■ apply five steps to calculate the monetary value of benefits for a program.

The Importance of Converting a Measure to Money

The need to convert data to monetary amounts is not always clearly understood. A program can be shown to be a success just by providing business impact data, which show the amount of change directly attributable to the program. For example, a change in quality, cycle time, market share, or customer satisfaction could represent improvement that is linked directly to a program. Sometimes, this information is sufficient; however, many program sponsors require the actual monetary value, particularly when they want to compare program benefits to costs.

Value Equals Money

For some stakeholders, the most important value of any program is its monetary contribution. Executives, sponsors, clients, administrators, and other leaders are concerned with the allocation of financial resources and want to see evidence of program contribution in financial terms. Often, for these key stakeholders, outcomes stated in any other terms are insufficient.

Money Normalizes Program Benefits

For some programs, the impact of a program is more understandable when it is stated in terms of monetary value. Consider, for example, the impact of a major program to improve the creativity of an organization's employees and, thereby enhance the innovation of the organization. Suppose this program involved all employees and had an impact on various measures. The easiest way to understand the value of such a program is to convert the individual outcomes of this new creativity to money. Totaling the monetary values of all the innovations can provide a sense of the total value of the program and allow stakeholders to make comparisons among the different outcomes.

Money Is Often the Reason for Programs

Sometimes, the monetary value of a particular issue provides the impetus for a program. For example, a company might be incurring fines due to compliance violations, so management holds a program to prevent further violations. Another example may be in the case of excessive accidents. When converted to monetary value, the magnitude of this problem becomes more evident, leading to new programs. The best way to get the attention of a potential sponsor for a program is to place the problem or opportunity in the context of money.

Monetary Value Is Vital to Organizational Operations

With global competitiveness and the drive to improve the efficiency of operations, awareness of the costs related to particular processes and activities is essential. In the 1990s, this emphasis gave rise to activity-based costing (ABC) and activity-based management. ABC is not a replacement for traditional general ledger accounting. Rather, it is a translator or medium between cost accumulations—that is, the specific expenditure account balances in the general ledger—and the end users who must apply cost data in decision making. In typical cost statements, the actual cost of a process or problem is not readily discernible. ABC converts inert cost data to relevant, actionable information. ABC has become increasingly useful for identifying improvement opportunities and measuring the benefits realized from performance initiatives (Cokins, 1996). Understanding the cost of a problem and the payoff of the corresponding solution is essential to properly managing a business.

Monetary Benefits Are Necessary to Calculate ROI

Return-on-investment (ROI) is a fundamental accounting term that compares the annual monetary benefits of a program or project to its costs. To develop the ROI, the benefits of a program must be converted to money before they can be compared to the program costs. Only by converting benefits to the same type of measure as program costs (which is money) can the two can be mathematically compared. The concept of ROI is discussed in detail in chapter 16, Calculating the Return-on-Investment.

Techniques to Convert a Measure to Money

Converting measures to money is not new. For centuries, monetary values have been placed on a variety of measures, including the benefits of public parks, the value of human life, improvements in productivity and quality, and the lifetime value of customers. The key to converting measures to money is to first understand the techniques available.

Standard Values

Perhaps the best news about converting data to monetary values is that it has already been done for most of the measures that matter in an organization. An estimated 80 percent of the measures that are important to an organization have been converted to monetary values (Phillips and Burkett 2008). That is, if it is important enough to drive a program or project, then someone has been concerned enough about it to convert it to a monetary value. Standard values are used to convert output data, quality measures, and employee time to money.

Converting Output Data to Monetary Value. When a program has produced a change in output, the value of the increased output can be determined from the organization's accounting or operating records. Output measures include revenue and productivity measures. For organizations operating on a profit basis, this value is the marginal profit contribution of an additional unit of production or unit of service provided. For performance-driven programs versus revenue-generating programs, the value of increased output is reflected in the savings accumulated when additional output is realized without increasing input requirements.

Converting Quality to Monetary Value. Because quality is a critical issue, its cost is an important measure in most manufacturing and service firms. And because many programs are designed to improve quality, the program staff must place a value on improvement in relevant quality measures.

⚙ **Practitioner Tip** ⚙

Get to know your gatekeepers in advance of when you need the data.

- Schedule a meeting to review your analysis plan.
- Ask them to show you how their measures are gathered and reported.
- Ask how the measures are used in their business.
- Find out how the data are associated with other important values.
  - Associated or matched to individuals?
  - equipment?
  - work shifts?
  - work areas?
  - supervisors or managers?
  - locations or regions?
- Ask how these measures get converted to money. Are the conversions based on cost per
  - unit of time?
  - percentage point change?
  - unit produced?
  - rework/defect?
  - process step?
  - complaint or incident?
- Ask about the frequency with which data are collected and reports run.
- Ask if the gatekeeper can run special/customized reports for you.
- Ask if you can receive a copy of the data so that you can sort and manipulate them as needed.
- Discuss data trending with the gatekeeper. How much baseline data will you need to determine a trend line?
- What can the gatekeeper tell you about any cyclical/seasonal changes in the data that may need to be accounted for?
- Ask the gatekeeper if he/she will be willing to meet with you periodically to answer questions and review your work.
- Honor your data gatekeepers as if it were their birthday every day you communicate with them!
- Acknowledge the data gatekeeper's contribution to your project.

—Darell Provencher
Director, Professional Development, Global Talent Development
Nike, Inc.

Converting Employee Time to Monetary Value. Reducing the use of employee time is a typical objective for many programs. Although there are various benefits to saving time, the most obvious value involved in employee time-savings is reducing the labor costs of performing the work. The monetary savings are found by multiplying the hours saved by the labor cost per hour. For example, after attending a time management program, participants estimated that they saved an average of 74 minutes per day, worth $31.25 per day or $7,500 per year. These values for the time savings were based on the participants' average salary plus benefits.

Ensure that the time saved as a result of a program is being used productively. If not, the value of the time saved to the organization is nil.

Historical Costs

Sometimes, historical records contain the value of a measure or reveal the cost (or value) of a unit of improvement. This technique involves identifying the appropriate records and tabulating the cost components of the measure in question. For example, a large construction firm implemented a program to improve safety performance. The program improved several safety-related performance measures, ranging from OSHA fines to total workers' compensation costs. Using one year of data from the company's records, the staff calculated the average value of improvements in each safety measure.

Internal and External Experts

When historical costs are unavailable, another technique to convert a measure to money is using internal or external experts. Sometimes, a resident expert in an area can provide the monetary value for a measure. For example, labor relations experts may know the value of grievances by labor union members.

Databases

Google, Yahoo, Ask.com, Ebscohost and others are your friends when it comes to converting measures to money. There has never been such plethora of data with regard to data conversion, and the advantages the Internet, your local library, and local university offer are immense. For example, if you work in the hospitality industry and are interested in the cost of turnover of room service wait staff, go to Google, as we did for a client. There, we found a study conducted by Cornell University's School of Hospitality Management (Hinkin and Tracey, 2000) that provided the needed information.

Statistical Calculations

Another technique used to convert data to money is the use of statistics, particularly through gathering survey data and conducting analyses to determine correlations between measures. This classic approach can be relatively simple, if the data are readily available. Otherwise, use another method to be more efficient because the cost of converting a measure using this technique can outweigh the cost of the evaluation, and even the cost of the program.

Estimates

Although some people hate to think of using estimates, the fact is that most data used in any type of research is based on estimates. Nevertheless, using estimates of participants, managers, and supervisors to convert a measure to money is somewhat more subjective than the previously described techniques. When using estimates, the key is to obtain input from the most credible source—the person or persons who know best about the measure under review. These sources of data are asked to provide three pieces of information:

- their estimated value for the measure
- the basis for their estimated value
- their confidence in their estimated value.

Figure 14-1 describes this process in an example.

Table 14-1 provides examples of how each of the above techniques has been applied.

Five Steps to Convert an Improvement in a Measure to Money

Once the value of a measure is known, the process to convert the improvement in the measure to monetary benefits requires a few simple steps:

1. Identify the unit of measure.
   This is a Level 4 impact measure targeted for improvement by the program. The unit of measure is typically identified during the evaluation planning process and established as an objective.
2. Determine the value of the measure (V).
   The value of the measure is the unit value. This value is determined using one of the techniques described previously. It could represent profit, cost savings, or cost avoidance.
3. Determine the change in performance in the measure due to the program (ΔP).
   This is the improvement in the measure, or the Level 4 business impact results. Remember that this is the improvement caused by the program, accounting for other influencing factors, rather than the total improvement (see Chapter 13, Isolating the Effects of the Program).
4. Annualize the change in performance of the measure ($A\Delta P$).
   When reporting the monetary benefits of a program, it is customary to report them in terms of annual monetary benefits. So, if your measure is reported monthly, to annualize it you simply multiply improvement by 12. If reported weekly, the measure is multiplied by the number of weeks worked in one year. Forty-eight is the typical number used.
5. Calculate the annual monetary benefit ($A\Delta P \times V$).
   To develop the total monetary benefits of a program, simply multiply the annual change in performance (step 4) by the value of one unit of the measure (step 2). The product

Figure 14-1. Example of Using Estimates

Converting Unexpected Absence to Monetary Value Using Supervisor Estimates

Unexpected absences caused problems in a local plant. The performance team instituted a new program to reduce these absences. Due to its cost, an ROI study was conducted to show the value of the program.

To calculate the ROI, the monetary value of improvement in unexpected absences had to be developed. Because there were no standard values, historical costs, or databases with an acceptable value, the supervisors who had to deal with these absences would be the best source to provide an estimate.

In a focus group of five supervisors in the plant, the evaluator asked each supervisor three questions. These questions were:

- What happens when an unexpected absence occurs in your work unit?
- Given what happens, how much do you think one absence per one day costs you?
- How confident are you that your estimate is correct?

As shown below, each estimate was adjusted for confidence. The adjusted per absence costs were totaled then averaged. The average cost of a single absence was calculated as $1,061.

Supervisor	Estimated Per Day Cost	% Confidence	Adjusted Per Absence
1	$1,000	70%	$700
2	$1,500	65%	$975
3	$2,300	50%	$1,150
4	$2,000	60%	$1,200
5	$1,600	80%	$1,280
			$5,305
Average adjusted per day cost of 1 absence			**$1,061**

represents the annual profit, cost savings, or cost avoidance contributed by the program. When calculating the ROI , this value is placed in the numerator of the ROI equation (see Chapter 16, Calculating the Return-on-Investment).

Figure 14-2 explains the application of these five steps in a case study.

The five steps described above will help you identify the monetary benefits of a program. However, there will be some measures in which we decide not to convert to money—these measures are the intangible benefits.

Table 14-1. Examples of Application of Data Conversion Techniques

Data Conversion Techniques	Examples
Standard Values • Output to Contribution • Cost of Quality • Employee Time	• Sales—**profit margin** • Donations—**overhead margin** • Unproductive man hours—**hourly wage*** • Repackaging—**standard value based on time savings (hourly wage)** • OSHA fines—**fines associated with incident** • Unit per person hour—**profit of one additional product produced per person per hour at same cost**
Historical Costs	• Sexual harassment grievances—**litigation costs** • Food spoilage—**cost to replenish food inventory** • Turnover of marine engineers—**average replacement costs plus separation costs**
Internal / External Experts	• Electric utility rate—**internal economist** • Life**—**internal risk manager**
External Databases	• Turnover mid-level manager—**ERIC** • Turnover restaurant wait staff—**Google**
Statistical Calculations	• Employee satisfaction—**linked to customer satisfaction linked to profit** • Customer complaints regarding baggage mishandling—**percent complaints linked to percent who will not repurchase seat on airline linked to lost revenue**
Estimations • Participant • Supervisors/Managers • Staff	• Unexpected absence—**supervisor estimate (basis provided) x confidence adjustment** • Unwanted network intrusions—**participant estimate (basis provided) x confidence adjustment**

*Hourly wage includes hourly salary plus benefits factor.
**Economists have developed two methods to value a human life: estimate the individual's lost earnings for his or her remaining life, or consider people's acceptance of higher-risk jobs and their related higher salaries as payment for a higher probability of death.

Intangible Benefits

Program results usually include both tangible and intangible measures. Intangible measures are those business measures not converted to monetary value. A four-part test helps in making this decision. Table 14-2 includes four questions to be answered when considering whether or not to convert a measure to money.

Figure 14-2. Case Application

Case Application: Grievance Reduction

A large electric utility implemented a new policy to reduce grievances. The value of the grievance, based on input from labor-relations experts within the organization was $6,500 per grievance. Six months after the policy was implemented, the human resources function found that grievances had gone down, on average, to 10 per month. Because they knew this reduction was not entirely due to the program, they took steps to isolate the effects of the policy on the grievance reduction. The results showed that a reduction of seven grievances per month was actually due to the policy implementation.

The annual monetary benefit of the policy implementation was calculated by multiplying the value of one grievance by the number of grievances reduced in one year. Below is the calculation:

- The unit of measure is one grievance.
- Value of a grievance is $6,500 as defined by the internal expert.
- Change in performance due to the policy is seven grievances per month.
- Annual improvement in grievances is 7 x 12 = 84 grievances per month.
- Annual monetary benefit is $6,500 x 84 = $546,000.

Source: Phillips and Phillips (2005).

Table 14-2. Questions to Answer When Considering Converting an Intangible Measure

1. **Is there a standard value?**
   If yes, the measure is converted to money. If no, then answer the next question.

2. **Is there a technique to convert the measure?**
   Earlier in this chapter, a variety of techniques to convert measures to money were described. If one of these techniques will not work, then report the improvement in the measure as an intangible benefit. If one or more of the techniques will work, then answer the next question.

3. **Can the chosen technique(s) be implemented using minimum resources?**
   You do not want to spend more on data conversion than the evaluation itself. Thus, if it will cost too much money or consume too many resources to convert the measure to money using the chosen technique, report the measure as intangible. If you can convert the measure to money using minimal resources, then answer the final question.

4. **Can you convince your executive in two minutes or less that the value reported is credible?**
   Although high monetary benefits for a program are desirable, be sure to maintain the credibility of the calculation. Try to report acceptable and credible monetary benefits along with important intangible benefits rather than convert all measures to money just to show a large monetary contribution. Heeding this advice will enhance the credibility of your results and approach, as well as support the integrity of an ROI if calculated.

Guidelines for Converting Measures to Monetary Value

Converting measures to money is an important step in the measurement and evaluation process when you want to

- know financial benefits of programs
- normalize benefits so comparisons can be made
- give quantitative meaning to a benefit
- calculate the ROI in training investment.

By following the guidelines below, you should be confident as you move forward with converting measures to money:

- Plan ahead. If you are planning to report monetary value for improvement in your program, obtain agreement early as to your approach for obtaining the value of a measure.
- If you have standard values for measures, use them.
- Use the most credible source for data.
- If no improvement data are given, assume little or no results. This is the conservative approach that enhances the credibility of your results.
- When using estimates, adjust for error in the estimate by asking sources to provide you their level of confidence in their estimated values.
- Extreme measures and unsupported claims should be thrown out. If someone provides an estimated monetary value that is well beyond the norm, rather than skew your data, throw it out. If they do not provide a basis for their estimate, don't guess at how they developed it—throw it out.
- For short-term programs, assume only first-year benefits.
- When in doubt, leave it out. The key is to follow conservative standards. If you are unsure of the credibility of a value or if it costs you too much to convert a measure to money, report the improvement as an intangible benefit.

Knowledge Check: Converting Program Benefits to Money

Now that you have read this chapter, try your hand at converting the benefits of a program to monetary value. Check your answers in the appendix.

Wines-by-the-Glass is a growing franchise of wine boutiques located throughout the United States. Although they sell bottles and relevant accessories, their niche is in selling fine wines by the glass. This wine bar concept has increased in popularity in large cities, where the median age is around 40 years old. With 250 stores and growing, the chain has exceeded expectations.

The slowing economy has had a slight impact on these stores, although not to the extent of other retail stores. Nevertheless, the general manager of the chain invited shop owners with the weakest sales to attend a two-day training on marketing techniques to help boost sales. Forty shop owners attended this training in Atlanta. Three business objectives were established:

- Increase sales to existing customers by 5 percent within six months of the training
- Increase the number of new wine club memberships by an average of five per month per store within six months of training
- Increase sales for accessories by 10 percent within six months of the training

Six months after the training, an evaluation was conducted to see how the training contributed to achieving the objectives. With regard to the wine club memberships, the evaluation team found that new wine club memberships increased on average seven per month for each of the 30 stores reporting data (that is, seven memberships per month per store). By asking the shop owners a series of questions, the evaluators found that only 40 percent of the sales was due to the training; the remaining 60 percent of sales were due to factors such as advertising, promotion, new stores opening in the general area, and an overall boost in economic conditions. The sale of a membership is $45 per month. The profit margin for the membership is 60 percent.

Following the five steps described in this chapter, what is the annual monetary benefit to Wines-by-the-Glass for increasing new wine club memberships through training?

1. Identify the unit of measure.
2. Determine the value of the measure (V).
3. Determine the change in performance in the measure due to the program (DΔP).
4. Determine the annual change in performance (AΔP).
5. Calculate the annual monetary benefit (AΔP x V).

About the Author

Patricia Pulliam Phillips, PhD, is president and CEO of the ROI Institute, the leading source of ROI competency building, implementation support, networking, and research. She can be reached at patti@roiinstitute.net.

References

Cokins, G. (1996). *Activity-Based Cost Management: Making It Work—A Manager's Guide to Implementing and Sustaining an Effective ABC System.* New York: McGraw-Hill.

Hinkin, T. R. and J. B. Tracey. (June 1, 2000). "The Cost of Turnover." *Cornell Hotel & Restaurant Administration Quarterly,* 14–21.

Phillips, P. P. and J. J. Phillips. (2005). *Return on Investment Basics.* Alexandria, VA: ASTD, p. 124.

Phillips, P. P. and H. Burkett. (2008). *Data Conversion: Calculating the Monetary Benefits.* San Francisco: Pfeiffer.

Additional Reading

Kee, J. E. (2004). Cost-Effectiveness and Cost-Benefit Analysis. In Wholey, J. S., H. P. Hatry, and K. E. Newcomer eds., *Handbook of Practical Program Evaluation,* 2nd ed. San Francisco: Jossey-Bass.

Kida, T. (2006). *Don't Believe Everything You Think: The 6 Basic Mistakes We Make in Thinking.* Amherst, NY: Prometheus Books.

Koomey, J. G. (2008). *Turning Numbers into Knowledge.* Oakland, CA: Analytics Press.

Rucci, A. J., S. P. Kim, and R. T. Quinn. (January–February 1998). "The Employee-Customer-Profit Chain at Sears." *Harvard Business Review.*

Chapter 15

Identifying Program Costs

Judith F. Cardenas

In This Chapter

This chapter explores the most relevant techniques for identifying program costs. Upon completion of this chapter, you will be able to

▪ articulate the importance of developing and monitoring costs

▪ identify types of values associated with programs and initiatives

▪ identify the challenges of capturing costs

▪ identify sources of program costs.

The Importance of Identifying Program Costs

Managers are being called to provide accurate and timely information related to the cost of programs and projects. No longer is the total program cost sufficient because increasingly more managers are asking for how and why money is spent. A cost profile, which includes both direct and indirect costs, becomes a critical decision-making tool. Cost information is used to monitor and manage resources, develop standards, and study the pros and cons of alternative delivery processes.

Tabulating program costs is an essential step in measuring and evaluating training, particularly if one wants to calculate the return-on-investment (ROI) in training. With the challenges and pressures to use resources wisely, organizations must carefully monitor, report, and forecast cost in a timely and transparent manner. Table 15-1 presents a variety of reasons to develop costs.

Pressure to Disclose All Costs

In the past, training costs were associated with training budgets. Today, more than ever, training is touted as an investment rather than viewed as a cost. Organizations with the investment view of training expenditures look beyond the budget when identifying program costs. Training as an investment considers all costs related to assessing, designing, developing, implementing, and evaluating a training program. For example, the cost associated with the time participants are involved in a program includes the salary plus the benefits earned during the timeframe of the given program. To accurately and appropriately reflect the entire cost of a particular program, indirect as well as direct costs must be accounted for within the total calculation of program cost.

Fully Loaded Costs

Evaluators recommend training costs be fully loaded. This is especially important when calculating the ROI in training, because it ensures the most conservative and credible ROI will be developed. Fully loaded costs include those direct and indirect costs. If the cost is questionable as to whether or not it should be included, include it, even if the cost guidelines for the organization do not require it.

The Danger of Costs Without Benefits

Take care when communicating costs without benefits. Senior executives recognize training costs are quite high. Blatantly communicating that information does not necessarily help the training cause. When most executives receive training costs, a logical question comes to mind: What benefit was received from the program? This is a typical management reaction, particularly when costs are perceived to be high.

Table 15-1. Reasons to Develop Costs

- Determine overall training expenditures
- Determine relative cost of each program
- Predict future program costs
- Calculate ROI of a program
- Evaluate alternatives to a proposed program
- Plan and budget for next year's operation
- Develop a cost pricing system
- Integrate data into other systems

Cost-Monitoring Issues

The most important task is to define which specific costs are included in a training costs profile. Costs come from a variety of sources. When developing costs, some are prorated, whereas others are expensed.

Sources of Program Costs

Program costs can be captured and categorized into three major sources of program cost:

- Staff expenses. These costs often represent the greatest portion of training costs and often are transferred directly to the client or program sponsor.
- Participant expenses. These costs include direct costs and indirect costs.
- External resources. These costs include payments to external training venues such as hotels and conference centers, equipment, suppliers, and providers of services prescribed in the program.

Unfortunately, the costs in these categories are often understated. Financial and accounting systems should be able to track and report the costs from these sources.

Prorated versus Direct Costs

Once a program has been developed and implemented, the costs related to the program are captured and expensed to the specific program. However, three categories are often prorated over several sessions of the same program. These categories include needs assessment, design and development, and acquisition. The cost for these categories should be prorated over the life of a program. A program's life should be short if the manager evaluating the program uses a conservative approach. The timeframe of prorating such costs differs among organizations. Some organizations will prorate program costs over one year of operation; others may prorate costs over two or three years (Phillips and Zúñiga, 2008). Figure 15-1 presents an example of how costs may be prorated.

Major Cost Categories

The most important task in a tabulation of program costs is to define which costs should be included. Table 15-2 shows the recommended cost categories for a fully loaded, conservative approach to estimating costs (Phillips, 1983; Phillips and Zúñiga, 2008). Each category is briefly described in this section.

Needs assessment and analysis. It is important to capture the costs associated with conducting a needs assessment. In some programs, this cost is zero because the program is conducted without a needs assessment, but for other organizations, the cost is significant.

Figure 15-1. Example of Prorated Costs

In a large pharmaceutical company, a program was developed at a cost of $150,000. It was anticipated that the program would have a three-year life before it would need to be updated. About 900 participants would be involved in the program over the three-year period. The training department wanted to prorate the cost over the life of the program. To be conservative, the total cost should be written off at the end of three years. Therefore, the $150,000 development cost would be spread over the 900 participants as a prorated development cost of $167 per participant.

- $150,000 development cost
- Three-year program life
- 900 participants expected to attend over the program life
- Per person cost to develop the program = $150,000 / 900 = $167 per person.

An evaluation that included an ROI calculation was conducted for 50 participants. The development cost used in the ROI calculation was $167 x 50 = $8,350.

Table 15-2. Training Program Cost Categories

Cost Item	Prorated	Expensed
Needs Assessment	✔	✔
Design and Development	✔	✔
Acquisition	✔	✔
Delivery		
• Salaries/Benefits—Facilitators		✔
• Salaries/Benefits—Coordination		✔
• Program Materials and Fees		✔
• Travel/Lodging/Meals		✔
• Facilities		✔
• Participants Salaries/Benefits		✔
• Contact Time		✔
• Travel Time		✔
• Preparation Time		✔
Evaluation	✔	
Overhead/Training and Development	✔	

All costs associated with the needs assessment include the time of staff members who conduct the assessment, direct fees, expenses of external consultants who conduct the assessment, and internal services and supplies.

Design and development. One of the most significant cost categories is the cost associated with designing and developing a program. These costs may include internal staff time for design and development, cost of supplies, videos, software, and other materials directly related to the program. These costs may also include external fees for consultation and support.

Acquisition. Some organizations lack the staff or expertise to internally develop programs. Such organizations purchase programs to use directly or in a modified format. The acquisition cost associated with such programs includes the purchase price for facilitator materials, train-the-trainer sessions, licensing agreements, webinars, assessment tools, and other costs for rights to deliver the program.

Technological support. Some programs require technological support. For example, online assessments may be required of the participants prior to program participation. Additionally, many programs are offered in a hybrid format, in which a portion of the training is offered using a variety of technology platforms.

Delivery and implementation. The delivery and implementation of a training program often represents the largest segment of program cost. Five major subcategories must be considered when capturing all program cost.

- **Facilitators' and coordinators' salaries and benefits.** Proportionally allocated salaries of facilitators or program coordinators should be included in the program's cost based on the amount of time spent on the particular program. These costs include internal facilitators and coordinators, as well as external facilitators and consultants. When calculating labors costs for internal staff, the benefits factor should be used to figure the cost of employee benefits so that it can be included. The benefits factor is usually in the range of 30 to 50 percent in the United States.
- **Participants' salaries and benefits.** The salaries and benefits of participants are an expense that should be included in the program cost. This cost represents the cost of taking employees off the job to attend a training program. The amount allocated should be directly calculated based on the amount of time spent on the given program.

- **Travel, lodging, and meals.** Direct travel costs for participants, facilitators, and coordinators should be included in the program cost. All expenses related to lodging and meals for participants, facilitators, and coordinators during travel, as well as during the entire time of the program offering should be included. If refreshments are offered throughout a particular training session, the cost should also be captured and recorded as well.
- **Facilities.** The cost of the facilities used during a training session should also be captured, regardless if the session was offered at an external facility or inside the organization itself. For meetings or sessions held at external facilities, this cost is the direct charge from the conference center or hotel. If the program is conducted in-house, the use of the conference room represents a cost for the organization, and that cost should be estimated and included, even if it is not the practice within the organization to include in-house facilities costs in other reports. The cost of internal facilities can easily be obtained by the facilities manager or estimated by obtaining the rental rate of a room of the same size at a local hotel.
- **Program materials and fees.** Specific program materials such as notebooks, textbooks, how-to manuals, instruction guides, software, case studies, exercises, CDs, DVDs, jump drives, and participant workbooks should be included in the delivery costs of a program. In addition to these costs, license fees, user fees, and royalty payments along with pens, paper, certificates, calculators, and personal copies of software are also included in this category.

Evaluation. Program evaluations should be included in calculating the program cost. Evaluation costs include the cost associated with developing the evaluation strategy, designing instruments, collecting data, data analysis, and report preparation and distribution. Cost categories include time, materials, hardware or software used to collect or analyze data, and purchased instruments or surveys.

Overhead. A final cost category is overhead. The overhead costs are the additional costs within the training department that are not directly related to a particular program. Typical overhead items include the cost of administrative support, departmental office expenses, salaries of managers, and other fixed costs. Figure 15-2 presents an example of how to pro-rate the cost of overhead across the number of training days. Remember that the cost of overhead may also be divided by the number of people trained during a year, the number of programs offered during a year, or the number of training hours per year.

The key to allocating overhead is to use a simple approach that logically and systematically allocates the costs in the department that are not allocated to specific programs. Also, it

Figure 15-2. Overhead Allocation

An organization with 50 training and development programs tabulated all the expenditures in the budget not allocated directly to a particular program ($548,061). This part of the budget represented total overhead. Next, this number was divided by the total number of participant days (for example, if a five-day program is offered 10 times a year, 50 days would be put in the total days category). Participant days for the year totaled approximately 7,400. The total unallocated overhead of $548,061 was divided by 7,400 days to arrive at $74. Therefore, $74 is charged for overhead for each day of training.

- Unallocated budget = $548,061
- Training days = 7,400
- Overhead cost per training day = $74

The organization calculated an ROI study on a three-day leadership program. The overhead allocation to that particular study was $222 ($74 x 3 = $222).

is important not to spend too much time on this issue. Estimates are appropriate in most situations. Some organizations estimate an amount of overhead for a program, using some logical rationale, spending no more than 10 or 15 minutes on the issue.

Cost Estimation

Cost estimations are developed by many organizations in an effort to track training costs. Table 15-3 displays an example of a cost estimation worksheet. The worksheet summarizes analysis, development, delivery, operations and maintenance, and evaluation costs. The worksheet contains a few formulas that make it easier to estimate the costs.

In addition to cost estimating worksheets, organizations often provide the current rates for services, supplies, and salaries. These data become outdated quickly and are usually updated periodically. The most appropriate way to predict costs is by tracking the actual costs incurred in all phases—from analysis to evaluation—of all programs. This way, it is possible to see how much is spent on programs and how much is being spent in the different categories. Until adequate cost data are available, however, detailed analysis on the worksheets for cost estimation will be necessary.

Summary

Capture and reporting costs is a critical part of measuring and evaluating training. This is particularly true when an ROI calculation is planned. Historically, capturing costs provided a synopsis of expenses related to a particular program or event. Today, managers use cost

Table 15-3. Cost Estimating Worksheet

Analysis Costs	
Salaries and employee benefits—function staff (no. of people × average salary × employee benefits factor × no. of hours on project)	_____
Meals, travel, and incidental expenses	_____
Office supplies and expenses	_____
Printing and reproduction	_____
Outside services	_____
Equipment expenses	_____
Registration fees	_____
Other miscellaneous expenses	_____
Total Analysis Cost	_____
Development Costs	
Salaries and employee benefits (no. of people × avg. salary × employee benefits factor × no. of hours on project)	_____
Meals, travel, and incidental expenses	_____
Office supplies and expenses	_____
Program materials and supplies	_____
Printing and reproduction	_____
Outside services	_____
Equipment expenses	_____
Other miscellaneous expenses	_____
Total Development Costs	_____
Delivery Costs	
Participant costs, salaries, and employee benefits (number of participants × average salary × employee benefits factor × hours or days of meeting or training time)	_____
Meals, travel, and accommodations (number of participants × average daily expenses × days of training)	_____
Program materials and supplies	_____
Participant replacement costs (if applicable)	_____
Lost production (explain basis)	_____
Facilitator costs	
Salaries and benefits	_____

Delivery Costs (continued)

Facilitator costs (continued)

    Meals, travel, and incidental expenses   _____

    Outside services   _____

Facility costs

    Facilities rental   _____

    Facilities expense allocation   _____

Equipment expenses   _____

Other miscellaneous expenses   _____

    Total Delivery Costs   _____

Operations/Maintenance

Salaries and employee benefits—function staff (no. of people $\times$ avg. salary $\times$ employee benefits factor $\times$ no. of hours on project)   _____

Meals, travel, and incidental expenses   _____

Participant costs   _____

Office supplies and expenses   _____

Printing and reproduction   _____

Outside services   _____

Equipment expenses   _____

Other miscellaneous expenses   _____

    Total Operations/Maintenance Costs   _____

Evaluation Costs

Salaries and employee benefits—function staff (no. of people $\times$ avg. salary $\times$ employee benefits factor $\times$ no. of hours on project)   _____

Meals, travel, and incidental expenses   _____

Participant costs   _____

Office supplies and expenses   _____

Printing and reproduction   _____

Outside services   _____

Equipment expenses   _____

Other miscellaneous expenses   _____

    Total Evaluation Costs   _____

General Overhead Allocation   _____

TOTAL PROGRAM COSTS   _____

Source: Phillips and Phillips (2005).

data to compare programs, internally and externally; track resources; and monitor efficiencies. Tracking costs helps program staff manage resources carefully, consistently, and efficiently. A strong understanding of the different cost categories and different methods of extrapolating cost data provides a stronger evaluation framework.

Knowledge Check: Prorating Development Costs

Now that you have read this chapter, try your hand at prorating development costs. Check your answers in the appendix.

A large financial institution plans to evaluate a major leadership development program. They are interested in prorating the development program costs over the life of the program. The leadership program will last approximately 18 months. The intent is to run 200 supervisors and team leaders through the program. The development costs were $250,000. This is a high profile project and the senior leaders are interested in seeing an ROI for at least one group of 25 participants. The data are summarized as follows:

- Development costs = $250,000
- Program life = 18 months
- Number of participants = 200
- Number of participants included in ROI study = 25

What is the per person cost of developing the leadership development program?

How much in development cost will be included in the ROI study?

About the Author

Judith F. Cardenas, PhD, CPLP, CRP is the founder and CEO for the Center for Performance and Accountability. She has worked in many diverse work settings and has held positions of president and vice president in higher educational institutions. Cardenas received her doctorate in education administration from Baylor University in 1995, as well as a doctorate in training and performance improvement from Capella University in 2007. She also possesses significant expertise in measuring results and accountability. She is certified as an ROI Professional (CRP) and has completed a variety of postdoctoral training, including leadership development, Harvard University John F. Kennedy School of Government; human performance improvement, ASTD; and advanced ROI methodology, Villanova University. In addition, she holds the designation of RCC (Registered Corporate Coach). She can be reached at judcard@att.net.

References

Phillips, J. J. (1983). *Handbook of Evaluation and Measurement Methods,* 3rd ed. Boston: Butterworth-Heinemann.

Phillips, J. J. and L. Zúñiga. (2008). "Costs and ROI: Evaluating at the Ultimate Level." In Phillips, P. P. and J. J. Phillips, *Measurement and Evaluation Series.* San Francisco: Pfeiffer.

Phillips, P. P. and J. J. Phillips. (2005). *Return on Investment Basics.* Alexandria, VA: ASTD, p. 124.

ROI Institute. 2005. *ROI Certification Handbook.* Birmingham, AL.: ROI Institute.

✍ **Chapter 16**

Calculating the Return-on-Investment

Patricia Pulliam Phillips

··· **In This Chapter** ···

This chapter describes the importance of and the steps to calculate the return-on-investment (ROI) for training programs. Upon completion of this chapter, you will be able to

▪ calculate the ROI given the monetary benefits and costs of a program

▪ report ROI in the context of other measures of performance

▪ identify programs suitable for evaluation to ROI.

The Importance of ROI

"Show me the money." There's nothing new about this statement. Organizations of all types want to show the financial return for investments of many of their programs (Phillips and Zúñiga, 2008):

▪ The U.S. Air Force developed the ROI for an information assurance program to prevent intrusion into its computer databases.

▪ Apple computer calculated the ROI for its process improvement teams.

▪ Sprint/NEXTEL computed the ROI on its diversity program.

- The Australian Capital Territory Community Care agency forecast the ROI for implementing a client relationship management system.
- Accenture calculated the ROI on a new sales platform for its consultants.
- A major hotel chain calculated the financial value and ROI of its coaching program.
- The cities of New York, San Francisco, and Phoenix showed the monetary value of investing in programs to reduce the number of homeless citizens on the streets.
- Cisco Systems measured the ROI for its key meetings and events.
- A major U.S. Department of Defense agency calculated the ROI for a master's degree program offered by a major university.

Program value is determined by stakeholders' perspectives, which may include organizational, spiritual, personal, and social values. Although some people are concerned that too much focus is placed on economic value, economics—that is, money—is what allows organizations and individuals to contribute to the greater good. Monetary resources are limited; they can be put to best use, or they can be underused or overused. Organizations and individuals have choices about where they invest their resources. To ensure that monetary resources are put to best use, resources must be allocated to the programs, projects, and initiatives that yield the greatest return. For example, if a process improvement initiative is designed to improve efficiencies and it subsequently does improve efficiencies, one might assume that the initiative was successful. But if the initiative cost more than the efficiency gains are worth, has value been added to the organization? Could a less expensive process have yielded similar or even better results, possibly reaping a positive ROI? Questions like these are routinely asked. No longer does activity suffice as a measure of success. A new generation of decision makers is defining value in a new way, by measuring programs' impact on business performance, including showing the return-on-investment.

Despite its extensive use, there is still some confusion around the ROI definition.

ROI Defined

ROI is a financial metric. It compares the monetary benefits of a program to the cost. ROI is considered the ultimate measure of program success for various reasons, one of which is that it defines program benefits and program costs in the same terms—money—so that the two can be equally compared. In this one metric, economic contribution is apparent. There are several metrics used to compare monetary benefits to costs.

Benefit-Cost Ratio (BCR)

Among the economic metrics reported, the benefit-cost ratio (BCR) is one of the oldest. An output of cost-benefit analysis, the BCR compares the monetary benefits of an investment to the investment, resulting in a ratio. Grounded in welfare economics and public finance, cost-benefit analysis historically served as a feasibility tool to justify government involvement in the economy and to examine the extent of government's influence on the private sector and its effect on the welfare of society at large (Nas, 1996).

The fundamental equation to calculate the BCR is

$$\textbf{BCR} = \frac{\text{Benefits}}{\text{Costs}}$$

To calculate the benefit-cost ratio

- identify the annual benefits or gains due to implementing a program
- convert benefits to monetary value using either profit, cost savings, or cost avoidance associated with the investment (see data conversion techniques described in chapter 14)
- determine the cost (or investment) of the program (see cost categories described in chapter 15)
- identify the intangible benefits of program implementation
- compare the monetary benefits to the program costs
- compare the result to some alternative program or a standard for acceptance.

Reported as a ratio, the BCR describes how annual monetary benefits returned compare to the cost. For example, if a program returns $350,000 in monetary benefits from profit, cost savings, and/or cost avoidance and cost of the program to the organization is $250,000, the BCR is

$$\textbf{BCR} = \frac{\$350,000}{\$250,000} = 1.4{:}1$$

This BCR says that for every $1 invested in the program, $1.40 is returned. The classic decision-making criteria for the BCR is that anything over a 1:1 BCR is acceptable.

Return-on-Investment

Return-on-investment is the ultimate measure of profitability returned on investments and the classic tool used to report this profitability. Applied for centuries by financiers, the metric did not become widespread in industry for measuring operating performance until the 1960s (Horngren, 1982). Today, this simple metric is standard in business and now an important metric used in nonbusiness settings when reporting economic contribution of all types of investments, including those made in training.

Whereas BCR was historically used as a feasibility tool, ROI classically is based on historical data. Today, the BCR is commonly used as a measure of actual results, whereas the ROI is often forecasted prior to investing in a program or project (see Chapter 17). ROI compares annual earnings (or net program benefits) to investment (or program costs). Unlike its cousin BCR, ROI is reported as a percentage and represents the annual net benefits returned over and beyond the initial investment. The steps to develop the data necessary to calculate the ROI are similar to those used to calculate the BCR, however, the difference is in the equation. The numerator for the ROI equation is developed using the net benefits (benefits-costs). To calculate the ROI, the net benefits are divided by the costs; the quotient is then multiplied by 100 to calculate the percentage return-on-investment:

$$\text{ROI} = \frac{\text{Net Benefits}}{\text{Costs}} \times 100$$

Using the earlier example, the ROI for a program achieving $350,000 monetary benefits and requiring an investment of $250,000, the ROI is

$$\text{ROI} = \frac{\$350{,}000 - \$250{,}000}{\$250{,}000} \times 100 = 40\%$$

The resulting ROI explains that for every $1 invested in the program, that dollar is returned plus there is a gain of $.40. The 40 cents represents the *return* on the investment. Although this seems like a reasonable return, acceptance of a 40-percent ROI depends other factors, such as the ROI of other investments or the standard to which this ROI is compared.

Payback Period (PP)

Periodically, it may be important to estimate the time at which an organization will recoup the investment in a program. This payback period is calculated by comparing the initial investment with the annual cash flows or monetary benefits due to the program. The equation is simply a reverse of the BCR.

$$\text{PP} = \frac{\text{Costs}}{\text{Benefits}}$$

Payback period is reported in terms of number of months or years. Using the earlier example, the payback period for a program reaping $350,000 in monetary benefits and costing the organization $250,000, the payback period is

$$\text{PP} = \frac{\$250{,}000}{\$350{,}000} = .71$$

By multiplying .71 times 12 months, the payback period for this program is 8.52 months. This tells decision makers they can expect to recover their investment in less than one year. This payback period is compared to that of other potential investments or to a predetermined standard.

ROI, BCR, and PP are appropriate when comparing the monetary benefits of investing in developmental opportunities for people. Although assets to an organization, people are

---

❧ **Practitioner Tip** ❧

Create a vision for what will be different as a result of your ROI story. Your stakeholders should be inspired by the value this new information brings and compelled by the business need to support your efforts.

Kris Potrafka
Director, Marketing Professional Effectiveness
Cisco Systems

---

not treated on the accounting books as other assets like equipment, land, and buildings. Also, most training programs are short term in nature, meaning, they take only a few months, weeks, or days to fully implement. Bearing this in mind, remember that a payoff within the first year of such an investment is desirable, if not required (Phillips and Phillips, 2008, 2009).

Net Present Value (NPV)

Net present value (NPV) is a commonly used technique in making capital budgeting decisions. While not useful in evaluating typical people development programs, it is useful when analyzing the value of long-term investments such as equipment, plants, products, or research and development. Questions about net present value and discounted cash flow methods often arise when discussing ROI in training and development, so it is appropriate to briefly address it here. NPV is one of several discounted cash flow (DCF) methods that account for the time value of money and is used for long-range decisions.

Using NPV, expected cash inflows (program benefits) and outflows (program costs) are discounted to the present value given a point in time, using a preselected discount rate. The assumed benefits over time (discounted at the determined hurdle rate) are added together, and the initial investment is subtracted. The future benefits and costs are reduced to a single present dollar value. If the present value of benefits is greater than the investment, the program is assumed to be a good investment (Friedlob and Plewa, 1996; Nas, 1996).

Take a simple example of how this technique may be applied: Assume a learning management system (LMS) is to be purchased. The cost of a three-year cumulative license for 5,000 learners is $150,000. The $150,000 will be invested in total at the outset (year 0) with no benefits occurring until the following year (year 1). Maintenance and operations costs will be $15,000 per year for the two years. The assumed benefit is a reduction in labor savings of $100,000 for each of the next two years. Table 16-1 presents these data.

Table 16-1. LMS Benefits and Costs

	Year		
	0	1	2
Benefits	—	$100,000	$100,000
Costs	$150,000	$15,000	$15,000

The initial outlay (I_0) is $150,000. A stream of net benefits for the next two years is $85,000 ($100,000 − $15,000 = $85,000). The future stream of net benefits (NB_n) is discounted to calculate the present value, which will be deducted from the investment to determine the NPV. Assume a discount rate of 8 percent. The equation for calculating the NPV is

$$\textbf{NPV} = -I_0 + \sum_{n=1}^{N} \frac{NB_n}{(1 + r)^n}$$

For our example, the NPV would be

$$\textbf{NPV} = -150,000 + \sum_{n=1}^{N=2} \frac{\$85,000}{(1 + .08)^n} = \$1,577.50$$

Breaking down the math, first calculate the present value of future net benefits:

$$
\begin{aligned}
\text{PV} &= \$85,000/(1 + .08)^1 + \$85,000/(1 + .08)^2 \\
&= \$78,703.70 + \$72,873.80 \\
&= \$151,577.50
\end{aligned}
$$

The present value of future net benefits exceeds the $150,000 initial investment resulting in an NPV of $1,577.50. The decision whether or not to invest in the LMS is made based either on the fact that the NPV is positive, on how the NPV compares to that of an alternative LMS, or on how it compares to some established objective or standard.

NPV, although useful in some circumstances, is inappropriate for calculating the return-on-investments in people development programs; when calculating the ROI in people development programs, the standards are the ROI percentage or the BCR.

ROI Targets

As with any measure, an ROI is only as good as the objective to which it is compared. Setting an ROI objective gives the metric relevance. Otherwise, the measure is meaningless, other than to say how the monetary benefits compare to the costs. Below are considerations in setting an ROI target:

- Set the ROI target at the same level as that of other investments. For example, if your organization is getting 15- to 18-percent return on other investments, it may be feasible to set the ROI objective for your training program at the same level.
- Set the ROI target slightly above that of other investments. If the right people are in the right program for the right reason, training can have a tremendous effect on the organization. Based on the number of studies in which members of the ROI Institute have been involved, 25 percent is a good target for training investments.
- Set the ROI target at break even. This translates into an ROI of 0 percent or a BCR of 1:1. Break even is often the target set by government and nonprofit organizations.
- Let the client help establish the ROI target. As you are working with your client, determine the economic opportunity to make money, save money, and/or avoid cost. Then consider the type of solution available to help achieve the business objectives. By looking at the financial opportunity, the cost of the program, and the likelihood the program will have an effect, you and your client can set a reasonable ROI target.

ROI in the Context of Other Measures of Performance

Reporting an ROI against a target is important, but reporting the ROI in the context of other measures of performance is equally important. ROI presents the economic contribution of a program. Reported alone, stakeholders cannot discern how the program achieved the reported ROI, improvements to the program cannot be made, and intangible benefits cannot be highlighted. For example, if an ROI resulted in a –85 percent, without additional information, you would not be able to explain how this occurred. If an ROI calculation resulted in a 200-percent return, without additional data, you would not be able to explain how a training program made such a large economic contribution. A chain of impact occurs as people are involved in programs and projects. Figure 16-1 presents this chain of impact in the context of the five levels of evaluation (Phillips, 1983).

The ROI calculation represents one of six types of data represented in this chain. ROI is the ultimate, but not the only, measure of program success. Other important outcomes occur as programs are implemented. Reporting ROI in the context of other measures of performance gives the measure additional meaning and provides all stakeholders information they can use to make decisions about the program.

Figure 16-1. Chain of Impact

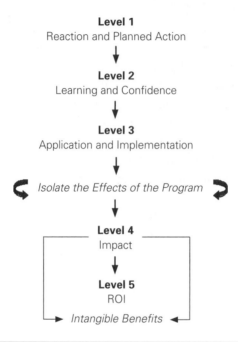

Programs Suitable for ROI Evaluation

ROI is not calculated for all programs. This does not mean it can't be calculated, but rather that it probably should not be calculated for all programs. ROI is appropriate for programs that

- have a long life cycle; at some point in the life of the program, this level of accountability should be applied
- are important to the organization in meeting its operational goals; these programs are designed to add value, and ROI may be helpful in showing the value
- are closely linked to the organization's strategic initiatives; anything this important needs a high level of accountability
- are expensive to implement; an expensive program that uses large amounts of resources should be subject to this level of accountability
- are highly visible and sometimes controversial; these programs often require this level of accountability to satisfy the critics

- have a large target audience; if a program is designed for a large number of employees, it may be a candidate for ROI
- command the interest of the top executive group; if top executives are interested in knowing the benefits of the program and how they compare to the costs, the ROI should be applied.

After completing this chapter, work with your team to assess your programs. Rate each against the criteria above. Determine how many programs are candidates for ROI. In the past, I have found that only about 5 to 10 percent of all programs of a given training department should go to ROI. Although I am seeing the percentage of ROI candidates increase due to the decreasing total number of training programs and the increasing number of programs targeting specific business objectives, 5 to 10 percent is still a good target.

Guidelines for Calculating ROI

Calculating the ROI for training programs is a standard practice in many organizations. By following a few guidelines, you can develop meaningful and credible ROI measures for programs in your organizations that drive business outcomes:

- Stick with the ROI calculation your finance and accounting staff knows (for example, ROI means return-on-investment, ROE means return-on-equity, ROA means return-on-assets, and so forth). Although some definitions may be clever and have meaning within a specific function, you should know and use business standards.
- Keep your calculations conservative. Consider first-year benefits only for short-term programs. By its very nature, ROI includes several assumptions. By using conservative standards, you can be assured that the ROI you calculate will be believable.
- Set a target for success. When presenting an ROI calculation, present it in the context of an objective. This objective may be one set by the guidelines presented in this chapter. It may also be an ROI calculated for an alternative solution.
- Report the ROI in the context of other measures of performance. If you will report your ROI in the context of other measures of success, stakeholders will clearly understand how the ROI was developed and what steps must be taken to improve it over time. ROI is only one piece of an important story. Tell the complete story of program success so all stakeholders can make good decisions about the training program.

Knowledge Check: Calculating the ROI

Now that you have read this chapter, try your hand at calculating the BCR, ROI, and PP. Check your answers in the appendix.

- The annual monetary benefit of an absenteeism reduction program is $237,800.
- The cost of the program is $175,000.

1. What is the BCR? What does this tell you?
2. What is the ROI? What does this tell you?
3. What is the PP? What does this tell you?

About the Author

Patricia Pulliam Phillips, PhD, is president and CEO of the ROI Institute, the leading source of ROI competency building, implementation support, networking, and research. She can be reached at patti@roiinstitute.net.

References

Friedlob, G. T. and F. J. Plewa. (1996). *Understanding Return on Investment: Getting the Bottom of Your Bottom Line.* New York: Wiley.

Horngren, C. T. (1982). *Cost Accounting: A Managerial Emphasis,* 5th ed. Englewood Cliffs, NJ: Prentice-Hall.

Nas, T. F. (1996). *Cost-Benefit Analysis: Theory and Application.* Thousand Oaks, CA: Sage.

Phillips, J. J. (1983). *Handbook of Evaluation and Measurement Methods,* 3rd ed. Boston: Butterworth-Heinemann.

Phillips, P. P. and J. J. Phillips. (2008). *The Value of Learning: How Organizations Capture Value and ROI.* San Francisco: Pfeiffer.

Phillips, J. J. and P. P. Phillips. (2009). *Measuring for Success. What CEOs Really Think about Learning Investments.* Alexandria, VA: ASTD.

Phillips, J. J. and L. Zúñiga. (2008). Costs and ROI: Evaluating at the Ultimate Level. In P. P. Phillips and J. J. Phillips eds. *Measurement and Evaluation Series.* San Francisco: Pfeiffer.

Additional Reading

Niedermann, D. and D. Boyum. (2003). *What the Numbers Say: A Field Guide to Mastering Our Numerical World.* New York: Broadway Books.

∾ Chapter 17

Estimating the Future Value of Training Investments

Daniel McLinden

In This Chapter

Much of program evaluation is looking back—a retrospective measurement of the success (or lack thereof) of a program. Prospective evaluation complements retrospective evaluation with a look forward at the future impact of programs, including forecasting the economic impact. This chapter will provide you with the tools to apply forecasting methods to training investments. Upon completion of this chapter, you will be able to

- explain the rationale for estimating the future value of training investments

- describe the effect of timing in the estimation process

- apply the return-on-investment (ROI) method to forecast a program's economic impact

- describe other methods for estimating the future value of a training and development investment.

The Rationale for Estimating the Future Value of Training Investments

Organizations need to consider the value of multiple investments, including those in the development of their workforce. Swanson and Gradous (1988) were among the early advocates of and contributors to both prospective and retrospective evaluation and the rationale of forecasting. Although not new, estimating the future economic value of training investments is underused. Using measurement tools for forecasting allows decision makers to make investment decisions and avoid critical problems, including

- overlooking projects that could yield a high impact
- funding projects with minimal or negative impact
- continuing a project when it's better to divert funding to a more productive use of capital.

In addition to avoiding problems, forecasting has positive benefits:

- It focuses resources. A comprehensive analysis provides the evidence needed to set priorities and determine which program will contribute the most to the organization's goals.
- It enables consistency with other functional areas of the organization. In most organizations resources are limited and stakeholders demand a clear economic rationale for the use of these limited resources. The training and development function needs to similarly approach investments in the development of human capital with the same level of rigor.

Timing: The Evaluation Continuum

Evaluating program impact and forecasting program impact are part of the same continuum (see figure 17-1). Evaluation looks back and answers the question, "What was the merit and worth of this program?" Forecasting looks forward and addresses different questions: "Is this investment prudent?" "Should the intervention be changed to improve value?" "What is the likely future outcome from this investment?" To answer these and similar questions, forecasts are created at different points in time during the lifecycle of a program—during planning for the intervention, during program development, and during program delivery. (For a detailed discussion of the effects of timing and the utility of data obtained at different times on the analysis of costs and benefits, see Boardman and others, 2006.)

Figure 17-1. The Forecasting and Evaluation Continuum

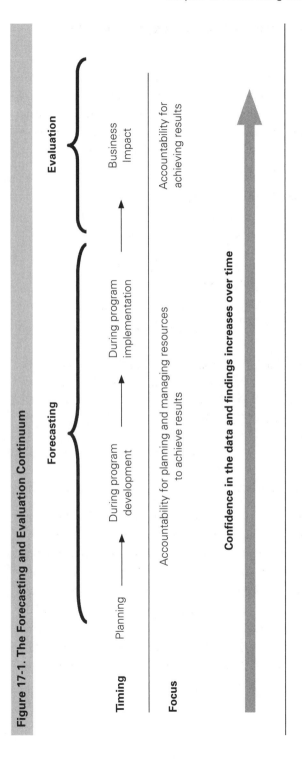

Timing: Evaluating Costs and Benefits During Planning

Estimating costs and benefits during planning clarifies and quantifies assumptions about the planned investment. An economic analysis, at this point, has multiple purposes, including

- reducing ambiguity and misunderstanding about the intervention. All stakeholders have the same understanding of the program—both the features of the program and the outcomes that will result. Because program costs and benefits are quantified, the elements that drive both costs and benefits need to be clearly stated and the result is a shared understanding of the program.
- prompting a thorough review of the investment. Results at this time may lead to a go or no-go decision or cause revisions to the investment's goals and cost structure, making a more favorable economic outcome.
- adding precision to the consideration of multiple alternatives. Multiple training investments can be compared and training investments can be compared to other nontraining investments and evaluated on a common metric, a financial metric, to determine the best and most productive use of limited resources.

Timing: Evaluating Costs and Benefits During Implementation

Similar to evaluating costs and benefits during planning, you'll also benefit from evaluation during implementation, both during program development and program delivery. Once the investment decision has been made, the program needs to be developed or purchased off-the-shelf or, possibly, a combination of both. During this period, the costs become clear as developers charge time to a project and invoices are paid. These data may confirm or revise cost assumptions in the planning forecast and, as a result, increase the accuracy of the program's cost. More accuracy in the cost analysis minimizes uncertainty about the cost structure for decision makers and provides an opportunity to consider the economic impact of any changes to the project plan (for example, scope increases).

At the point of program delivery, development is complete, development costs are invested, and delivery is in process. Options to affect the program's economic impact through changes to the costs are limited; however, there is an increased opportunity to affect change based on a clearer understanding of the benefits. Evaluation data that become available during the initial delivery of a program can provide preliminary evidence about the benefits that will (or will not) be achieved. For example, McLinden, Davis, and Sheriff (1994) used preliminary evaluation data to conclude that a training program was done well, participants learned, and were ready and able to apply what they learned. Preliminary data also showed, however, that training participants were not applying what they learned. Specifically, training participants were being discouraged from applying new practices they learned and encouraged to stay with former practices. A forecast during the delivery phase of the program showed that, at the current rate of application, the economic impact from this program would be negative. This forecast made clear to key stakeholders the need to intervene to remove barriers to ensure a positive economic impact.

Applying the Return-on-Investment (ROI) Process to Forecast Impact

The steps in forecasting the ROI of a training and development investment are similar to the ROI evaluation method (Phillips, 2003) applied retrospectively. An ROI forecast can be accomplished in three key steps:

1. defining the costs
2. defining the benefits
3. calculating the ROI as well as assessing sensitivity.

Step 1: Defining the Costs

A forecast should be able to withstand scrutiny. This means that all of the sources of cost should be incorporated into the analysis. Briefly, sources of cost include those associated with planning, development, or acquisition; delivery; and evaluation, including the effort invested in forecasting. An issue in forecasting is the tendency for stakeholders to underestimate costs. It is not uncommon to see project plans reflect the best-case outlook for the development of a program. For example, in one project, a key stakeholder had extolled potential of a sales training program based on a very favorable ratio between costs and benefits (that is, increased sales). Once the evaluators became involved, they discovered that although the benefits were reasonable, the costs only included the cost for delivery by faculty for this purchased program. Missing from the cost analysis was an accounting for other delivery costs, including the cost of time and expenses for training participants and costs associated with the ongoing administration of the program. Including these and other elements in a more thorough cost analysis and then forecasting the annual return led to a finding that the ROI would be negative. The more accurate analysis led to a significant revision of the program. The role of the evaluator is critical to ensuring that substantive costs are not missed.

Step 2: Defining the Benefits

To convert benefits to a monetary value, benefits need to be explicit. It is not uncommon early in a program's lifecycle to encounter stakeholders who have not articulated clear and specific expectations about the program's impact and who have difficulty responding to questions about impact, such as "Which business outcomes will change as a result of this program?" "How much will these outcomes change?" "How will this training and development investment cause the change in outcomes?" The evaluator is in the unique position to assist stakeholders in answering these questions. However, typically a structured process is required so that the evaluator can facilitate the effort by stakeholders to explicitly identify the expected impact of the program. Methods such as objective mapping (Hodges, 2002), and logic models (McLaughlin and Jordan, 2004) provide a structured approach to help stakeholders define specific changes that will occur as a result of the intervention. For example, stakeholders involved in a leadership program indicated that, as a result of attending the program, managers will have greater value for the organization. The evaluator in this situation noted that this outcome may indeed be true but was too ambiguous and could not be converted to a monetary value. The evaluator facilitated a session with stakeholders to create a map linking elements of the training program to specific and measurable outcomes. In a facilitated session between the evaluator and program stakeholders, the group was able to articulate more specific outcomes that included decreased attrition and developing depth in the management ranks. In turn both of these outcomes would lead to reduced recruiting costs and more rapid staffing of open positions. Unlike the ambiguous goal that was the starting point, recruiting and attrition were outcomes that could both be monetized and the next step in this and other forecasts was to convert benefits to a monetary value.

Convert benefits to monetary values. As is the case with a retrospective ROI evaluation, the forecast benefits need to be converted to a monetary value. Once converted, these benefits are directly comparable to costs because both are expressed as the same measurement units. This topic is covered in more detail in chapter 14, Converting Measures to Monetary Value.

Isolate impact. Multiple methods, including experimental methods, statistical approaches, and stakeholder estimates can be used to isolate the benefits of a training and development program so that these benefits can be attributed to the training program. These methods are necessary to separate the impact of the training and development intervention from other factors that may also influence the outcome. In this chapter we will confine our focus to estimation methods; estimation methods are widely applicable, commonly used, acceptable to executive stakeholders, and will withstand scrutiny. To supplement this perspective, in concluding statements for this chapter two other approaches will be mentioned, utility analysis and system's modeling, which may be of interest to the reader wishing to explore other models appropriate to forecasting.

Estimate benefits at different points in the program's lifecycle. Benefits can be estimated at different points of the program including during planning and during implementation.

- Planning forecast. In a forecast developed during a project's planning phase, methods to isolate the cause of the impact are not typically required. By virtue of how the question is posed, for example "What is the impact of this program on desired outcomes?" isolation is already part of the answer. It is, however, worthwhile to ensure that the "program as the cause" is communicated to estimate providers. At other times the forecast should include a method of isolation.

- Forecasting with preliminary application data during implementation. After the delivery of a program, preliminary data about the intended application or even the actual application may be available and these data can be used to forecast the future economic outcome. For example, McLinden and others (2010) reported on a project in which employees learned a new work process. Shortly after training was completed, preliminary data showed that the new process was being implemented. When compared to the previous process, this new process was more efficient and less prone to errors. The decrease in errors was treated as an intangible benefit and not monetized. Staff efficiency was treated as a monetary benefit and converted into a monetary value. Project evaluators reviewed the preliminary application data with multiple stakeholders and asked them to estimate the extent to which the educational program was responsible for the benefit. Results included

  - stakeholders estimated the extent to which the training program was a likely cause of the benefits, which could range from 0 percent (equivalent to attributing no impact) to 100 percent (equivalent to training being the only reason for impact)
  - stakeholders estimated their confidence in this attribution, with 0 percent equal to no confidence and 100 percent equal to complete confidence.

The estimates were averaged and the value of the benefit was multiplied by the impact and then by the estimated confidence to obtain a conservative estimate of the benefit's monetary value so it could be attributed to the training program. This value was then extrapolated for a year to forecast an annualized ROI.

Step 3: Calculating the ROI and Assessing the Sensitivity

The formula used to calculate the ROI is the net benefits (benefits – cost = net benefit) divided by the cost (ROI=net benefits/cost) and the result of the calculation is a single number. However, because a forecast is built about assumptions and estimates it is fair to ask what if a lower estimate of benefits is more realistic or what if the cost of development is higher? Sensitivity analysis is a process of asking and answering "what if" questions and determining how sensitive the results are to changes in the assumptions (Kee, 2004). Obviously, the ROI would be lower if the estimated cost was higher, but would that make a difference regarding program decisions? For example, one could increase the cost of program delivery as well as decrease benefits while keeping acquisition costs constant. Or, increase the travel expenses for program that requires centralized training while increasing the value of benefits. The key point is that the value of the benefit or the cost or an ROI value should not be considered as a single point estimate; multiple calculations should be developed.

Case Example: A Planning Forecast Scenario

A customer service organization was considering an investment in a training program that was intended to improve the employee skills. Employees worked with customers by phone to complete a variety of transactions. The cost of each transaction was largely the result of the time required for the service representative. This organization was interested in programs that would help service representatives become more efficient; in other words, handle more transactions and still maintain service quality. Given the large number of customer interactions, even a small improvement had the potential to yield significant positive benefits. Stakeholders considered a training investment that had the potential to increase efficiency and decided to invest in a preprogram forecast to determine the ROI that might be possible.

Step 1: Defining the Costs

The potential investment was a purchased program that required an annual licensing fee and all instructors be certified at delivery of the program in a train-the-trainer session. Assuming that 30 sessions could be conducted in a year, the cost of participants and instructor time was projected for the year. The estimated cost in year one was $154,000 (see table 17-1).

Step 2: Defining the Benefits

Each representative could start and finish an average of six transactions per hour. After a discussion, a conservative estimate of impact was reached and the stakeholders decided

Table 17-1. Define the Costs

Project Phase	Cost Elements	Value
Design	Forecasting and management time for negotiation for a purchased program.	**$5,000**
Development	Annual certification fees for a purchased (off-the-shelf) program	$5,000
	Compensation (salary and benefits) for instructor attendance at train-the-trainer sessions	$3,000
	Travel and housing	Does not apply
	Supplies	Does not apply
	Other expenses	None
	Total development	**$8,000**
Delivery	Faculty salary for preparation and delivery per session; assumes one instructor	$500
	Training participants—cost of salary and benefits per session; assumes 15 participants per session	$2,400
	Travel and housing of faculty and participants	Does not apply
	Classroom space	$700
	Supplies per session	$900
	Catering per session	$200
	Total delivery per session	**$4,700**
Summary	**Total year 1 costs for design, development and delivery of 30 sessions.**	**$154,000**

that an increase of one transaction per hour would be a reasonable goal. Based on the compensation ($20/hour including salary and benefits) of staff performing the job, the average cost per call was $3.33. An additional call per hour would improve that average to $2.86 per call and would be an improvement of $0.47. ($3.33 – $2.86). As a further measure to ensure the benefits' estimates were conservative, the team decided to assume that no representative could maintain this level of effort the entire year. Employees had other responsibilities so the value of the benefit ($0.47) was applied to approximately half of the work year, or 1,000 hours per person, and the resulting value of the improvement was $211,500 (1,000 hours × 450 staff × $0.47).

Step 3: Calculating the ROI and Assessing the Sensitivity

The net benefits equalled $57,500 ($211,500 – $154,000 = $57,500) and resulted in an ROI of 37 percent (net benefits/cost = 57,500/154,000 = 37 percent). The return was sufficiently positive to proceed with the investment and ultimately that is what the organization decided to do. Sensitivity analysis, however, revealed numerous risks.

If the number of hours to which this level of productivity applied was reduced much further, the ROI would be negative. Specifically, by changing the 1,000 hours to 700, the ROI was –3 percent. If projections about the number trainees were reduced from 450 to 300, the ROI would be negative.

Other Methods of Estimating Future Value

In this chapter, the focus has been on an ROI approach to assessing the future value of training and development investments. This method is not the only approach but this method is well known and well accepted in the industry and will withstand the scrutiny of executive stakeholders. This method is also accessible to a wide audience and requires no specialized software other than, perhaps, a spreadsheet. Other techniques do exist, however, and we briefly describe several here for readers who may wish to explore complementary methods.

Statistical Projections

Statistical estimation methods such as regression techniques use past data to project future values. For example, using past data about revenue, McLinden, Davis, and Sheriff (1994) statistically estimated the future trajectory of business revenue in the analysis of a training intervention. Among the weaknesses of the regression approach is that it assumes a straight line projection—when past performance continues on the current trajectory. Other more sophisticated statistical techniques exist that overcome this limitation and other limitations of the regression approach but these are not widely applied because training and development initiatives seldom meet the data requirement of these sophisticated statistical methods.

Systems Modeling

Systems models may hold promise for estimating future states. System models can incorporate both economic and other variables to create "flight simulators." These sophisticated simulations allow the evaluator to incorporate many interacting variables, model nonlinear relationships between variables, include feedback loops, and generally model the complexity of organizational systems. These models allow stakeholders to quickly test multiple scenarios and simulate the effects of decision on future states (see Sterman, 2000, for an overview of applied simulation). This approach is particularly appropriate when there are multiple programs where changes in one program affect the outcomes in other programs, requiring that multiple variables be considered simultaneously—a situation that does not lend itself to analysis by a single equation. For example, when confronted with situation that involved multiple programs, lost opportunity costs that varied over time, readiness to learn, and other variables, McLinden, Phillips, and Helbig (2008) used systems modeling to simulate the economics associated with varying decisions about the timing of multiple required training programs. Although this approach may hold promise in some situations, the underlying model development can get quite complex and requires specialized software.

Utility Analysis

Utility analysis is a method of calculating the value of a program that may be an appropriate complement to ROI estimation. Although rigorous, this approach is accessible and does not require knowledge of esoteric analytical techniques or specialized software. This approach has previously been widely applied in personnel selection and has been modified to apply to training decisions (see Cascio, 1989; Cascio and Boudreau, 2008). The formula to calculate the Utility, U, is $U = (N)(T)(SDy)(d)-C$. The elements of the formula are as follows: N is the number of people who participate in the program, T is the duration of the program's effects, SDy is the standard deviation of the variation in the value of job performance among untrained staff, d is the magnitude of the effect of the program, or the number of standard deviations that the training and development program will increase performance among staff, and C is the cost of the program. I have used this formula to create a sensitivity analysis by varying the multiple variables and determining the value that would be created under each scenario and then reviewing these values with stakeholders and discussing the reasonableness of the value that would need to be created for the program to be successful.

Final Points: A Forecast Is More Than a Calculation

Forecasting the future value of an investment is not an exact number, it is an estimate and the goal of forecasting is not to arrive at a single precise estimate but to "identify the full range of possibilities, not a limited set of illusory certainties" (Saffo, 2007). These are some additional considerations for forecasting:

- ROI value is not a single number but a range of values and a well done forecast will include a sensitivity analysis that incorporates changes to assumptions about costs and benefits.

- As the lifecycle of the program proceeds from planning to implementation, the data available to the evaluator will be more accurate and the forecast should be revised to incorporate new information.
- Stakeholders may have difficulty articulating specific benefits that can be converted to monetary values. The evaluator's role is to facilitate a process to help stakeholders be more precise about the outcomes that can be expected from the proposed investment.
- Stakeholders may have difficulty estimating the true costs of a program. The evaluator's role is to facilitate a conversation with stakeholders about the concept of fully loaded costs.

Knowledge Check: Estimating the Future Value of Training Investments

Answer the following questions, and check your answers in the appendix.

1. At what point in time can an estimate of the future value of a training and development intervention be developed?
2. There are many reasons to assess the future value of a training and development investment. In your opinion, what reason do you find most compelling?
3. A key stakeholder wishes to substantially decrease the length of participant time in the delivery program from the current eight hours to four hours. This change would increase the ROI by decreasing the cost. Develop a sensitivity analysis assuming that the value of the benefits is unaffected and the value of the benefits decrease by 0.5 transactions to 6.5 transactions. Use the following data to calculate the ROI. What recommendations could you make to this stakeholder?
    - Scenario 1: The cost of participant time is reduced by 50 percent resulting in a total cost of $118,000 and the value of benefits remains the same at $214,285.
    - Scenario 2: The cost of participant time is reduced by 50 percent resulting in a total cost of $118,000 and benefits are likewise reduced by reduced by 50 percent and the resulting value is $115,384.
4. There is a need to develop an economic forecast for multiple training programs. Additionally, stakeholders wish to explore how various levels of funding might affect noneconomic variables, such as participant learning and customer service quality to name a few. What method might complement an ROI analysis and include these other noneconomic variables and allow stakeholders to explore these issues?

About the Author

Daniel McLinden, EdD, has spent more than 20 years applying program planning and evaluation in both private and public sectors. In the private arena, he has worked with a number of industries and has substantial experience in the professional services and healthcare industries. In the public sector, McLinden has worked with the U.S. Department of Defense, the Department of Transportation, the National Institutes of Health (NIH), and the Centers for Disease Control and Prevention (CDC). He has authored and coauthored articles on training evaluation that have appeared in multiple trade and professional journals. He also coauthored chapters on training evaluation in *Return on Investment in Human Resource Development* (volume 1) and *Implementing Evaluation Systems and Processes*. McLinden is currently an assistant vice president in the Education and Training Department at Cincinnati Children's Hospital Medical Center. He is also a field service assistant professor in the Department of Pediatrics at the College of Medicine of the University of Cincinnati. McLinden may be reached at daniel .mclinden@cchmc.org.

References

Boardman, A. E., D. H. Greenberg, A. R. Vining, and D. L. Weimer. (2006). *Cost-Benefit Analysis*. Upper Saddle River, NJ: Pearson Prentice Hall.

Cascio, W. F. (1989). Using Utility Analysis to Assess Training Outcomes. In I. L. Goldstein ed. *Training and Development in Organizations*. San Francisco: Jossey-Bass. 63–88.

Cascio, W. F. and J. W. Boudreau. (2008). *Investing in People: Financial Impact of Human Resource Initiatives*. Upper Saddle River, NJ: Pearson Education, Inc.

Hodges, T. (2002). *Linking Learning and Performance: A Practical Guide to Measuring Learning and Performance*. Boston: Butterworth-Heinemann.

Kee, J. E. (2004). Cost-Effectiveness and Cost-Benefit Analysis. In J. S. Wholey, H. P. Hatry, and K. E. Newcomer eds. *Handbook of Practical Program Evaluation*. San Francisco: Wiley.

McLaughlin, J. A. and G. B. Jordan. (2004). Using Logic Models. In J. S. Wholey, H. P. Hatry, and K. E. Newcomer eds. *Handbook of Practical Program Evaluation*. San Francisco: Wiley.

McLinden, D. J., M. J. Davis, and D. E. Sheriff. (1994). Impact on Financial Productivity: A Study of Training Effects on Consulting Services. In J. Phillips ed. *Return on Investment in Human Resource Development: Cases on the Economic Benefits of HRD—Volume 1*. Alexandria, VA: ASTD Press, 133–46.

McLinden, D., R. Phillips, and A. Helbig. (2008). *Evaluating Opportunities to Optimize Learning and Economic Impact: Applying System Dynamics to Model Training Deployment in a Medical Center*. Denver, CO: American Evaluation Association.

McLinden, D., R. Phillips, S. Hamlin, and A. Helbig. (2010). Evaluating the Future Value of Educational Interventions in a Healthcare Setting. *Performance Improvement Quarterly* 22(4): 1–11.

Phillips, J. J. (2003). *Return on Investment in Training and Performance Improvement Programs.* Boston: Butterworth-Heinemann.

Saffo, P. (2007). Six rules for effective forecasting. *Harvard Business Review* 85, 122–31.

Sterman, J. D. (2000). *Business Dynamics: Systems Thinking and Modeling for a Complex World.* Boston: Irwin McGraw-Hill.

Swanson, R. A. and D. B. Gradous. (1988). *Forecasting Financial Benefits of Human Resource Development.* San Francisco: Jossey-Bass.

Measurement and Evaluation at Work

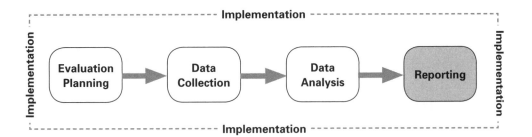

Section IV describes the last two steps in the measurement and evaluation process: reporting and implementation. These two steps put evaluation to work. We can plan an evaluation to the nth degree, we can collect data using textbook protocols, and we can analyze the data until we have nothing left to analyze. But, if no action is taken as a result of all these efforts, the evaluation process becomes just another activity.

The first step toward putting measurement and evaluation to work is reporting the results. Quantitative data show the results obtained through the evaluation; qualitative data tell the story. Together, these two types of data develop a powerful profile of what is working and what is not working with training programs. The key is to present relevant results in such a way that the audiences believe and accept them as well as feel compelled to take action.

To make evaluation work, data must be used to improve processes. When we speak of evaluation we often focus on program success. But using the results to improve programs and process is the way to achieve positive return on the evaluation investment. To effectively use evaluation data, systems must be in place to support its implementation. This requires technology as well as an instructional design approach that puts evaluation first rather than last (see Section I). Additionally, applying evaluation to a variety of types of programs provides an across-the-board look at how training is doing.

Section IV will provide you insights into

- reporting evaluation results
- selecting technology that will support your evaluation efforts
- using evaluation data to provide evidence of training success
- applying measurement and evaluation processes to different types of programs.

∞ **Chapter 18**

Reporting Evaluation Results

Tom Broslawsky

In This Chapter

Communicating evaluation results is as significant as achieving them. This chapter will explain the importance and challenges of communicating your results to diverse levels of management in an unbiased and objective manner. In this chapter you will learn

■ the importance of communication

■ the main principles for communicating results

■ how best to design your impact study results

■ how to communicate results to different stakeholders.

Why Reporting Results Is Critical

Each step in the evaluation process model requires planning and great attention to detail so one can achieve the desired outcomes of the evaluation project. Yet, the communication step does not always receive the attention it requires because it is multifaceted and somewhat complex. Evaluating data and producing a successful outcome are meaningless unless the findings are communicated properly and in a timely manner to stakeholders so that actions can be taken accordingly. There are three foundational reasons for making this step a high priority.

Communication Is Necessary to Make Improvements

The timeliness and quality of communications are critical when adjustments and improvements are needed. One must deliver updates to the appropriate groups throughout the process for timely adjustments. Communication of the final report provides comprehensive data for enhancing current or future programs aggressively.

Communication About Results Is a Sensitive Issue

Never assume that the results of your study will be greeted with praise by all, particularly in tough economic times. A program that is tied to internal political issues or the performance of others may distress some individuals but gratify others.

Different Target Audiences Require Different Information

A "one-size fits all" report most likely won't meet the individualized needs of your stakeholders. Consider the information each group requires, the format/media, and the appropriate time for discussing the results. The composition of the target audience determines which communication process is most appropriate.

Principles for Communicating Results

Style can be as important as substance when reporting results. Managing the complexity of the message, audience, or delivery medium can be demanding, but you can achieve exceptional results by following a few general principles outlined here.

Timely Communications

Timing the communication of results can affect how well they are accepted and how effectively and quickly the findings are acted upon. Communicate results as soon as they are known so that decision makers can take immediate action. Realistically, however, it may be best to communicate at a time that is most convenient to the audience in an effort to maximize the effects of the study. Is the audience prepared for the results given their current work environment or other events affecting the business? Are they expecting the results?

I once scheduled the review of a nine-month return-on-investment (ROI) study with a product marketing team who had demanding schedules. The day before the session, a major issue developed with a leading product, and an "all hands" meeting was scheduled before our review session. The response to the ROI study results, as expected, was met with vague indifference. Several key players were not present, and those who did attend were distracted.

❧ **Practitioner Tip** ❧

Maximize the evaluation study's results by ensuring that the greatest number of key stake-holders will attend the presentation and that the current work environment is favorable to a robust discussion of the findings.

Targeted Communication

Communication will be more effective if it is designed early in the planning process with a particular group in mind and tailored to their interests, needs, and expectations. The program results discussed in this chapter mirror outcomes at all levels, including the six types of data discussed in previous chapters: reaction or satisfaction, learning, job application, business impact, ROI, and intangible benefits. Some data are gathered early in the project and communicated as soon as possible to implement changes, whereas other data are collected after implementation and communicated in a follow-up study. The results, in the broadest sense, may range from early feedback in qualitative terms to ROI values in varying degrees of quantitative terms.

Appropriate Media Selection

Selecting the correct media is important because the proper form of communication can determine the effectiveness of the message. The more directly your audience is affected by the results, the more personal the media should be. Also, whenever appropriate, direct communication is the preferred method to ensure that the intended message is received. In other cases, a traditional memo distributed to select top executives may be more effective. Company publications offer an opportunity to tell the story of training success, as do detailed case studies.

❧ **The Value of Case Studies** ❧

Developing case studies based on evaluation results can provide a great teaching tool for your audience because they will take the conceptual model of gathering data and apply it to authentic business situations. Supporters of the case study method point out that these studies turn out a more comprehensive report than one generated by only using statistical or data analysis. The audience for case studies based on evaluation data can convincingly debate that although the case study may be founded on one organization's key business metrics, the final study is more robust because it addresses conditions that go beyond the numbers, such as corporate vision, economic environment, or leadership mandates.

Unbiased Communication

Let objective, credible, and accurate results speak for themselves. Sometimes, in the excitement of "wanting to make a splash," over-inflated or controversial opinions may leak into a report. Although these declarations may get attention, they can detract from the accuracy of the results and turn off the recipients. Use the following pointers in developing your communication process:

- focus on the training *process*, not the program or training department
- give credit to participants and their supervisors
- fully address evaluation methodology to give credibility to the findings
- clarify data sources and explain why they are credible
- state any assumptions made during the analysis and reporting and clarify why these assumptions were made
- be pragmatic and make no claims that are not supported by the data.

Testimonials from Respected Individuals

Testimonials from individuals with recognized stature, leadership ability, or influence can have a strong bearing on how effectively messages are accepted. Opinions of your audience can be strongly swayed with this level of support. Conversely, testimonials from individuals who command little respect can have a negative effect on the message.

Communication Strategy Shaped by the Audience's Opinion of the Program Team

Consider the credibility of the program team when developing the communication strategy. A reputation for integrity and reliability will make it easier to get buy-in from decision makers. However, if the program team has a weak reputation and low credibility, then presenting facts alone may not be enough to change perceptions. Facts alone may strengthen the voice of those who already agree with the results.

Communication Plan

Strict attention to detail is required to ensure that each targeted audience receives the proper information in a timely fashion and that appropriate actions are then taken. There are four basic steps to planning the communication of your evaluation project:

1. analyze the need for communication
2. identify the target audience
3. develop communication documents
4. deliver reports through appropriate media.

Table 18-1 describes the communication documents, targets, distribution method, and reasons for the communication.

Perhaps the most important audience member is the sponsor. This individual (or group) initiates the program, reviews the data, and weighs the final assessment of the effectiveness

Table 18-1. Communication Plan

Communication Document	Communication Target(s)	Distribution Method	Reason for Communication
• Complete report with appendices	• Program sponsor	• Distribute and discuss in a special meeting	• To secure approval for the project • To drive action for improvement • To show the complete results of the project • To underscore the importance of measuring results, if applicable • To explain techniques used to measure results
	• Workplace learning staff		• To secure approval for the project • To drive action for improvement • To underscore the importance of measuring results
	• Team manager		• To gain support for the project • To prepare reinforcement of the process • To create desire for a participant to be involved
• Executive summary (eight pages or less)	• Senior management in the business units	• Distribute and discuss in routine meeting	• To secure support for the project

(continued on next page)

Table 18-1. Communication Plan (continued)

Communication Document	Communication Target(s)	Distribution Method	Reason for Communication
• Executive summary (eight pages or less) (continued)	• Senior corporate management	• Distribute and discuss in routine meeting	• To secure support for the project • To build credibility for the learning and performance process • To stimulate interest in the workplace learning team
• General interest overview and summary without an actual ROI calculation, if applicable	• Participants	• Mail with detailed explanatory letter	• To secure agreement with the issues • To enhance results and quality of feedback
• General interest article (one page)	• All employees	• Publish in company publications	• To demonstrate accountability for all expenditures
• Brochure highlighting program, objectives, and specific results	• Team leaders with an interest in the program	• Informational brochure	• To gain support for the project • To secure agreement with the issues
	• Prospective sponsors	• Include with other marketing materials	• To market future projects

of the program. Senior management is responsible for allocating resources to the program and needs information to justify expenditures and gauge the effectiveness of efforts. Selected groups of managers (or all managers) are important to increase both support and credibility. Communicating with the participants' team leaders or immediate supervisors is essential because they will most likely be in a position to encourage the participants to put the proposals into practice and reinforce the objectives of the program.

Analyze for Communication

The program, the setting, and the sponsor's unique needs will dictate the specific reasons for communicating program results. The most frequent reasons are

- securing approval for a program and allocating time and money
- gaining support for a program and its objectives
- enhancing the credibility of a program or a program team
- reinforcing the processes used in the program
- driving action for program improvements
- preparing participants for a program
- showing the complete results of the training program
- underscoring the importance of measuring results
- explaining techniques used to measure results
- marketing future projects.

Although this list is fairly inclusive, there can be other reasons based on the individual situation, context, and audience.

Select Audience

As part of developing the overall communication plan, one should give significant thought to who should receive results of a program. The audience targeted to receive information is likely to be diverse in terms of job levels and responsibilities, so communication pieces should be delivered accordingly. Examining the reason for the communication is always a sound basis for determining audience selection.

Preliminary Issues

A helpful exercise for developing these lists is to ask the following questions:

- Does the audience have interest in the program?
- Does the audience want to receive the information?
- Has a commitment been made to this audience about receiving the communication?
- Is the timing right for communicating with this audience?
- How would this audience prefer to receive the results?
- Is this audience likely to find the results threatening?
- Which medium will be most convincing to this audience?

When scrutinizing each member of the audience, consider these three actions:

- The project manager should know and understand the target audience.
- The program team should examine what its specific needs are and why. Each group will have its own level of detail relative to the information desired.
- The program team should try to understand any audience bias or differing views. Although some will immediately support the results, others may be skeptical or impartial.

The Communication Document

The type of formal evaluation report will correlate with the level of detailed information presented to the different audiences. Brief summaries of results with appropriate charts may be sufficient for some communication efforts. Projects that require a high level of approval and considerable funding will necessitate a much more comprehensive write-up, possibly a full-blown impact study. The flow of your communication should address the following issues:

- why the program is being studied
- why the evaluation is being designed
- the evaluation methodology used
- the results generated
- conclusions and recommendations achieved.

An example of a comprehensive impact study is outlined in figure 18-1.

A few last things to consider:

- give credit for success entirely to the participants and their immediate leaders
- avoid bragging about results
- ensure that the methodology is well understood.

Select Media

Even the most positive program results can be sent awry if they are not delivered in the appropriate format or setting. Certain media may be more effective for a particular group than others, such as face-to-face meetings, special bulletins, memos, or company newsletters.

An array of electronic media has exploded in the past few years with the advent of wikis, blogs, and Twitter. Case studies represent an effective way to communicate the results of a project, particularly when explaining the measurement methodologies in a group setting.

Scorecards

Scorecards are a performance management tool that concentrate on various performance indicators that can include financial outcomes, operations, marketing, process performance, customer perspective, or any other appropriate measure. In fact, in many organizations, each business unit will develop its own scorecard and incorporate each into

Figure 18-1. Format of Impact Study Report

- Executive summary
- General information
  - Background
  - Objectives of study
- Methodology for impact study
  - Levels of evaluation
  - Collection procedures
  - Data analysis procedures
    - Isolating the effects of training
    - Converting data to monetary values
    - Assumptions

Builds credibility for the process

- Program categories
- Results: general information
  - Response profile
  - Success with objectives
- Results: reaction and satisfaction
  - Data sources
  - Data summary
  - Key issues
- Results: learning
  - Data sources
  - Data summary
  - Key issues
- Results: application and implementation
  - Data sources
  - Data summary
  - Key issues

The results with six measures: Levels 1, 2, 3, 4, 5, and intangibles

- Results: business impact
  - General comments
  - Links with business measures
  - Key issues
  - Barriers and enablers
- Results: ROI and its meaning
- Results: intangible measures
- Conclusions and recommendations
  - Conclusions
  - Recommendations
- Exhibits

one that ultimately reflects the vision of the whole business. Robert Kaplan and David Norton first explored the concept behind scorecards in their pioneering book *The Balanced Scorecard*. Kaplan and Norton suggest that data can be organized in the four categories of process, organizational, financial, and growth.

The scorecard method provides a snapshot comparison of key business impact measures and how they align with overall corporate strategies. Whether the scorecard is a step up with numerical indicators, a traffic light configuration (green—success, yellow—mixed results, red—unsatisfactory) or a dashboard design, the purpose is to reflect the current conditions of the organization. Also, many corporations now use the terms scorecard and dashboards interchangeably because both convert strategies into accountability and measure progress to date. Figure 18-2 shows a SenseiROI dashboard depicting the results of impact studies on line manager absenteeism.

Routine Feedback on Project Progress

Routinely collecting reaction and learning data provides feedback promptly so that adjustments can be made throughout the project, possibly to several different audiences using various media. This process becomes complex and must be proactively managed.

Figure 18-2. Sample Dashboard

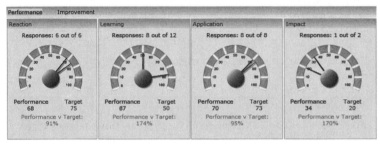

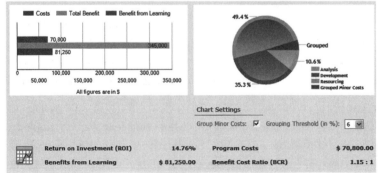

© Gaelstorm Software Solutions, 2009. Used with permission.

The following steps, some based on the recommendations of Peter Block in his book *Flawless Consulting*, are suggested for providing feedback and managing the overall process:

- communicate quickly and appropriately
- simplify the data
- examine the role of the project team and the client in the feedback process
- use negative data in a constructive way
- use positive data in a cautious way
- ask the client for reactions to the data
- ask the client for recommendations
- use support and confrontation carefully
- react to and act on the data
- secure agreement from all key stakeholders.

Following these steps will help move the project forward and generate useful feedback, often ensuring that adjustments are supported and can be executed.

Presenting Results to Senior Management

Presenting the results of an evaluation study to senior management can be one of the most challenging and possibly stressful types of communication. The challenges are convincing this highly intuitive group that outstanding results have been achieved (assuming they have), addressing the salient points clearly and concisely, and ensuring the managers understand the process.

Two potential reactions can create problems. An initial reaction may be that the results are impressive and it may be difficult to persuade the managers to accept the data. Conversely, if the data are negative, you cannot ensure that managers won't overreact to the results. The following guidelines can ensure that this process is planned and executed properly.

Arrange a face-to-face group meeting with senior team members to review results and ensure they understand the process, even though they may be familiar with the measurement methodology. Although this presentation can consume precious executive time, an executive summary may suffice after receiving a methodology presentation a few times.

Bottom-line results should never be disseminated until the end of the session to allow adequate time to present the process and collect audience reactions. If additional accuracy is an issue, illustrate how the trade-off for more accuracy and validity can often be greater expense. Address this issue when necessary, agreeing to add more data if required. Gather concerns, reactions, and issues involving the process and make adjustments accordingly for future presentations.

✂ **Practitioner Tip** ✂

Present results in an organized and focused manner. Make sure that the project team understands the importance of explaining the measurement methodology, data gathering, and data analysis steps before sharing final results because this may minimize the full effect of the findings.

Reactions to Communication

The level of commitment and support expressed by the managers, executives, and sponsors will mirror how successfully the results of a project have been communicated. Top management may also reflect their positive perception of the results by allocating requested resources and voicing their commitment. A final measure will be the comments, nonverbal language, and attitudes expressed by the audience.

When major project results are communicated, sometimes a feedback questionnaire is administered to the audience or a sample of the audience to evaluate their understanding and/or acceptance of the information presented.

Summary

The communication step does not always receive the attention it requires because it is multifaceted and somewhat complex. Effectively communicating results is a critical step in the overall evaluation process. If this step is not executed properly, the full effect of the results will not be realized, and therefore the value of the study may be lost.

Knowledge Check: Reporting Evaluation Results

In the first quarter of last year, you joined a project team to develop marketing plans for increasing the percentage of environmentally green goods sold by the household cleaning business unit. Because the effect on the company's bottom line was potentially dramatic, the team included senior managers, marketing reps, sales training, human resources, and workplace learning and performance staff, along with a few high-performing sales reps. A senior marketer had agreed to be the project sponsor.

A major part of the strategy was a product training course for the sales team. After three weeks of home study, 500 representatives were brought to corporate headquarters for a week of training on new products, competition, and business planning.

During the initial strategic planning session, a comprehensive study on the training was conducted to gather results from reaction through business impact. Because all representatives were required to undergo training, an experimental and control study to measure impact was not feasible. Results would best be measured by using the participants' estimate of impact on key business metrics.

A reaction and learning evaluation was completed by all participants at the end of the home study and in-house training. Three months after the in-house training, the evaluation team emailed a comprehensive behavioral change evaluation, which included questions on estimation and confidence. In all, 366 of the 500 participants completed the evaluation.

Finally, after eight months, a report was emailed to all containing some results, partial recommendations, and promises of a more comprehensive report later in the fourth quarter.

1. As someone involved in this training and study would you consider the reporting of the evaluation results acceptable? If not, why?
2. If *you* were on the team designing the measurement study how would you have designed the communication plan?

Check your answers in the appendix.

About the Author

Tom Broslawsky, BSIE, is the owner of Managing thru Measurement, LLC, a company that specializes in assisting corporations and institutions to develop measurement programs that align training objectives with strategic corporate business goals. He has international experience as a consultant, speaker, author, and facilitator with expertise in the Phillips ROI Methodology, along with 30 years' experience in education, training, healthcare, wellness, pharmaceuticals, and manufacturing. His most current venture is as the U.S. account manager for SenseiROI, a one-of-a-kind software product that incorporates the Phillips ROI Methodology into a simple, sustainable, and cost-effective measurement tool. He can be contacted at tbroslawsky@yahoo.com.

References

Block, P. (1981). *Flawless Consulting.* San Francisco: Pfeiffer.

Kaplan, R. S., and D. P. Norton. (1996). *The Balanced Scorecard: Translating Strategy into Action.* Boston: Harvard Business School Press.

Phillips, J. and P.P. Phillips. (2007). *Show Me the Money: How to Determine ROI in People, Projects, and Programs.* San Francisco: Berrett-Koehler.

Phillips, P. P., J. J. Phillips, R. D. Stone, and H. Burkett. (2006). *The ROI Fieldbook: Strategies for Implementing ROI in HR and Training.* Burlington, MA: Butterworth-Heinemann.

Phillips, J. J. and W. F. Tush. (2008). *Communicating and Implementation-Sustaining the Practice.* San Francisco: Pfeiffer.

✑ Chapter 19

Giving CEOs the Data They Want

Jack J. Phillips

In This Chapter

This chapter emphasizes that the executive point of view is the most critical perspective for today's learning and development manager. After completing this chapter, you will be able to

- identify eight types of data that can be reported to executives

- explain why executives appreciate and do not appreciate certain types of data

- identify specific actions to improve each type of data as it is reported to executives.

Setting the Stage

Regardless of what you may have heard, opinions do matter. The executive viewpoint is essential, particularly regarding learning and development. This chapter presents the executive's view, using research data, details, examples, and action items. Now more than ever, one needs to understand executives' views of learning and development that are based on their actual input, not just perceived assumptions.

Sources of Data

Various sources provide input into developing a profile of reliable, CEO-friendly data. The four key sources of data include executive surveys, executive interviews, executive briefings, and impact studies.

Executive survey. We targeted 401 *Fortune* 500 companies and 50 large private organizations; 96 CEOs gave insight into their perceptions, as the most senior executive in their organization, of learning and development measures of success.

Executive interviews. Structured interviews complemented the surveys and allowed us to probe for details. These interviews provided insight into executive concerns, desires, and opportunities.

Executive briefings. Almost 3,000 individuals have earned their Certified ROI Professional credential through the ROI Certification process. In some cases, individuals sought assistance from the ROI Institute in presenting an ROI study to his or her executive team. During this process, we received feedback yielding comments, discussions, and even lively debate about results and the need for additional results.

Impact studies. The ROI Institute has conducted hundreds of studies in the last two decades and presented the results to senior executive teams. Some of these presentations have been to *Fortune* 500 CEOs and boards of directors. These discussions served as data sources of insights into executive concerns and reactions.

Why It Matters

The dilemma surrounding the evaluation of learning is a source of frustration for many senior executives. They intuitively think that providing learning opportunities is valuable, and they logically anticipate a payoff in important, bottom-line measures, such as productivity, quality, cost reductions, time savings, and improved customer service. Yet, they are also frustrated by the lack of evidence showing that learning programs work. They assume, when soft-skills programs are involved, that the outputs can neither be measured nor credibly connected to the business. More rigorously calculated evidence must be reported or executives may feel forced to reduce future funding. The success of learning and development can be measured in ways that are credible, economical, and realistic within the resource boundaries of most learning and development functions.

The Investment Level: The Starting Point

Ultimately, top executives set the investment level for learning and development. Although some rely only on benchmarking, others adopt more well-defined strategies. In the CEO survey, five basic strategies for determining the investment level in learning and development were identified.

- Some executives (4 percent) take a passive role when investing in employees, attempting to avoid the investment altogether, employing competent employees who need minimal exposure to developmental opportunities, or using contract and temporary employees rather than permanent staff.
- An alternative strategy for some CEOs (20 percent) is to invest only the minimum in learning and development, providing training only at the job skills level with almost no development and preparation for future jobs.
- Many executives (39 percent) prefer to invest in learning and development at the same level that others invest, collecting benchmarking data from a variety of comparable organizations, often perceived as implementing best practices.
- Some CEOs (10 percent) operate under the premise that more is better, over-investing in learning and development beyond what is needed to meet the goals and mission of the organization.
- A growing number of CEOs (18 percent) prefer to invest in learning and development when there is evidence that the investment is providing benefits. This strategy is becoming more popular following the increased interest in accountability, particularly with the use of return-on-investment (ROI) as a business evaluation tool. With this strategy, all learning programs are evaluated with a few key programs evaluated at the ROI level.
- The remaining CEOs (9 percent) did not know the investment level or just decided not to respond.

The Executive View

The views on learning and development were obtained from the CEO survey. Ninety-six CEOs responded, representing 21.3 percent of the 451 targeted. This level of response is impressive when considering the difficult economic circumstances during the time the survey was conducted (2009). We wanted to know what measures were being reported now, what measures were missing but should be reported in the future, and how the executives would rank them in terms of value on a 1 (low ranking) to 8 (high ranking) scale. Table 19-1 shows the responses.

Table 19-1. Survey Responses

Measure	We Currently Measure This	We Should Measure This in the Future	My Ranking of the Importance of This Measure	
			Average	Rank
Inputs: Last year, 78,000 employees received formal learning.	(90) 94%	(82) 86%	6.73	6
Efficiency: Formal learning costs $2.15 per hour of learning consumed.	(75) 78%	(79) 82%	6.92	7
Reaction: Employees rated our training very high, averaging 4.2 out of 5.	(51) 53%	(21) 22%	7.15	8
Learning: Our programs reflect growth in knowledge and skills of our employees.	(31) 32%	(27) 28%	4.79	5
Application: Our studies show that at least 78% of employees are using the skills on the job.	(11) 11%	(59) 61%	3.42	4
Impact: Our programs are driving our top five business measures in the organization.	(8) 8%	(92) 96%	1.45	1
ROI: Five ROI studies were conducted on major programs yielding an average of 68% ROI.	(4) 4%	(71) 74%	2.31	2
Awards: Our learning and development program won an award from ASTD.	(38) 40%	(42) 44%	3.23	3

The first column in the table provides the percentage of CEOs who checked each item as a measure being reported, the second column gives the percentage indicating that it should be reported, and the third column gives the average ranking number for the group. As shown, inputs and efficiencies ranked 6 and 7 respectively; these types of data are always reported. Reaction is ranked the lowest, although it's the number 1 measure reported to executives. This particular measure could be improved with more focus on content. Awards ranked 3, which was higher than we expected. The highest-ranking categories were impact (8) and ROI (9). CEOs always want to see these types of data, especially during tough economic times. These are the least-reported data sets, yet are of the most value to executives.

Reaction Measures

Although participant feedback can be powerful data, the measures taken are often those of convenience versus quality. Executives rate this level of data as least valuable to them. Yet, reaction data are more likely to be reported to executives than any other type of data.

What's Wrong with Them?

Here are a few issues related to reaction data.

Image problem. Often referred to "happy sheets," "smiley feedback," or "happiness ratings," the feedback from these tools is perceived to measure the happiness of participants. Although happiness can be a rating, it has very little use when trying to predict learning and even less use when predicting application and impact.

Not taken seriously. Most stakeholders do not take reaction data seriously. Participants rarely provide quality feedback and often take little or no time to respond to a reaction questionnaire.

Too much data. At least 90 percent of programs are measured at the reaction level. This is too much data collection when compared with the value of the data. The process consumes precious resources, leaving many organizations without the resources to collect and analyze data higher on the value chain.

How to Make Them Executive Friendly

Although executives responding to the survey placed little value on these data, they do recognize their importance, because they help the learning and development team. Several tactics can be undertaken to create a renewed appreciation for reaction measures.

Manage the measures. Report to executives those measures that reflect the contribution of the program. Content-related measures have more meaning to the executives and other key stakeholders.

Use the data. Unfortunately, reaction data are often collected and immediately disregarded. The information collected must be used to make adjustments or validate early program success; otherwise, the exercise is a waste of time.

Forecast. Collect information related to improvement. Consider collecting data about results, including effect and monetary contribution. These data forecast value.

Learning Measures

Understanding how much learning has occurred is important, particularly in programs with significant skill building. Measuring learning has its share of problems.

What's Wrong with Them?

Besides being an essential part of the comprehensive evaluation system, measuring learning is often misunderstood and misused.

Measuring learning does not equal taking a test. Measuring learning is sometimes equated with testing, and participants fear or resent being testing. The challenge is to make testing (or learning measurement) less threatening, and rarely, if ever, have testing scores affect a job situation.

Measuring learning requires resources. With tight budgets, spending excessive amounts of resources on developing and administering tests may be an issue of resources given the measures taken. There is always a tradeoff between resources and the accuracy of data desired by some individuals.

How to Make Them Executive Friendly

Executives do not rank learning measures very high. They see these data as important for the learning and development team, but not important enough to judge the success of learning and development. To make learning measures more relevant and executive friendly, several actions are possible.

Use formal measures sparingly. Formal measures are important in critical jobs involving safety and health, critical operational issues, and customer-facing jobs. The dilemma of having formal measures is that it commands resources to ensure that a test is both valid and reliable. It's important to know when formal testing is necessary and when it is not.

Use informal measures. This involves a self-assessment for participants, ideally taken anonymously in a nonthreatening environment. This also may involve team assessments or, in some cases, facilitator assessments. Try building a learning measure into your scorecard. Because executives need only one or two measures on learning, it may be helpful to capture these types of data on a self-assessment basis and roll it into the scorecard.

Consider an ROI forecast with learning data. If there is a statistically significant relationship between test scores and on-the-job performance, and the performance can be converted to monetary units, then it is possible to use test scores to forecast the ROI from the program.

Application Measures

For some programs, measures of application represent the most critical data set. This level of results provides an understanding of successful implementation, along with the barriers and enablers that influence success. Many learning and development programs fail because of breakdowns in application.

What's Wrong With Them?

This level of measurement is not without its share of issues. Executives have interest in this level of data (61 percent of CEOs say they should be receiving it). They also have concerns about it.

Not enough data. This important data category is essential to understand on-the-job behavior. Even in the best practice organizations, only about 30 percent of learning and development programs have any type of follow-up at the application level. Without the level of data, there is no evidence that learning and development is making a difference in the organization.

Much is perception. Because this evaluation often involves behavior change and specific actions taken, the data are based on perception. Even an observation taken by others is subject to error and misinterpretation.

No standards. Unlike some of the other levels, there are no standards at this level, at least, none that are accepted in the industry. Knowing what to ask and how to ask it is not standard, which makes it impossible to compare data across programs, even with other organizations.

How to Make Them Executive Friendly

Almost every executive would agree that behavior change is an important output of learning and development. After all, many of them are attempting to shape the behavior of the organization through development programs, change management programs, and leadership development efforts. However, most executives quickly point out that activity does not always translate into results. A few changes help.

Report only a few measures. Executives may find helpful some simple measures that reflect on-the-job behavior or actions across programs that bring a sense of success to the entire organization.

Address the transfer of learning issue. One of the important reasons for collecting data at this level is to uncover the barriers to, and enablers of, using skills and knowledge. Identify barriers and take actions to minimize, remove, or go around the barrier. Along with barriers are the enablers, which are the supporters or enhancers of the transfer of learning. Working on barriers and enablers with the executives provides an opportunity to make improvements beyond the success that was already achieved.

Use the data. Data become meaningless if not used properly. As we move up the levels of results, the data become more valuable in the minds of the sponsors, key executives, and other stakeholders who have a strong interest in the program.

Develop ROI with Level 3 Data. Although using skills on the job is no guarantee that results will follow, there is an underlying assumption if the knowledge and skills are applied, positive results will occur. A few organizations attempt to take this process a step further and measure the value of on-the-job behavior changes and calculate the ROI. If there are no plans to track the actual effect of the program in terms of specific, measurable business results (Level 4), then this approach represents a credible substitute.

Build the executive scorecard. As with the previous level, it is necessary to capture data at Level 3 to use on the macro-level scorecard. Specific questions that must be identified are always asked at this level of evaluation, whether the data collection is by survey, questionnaire, interview, focus group, or action plan. These questions are then transferred to the macro-level scorecard.

Impact and ROI Measures

For most executives, the most important data are impact. Today, a growing number of executives seek, request, and require impact and ROI. This is a typical executive comment regarding the kind of data they want to see: "Although the activities are reported, I'd prefer to see the business results. To me, it's not so much what they're doing that makes a difference. I'd like to see a connection to our major business goals."

What's Wrong With Them?
To explore what is wrong with this level, the focus is not the measures themselves, but the credibility of the data and the issues surrounding collection and presentation.

Not enough data. For various reasons, it is not a common process to connect major programs to business measures, and even less common to show the ROI. More is needed.

Improve the front-end analysis. Problems are sometimes tracked back to the beginning of a program. A new program should start with the end result in mind. This specified business need can be met if the solution is linked to that need to some way. This requirement shifts the traditional front-end analyses away from classic skills and knowledge assessment, to starting with the business, linking to job performance needs, and finally, to identifying learning needs.

Use higher level of objectives. The learning and development team is very capable of developing appropriate learning objectives but they are not enough. Higher levels of objectives, including application and impact objectives, are now required to give proper focus to the learning program.

Is the ROI credible? Assumptions about the ROI calculation must be understood by the audience. Otherwise, credibility is lost. In essence, there must be standardized assumptions with a conservative flair to make ROI data credible, and ultimately, believable by the audience.

How to Make Them Executive Friendly

This category of data makes the business connection. The measures that are reported clearly are the business measures that often represent key performance indicators of the executive and illustrate business alignment. However, many executives rarely see this being done, and in more cases, not at all, which has left them confused and frustrated. Here are a few ways to ease executive frustration.

Create a discipline and culture for sustainability. As this level of evaluation is pursued, a culture of accountability is created, where the results are expected from programs and actions must be taken through the process with a results-based focus. Measurement and evaluation is systematic, routine, and not necessarily an add-on process. Collecting and analyzing data and using the results becomes systematic.

Isolate the effects of programs. In this step, evaluation planners explore specific techniques for determining the amount of impact directly related to the program such as a control groups, forecasting models, estimates, and expert opinion. Collectively, these techniques provide a comprehensive set of tools to address the critical issue of isolating the effects of a program.

Convert data to money. Calculate the return-on-investment by converting impact data to monetary values and compare the values with program costs. For some programs, the impact is more understandable when the monetary value is developed. Many techniques for converting data to monetary values are available; which technique is appropriate depends on the type of data and the situation.

Treat intangibles with respect. In addition to tangible monetary benefits, most programs will have intangible nonmonetary benefits. The ROI calculation is based on converting both hard and soft data to monetary values. Intangible benefits are program benefits that individuals choose not to convert to monetary values. Sometimes, intangible nonmonetary benefits are extremely valuable, carrying as much influence with executives as the hard data items.

Use forecasting. Before a program is developed, forecasting can be used to anticipate what impact may occur, or what ROI may be generated. Also, the forecast can be conducted when the program is implemented with data collected at the end of the program, essentially using the reaction data. These time frames are very helpful for executives to see the value of projects before they are developed, or at least in the initial stages of implementation.

Executives are interested in impact and ROI, particularly for large-scale programs that are expensive and strategic. Because of the costs, both in time and money, and their perceived connection to results, executives often want to see the ultimate level of accountability. When this is the case, it must be pursued.

Call to Action

Results and measures of value can be developed and communicated to senior executives to influence their perception of and decisions about learning and development. To ensure this influence, the learning and development team must focus on six important actions.

Spend wisely. There is no room for waste, which means programs should be connected to business objectives.

Respond professionally. Quick, professional responses while delivering impeccable service and building professional relationships within the organization are a must.

Operate proactively. The connection to the business should consist of understanding its problems and opportunities as well as being able to examine, explore, and recommend programs that may solve problems before they are requested.

Build productive partnerships. Work with executives and understand their issues, while delivering value that they appreciate. This effort will help make a partnership productive and earn the respect necessary for the success of the learning and developments process.

Show results. Pursuing a results-focused approach will have a tremendous influence on executives' attitudes toward and perceptions of the learning and development process.

Take risks. All executives take risks, and the learning and development team should follow suit. But the team can mitigate these risks by aligning potential programs with business objectives and by making immediate changes as needed.

Knowledge Check

Answer the following questions. Check your answers in the appendix.

1. What is the gap between what learning and development professionals provide to executives and what they want to see in terms of results? Be precise.
2. What are the implications of the gaps for business impact and ROI?
3. What are the implications of 18 percent of executives setting the investment level based on the payoff they see from the investment?

Actions to Bring More Executive Accountability to Learning and Development

1. Discover your gaps—have executives take the survey.
2. Review why top executives invest in learning and development. Identify the strategy your executives take.
3. Consider developing an executive-friendly learning scorecard.

About the Author

Jack J. Phillips, PhD, is a world-renowned expert on measurement and evaluation and chairman and cofounder of the ROI Institute. Through the ROI Institute, Phillips provides consulting services for *Fortune* 500 companies and major global organizations. Phillips has served as training and development manager at two *Fortune* 500 firms, senior HR officer at two firms, president of a regional federal savings bank, and a professor of management at a major state university. His academic accomplishments include degrees in electrical engineering, physics, and quantitative methods, and he has a PhD in human resources.

He is the author or editor of more than 50 books, and he conducts workshops and presentations at conferences in 50 countries. His most recent books include *Measuring for Success: What CEOs Really Think about Learning Investments* (2010); *The Consultant's Guide to Results-Driven Proposals: How to Write Proposals that Forecast Impact and ROI* (2010); *Show Me the Money: How to Determine ROI in People, Projects, and Programs* (2007); and *The Value of Learning* (2007). He can be contacted at jack@roiinstitute.net.

Recommended Reading

Phillips, J. J. and P. P. Phillips. (2007). *The Value of Learning: How Organizations Capture Value and ROI and Translate It into Support, Improvement, and Funds.* Hoboken, NJ: Wiley.

Phillips, J. J. and P. P. Phillips. (2010). *Measuring for Success: What CEOs Really Think about Learning Investments.* Alexandria, VA: ASTD Press.

 **Chapter 20**

Using Evaluation Results

James D. Kirkpatrick and Wendy Kayser Kirkpatrick

In This Chapter

This chapter presents the idea that unless evaluation results are effectively used, you have likely expended a lot of energy but have stopped just short of realizing the ultimate purpose of training and learning—to improve organizational effectiveness. Upon completion of this chapter, you will be able to

- identify the results most meaningful to each key partner group

- approach each audience in the most effective way to share relevant results with them

- use results to improve the effectiveness of training program delivery, on-the-job application, and related businss results.

Your Job Is Not Done Until You Create, Demonstrate, and Present Value

For decades, learning professionals have believed that their job is to design, develop, and deliver training programs. They have believed their work was done when program participants left the classroom or completed their e-learning modules. Many still believe they are truly effective when they fill classrooms, get 4.7 out of 5.0 on their reaction sheets, and close "skills gaps." Although designing, developing, and delivering training programs are indeed important parts of the training discipline, they are not enough on their own. Extending learning into the business and creating and demonstrating value to business stakeholders is critical for training professionals who wish to remain viable into the future. Training professionals no longer have the luxury of just concerning themselves with learning events, if they ever did. Evaluation is key to being able to demonstrate business value by contributing to organizational effectiveness.

Leverage Data and Information

Using evaluation results to improve programs and show value is not a new concept. Rather, it supports the underlying purpose of training. According to the *ASTD Competency Study: Mapping the Future* (Bernthal and others, 2004), [measurement and evaluation is about] gathering data and information to answer specific questions regarding the value of learning and performance solutions; focusing on the impact of individual programs and creating overall measures of system effectiveness, leveraging findings to provide recommendations for change and to increase organizational effectiveness.

Our job as learning professionals is to "provide learning and performance solutions" and to "increase organizational effectiveness." Thus, our job is to take the data and information we gather while conducting various learning events and, afterward, turn them into something useful for all.

Results Go Beyond Training

A historic problem with training evaluation is that trainers too often define "results" at Kirkpatrick Levels 1 and 2. Level 1 reaction sheets and Level 2 pre- and posttest results may tell a lot about the *delivery* of programs, but they are not a measure of *value* to the business. Data and information must be gathered at higher levels of evaluation (Kirkpatrick Levels 3 and 4) to show business value and justify training budgets. Figure 20-1 gives a brief summary of each of the Kirkpatrick four levels.

As you have learned in previous chapters, if you wait until after a training event is over to determine what data to collect, you have compromised your ability to not only measure the value of the program you have delivered, but to create it in the first place. You must build your evaluation plan into the design and development of your programs. Also, make sure that facilitators and trainers inform participants how evaluation will take place *after* training. Participants will be more comfortable because they will be expecting the reinforcing, monitoring, measuring, and encouraging activities back on the job. It also supports learning, because if training participants know there will be accountability for what they learned, they are more likely to stay engaged during class.

Figure 20-1. Kirkpatrick Four Levels

Level 1: Reaction	To what degree participants react favorably to the learning event. Common measurement tools • reaction sheet / survey • focus group • interview
Level 2: Learning	To what degree participants acquire the intended knowledge, skills, and attitudes based on their participation in the learning event. Common measurement tools • written knowledge test • role play and simulation • activities and games
Level 3: Behavior	To what degree participants apply what they learned during training when they are back on the job. Common measurement tools • survey, interview, or focus group • observation • work review
Level 4: Results	To what degree targeted outcomes occur as a result of the learning event(s) and subsequent reinforcement. Common measurement tools • borrowed metrics (that is, existing company and human resource reports) • survey • focus group

"Results" are not always about Kirkpatrick Level 4 business results, like sales numbers, cost savings, customer retention, or human resource results, like the retention of top talent. Results in this chapter are defined more broadly, encompassing all four Kirkpatrick levels. This chapter will outline how to use results from all four levels most effectively.

Effective Training versus Training Effectiveness

Results can generally be divided into two types:

- those that can be used to improve programs (effective training)
- those that can be used to improve organizational effectiveness (training effectiveness).

You first want to ensure that your training is effective, or in other words, that the training program results in the successful imparting of the intended knowledge, skills, or attitudes to the participants. If you think there is room for improvement when you deliver your programs, first use lower level results to enhance your training programs before turning your attention to business results. Be sure to do this as efficiently as possible, however; your business leaders will likely not wait long to for you to show them business impact. Statistically, in most cases, lack of training effectiveness is not due to the delivery of training programs.

Your next and larger concern is that you accomplish training effectiveness so that the knowledge, skills, and attitudes learned during training are applied on the job and yield a measureable business result. The majority of the breakdowns occur at this stage. If you are in this majority and feel confident that you are delivering good quality training programs, continue to monitor the lower levels of evaluation (reaction and learning), but focus your attention on whether the training is yielding the desired behaviors and results.

Results Most Relevant to Each Key Partner Group

To create a cohesive training effort, share a summary of the results of a training program with everyone involved. This should be brief and high level. Then give each group the results that are most important to them. Different results will be most relevant for different groups in creating positive business impact, so emphasize the key results for each group accordingly.

The key partner groups that will use training results include

- training participants
- instructional designers and trainers
- training leaders and consultants
- business supervisors and managers
- business executives.

If you made good decisions when building and delivering your various learning events, you will have results that can be useful to each of these groups. In addition to knowing what results to share with each group, you should also be clear about why the results are being shared and how they can be used.

Results for Training Participants

Strategy is executed one employee at a time, and training affects one employee at a time. The degree to which individuals are engaged, learn, and then apply what they have learned is the key to performance, confidence, engagement, retention, customer satisfaction, and business success. Therefore, it is wise to go over individual Level 1 and 2 results with participants to remind them of and reinforce the reasons they attended training in the first place: to learn, perform, and contribute to the organization. This means asking them about their reaction to the training program and any recommendations for improvement they may have. It also entails reviewing their own Level 2 learning scores for tests, activities, or demonstrations they performed during the class.

Results for Instructional Designers and Trainers

Instructional designers and trainers are primarily responsible for the quality of the training program itself and any required improvements, including both the content and delivery. Provide them with Level 1 reaction sheet data and Level 2 information from all in-class testing, activities, and other skills practice for this purpose.

Here is a list representative of the types of results that can help instructional designers build stronger programs and trainers deliver that material more effectively:

- the degree to which participants were engaged during the event
- the degree to which participants found the training relevant to their jobs
- the degree to which participants learned what was targeted
- the adequacy of time to practice key skills during the course
- the ease of navigation of e-learning modules
- the degree to which participants used social learning methods to enhance learning.

What often seems to happen with Level 1 and Level 2 results is that trainers glance over the data immediately after a program to see if participants say nice things about them, or if there are "reasonable suggestions" for improving programs. Instead, instructional designers and trainers should study the information to look for patterns. If the data suggest something is not strong—relevance, engagement, learning, and so on—dig deeper. Consider using stronger evaluation methods, such as interviews or focus groups, to determine exactly what is sub par. Then, you will be able to make the proper improvement to the course.

Too often, reaction sheets and learning data are gathered during class only to collect dust in the corner of someone's office. With proper analysis, this information can be extremely useful to ensure that the learner achieves the foundational knowledge, skills, and attitudes that will set the table for performance results down the road.

Results for Training Leaders and Consultants

The most critical results for training leaders, such as managers, directors, consultants, and chief learning officers, to study in detail are Levels 3 and 4. There is a very critical cause and effect chain involving required drivers, critical behaviors, and desired results. In short, the degree to which required drivers are used determines how consistently critical behaviors are performed. The more consistently critical behaviors are performed, the more likely you are to accomplish the desired results.

Required Drivers. Processes and systems that reinforce, monitor, encourage, or reward performance of critical behaviors on the job.

Critical Behaviors. The few key behaviors that employees will have to consistently perform on the job to bring about targeted outcomes.

Consider this example that illustrates the cause and effect chain. Training participants have just completed a class where they learned how to use a new order entry system. The order entry system will reduce order entry time, saving the company $2 million annually once fully up and running. The new order entry portal has been loaded on customer services representatives' computers, but the old system remains there as well during a transitional period. However, just because people learn a new skill doesn't mean they are eager to apply it, particularly if there is a more familiar or easier way to accomplish a similar end. So in this case, drivers will be critical to make sure that the training graduates enter orders using the new system. Drivers could be a scoreboard of number or percentage of orders entered in the new system, coaching and encouragement from supervisors to use the new system, and an incentive to enter 100 percent of orders in the new system by a certain date. Training leaders should ensure drivers like these are in place and are getting used when the training program is complete.

Training leaders and consultants also should ensure that the programs for which they are responsible are being delivered effectively from a high level. They should review the Level 1 and 2 summary data and ensure that the instructional designers and trainers make any required content or delivery improvements.

Here are some examples of higher-level results that training leaders and consultants can monitor, analyze, and use as the basis of sound decisions:

- action plan progress
- coaching frequency
- incidences of noncompliance
- performance rates for critical on-the-job behaviors
- reasons for lack of application
- rewards for positive application
- early business results
- early human resource results.

Higher-level results can be used to make good decisions to maximize on-the-job application. For example, use data to identify and remove barriers to application and create focus on critical behaviors. This will directly influence the desired Level 4 results.

Results for Business Supervisors and Managers

To improve organizational effectiveness, learning professionals need to get the data and information into the hands of business people who affect execution—the front line leaders. Business supervisors and managers need to see Levels 3 and 4 results to ensure that they reinforce the key behaviors that will generate the targeted business results.

Supervisors and mid-level managers like to see these kinds of results:

- applying knowledge and skills on-the-job
- identifying and eliminating performance barriers
- taking employee engagement scores
- accomplishing action plans
- demonstrating individual key performance indicators (KPIs)
- showing operations efficiencies
- executing cost savings
- contributing to overall strategy.

Sometimes business managers and supervisors want specific suggestions on how to improve performance, and sometimes they don't. If they do, that's great. Talk with them and provide recommendations for action along with the potential results. If they don't, give them what they do want. However, you might consider doing some "client shaping"; gently but clearly show them how you might be able to offer them more targeted recommendations in the future. Always keep in mind that they are your customers and it is your job to make their job of coaching and reinforcing learning as easy as possible.

Results for Business Executives

Business executives are at the highest level in the organization. It follows that results of training at the highest level are of the most interest to them. When providing data to the executive level, it is appropriate to focus on Levels 3 and 4. There are three reasons for this. First, business executives can influence change and growth in the organization more than any others. Second, this connects training directly to executing business strategy. Finally, it helps to dispel the common yet false belief that evaluation is no more than "smile sheets" and pre- and posttests.

Many training professionals regrettably provide Level 1 and 2 results to executives in great detail. This is what has created the myth that training can only yield results on those levels.

Resist the urge to share data like number of courses available, sessions held, people trained, and hours of training completed with your executives. Focus on presenting to what degree information learned is being applied on the job and what key business results those actions are supporting.

To find out what types of ultimate results your senior sponsors and other executives are looking for, you will have to talk with them. A key question to ask them to get the information you need is, "What will success look like to you?" Here are some examples of results that balance being pleasing to executives and realistic to achieve:

- efficient operations
- compliance
- retention of top talent
- customer satisfaction scores
- sales volume.

Summary of Key Results for Key Partner Groups

Every group that uses the results of training evaluation data should see all results in a high-level summary. However, certain results will be of the most interest for each group. Figure 20-2 provides a summary of the level of results that will be most useful and compelling to each of your key groups, along with representative decisions they can make using the information.

As you move further up the corporate ladder, so you move up the Kirkpatrick levels in terms of what type of information is appropriate and most meaningful to emphasize. Focusing your presentation of data following this guide will show both your sensitivity to limited resources and your business acumen.

Providing Evaluation Data to Each Group Effectively

Each group requires different evaluation data. Requirements for all groups, training participants, instructional designers and trainers, business supervisors and managers, and business executives are discussed in the following sections.

All Key Partner Groups

For any initiative, everyone involved should know the highest-level objective that the program supports. Using the example of the new order entry system from the last section, training participants should know that the reason they are learning a new way to enter orders is to save the company $2 million. This adds a higher level of meaning to the training

Figure 20-2. Results Most Important to Each Key Group

Kirkpatrick Level	Key Partner Group	Targeted Decisions
Level 1: Reaction **Level 2: Learning**	Instructional designers and trainers	• Improving program development and delivery • Ensuring training is targeted to strategic goals
Level 3: Behavior	Training leaders and consultants	• Improving follow-up and reinforcement to increase on-the-job application • Improving business partnerships
	Business supervisors and managers	• Improving decisions about training choices for direct reports • Enhancing engagement of direct reports through support and accountability • Improving performance of direct reports
Level 4: Results	Training leaders and consultants	• Ensuring training offered is in alignment with key strategic initiatives and company goals • Reducing costs by trimming nonstrategic training
	Business supervisors and managers	• Improving department / division KPI metrics
	Business executives	• Communicating strategic objectives to focus training and reinforcement efforts • Modeling and communicating the business partnership approach to training, performance, and strategy execution

that typically results in better learner engagement, which in turn, supports higher retention and application.

A good way to communicate the overall meaning of a program to all audiences is through a compelling Chain of Evidence. This links the intended outcomes at each of the Kirkpatrick levels to show how one supports the other. This takes a training initiative from being just a class to something that supports the highest organizational goals. Figure 20-3 presents an example of the Chain of Evidence for the new order entry system. In this example, the program is complete. At the onset of the program, the same Chain of Evidence can be used to show the cascading goals the organization hopes to achieve. The rest of this section is dedicated to explaining how to expand on the high-level Chain of Evidence to provide more detail to each key partner group for the areas of the most interest and use to them.

Training Participants

Training participants typically need to know just their individual results. Often, they know these before they leave the classroom. If feasible, the trainer, a peer, or a supervisor can meet with them individually after the program to talk about future actions for individual improvement and higher-level contributions. A career opportunity discussion can also be part of the conversation if relevant and appropriate. Personalized conversations, when possible, yield many benefits. For the participant, it makes them feel important. For the training organization, it punctuates the importance of training. For the organization as a whole, it increases employee engagement and satisfaction.

Figure 20-3. Chain of Evidence Example

Chain of Evidence

Level 1	Level 2	Level 3	Level 4
Reaction	Learning	Behavior	Results

New Order Entry System Implementation Initiative

Level 1: Reaction	Overall course rating: 4.6 / 5.0
Level 2: Learning	Hands-on practice participation: 100% Posttest average score: 92%
Level 3: Behavior	Percentage of orders entered in new system: November: 48% December: 79% January: 99%
Level 4: Results	Cost savings that resulted from reductions in order entry hours: November: $83,250 December: $132,000 January: $149,000

Instructional Designers and Trainers

Instructional designer and trainer efforts need to be in alignment, so we advise meeting with them as a group to review evaluation results. Look for and generate action steps to improve engagement, learning, and follow through for participants. Taking the time to meet with these groups of people will eliminate any possibility that the results are skimmed over and then set aside. Take the initiative to make sure that results are used for future program improvements if indicated.

Business Supervisors and Managers

When working with business supervisors and managers, discuss what needs to be done collaboratively. Review data and information with them in the context of executing the strategy of their department in relation to employee engagement and contribution, and to corporate goals and directives. Constantly remind business supervisors and managers of the connection between training, their direct reports' learning and performance, and their own support and accountability. Don't think you can just email them a report and they will take it from there. The personal relationship that you maintain with the managers and supervisors who will reinforce, monitor, encourage, and reward the performance of critical behaviors on the job is key to training success.

During Jim's time as the training director for First Indiana Bank, he found that he spent most of his time working with supervisors and managers at all levels. He constantly supplied them with data and information that, in his opinion, could help them improve the morale and/or productivity of their employees. At first he thought it would be enough to send this information and, surely, they would see things the way he did and make the indicated changes. He quickly found, however, that to really create change, he needed to make a business case to managers and supervisors that these were opportunities to actually execute their strategies and improve their department's KPIs. He also learned that they wanted more than data. They wanted to know how to interpret it in relation to changing behavior and positively affecting future results.

In between personal meetings with key supervisors and managers, dashboards are an efficient and effective way to communicate program progress. The "stoplight variety" (green for actual results on target, yellow for results somewhat below target, red for results significantly below target) is an effective way to visually communicate program status. We recommend the metrics in the dashboard include measures of learning, drivers, and critical behaviors. They should be sequenced to show a cause-and-effect relationship among training, learning, reinforcement, performance improvement, and lower and upper tier results. This allows managers and training professionals to use the results to determine what to

Table 20-1. Dashboard Example

New Order Entry System Usage		
	Target	**Actual**
Training completed for all associates	November 1	October 15
Orders entered in new system:		
November	50%	48%
December	75%	79%
January	100%	
Order accuracy:		
December	95%	92%
January	98%	

continue to support, and where to intervene to improve learning, performance, and subsequent results. Table 20-1 shows an example of a dashboard that could be used for the previously mentioned new order entry system training initiative.

Business Executives

As you have read in previous chapters, it is critical to negotiate expectations and reporting formats ahead of time with executives. Rather than automatically sending them dashboards, scorecards, and "executive reports," determine what results they want and need to see, and how often. Two categories of results that interest business executives are

- ongoing results that show progress (or lack thereof) with specific strategic initiatives
- a final Chain of Evidence that presents a story of ultimate value to the business.

Ongoing results that show the progress of an initiative are often overlooked. A dashboard or some other simple reporting method should be used regularly (typically monthly) to show program sponsors and other interested stakeholders to what degree things are moving along toward the ultimate goals. This is important for two reasons. One, when key indicators of progress fall below standard, you will likely need executive influence to get back on track. Two, this is a way of reassuring them that all is well. It is unwise to wait months for final Level 4 results to arrive to be able to demonstrate your value. Worse, if the initiative becomes derailed for any reason during the execution, you want to identify and correct the issues as quickly as possible so the initiative doesn't fail to produce the intended results.

When a program is complete, you may need to present evidence that your efforts have brought value to the bottom line. This may be for key company initiatives or those where the value is being questioned. The emphasis is not to rely solely on ultimate business and human resource metrics, but instead, to show results at all four levels with your Chain of Evidence. This demonstrates the power of everyone working together and solidifies the role of training in a business partnership.

If you are asked to present the results of a training program, request the opportunity to do so in person. If you are granted this privilege, you will have the best chance of showing how the Chain of Evidence and training support the business goal in question. A conversation about the program in general also gives you the chance to build your business partnership with the executive level and keep the pump primed for receiving the information you need for future training initiatives. Positioning yourself as a business partner in this way will help you as a training professional, and ultimately your entire organization as you align to meet the highest objectives of the company. See figure 20-4 for an example of how a training professional can support business managers.

Figure 20-4. Example of Successful Trainer-Business Manager Cooperation

Linda Hansen works as a high-level training manager at a large mid-west healthcare network. She led the learning and development arm of a program to increase the incidences of nurses completing electronic patient charting entries. These entries were an important component in the effort to increase patient safety. The training for this skill went off without a hitch. Attendees not only responded to the training with high Level 1 engagement and satisfaction scores, but also high levels of knowledge and competencies at Level 2. The key to ultimately improving patient safety at Level 4 was to get the nurses to actually perform their newly developed skills on the job (Level 3).

Linda spent time both before and after training ensuring managers at all levels were on board with this initiative, knowing that training in and of itself would not bring about enough change and subsequent results. She and her team partnered with the information technology department and developed and administered an automated Level 3 assessment, which indicated that the amount of on-the-job application was below standards. They queried the nurses' supervisors, who responded, "Yes, we know they are not doing it, but if we watch them, they will, and then when we don't, they won't." In short, the supervisors had no data to tell them who was and who wasn't complying.

To resolve the problem, she provided the data to the supervisors showing them who was compliant and who wasn't. Because the degree that the nurses used the application on the job significantly affected the supervisors' and managers' key performance indicators, they were only too glad for the specific data. They immediately went to work ensuring all were in compliance at Level 3, thus leading to success at Level 4.

Case Example: Using Evaluation Results at 7-Eleven

Field Consultant Certification Training (FCCT) is one of 7-Eleven's most important initiatives. The program, which has been running since February 2007, is designed to prepare business consultants to effectively produce results for the organization. In each of the three distinct training phases, the company's focal team members gather for a week at the corporate headquarters in Dallas, Texas, to learn about leadership skills, the core processes involved in doing their job correctly and efficiently, and the analytical skills necessary to produce tangible results to the bottom line.

As with all graduation programs, the end truly is the beginning for business consultants who attend this training program. The graduation marks a new way of doing business. The intensive certification process ensures that the training the business consultants received in Dallas is applied and verified back on the job.

Results of this program at all four Kirkpatrick levels are tracked diligently, and monitored monthly by senior leadership to ensure the significant cost associated with the program is producing suitable results. Scorecards for all functions involved in this program include metrics designed to capture performance, looking more for the applicative results rather than simply tracking the number of people who complete the training. Measured performance is targeted directly at those behaviors and results associated with the strategic objectives and tactics on the 7-Eleven strategy map. Table 20-2 provides a summary of the metrics tracked for this initiative.

Table 20-2. Summary of Field Consultant Certification Training Metrics

Metric Definition	Who Tracks?	Who Receives?	Purpose of Metric
Level 1: Reaction			
Participant Daily Course Evaluations	Facilitator Team	1. Facilitator Team 2. Learning Management 3. Learners	1. Help facilitators improve training delivery. 2. Help learning management team verify facilitator performance and monitor participant satisfaction. 3. Show learners that their feedback is valued and used to improve future programs.
Level 2: Learning			
Knowledge Verification	Facilitator Team (Using online assessment tool)	1. Learners 2. Managers 3. Facilitator Team 4. Development Team	1. Pretest focuses learner on knowledge gaps, maximizing learning. 2. Provide supervisors and managers with individual learner reports for each of their direct reports to help them coach more effectively. 3. Give the facilitator team information to verify they are covering material adequately, or indicate places where material or delivery should be modified for more effective learning. 4. Give the development team the information to gauge entering and exiting participant knowledge to tailor course materials to their needs, while meeting stakeholder expectations of content mastery.
Level 3: Behavior			
Business Plan	Supervisors/ Managers, Facilitator Team	1. Learners 2. Supervisors 3. Learning Team 4. Senior Leadership	1. Learners are provided valuable feedback from various sources (division vice president, merchandising, their supervisor, human resources, training, and others) on their performance of a major job component (business planning).

(continued on next page)

Table 20-2. Summary of Field Consultant Certification Training Metrics (continued)

Metric Definition	Who Tracks?	Who Receives?	Purpose of Metric
Level 3: Behavior (continued)			
			2. Supervisors use the Business Plan opportunity in a variety of ways, including verifying current performance and coaching learners for improved performance. 3. The learning team uses the information as part of the verification of whether the training program was effective in changing behavior on the job.
Level 4: Results			
Store Sales Results (six months after certification)	Financial Planning, Training Team	Senior Leadership, Financial Planning, Supervisors	1. Sales are tracked to make sure that certification impacts sales. (i.e, those who are certified have higher sales increases than those who are not). Senior leadership (and the learning team) use these results to verify that the program is working. 2. Financial Planning uses this information to justify the training cost to the organization/senior leadership. 3. Supervisors use this information to justify the expense (even though it is not theirs) of sending their employees to training.

Knowledge Check: Measuring the Value of a New Hire On-Boarding Program

You are the leader of the learning and development team for a large consumer products manufacturing company. The company has found an exciting new market niche and will therefore be hiring new employees in the coming months.

Until now, new hires were trained with an orientation program through the human resources department. You made the case for a different program run by the training department called the new hire on-boarding program. You have been granted the chance to pilot the program with the understanding that you will report program results throughout the implementation, and make a formal report to the executive committee in six months.

The targeted success outcomes of the new program are

- increased new employee engagement scores
- decreased employee turnover during the first year
- shortened time to targeted performance levels
- improved unit productivity.

For each of the following groups, what level of targeted results will you gather and share and what targeted decisions can be made from the results provided to each group? Check your answers in the appendix.

1. Instructional designers and trainers
   Level of results:
   Targeted decisions:

2. Training leaders and consultants
   Level of results:
   Targeted decisions:

3. Business supervisors and managers
   Level of results:
   Targeted decisions:

4. Business executives
   Level of results:
   Targeted decisions:

About the Authors

James D. Kirkpatrick, PhD, is a senior consultant with Kirkpatrick Partners. He provides workshops and consulting for *Fortune* 500 companies around the world on the topics of business partnership and four-level evaluation. His clients include Harley-Davidson, Booz Allen Hamilton, L'Oreal, Clarian Health Care, Edward Jones, Ingersoll Rand, Navy Federal Credit Union, Honda Manufacturing, the Federal Reserve Bank of St. Louis, the U.S. Department of Defense, the Royal Air Force, Petronas Oil Company, and the Abu Dhabi Police Department.

Kirkpatrick's approach goes beyond the science of training, reinforcement, and evaluation. His emphasis is on the art of developing and sharing business cases with would-be partners on the benefits of and need for a business partnership approach. He uses metaphors and the testimonials of successful employees and managers to bring his message to life.

Kirkpatrick has cowritten three books with his father, Don Kirkpatrick, the developer of the Kirkpatrick four levels. He has coauthored two books with his wife and business partner Wendy: *Kirkpatrick Then and Now* (2009) and *Training on Trial* (2010). He can be reached at jim.kirkpatrick@kirkpatrickpartners.com.

Wendy Kayser Kirkpatrick is the founder of Kirkpatrick Partners, LLC, a company dedicated to helping organizations become more effective through business partnership. She applies her skills as a certified instructional designer and expert presenter and facilitator to lead companies to measurable success.

Kirkpatrick's results orientation stems from her career beginnings in retail, holding positions in merchandising, direct importing, and product development with Venture Stores and ShopKo Stores. From there she held marketing positions with Springs Industries and Rubbermaid. Most recently she was a training manager for Hunter Douglas Window Fashions, managing the curriculum for 1,500 sales and customer service representatives in North America. She can be reached at wendy.kirkpatrick@kirkpatrickpartners.com.

References

Bernthal, P. R., K. Colteryahn, P. Davis, J. Naughton, W. J. Rothwell, and R. Wellins. (2004). *ASTD Competency Study: Mapping the Future.* Alexandria, VA: ASTD Press.

Additional Reading

Brinkerhoff, R. O. (2003). *The Success Case Method.* San Francisco: Berrett-Koehler.

Kirkpatrick, D. L. and J. D. Kirkpatrick. (2007). *Implementing the Four Levels.* San Francisco: Berrett-Koehler.

Kirkpatrick, J. K. and W. K. Kirkpatrick. (2009). *Kirkpatrick Then and Now.* St. Louis, MO: Kirkpatrick Publishing.

Kirkpatrick, J. K. and W. K. Kirkpatrick. (2010). *Training on Trial.* New York: AMACOM.

Phillips, J. J. and P. P. Phillips. (2007). *Show Me the Money.* San Francisco: Berrett-Koehler.

Chapter 21

Implementing and Sustaining a Measurement and Evaluation Practice

Debi Wallace

.... **In This Chapter** ....

This chapter describes how to develop, implement, and sustain a measurment and evaluation practice focused on results. Upon completion of this chapter, you will be able to

- identify the critical components of a comprehensive assessment, measurement, and evaluation strategy

- create an action plan with critical milestones for successful implementation

- develop a plan to gain support for measurement and evaluation in your organization.

There are many paths you could have taken to get to this point of aspiring to develop and implement a comprehensive measurement and evaluation practice in your organization. You could have received a mandate from a senior leader to justify the budget for training in your organization and are currently sifting through volumes of data on participation, staffing, and financials to react to this request. You desire to start running the business of training in such a way that demonstrates the value of learning and development to your organization, seeking to position yourself with the information you need in advance of being asked. You could be concerned about whether your learning programs are truly targeting the right issues and performance goals and want to ensure that training is prescribed and delivered when appropriate, along with a plan to affect results. You could be involved in a major change initiative in your organization and want to ensure that team members don't revert to previous processes or behaviors, but rather apply what they've learned on their jobs to achieve measurable results. You may have already engaged in one or more measurement projects, or you may just be at the beginning of your journey. Regardless of what brought you to this point, developing and implementing assessment, measurement, and evaluation processes as a systemic part of the learning process will improve the learning and development team's effectiveness and reputation as valued business partners. Carefully consider the following to develop the right plan for your company.

Create a Strategy for Measurement in Your Organization

Creating a strategy for measurement in your organization is important. To do so, you need to determine what you want to do, identify what to avoid, and develop specific outcomes.

Develop Goals

Determining what you want to be able to do is a critical first step. Carefully select colleagues and leaders in your learning organization that you know are both supportive of and skeptical about measuring and evaluating learning, and collaborate with them to answer the following questions:

- What do you want to know?
- Why are you interested in measuring learning?
- Who wants to hear (or do you want to tell) about measurement results, and why?
- How will measurement information be used? What decisions will be made?
- When is measurement needed?

Identify What You Want to Avoid

Equally important to knowing what you want to be able to do is to identify what to avoid. By deliberately exposing any barriers or baggage in your organization that could hinder your progress with measurement and evaluation, you will save time and significantly increase your chances of sustaining what you're about to work hard to design and implement. Answer the following questions with this same group of colleagues and leaders:

- Have there been previous measurement efforts that have left organizational baggage behind?
- Are there particular elements of fear with partners or stakeholders?

Develop Specific and Measurable Outcomes

Finally, you should develop specific and measurable outcomes you expect to achieve. This final step in defining your goals will allow you to not only define success, but will also assist you as you define the organizational scope of your efforts. Questions to consider include

- What are you currently experiencing in which you expect to see a difference?
- How do senior leaders currently view learning and development processes, programs, services, and results?
- What type of partnership do you experience with business unit leaders when implementing a new learning program?
- What are you hoping to achieve with programs, curriculum, and overall learning results?

Once you've compiled a draft of your goals, test them with colleagues in learning and development, human resources, and business unit leaders. Then, make revisions based on their input. Use these goals to equip you as you design a comprehensive measurement and evaluation practice tailored to your organization's needs and gain much needed advocacy and support.

Gain Advocacy and Support

It is likely that during your work to define goals for measurement and evaluation in your organization, you identified individuals in learning and development; broader human resources; and hopefully, business units eager to begin working with information that equips them to partner and improve their group's performance. These individuals can become early advocates and champions to provide the support necessary to secure resources and make this work an organizational priority.

Develop Individual and Organizational Experience

To gain individual and organizational experience, select a challenging problem or opportunity to measure, creating a chain of impact from the learning event all the way through to business impact and ROI. Use results from this effort at appropriate points in time along the way to "show" rather than "tell" colleagues and leaders about the value of measurement and evaluation. Consider the following questions to help you select your first project:

- Where is the organizational or business unit pain?
- Can operational or strategic objectives be clearly defined?
- Are senior leaders eager and committed to resolving this problem or pursuing this opportunity?

- Will solving this problem or opportunity require a large investment of time and/or money?
- Do data exist or can you collect data to analyze?
- How many people will be involved or affected?
- Have skill or knowledge gaps been identified as part of the problem or opportunity?

As you assess the problem or opportunity, ensure that skill or knowledge needs to be acquired by your target audience. If not, the program may be a good candidate for evaluating from an overall human performance improvement perspective, but it won't help you show the value of training and development. Additionally, being able to link the program to specific business unit objectives, having access to obtain or collect related data, and getting active senior leader interest and commitment are critical for your first measurement and evaluation effort.

Select a Subject Matter Expert with Whom to Partner

Once you've selected a project, engaging a subject matter expert with whom to partner provides important experience to guide the work, as well as produces results that are often more credible in the early stages of implementation. These experts can be engaged in a way that enables your long-term capability by not only leading this initial project, but also by coaching and mentoring individuals in your organization as they develop necessary skill and knowledge. Consider the following questions when selecting a subject matter expert:

- Do you have experts internally that can partner with you to implement your study?
- Do you want this expert to transfer the ability to you or other team members to complete similar analysis in the future? If so, what type of training and implementation support do they offer?

✑ Practitioner Tip ✑

Because companies spend large sums of money on new hire training, this topic is often chosen for initial measurement efforts. This is not the place to start for measuring business impact, however, unless you are measuring the difference between a former and new program, or measuring the difference between training or not training a group of new hires. That is not to suggest that new hire training should not be measured and evaluated, because it can be critical to ensure that learning has occurred, that individual team members are prepared to apply what they've learned on their jobs, and that they do in fact perform at an appropriate level once on the job. Without something to compare your results to, however, business impact and ROI results will lack credibility.

- Does the expert have a documented and proven business process, or is it a theoretical model?
- Does the expert use processes that position you to gain credibility as a business person, producing results your leadership team can relate to, or use language that are unique to human resources?
- Does the expert have resources and a proven track record to ensure he or she will deliver on their commitments to you and your organization?

Seek experts who use a process that is both simple and consistent with other processes your business unit leaders are familiar with. If you're calculating a metric like the return-on-investment of a human performance improvement program, you should use the same formula an executive would use to calculate ROI on a business unit initiative. If multiple interventions are developed and executed to achieve the desired performance improvement (for example, training, plus a change in a compensation plan, plus new marketing tools), expect the expert to have valid methods to measure and attribute that portion of the improvement resulting from training and the other interventions separately. Whomever you partner with should be able to clearly and concisely articulate how their approach will achieve your goals, the process(es) they will use during the engagement, key deliverables and related timing, and demonstrate flexibility given your unique set of circumstances. Be skeptical of experts who build themselves up by tearing other experts down, and always ask for and review relevant examples and references.

Secure Senior Leader Involvement and Engagement

Having access to individuals who either have specific subject matter expertise in the business unit (for example, product specialists), or being assured of leadership support to both set expectations and inspect results are critical to any successful training and development effort. For measurement and evaluation efforts, it can make the difference between having or not having access to the information you need to engage. For any measurement project you participate in, be sure to answer the following questions:

- Who do you need access to in the business unit to offer expert input and insight for planning efforts?
- What types of communications do you need to contract with senior leaders for in advance?
- How can you demonstrate strong business acumen versus overwhelming with "HR speak"?
- How will information be used at each step to focus on improving results?

Consider asking the most senior leader involved in your program to introduce the learning opportunity either in writing or by kicking off the session. Contract with them to make the program a topic of discussion at lead team meetings before, during, and after the learning event. Set expectations with them for specific communications, and solicit their support for securing assistance from other teams if necessary to collect and report on required data.

Follow Through with Concise and Targeted Communication

How you communicate results has both short- and long-term effects on your implementation. Because some colleagues may have had experience with measurement processes that didn't equip them with information they could tangibly use to facilitate performance improvement, or they may view measurement as an academic process and not a business process, it's very important to develop communications that "show," not just "tell." Use measurement results along the way to inform and equip leaders to intervene if necessary where there is concern and to encourage and reward where things are progressing as planned. Carefully plan and execute your communications considering the following questions:

- What types of data will you collect along the way?
- How will you communicate the "so what"? Given all the data you're likely to have available, what do they really mean, and what do the various partners or stakeholders need to know?
- How will you use findings to affect the probability of a positive change in performance and business results?
- When do partners and stakeholders need to have the information to affect results?
- How will you share overall final results with partners and stakeholders, and who needs to be involved?
- In the event the program's results are negative, how and to whom will you communicate? Will this change your overall communication plan?

❧ Practitioner Tip ❧

Every organization discovers programs that do not achieve intended results, and communicating with leaders in these situations can drive needed change. These situations often expose other issues in the organization that need to be addressed, ranging from how needs were assessed, to how decisions were made to develop training as a solution to the performance issue, to organizational communication about changes that could drastically affect employee morale or even the target population. Although you should navigate carefully to avoid unnecessary repercussions, these opportunities should be addressed with candor and transparency, not with fear and blame. You will likely be surprised at how much support for measurement will result from these often dreaded but truly opportunistic situations.

Finally, don't forget about those individuals you identified in step one who could be classified as "skeptics" for pursuing this important work. If they remain skeptical, their opinions could create unnecessary obstacles, or even sabotage your efforts. You should deliberately seek opportunities to engage them in the work in such a way that they experience the business value of information produced, perhaps even equipping them with information that will allow them to facilitate critical communications at some appropriate point in the project. It is not uncommon for them to become some of the greatest and most outspoken champions, with relevant and compelling testimonies that develop advocacy and support.

Identify Necessary Processes and Adapt Them to Your Organization

Assessment, measurement, and evaluation span the entire performance improvement cycle from the initial assessment of the performance issue, to the final analysis and reporting of business results. If your processes are not integrated, you risk designing and implementing programs that are not linked with the problem or opportunity and will struggle to develop an effective measurement plan. Consider figure 21-1 for overall performance improvement, and answer the following questions to discover where your organization should develop more robust processes to support this work:

- How do you know what leaders are aspiring for, or where the organization's pain points are?
- How do you identify opportunities to improve efficiency or effectiveness?
- What reactions have you gathered from human resources colleagues or business unit partners and stakeholders about how performance issues are assessed? Is the current situation viewed as effective or ineffective, and why?
- How do you conduct training needs assessments? Are they aligned to specific organizational or business needs?
- At what point in the training design and development process do you plan for measurement and evaluation?

Figure 21-1. Overall Performance Improvement

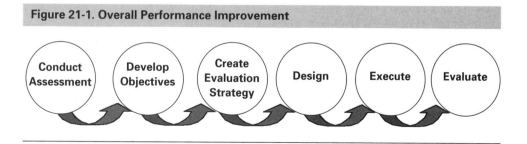

- Are objectives developed for the various types of performance, that is, readiness, learning, on-the-job application, business impact, and ultimately ROI?
- Are measurement data collected, analyzed, reported on, and used with partners throughout the performance improvement cycle, or only at the end when final results are determined?

Maintaining a focus on overall performance improvement as you identify and adopt required processes is critical to your success. Remember, you want the processes to support the work and the information gained from applying the processes to be used to achieve improved performance for your clients and partners.

Identify Resources and Roles Needed to Support Implementation

You'll require a variety of resources to implement your measurement strategy, including human resources and technology.

Identify Human Resources Required to Support Your Strategy

The implementation of a results-based approach may require updated roles and responsibilities for all individuals and groups involved in initiating, designing, developing, delivering, and supporting learning in the organization. Human resources partners must assess performance problems and opportunities and prescribe relevant performance improvement interventions targeting specific business measures. During the design and development of training, designers and vendors must develop materials directly linked to the measurable and criterion-referenced performance and learning objectives. Facilitators must focus their presentations, exercises, and activities on relevant business issues and collect information required to measure readiness and learning. Managers must support and reinforce the learning process by expecting and inspecting behavior change. The ultimate responsibility for the success of a learning opportunity must rest with business unit leaders, and the learning organization must support them with performance data to guide them to specific action. Consider the following questions to determine the effect on roles in your organization:

- Who is currently involved in assessing performance issues, measuring human reource initiatives, or consulting with partners and stakeholders?
- Will business unit leaders be required to take different actions or behave differently?

- What skill sets are needed by those involved to effectively engage in the new processes and use results produced?
- How will processes for assessing, measuring, and evaluating programs be linked to existing work processes?
- How will you ensure that these new processes become systemic in your organization?

Identify Technology Required to Support Data Collection and Communication

Technology has enabled efficient data collection in most companies, while mergers and acquisitions have created data quality issues because of multiple systems of record, data redundancy, and lack of consistent data standards. Having data to analyze is required, and should be collected from various sources. Consider the following questions to identify potential technology needs to support data collection:

- How do you collect survey data? Do you have access to raw data that can be integrated with other types of human resource and performance data?
- How do you collect assessment data and who are your sources for this information?
- How will you collect performance data? Do you need special access to secure it?
- How will you track costs? What will you include to "fully load" expenses?

Carefully identify, plan, and budget for technology to ensure you are able to collect or secure the data you need. To learn about deciding on the appropriate technology for your evaluation needs, read chapter 22, "Selecting Technology to Support Evaluation."

Determine the Effect on Organizational Structures

To implement and sustain a comprehensive measurement and evaluation practice, human resources must be aligned and equipped to offer support and develop expertise. Consider the following questions to determine the best approach for your organization:

- Is centralized leadership necessary to support consistent implementation and application?
- How will you keep the work close enough to the business units to facilitate necessary customization and flexibility, yet ensure consistent enterprise results?
- If you choose to have centralized and decentralized human resources, how will they work together to achieve and support your overall goals?

Develop Implementation Plan and Execute

At this point, you have considered a wide range of issues to define your goals for measuring and evaluating learning in your organization, gaining advocacy and support for the work, and have identified new processes and resources required to support your implementation. You are ready to develop an implementation plan covering the following milestones to ensure a successful execution:

- secure approval for strategy
- communicate to all partners and stakeholders involved
- secure resources (human and financial) as necessary
- develop and implement new governance and process
- develop and implement required learning
- develop and implement new technology
- develop rollout plans and measurement criteria for each business unit
- address any barriers to implementation as necessary
- create and support the measurement community
- share status updates and success stories throughout the organization
- communicate results to partners and stakeholders
- continuously improve your process.

This work is about so much more than collecting data and producing reports; rather, it is about equipping individual learners and leaders in your company with the information they need to know, whether they are well positioned to succeed or are at risk of not achieving desired results. Many great ideas and valiant efforts result in little more than good intentions and significant time spent trying to implement them. Diligently consider the questions in this chapter and the checklist in table 21-1, and allow your discoveries to establish a reasonable plan for using measurement and evaluation results to drive greater accountability and improved results in your company's learning organization.

Table 21-1. Checklist for Implementing and Sustaining a Measurement Practice

1. Create a strategy for measurement in your organization.
2. Gain advocacy and support.
3. Identify necessary processes and adapt them to your organization.
4. Identify resources and roles needed to support implementation.
5. Develop implementation plan and execute.

Knowledge Check

Align each activity listed below with one of the following key components of a comprehensive assessment, measurement, and evaluation practice implementation. Check your answers in the appendix.

Key Components:

1. Create a strategy for measurement in your organization.
2. Gain advocacy and support.
3. Identify necessary processes and adapt them to your organization.
4. Identify resources and roles needed to support implementation.
5. Develop implementation plan and execute.

Activities:

	Secure senior leader involvement and engagement.
	Create and support a measurement community.
	Develop measurement and evaluation processes.
	Develop goals.
	Select a subject matter expert to partner with.
	Identify technology required to support data collection and communication.
	Develop and implement required learning.
	Integrate new processes with existing program design and development processes.
	Develop specific and measurable outcomes.
	Determine the impact on organizational structures.
	Develop individual and organizational experience.
	Identify what you want to avoid.
	Develop rollout plans and measurement criteria for each business unit.
	Develop assessment processes.
	Identify human resources required to support your strategy.
	Follow through with concise and targeted communication.

About the Author

Debi Wallace has more than 23 years' experience in leading and evaluating strategic human performance interventions in the financial services industry, along with a strong analytics, learning and development, human resources, and communications background. She has led the strategic and tactical development and implementation of an enterprise assessment, measurement, and evaluation practice to measure the impact of learning and other human resource programs, conducting dozens of linkage and ROI studies since 1995. She most recently created and led Wachovia's Advanced Analytics and Research Practice in HR Workforce Analytics as a senior vice president in their human resources division, where she partnered with other leaders to set Wachovia's strategic analytical direction for HR-related information, striving to consistently demonstrate how to use HR data and measurement systems to drive fact-based decision making. Her team led HR business impact analysis projects, as well as complex enterprise analytics initiatives. She regularly speaks at industry conferences and has published a number of case studies on related topics. She can be reached at dwallace7@sc.rr.com.

Additional Reading

Blanchard, K. (2002). *Zap the Gaps.* New York: HarperCollins.

Phillips, J. J. (1998). *Implementing Evaluation Systems and Processes.* Alexandria, VA: ASTD.

Chapter 22

Selecting Technology to Support Evaluation

Kirk Smith

In This Chapter

This chapter looks at the different technologies designed specifically for training evaluation; technologies that can capture, store, retrieve, and report evaluation data. In this chapter, you will learn to

- discriminate among different tools
- develop criteria from which to make your decision
- select the most appropriate tool for your short-term and long-term evaluation needs.

Why Technology?

Evaluating training at a significant level can be an onerous job. On one hand, you want enough data to be able to make sound business decisions, and on the other hand, you do not want to create a measurement bureaucracy. You want actionable information—information that is going to improve your processes, job impact, and/or business results. Technology can make it easier for you, depending on what you are trying to accomplish. This requires asking the right questions.

Asking the Right Questions

The top three questions I have found to be most important are

- What do you want to know?
- How are you going to use it?
- Who are the intended users of the information?

Once you have asked these questions and understand the answers with your team, the next step is to identify and prioritize the intended uses of the information. These answers and actions will form the basis for developing the criteria to make the decision about the right technology tool for you and your organization.

Examples of criteria include

- keep costs to a minimum
- easy reporting
- good technical help desk
- customizable questionnaires
- access to raw data
- automated report distribution
- easy implementation.

Establishing your criteria for technology prior to discussing it is important. This type of decision analysis is not about identifying choices and making a case for one specific alternative. Instead, establish what needs to be accomplished, and then find the alternative that best accomplishes it (Kepner and Tregoe, 1997). Figure 22-1 provides a form to help you

---

☙ Tips for Developing Decision Criteria ❧

Ask

- What short- and long-term benefits or results do we want?
- What resources should we use or save?
- What restrictions influence this choice?
- What minimums must we meet?

Thought Starters

- Consider how time, cost, customers, management, and so on influence this choice.
- Be clear and specific.
- Use short statements—include measures.
- Involve those who will approve or implement.
- Stay away from objectives that are just features of alternatives.

---

develop a list of your decision criteria for technology to support evaluation (*Criteria* and *objectives* are used interchangeably).

The Technologies

Now that you are armed with your criteria, let's look at some alternatives. For the scope of this chapter, we have only chosen four alternatives out of many available. However, these four should give you a good idea of what is available and what the various options have to offer. A discussion of all possible is beyond the scope of this chapter, but we have selected alternatives in three categories: online survey software, stand-alone systems, and analytics modules within learning management systems (LMS).

SurveyMonkey (www.surveymonkey.com)

SurveyMonkey is probably the least expensive and easiest tool with which to get started. This online survey design tool allows you to quickly and easily design and administer your surveys. It is not specifically designed for the measurement and evaluation of training, but can be used—and is being used by many—to do so. If you are going to send out surveys with 10 or fewer items to 100 or fewer respondents, it can be free. Free is good. Three hundred dollars per year allows you to design as many surveys as you need with as many questions as you need. Most types of questions are supported, such as multiple-choice, Likert, and so on.

SurveyMonkey also collects responses for you and can be controlled by date or number of responses. The reporting allows you to show charts and graphs, but also allows you to drill down to individual responses. A filtering and cross-tabulation function allows you to view and report on segments of your respondent data. For more detailed analysis, you can download raw data into different formats, including spreadsheets.

Figure 22-1. Decision Criteria Exercise

Develop your own criteria below:

1. _____
2. _____
3. _____
4. _____
5. _____
6. _____

Metrics That Matter (www.knowledgeadvisors.com)

KnowledgeAdvisors was a pioneer in learning analytics when they introduced Metrics That Matter. It provided a technology-enabled way to capture, store, retrieve, analyze, and report on learning and development data. It is based upon Kirkpatrick's and Phillips' frameworks and includes concepts from Brinkerhoff's Success Case Method (2003). It is a one-stop shop that allows you to measure all aspects of enterprise learning, from activity metrics to return-on-investment (ROI).

The standard surveys are for postevent and follow-up and are sent via email or can be done manually. Multirater 360-degree feedback instruments are also available. The postevent and follow-up survey items are in seven categories:

- instructor
- environment
- courseware
- learning
- job impact
- business results
- ROI.

The standard reporting module contains more than 30 standard reports, and they are divided into four categories: ROI tools, executive tools, aggregate tools, and tactical tools. The ROI tools are based upon the Phillips ROI Methodology (Phillips, 2003). The executive tools provide a high-level look at results for senior management. The aggregate tools provide cumulative data, and the tactical tools are primarily to look at individual classes. Through filters, the reporting capability is virtually unlimited. Another useful and time-saving feature is that any report can be automated to be completed and emailed to individuals of your choosing regularly.

If you want to take data analysis to a more sophisticated level, you can perform raw data downloads. This is a fairly simple process within Metrics That Matter and allows you to import the data into spreadsheet programs and, from there, into statistical analysis programs. The active authoring feature offers you an opportunity to customize your surveys, develop other kinds of surveys, and write assessments for pre- and/or posttesting. Pricing is based upon the number of prospective users. KnowledgeAdvisors upgrades Metrics That Matter twice a year.

Sensei/ROI (www.senseiroi.com)

Sensei/ROI is a fairly new solution in the United States and is gaining ground. Developed by Galwey, Ireland-based Gaelstorm, this software is built exclusively on the Phillips' ROI

Methodology. It is extremely comprehensive in making sure all of the process steps of the ROI Methodology are followed. It is a process management tool that walks and coaches you through the entire ROI process. The administrative steps are automated so that you are free to spend more time at the higher-level objectives of the Kirkpatrick and Phillips frameworks and models. It allows you to more easily measure Level 3 application virtually 100 percent of the time. It makes it easier for you to customize and streamline your evaluation planning process by coaching you through the objective setting process that is so important in the initial stages of planning. Many of the input fields also have drop-down menus, which saves time as well. It uses customizable surveys to gather the pre- and postprogram data, including 360-degree multirater feedback instruments. The output is a clean, one-page summary of the ROI Methodology results, called a "Sensei Map." The Sensei Map can be high level enough for senior management's at-a-glance needs or detailed enough to be able to make business decisions based upon the data.

The Sensei/ROI process begins with planning and then follows the Phillips (2003) ROI Methodology process steps. The Sensei Map then shows, in a dashboard format, the results that can help make future decisions that align training to the business strategy.

Reports can be automatically completed and distributed. Most of the clients use the program hosted on Gaelstorm's servers, but in-house, behind the firewall, hosting is available. The pricing is on a pay-as-you-go system, based upon the number of studies conducted, with pricing breakpoints available for higher volumes.

Learn.com (www.learn.com)

Learn.com is a learning management system provider. Traditionally, LMS providers have included basic analytics capability within the system and now, in response to market demand, many LMS providers have expanded their analytics modules to include the capability to evaluate training effectiveness; not just activity and compliance (Bersin, 2009).

Learn.com's LearnCenter Performance Dashboard is based upon delivering at-a-glance, on-demand reporting to all levels of the organization. More than 60 standard reports are available. Because virtually everything done within training is captured inside the LMS, the amount of data is quite extensive and provides maximum reporting capability and flexibility. The robustness is increased dramatically by the access to Crystal Reports, allowing you access to disparate databases to merge into reports. Learn.com pledges an ROI guarantee for their clients. The guarantee promises a positive financial ROI in the first year of implementation. If that is not achieved, the second year fees are waived.

Direct learning effectiveness data are collected in the same way as the other technologies—through customizable surveys and questionnaires. Multirater 360 feedback capability is also included. The reporting and performance data can be also integrated into a client's performance management system. Reports can also be done for both teams with formal reporting relationships and ad hoc groups, such as project teams.

Pricing is based upon the number of users, along with volume breakpoint discounts. One of the disadvantages of Learn.com's LearnCenter Performance Dashboard module is that it is not a stand-alone system. It is available only within the LMS.

These four technologies represent some of the opportunities to support the training measurement and evaluation processes. Table 22-1 presents a list of other technologies available.

The Decision

Now that you have some basic information about four representative training evaluation technologies, how do you decide which one is for you? The rest of this chapter will be devoted to walking you through a decision analysis. The method will be based upon the work of Kepner and Tregoe (1997)—who present a rational process for making decisions. Here are the steps:

1. Develop objectives.
2. Classify them into musts and wants.
3. Weigh the wants.
4. Generate alternatives.
5. Evaluate the alternatives against the musts and wants.
6. Identify risks.

Table 22-1. Other Technologies

Technology	Type	URL
Zoomerang	Online surveys	http://www.zoomerang.com
Key Survey	Online surveys	http://www.keysurvey.com
C3 Analytics	Stand alone	http://www.c3analytics.com
SAS Analytics	Stand alone	http://www.sas.com/technologies/analytics
Sum Total	LMS	http://www.sumtotalsystems.com
Plateau	LMS	http://www.plateau.com

Classify Objectives

Let's go back to the objectives you developed earlier. The first thing you want to do is classify these objectives into "musts" and "wants." An objective is a must if you can answer yes to all three of these questions:

- Is it mandatory (required)?
- It is measurable (set limit)?
- It is realistic (can be met)?

Out of a set of six to 10 objectives, you might have one to three musts. Everything else is a want. As you will see, the musts tell us who gets to play, and the wants tell us who wins. Let's look at the sample criteria in table 22-2. The objective, "Keep costs to a minimum" cannot be a must, because it is not measurable with a limit. The word "minimum" is too vague to be a measurable limit. Anytime a phrase contains the words minimize, maximize, or optimize, it cannot be a must. The only must is "access to raw data." It is mandatory in this case. It is measurable with a limit; either you can download raw data or you cannot. It is realistic. You signify a must with an "M" in the first column. Everything else is a want.

Weigh the Wants

The next step is to weigh the wants. Wants do not all have the same importance, so you must attach relative numerical weights to each of them. You determine your most important want(s) and give it (them) a weight of 10. You can have more than one 10. The other wants are weighted relative to the 10s. For example, if another want is half as important as a 10, then weigh it with a 5. Do not weigh the wants in an ordinal manner (that is, 10, 9, 8, 7, and

Table 22-2. Must Objectives

	Objectives
☐	Keep costs to a minimum
☐	Easy reporting
☐	Good technical help desk
☐	Customizable questionnaires
M	Access to raw data
☐	Automated report distribution
☐	Easy implementation

so on). Keep in mind that you will more than likely be doing this with a group of people and facilitation skills are sometimes needed to come to agreement on weighting and alternative evaluation scores that are to come. Table 22-3 shows the weighting of your objectives.

Generate Alternatives

The next step is to generate your alternatives by identifying possible choices. To be fair and impartial, the alternatives are numbered and do not represent the technologies discussed above. This exercise is not to show you which technology to use, but a decision analysis method as a tool for you to decide. Then, you want to screen the alternatives against any must. If an alternative cannot satisfy the must, then it is eliminated from your choices. Remember, musts tell you who gets to play the game, and wants tell you who wins. Table 22-4 is a matrix with the alternatives across the top and your objectives in the first column after being screened through the must objective of having access to raw data. Alternative 3 is eliminated here.

Evaluate Alternatives

The next step is to compare alternatives against the wants, evaluating the relative performance for each want to determine which alternatives create the most benefit. This is done by asking how each alternative performs against each want objective. Score the best performing alternative for each want with a 10. Give the other alternatives scores relative to the best performer. It is possible, and sometimes likely, that there are ties for the best alternative. Then, multiply the performance score by the weighting of each want and total the weighted scores.

Table 22-3. Weighted Objectives

Weight	Objectives
7	Keep costs to a minimum
6	Easy reporting
7	Good technical help desk
10	Customizable questionnaires
M	Access to raw data
4	Automated report distribution
6	Easy implementation

Table 22-4. Screening Through the Musts

Weight	Objectives	Alternative 1	Alternative 2	Alternative 3	Alternative 4
7	Keep costs to a minimum				
6	Easy reporting				
7	Good technical help desk				
10	Customizable questionnaires				
M	Access to raw data	GO	GO	NO GO	GO
4	Automated report distribution				
6	Easy implementation				

For example, the top performer for the first objective, "Keep costs to a minimum," is alternative 1, so it gets a score of 10. Alternative 2 and alternative 4 rate scores of 7 and 4 respectively, based upon their costs relative to alternative 1. We then multiplied the weight (from the first column) of 7 by the performance scores to arrive at the totals for that objective; 70 for alternative 1, 49 for alternative 2, and 28 for alternative 4. After this process is done for every want objective, you add the total scores in each column to arrive at a total for each alternative. Table 22-5 shows the completed evaluation.

Identify Risks

You have a pretty clear winner in alternative 2, but there is still one step left. Identify any risks associated with the highest scoring alternative. If you can live with the risks, you have made your decision. If you cannot, you go to the next highest scoring alternative and do the same risk analysis. Some questions to ask during your risk assessment are

- What could go wrong in the short and long term if we implement this solution?
- What are the implications of being close to a must limit?
- What disadvantages are associated with this alternative?
- Did I make any invalid assumptions about this alternative?

For this exercise, we did not identify any intolerable risks, so the decision is made. To learn more about this decision analysis technique, see Kepner and Tregoe (1997).

Table 22-5. Completed Analysis

Weight	Objectives	Alternative 1	Alternative 2	Alternative 3	Alternative 4
7	Keep costs to a minimum	10/70	7/49		4/28
6	Easy reporting	5/30	10/60		8/48
7	Good technical help desk	3/21	10/70		7/49
10	Customizable questionnaires	10/100	10/100		10/100
M	Access to raw data	GO	GO	NO GO	GO
4	Automated report distribution	3/12	8/32		10/40
6	Easy implementation	10/60	7/42		3/18
	Totals	**293**	**353**		**283**

Summary

Measurement and evaluation of training programs is something all of us should be doing at some level and probably at higher levels than what you are doing now. Time constraints and lack of analytical skills are two of the main roadblocks to doing it. The right learning analytics technology can help you in both areas. There are several alternatives for the right technology for you, depending on what you are trying to accomplish. We briefly described four of them: SurveyMonkey, Metrics That Matter, Sensei/ROI, and Learn.com. The key is the same as in conducting an evaluation study; develop your objectives early in your planning stage and let them be your guide. We walked though a decision analysis using a rational process. Whether you use this method or another, it does not matter as long as you are as objective as you can be and take politics and emotion out of the decision process. A rational method helps you do this so you end up with the right evaluation technology for your needs.

Knowledge Check: Musts and Wants

Now that you have seen the decision process, how do you know whether a decision objective is a must or want? Check your answer in the appendix.

About the Author

Kirk Smith, PMP, CPT, CRP, is a freelance performance consultant and also an adjunct faculty member for three universities. He teaches organization performance; organizational communications; project management; research and evaluation methods in human resources; business, ethics, and society; and human resource development. His primary practitioner focus is on measuring and evaluating the effectiveness of performance improvement projects, human capital analytics, transferring critical thinking skills in client organizations, and facilitating issue resolution through systemic solutions. Smith has significant experience in analyzing the human performance systems in organizations to resolve performance improvement issues.

He is a PhD candidate in technology management with a specialization in human resource development and expects to defend his dissertation in 2010. His research interests are in measuring and evaluating informal learning, organizations as complex adaptive systems, and the role of network science in HRD. He is also a Project Management Professional (PMP) through the Project Management Institute, Certified Performance Technologist (CPT) through the International Society for Performance Improvement, and a Certified ROI Professional through the ROI Institute. He can be reached at kirk@wkirksmith.com.

References

Bersin, J. (2009). *The State of Learning and Talent Measurement.* Bersin and Associates.

Brinkerhoff, R. O. (2003). *The Success Case Method.* San Francisco: Berrett-Koehler.

Kepner C. H. and B. B. Tregoe. (1997). *The New Rational Manager.* Princeton, NJ: Princeton Research Press.

Phillips, J. J. (2003). *Return on Investment: In Training and Performance Improvement Programs.* San Francisco: Butterworth-Heinemann.

Additional Reading

Barnett, K. and J. Berk (2007). *Human Capital Analytics: Measuring and Improving Learning and Talent Impact.* Tarentum, PA: Word Association Publishers.

Davenport, T. H. and J. G. Harris (2007). *Competing on Analytics: The New Science of Winning.* Boston: Harvard Business School Press.

Fitz-enz, J. (2000). *The ROI of Human Capital: Measuring the Economic Value of Employee Performance.* New York: American Management Association.

Chapter 23

Evaluating mLearning

Cathy A. Stawarski and Robert Gadd

In This Chapter

This chapter focuses on evaluating formal and informal adult learning that is delivered via mobile devices (that is, mlearning) and on adapting traditional training evaluation methodology so that it can be applied to mobile learning. Upon completion of this chapter, you will be able to

- describe common data collection methods used to evaluate instructor-led training and mlearning using the Phillips ROI Methodology

- identify methods that can be used to collect mobile learning evaluation data at Levels 1, 2, and 3

- discuss the rationale for changing the approach at these levels when evaluating mlearning

- recognize variables and issues that evaluators must consider when evaluating mlearning (for example, data collection ethics).

A review of the literature highlights various definitions of mobile learning (mlearning). Many definitions emphasize that the learning occurs using a device that is not tethered to a specific location (Wikipedia, 2009). Authors such as Traxler (2007) prefer to explore definitions of the "underlying learner experience" and how mlearning differs from other forms of education and learning. The focus of this chapter is on evaluating formal and informal adult learning delivered via technology that is easily transported using mobile devices and either used in isolation (that is, pure mlearning), or as part of a blended learning solution. Regardless, the learning was developed in accordance with standard principles of instructional design. Specific learning objectives are expected to be accomplished, application of the learning is expected to occur, and potential for organizational impact exists. The primary goals of evaluation are to improve both training and participant performance.

Transitioning from Classroom to Technology-Enabled Learning

With the advent of technology-enabled learning, training material is now covered in virtual classrooms in less time than it was in traditional classrooms. As classroom training is converted to e-learning, common estimates are that classroom "seat time" is approximately twice as long as that of e-learning (for example, CellCast Solution Guide, 2009). Of course, this estimate can vary, depending on the complexity of the content and level of interactivity. Regardless, when training programs leave the classroom in favor of online learning, more is covered in less seat time. Now, as mlearning becomes more popular, we are finding that training is developed in even smaller chunks of information. Whereas in the past we measured classroom-training time in terms of hours or days, we now measure mobile learning time in terms of minutes. After all, most people's primary use and justification for owning and carrying a mobile device is on-the-go communications (phone calls and email), rather than as a learning appliance.

As mlearning evolves, it is transforming the definitions of training and education. With technological advances, approaches to training are becoming more creative. The popularity of mobile devices enables training developers to create material for learners on the go. Learners and workers are not limited to sitting at a desk. Personalized instruction can be delivered directly to mobile devices. Podcasts can be listened to at the gym, on a train, and in various other locations. Performance support tools, such as checklists, can be viewed and used on mobile devices. GPS coordinates can be accessed on mobile devices, providing opportunities to learn about locations as the learner is on location. With these advances in technology, instructional designers are creating tools and opportunities in such a way that

---

✑ Practitioner Tip ✐

mLearning units of instruction may be as short as two to five minutes.

✐ **Practitioner Tip** ✎

Evaluation techniques must keep pace with evolving definitions of training and education.

---

the concepts of training and education are broadening and the lines between formal and informal learning are blurring. When one incorporates using mobile delivery with Web 2.0 tools and techniques (for example, wikis, blogs, and social media), the use of technology is affecting the learning experience in unseen ways. It is important to use the evaluation results for continuous improvement of the instructional methodology and materials.

Some authors (Vavoula and Sharples, 2009) have discussed the challenges of evaluating mobile learning and have attempted to capture the learning context in their evaluation framework. Sharples (2009) makes the point that mobile learning may be distributed, involving multiple participants in many different locations that offer learning opportunities. But, when they occur in informal settings (for example, museums), we will neither know how learners will engage in the learning activity, nor have specific learning objectives to achieve, making it more difficult to evaluate the learning. Although these are the types of variables that evaluators of mobile learning need to consider in the future, it is not the purpose of this chapter to measure the influence of context, or to compare mlearning to other types of learning formats. The purpose of this chapter is to focus on techniques that can be used to measure the achievement of learning objectives and organizational impact of adult mlearning experiences. The discussion is focused on ways to adapt traditional training evaluation methodology so that it can be applied to mobile learning.

Traditional Training Evaluation Approaches

Kirkpatrick's four levels of evaluation (shown in table 23-1) comprise the most commonly used training evaluation framework (Kirkpatrick, 1998). Level 1, reaction, defines what participants thought of the program materials, instructors, facilities, and content. Level 2, learning, measures the extent to which learning has occurred. Level 3, job behavior, is defined as whether the participant uses what was learned on the job. Level 4, results, measures changes in business results, such as productivity, quality, and costs.

Although Kirkpatrick provided the initial framework for evaluating training and his work continues to be the most widely recognized (Twitchell, Holton, and Trott, 2000), Phillips attempted to move beyond Level 4 in the early 1980s. He redefined Levels 3 (application and implementation) and 4 (impact) to broaden their definitions by including transfer of

Table 23-1. Kirkpatrick's Four-Level Framework

Level	Measures
1. Reaction	Participant reaction to the program
2. Learning	The extent to which participants change attitudes, improve knowledge, and/or increase skills
3. Behavior	The extent to which change in behavior occurs
4. Results	The changes in business results

Source: Kirkpatrick (1998).

learning and outcomes to processes other than training (Phillips, 1995). He also focused on what he called Level 5, return-on-investment (ROI). Phillips' five levels, and common data collection methods used at each level, are shown in table 23-2.

Evaluating Traditional Training versus Evaluating mLearning

With instructor-led training or e-learning, one often uses extensive end-of-course surveys to measure reaction and learning. Tests or other class projects that demonstrate learning are also common. Further, supervisors are often contacted three to six months after training to determine whether learners have applied what they learned in class. Each of these data collection methods is time consuming for the learners and supervisors. When units of instruction become smaller and more numerous, as they are with

Table 23-2. Common Data Collection Methods Using the Phillips ROI Methodology

Level	Common Data Collection Method
1. Reaction	End of course survey, action plans
2. Learning	End of course survey, test, portfolio, facilitator assessment
3. Application and Implementation	Supervisor or participant survey, observation, focus groups, interviews, action plans
4. Impact	Variety of sources
5. ROI	Convert Level 4 data to monetary value using actual costs, extant data, other sources

mlearning, placing significant burden on the learner to provide evaluation data at the end of each unit is not desirable, nor is it appropriate to contact supervisors at the end of each mlearning unit of instruction to obtain feedback on application. Therefore, units either need to be bundled together in such a way that logical evaluation data can be obtained at the end of a bundle of units, or data collection needs to be streamlined at the end of each unit of instruction. One way to consider bundling units is by terminal learning objective.

When mlearning or e-learning units are accessed via the Internet, collecting data without the learner's knowledge is possible. For example, if you wish to know when, or how frequently, a participant accessed a specific learning unit to get a measure of whether the participant perceived the unit to be relevant, a password may be required to access each unit. Learning units (for example, podcasts or iPhone/BlackBerry/Android apps) that will be downloaded to mobile devices can also require a password to be downloaded for use on an individual's own schedule, while using a personal mobile device.

Levels 1 and 2: Traditional versus mLearning

As shown in table 23-2, the traditional methods used for collecting Level 1 data at the end of classroom training are end-of-course surveys and action plans. When collecting reaction data, we often ask the following content-related questions:

- Is the training relevant to your job?
- How much new information was provided?
- Would you recommend the training to others?
- Do you intend to use the information covered in class?
- How important is the information to your job? (Phillips and Phillips, 2007)

Common Level 2 data collection methods include end-of-course survey, test, portfolio, and facilitator assessment. Key questions to be answered at Level 2 include

- Is there evidence of learning?
- Do participants understand what they are supposed to do?
- Do participants understand how they are supposed to do it?
- Are participants confident to apply skills and knowledge learned? (Phillips and Phillips, 2007)

❧ Practitioner Tip ❧

Consider bundling mlearning units based on the targeted objectives.

✎ **Practitioner Tip** ✎

Evaluators should always be cognizant of the potential for survey overload and minimize the burden on participants.

Designing the common data collection instruments and answering surveys, completing portfolios, or taking tests can be fairly labor intensive for evaluators and program participants. As described, at least nine common questions should be answered when evaluating traditional learning at Levels 1 and 2. Imagine how disruptive it would be to include nine or more questions at the end of every mlearning unit to evaluate whether it was effective. Participants could spend more time addressing evaluation questions than going through the mlearning unit itself. Therefore, evaluators need to get creative in their approach to evaluation at Levels 1 and 2, while continuing to keep the goals and objectives of the learning module in mind.

When collecting mlearning reaction data (Level 1) consider asking just two questions:

- Is the training relevant to your job?
- Do you intend to use the information covered in class?

A positive response to these two questions indicates that the learner understands the relationship between the material covered in the class and his or her job responsibilities. Intent to use the information, or planned action, is a good predictor of future application of the information (Phillips and Phillips, 2007). You can either ask these questions directly or consider other ways of measuring reaction. For example, accessing the learning units or job aids multiple times may be considered an indication of perceived relevance.

Data regarding the date, time, and frequency of access can be tracked in a database based on when the password was entered and would not require asking participants any questions. Unless downloaded units contain access information that can be synchronized at the end of a unit and entered into a central database, it will be more difficult to track the frequency of timing of accessing such units, compared with the ease of tracking units that are delivered directly from the Internet. Certain mobile devices (for example, smartphones) that can be used for mlearning do have access to the Internet and can effectively

---

✎ **Practitioner Tip** ✎

Always consider ethical issues when evaluating mlearning.

---

transmit back to the central database usage information regarding each learning unit. Any attempts to track users should be fully disclosed to all learners before any action is taken. As with any good evaluation, evaluators should consider multiple methods of collecting the data they are seeking.

If you are tracking which students access mlearning modules, consider asking those who do not access the module, "Why didn't you access the module?" The answer to this question could give you information about student motivation and potential barriers in the environment.

When collecting mlearning Level 2 data, indicators of learning can be built into the learning unit or provided at the end of the unit. Correct answers to questions asked during or after the unit can be analyzed to determine whether learning is occurring. In addition, consider other methods of collecting data, such as asking participants to explain *how* they are supposed to use the information. Whereas simple multiple-choice responses indicate *recognition* of the correct answer, explaining how to use the information provides an estimate of *comprehension*, a higher level on Bloom's Taxonomy of Educational Objectives. Further, with the common practice of text messaging in today's society, a brief explanation typed into a mobile device will be a minimal burden on students.

As mentioned earlier, to minimize the burden on respondents, it is best to bundle learning modules, for example, based on terminal objectives. The end of an mlearning bundle may be a good opportunity to ask the participants how confident they are to apply the skills and knowledge learned in the bundle. This might also be a good time to provide a short series of quiz questions. Anytime/anywhere content delivery via mlearning also provides an opportunity to package, deliver, and track reinforcement for any concepts learned today and largely forgotten tomorrow, ensuring knowledge gained stays front and center and is reused and reconsidered proactively.

Level 3: Traditional versus mLearning

The key questions typically asked to determine application of learning, Level 3, include

- To what extent do participants apply the knowledge and skills they learned?
- How frequently are participants applying these knowledge and skills?
- What supports participant application of knowledge and skills?
- What barriers are preventing the application of knowledge and skills? (Phillips and Phillips, 2007)

Answers to these Level 3 questions should be collected from individuals who observe the participant's behavior and may include a self-report by the participant him- or herself. When we take these questions and apply them to a mobile learning application, data can be used to quickly customize training and improve performance if the data are collected online and monitored by the instructor.

For example, requiring participants to maintain an online journal or blog, answer regularly scheduled survey questions, or use an online performance support tool accessible on their mobile device can provide real time, or close to real time, application data. An online journal can be submitted as a text message and entered into a database or formatted as a blog. Depending on the specifics of the training, it may be appropriate to require a daily online journal that briefly summarizes application of learning that day and planned actions for the next day. By documenting planned actions for the next day, the participant may consider him- or herself more accountable for application, which may encourage more frequent application of learning. Barriers and enablers to application can be identified early when instructors monitor the journals and verify actual application or lack thereof. This provides an opportunity to intervene in the training program to either improve the overall learning module, or to customize the training pushed out to individuals who are encountering specific challenges. Because the goal of evaluation is to improve training and performance, real-time (daily) data collection and monitoring can provide opportunities to strengthen enablers and remove barriers or otherwise improve training in ways that ultimately improve performance.

If the instructor observes specific participants having challenges applying learning, he or she should ask simple survey questions regarding the barriers and enablers to application. Because text messaging is such a common behavior, responding to simple open-ended questions should provide a minimum burden to respondents. Depending on the length of your program and how long you monitor application, consider sending regular reminders to participants to update blogs or journals, or pushing out regularly timed (for example, weekly or monthly) survey questions.

If you ask supervisors for feedback on how their employees apply what they have learned, keep in mind that supervisors are very busy. Be judicious when deciding on the frequency with which you plan to contact them about their employees' application of learning. At a minimum, bundle questions to supervisors by terminal objectives. Larger bundles may be desirable.

❧ **Practitioner Tip** ❧

Bundle supervisor contacts as much as possible. .

Level 4: Traditional versus mLearning

When examining organizational impact, the key questions to ask are

- To what extent have key measures improved as a result of the program?
- What measure(s) improved the most as a result of the program?
- How do you know it was the program that caused the improvement? (Phillips and Phillips, 2007)

The Level 4 evaluation process for mlearning often will be the same as with traditional training delivery. You will need to review organizational level measures and extant data reflecting measures related to your key business objectives. These measures are likely to reflect indications of increases or decreases in output, productivity, quality, cost, or time. If mobile training includes an electronic performance support system or is otherwise focused on job performance using technology, there may be a way to automatically measure time or output. Consider monitoring those trends over time. Be sure to consider all impact measures, not just those monitored via technology.

How do you know changes in the impact measures were a result of the mlearning program? If you're following the Phillips ROI Methodology, you want to be sure to isolate the effects of the program in the same way you would with more traditional training delivery methods. Examples of common approaches to isolation include

- control/comparison groups
- trend-line analysis
- forecasting methods
- participant and/or manager estimation (Phillips and Phillips, 2007).

The method used to convert impact measures to monetary value is no different if training is delivered via mobile devices. Standard practices include using

- standard values
- participant and/or manager estimates
- historical costs
- internal/external estimates (Phillips and Phillips, 2007).

Level 5: Traditional versus mLearning

The ROI calculation will not change for training delivered via mobile devices. As shown below, calculate the benefits-cost ratio (BCR) by dividing the program benefits by the program costs. The return-on-investment (ROI) is then calculated by dividing the net program benefits by program costs and multiplying the result by 100 (see figure 23-1; Phillips and Phillips, 2007).

Figure 23-1. Phillips' ROI Calculation Formula

$$\text{Benefits-Cost Ratio} = \frac{\text{Program Benefits}}{\text{Program Costs}}$$

$$\text{ROI} = \frac{\text{Net Program Benefits}}{\text{Program Costs}} \times 100$$

Summary

Common training evaluation approaches, for example Kirkpatrick's four levels and Phillips' ROI Methodology, focus on the goals and objectives of the training. The focus of evaluating mlearning also should be on the goals and objectives of the training. Because mlearning units may be delivered in shorter segments than traditional classroom training or e-learning units, different approaches to collecting evaluation data may be warranted at Levels 1, 2, and 3; however, standard approaches to collecting data at Level 4 and calculating ROI are likely to be sufficient when evaluating mlearning. Also, because mlearning modules are delivered via technology, opportunities exist to use the technology to collect data. Timely data collection and monitoring can result in an evaluation system that enables customized individual training programs being delivered via mobile devices, potentially decreasing the time to performance improvement.

✑ Case Application: Sales Quenchers ✑

Sales Quenchers is a sales training organization that provides just-in-time reference materials to organizations. Their Mem-Cards were originally designed in traditional playing card format. The cards distill the core concepts and key techniques of leading sales experts. The Mem-Cards help busy salespeople learn new skills they can apply while selling. Unfortunately, the cards were difficult to update, reprint, and redistribute in their original format. It was also impossible to track who was using the cards. So, Sales Quenchers made the decision to convert the cards to a digital format. By going through this conversion, the Mem-Cards became mobile learning ready, and Sales Quenchers was able to offer a flexible subscription model and deliver its content to customers via cell phone, personal digital assistant, or computer. It also enabled supervisors to create and distribute custom content to their workforce, track completion of assignments, and measure retention of information.

Sales Quenchers used a mobile content and communications platform, CellCast Solution, from OnPoint Digital, to address its requirements. This fully integrated mobile content creation, delivery, and tracking platform supports mobile learning and information delivery initiatives, using essentially any telephone equipped with touchtone dialing. Managers, supervisors, and higher-level administrators can access, review, and analyze the collective results at any time. CellCast call tracking records time and frequency statistics for every interaction.

Level 1

The program was designed to include one or two interactive or open-ended survey questions gathering real-time feedback.

Level 2

Interactive open-ended survey questions are designed to measure knowledge retention. Test and survey questions are answered by pressing specified keys or giving verbal responses on the phone. Learners receive immediate feedback on test scores via email or text message. Managers receive test confirmations and can review scores and hear comments or read transcripts.

Level 3

The system facilitates just-in-time learning with search methods and tools integrated into the portal platform. The use of digital cards is tracked. The system also includes social networking capabilities. Comments can be monitored for evidence of application.

Level 4

Managers have access to call completion rates, best and worst performers, best and worst test scorers, top content contributors, monthly billing reports, and collective survey results and/or responses. This conversion to mobile learning is driving larger and broader sales into both current and new markets and sales channels for Sales Quenchers. Using the system to gain wisdom, insights, and a pep talk from industry-leading experts has translated to accelerated learning and increased sales.

Level 5

Although Sales Quenchers did calculate the cost savings when it converted to the digital format, a full cost-benefit analysis was not performed. Therefore, ROI was not calculated.

Source: Gadd (2008).

Knowledge Check: Designing an mLearning Evaluation Strategy

Now that you have read this chapter, try your hand at designing an evaluation strategy for a mobile learning unit. Check your answers in the appendix.

Flower Meadows is a garden store that has locations nationwide. They sell annuals, perennials, trees, gardening tools, and supplies. Their spring flowers are especially popular in cold climates. Sales have recently dropped more than would have been expected if it were simply due to difficulties in the economy.

Flower Meadows' headquarters has developed training materials that can be accessed on mobile devices used by nursery workers. The suspicion had been that the spring flower sales have fallen due to problems fertilizing and watering flowers in the nursery. The new training materials include instructions regarding scheduling of plant care in various zones throughout the Flower Meadows sales areas. Daily checklists are included in the materials, enabling nursery workers to indicate that each required task has been completed. All nursery workers were required to complete the training at least one week prior to the beginning of the spring planting season in each zone, and to complete checklists each Friday during the spring season in each zone.

Five business objectives were established. The goal was to achieve each of the following objectives during the first two months of the spring season in each zone:

* increase sales of perennials by 10 percent
* decrease the number of annuals that must be discarded due to poor condition (for example, disease, lack of water) by 10 percent
* increase sales of plant fertilizer by 5 percent
* increase the number of repeat customers (defined as customers who buy flowers early in the spring and then return at a later point for additional products) by 8 percent
* maintain a minimum customer satisfaction rating of 92 percent.

One month into the spring season in each zone, supervisors were expected to report interim results to management and make any necessary corrections. At the end of the spring season, supervisors were expected to report final results for the season and recommend whether a similar approach should be taken for the fall season.

Following the steps described in this chapter, how would you evaluate the mlearning taken by the nursery workers? How would you attempt to measure success of each of the business objectives?

About the Authors

Cathy Stawarski, PhD, is the program manager of Strategic Performance Improvement and Evaluation at the Human Resources Research Organization (HumRRO) in Alexandria, Virginia. Her current work is focused on program evaluation, training evaluation, and individual and organizational performance improvement. She is a certified practitioner in the ROI Methodology.

Stawarski is coauthor of "Data Collection: Planning and Collecting All Types of Data" in *Measurement and Evaluation Series: Comprehensive Tools to Measure the Training and Development Function in your Organization* (2008). She has also delivered numerous conference presentations on topics related to training evaluation issues. She can be reached at cstawarski@gmail.com.

Robert Gadd is president and chief mobile officer of OnPoint Digital, a leading supplier of online and mobile learning solutions to enterprise customers. Gadd oversees OnPoint's technology and strategic direction in the design and delivery of diverse learning models and enabling knowledge transfer through e-learning, mlearning, and social-enabled performance portals. He can be contacted at rgadd@onpointlearning.com.

References

Gadd, R. (July 2008). Sales Quenchers Case Study: Delivering Learning Nuggets by Smartphone. *eLearning Guild's Learning Solutions eMagazine*, 1–9.

Kirkpatrick, D. L. (1998). *Evaluating Training Programs: The Four Levels.* San Francisco: Berrett-Koehler.

OnPoint Digital, Inc. (2009). *CellCast Solution Guide.* Savannah, GA: OnPoint Digital, Inc.

Phillips, J. J. (Summer 1995). Corporate Training: Does It Pay Off? *William & Mary Business Review*, 6–10.

Phillips, P. P. and J. J. Phillips. (2007). *The Value of Learning.* San Francisco: Wiley.

Sharples, M. (2009). Methods for Evaluating Mobile Learning. In G. N. Vavoula, N. Pachler, and A. Kukulska-Hulme eds. *Researching Mobile Learning: Frameworks, Tools and Research Designs.* Oxford: Peter Lang Publishing Group, 17–39.

Traxler, J. (2007). Defining, Discussing and Evaluating Mobile Learning: The Moving Finger Writes and Having Writ.... *The International review of research in Open and Distance Learning* 8(2), available at http://www.scribd.com/doc/3115019/Traxler-Defining-Discussing-and-Evaluating-Mobile-Learning.

Twitchell, S., E. F. Holton III, and J. W. Trott Jr. (2000). Technical Training Evaluation Practices in the United States. *Performance Improvement Quarterly* 13(3): 84–110.

Vavoula, G. N. and M. Sharples. (2009). Challenges in Evaluating Mobile Learning: A 3-level Evaluation Framework. *International Journal of Mobile and Blended Learning* 1(2): 54–75.

Wikipedia. (October 24, 2009). *mLearning*, available at http://en.wikipedia.org/wiki/MLearning.

Chapter 24

Evaluating Leadership Development

Emily Hoole and Jennifer Martineau

In This Chapter

This chapter details a case study about a leadership training program for public libraries, the successes of the program, and the methods and processes used to evaluate it. Upon completion of the chapter, you will be able to

- recognize how to design an evaluation that targets behavior change and organizational impact as a result of a leadership development intervention

- identify how to successfully integrate multiple measures and perspectives to build a rich description of the program and triangulate the evaluation data

- become acquainted with how to benchmark programs against best practices in the field of leadership development for program improvement

- recognize how to present results to key stakeholders in a way that is aligned to their needs.

Background

The Executive Leadership Institute (ELI) program is a unique development opportunity provided by the Urban Libraries Council (ULC) and funded by the Institute for Museum and Library Sciences (IMLS) to libraries across the country. ULC contracted with the Center for Creative Leadership's Evaluation Center to conduct an external evaluation on the ELI program.

First, here is a bit about the program itself and the situation that led to the design and implementation of the ELI program. The context in which libraries and library leaders function is changing rapidly due to technological and societal changes. As society changes, so must libraries. For their institutions to remain relevant, library leaders will have to survive in competitive political and economic environments, manage in the context of changing information technology, guide significant organizational restructuring initiatives, and respond to customer and community dynamics.

Urban Libraries Council's ELI program used an action-learning model to help library leaders adapt to the changing environment in which they operate. ELI participants (called fellows in this program) engaged in challenging projects that provided an effective and appropriate practice ground for leadership development over an 11-month period. Twenty fellows engaged in learning lab projects in partnership with a sponsor from their library, three intensive face-to-face sessions, coaching, a national peer community, and reflective practice.

The overarching goals of the ELI program were to

- increase the leadership capacity and diversity of future public library leaders on a national basis
- support an expansive national network of new library leaders
- create opportunities for local library experimentation with new organizational structures and strategies that support leadership development
- create a national model and brand of effective public library leadership development.

Through the evaluation, we concluded that ELI was a powerful developmental and transformational program for individuals who participated. Fellows changed their behavior; experienced increased confidence in their leadership; and significantly shifted their viewpoints, vision, and professional approaches. The libraries that participated also experienced positive and potentially powerful shifts in service provision and strategy. Clearly, the communities these libraries serve are reaping the benefit from the fellow's and library's participation in ELI—through new programs and services, greater efficiency, and a library better connected to the community. The library field will also continue to benefit from the ELI program for years to come as these fellows influence others within their organization and across the field to provide strong leadership for addressing the many challenges libraries face in today's fast-changing society.

Guideline 1: Articulate Outcomes of the Leadership Development Intervention

ULC made it a priority to clearly articulate the outcomes of the intervention at each level because behavior change and organizational impact were desired targets of the program.

Articulating outcomes is critical, and the ideal timing for evaluation planning is alongside the needs assessment and design of the leadership development initiative itself. Integrating evaluation with program design allows for the outcomes of the program to be properly identified so that the program will be designed in a way that is likely to achieve the intended outcomes. Although CCL was not involved with ULC or the program director during the needs assessment and design phases, they articulated the skills areas and competencies for the individual leaders and specified the desired impact on the organizations.

At the point the evaluator is engaged, he or she should work closely with the program's sponsors to understand the program and its goals, outcomes, and objectives before designing an evaluation that will measure the extent to which these are reached. We try to cocreate with stakeholders the objectives for the evaluation itself, as well as the outcomes for the program.

The three primary objectives of the ELI evaluation are

- **Impact.** Provide evidence of leadership development of fellows, institutional changes, and community impact.
- **Benchmarking.** Identify the degree to which ELI makes use of processes, methodologies, and approaches that are considered best practice and/or are supported by the research on formal leadership development programs.
- **Program improvement.** Provide feedback that enables ULC to redesign the program for increased impact.

The evaluation design was based on two common frameworks. The first was Kirkpatrick's four-level model (1998), focused on reaction, behavior change, and impact. The second was Brinkerhoff's Success Case Method (2003), intended to understand the use of program content in relation to the outcomes, identify facilitators and barriers, and further document stories of impact.

In determining whether the ELI program's intended effect was achieved, they identified the following desired outcomes for participating fellows and libraries during the program's design phase (and were therefore assessed through the evaluation):

- increase the leadership capacity of future public libraries. Build skills in political relations, community planning, problem solving, and collaboration. Targeted competencies include
  — understanding the larger context of public libraries in communities
  — working effectively with community partners and leaders
  — working effectively as change agents in complex initiatives
  — having a vision about the future of the public library
- develop an effective learning community and valuable national network of colleagues, specifically relating to peer support and information exchange
- experiment with new library structures and strategies for leadership development within participating libraries
- evaluate learning lab projects for individual learning, organizational restructuring/revitalization, and new ways of connecting with the community
- create a national model and brand for public library leadership development.

Guideline 2: Think in Multiples

When evaluating behavioral and organizational changes, think in multiples. Multiple perspectives and multiple measures can be used to establish the type and magnitude of change to a greater degree than a single assessment of participant perspectives.

The design of the ELI evaluation used multiple methods and gathered multiple perspectives to substantiate the findings. Evaluations that collect data through multiple methods (for example surveys, interviews, reviews of existing project documentation) and from multiple perspectives (for example, program participants, participants' managers, program sponsors, organizational executives) are stronger than evaluations that do not because they are triangulating the data. That is, they are asking questions in multiple ways from multiple people to get the best representation possible of what actually occurred as a result of the program. When the data from multiple methods and multiple perspectives include consistent themes, the evaluators can make statements about the outcomes of the program with more confidence.

This evaluation included the fellows of two cohorts, as well as executives and sponsors related to both cohorts.

The evaluation design included the following components:

- online survey to gather data on behavior change, individual impact, organizational impact, value and usage of program content and components, utilization and value of the peer learning community, and learning lab project from two cohorts of fellows (N=38, response rate of 93 percent)
- online survey of sponsors and library CEO/executive directors for the two cohorts on behavior change, individual impact, organizational impact, learning lab project, and changes to the library's approach to leadership development (N= 36, response rate of 71 percent)
- identification of success cases and fellows who experienced less success:
  — interview fellows (21 interviewed)
  — interview CEO/executive directors and sponsors (eight CEO/executive directors and five sponsors interviewed)
- for benchmarking, review of program materials and interviews with ULC staff and program director.

Data were collected over several months using online survey software (see figure 24-1). Various software can be used—three of the more commonly known and used programs are SurveyMonkey, SurveyGizmo, and Zoomerang.

Through the online survey, fellows provided self-ratings, CEO/executive directors rated one or more fellows (some libraries had fellows in both cohorts), and sponsors rated the fellow they worked with during the intervention. We conducted one-hour telephone interviews with the fellows identified from the survey data and their corresponding CEO/executive directors and sponsors to gain multiple perspectives on the program's effect and relevant organizational and contextual variables.

We analyzed survey data and broke data down into ELI III and ELI IV data (referring to two cohorts). We compared frequencies and averages from the survey across cohorts and raters as well as to frequencies from the interview data. We content analyzed and themed interviews. We supported key evaluation questions by triangulating the data from both the survey and interview data (that is, do the data from both methods support the conclusions that are drawn regarding the answer to the question?).

We examined differences in data at the cohort level from various perspectives. Next, we considered changes in program design from one cohort to the next, along with differences in the composition of each cohort. This helped program staff understand if design changes had the desired effect for the subsequent cohort.

Figure 24-1. Example from Participant Survey

Reflect on your ELI experience and provide a rating of your *current* ability with regard to the following leadership behaviors and then rate how much your ability changed as a result of the ELI program.

Current ability rating scale: No ability, Not much ability, Some ability, Great ability, Very great ability
Changed ability rating scale: No change, A little change, Some change, A lot of change, A great amount of change

1. Lead organizational change: Ability to set direction, manage, and support organizational change.
2. Influence, leadership, power: Ability to inspire and promote a vision; persuade, motivate, and influence others.
3. Manage organizational politics: Ability to understand and negotiate political boundaries.
4. Solve problems and make decisions: Ability to analyze problems, formulate solutions, and make clear decisions.
5. Gather and understand information, identify problems: Ability to seek information, create order out of large quantities of information, and get to the heart of a problem.
6. Take risks, innovate: Ability to see new opportunities and consistently generate new ideas, effectively introduce and create needed changes, and think outside the box.
7. Think systemically: Ability to demonstrate understanding of the whole organization and how to move initiatives forward in that context.
8. Act systemically: Ability to effectively navigate the politics and processes of the organization, establish effective collaborative relationships, and create alliances throughout the organization.
9. Demonstrate openness to influence and flexibility: Ability to invite and consider ideas different from own, accept criticism, and listen with an open mind.
10. Demonstrate adaptability: Ability to adapt to changing community conditions and open to new ideas and methods.

Using the rating scale provided, please indicate the level of change that has occurred as a result of your participation in the ELI program.

Level of change rating scale: Significantly decreased or worsened, Decreased or worsened, Remained about the same, Increased or improved, Significantly increased or improved

My...

- self confidence has
- understanding of my strengths and limits as a leader has
- ability to effectively delegate work has
- ability to effectively manage projects has
- ability to gain the support of colleagues and peers has
- ability to gain the support of my superiors has
- ability to build effective relationships with others has
- ability to meet future leadership challenges has
- appreciation of the value of diverse perspectives has
- openness to feedback has
- vision of success for the leadership project has
- confidence to take risks has
- understanding of the national context of public libraries in communities has

326

- understanding of the context of my public library in my local community has
- ability to work effectively with community partners and leaders has
- ability to work effectively as a change agent in complex initiatives has

Using the rating scale provided, indicate the level of change that occurred in the part of the organization for which you are responsible.

In the part of the organization for which I am responsible...

Level of change rating scale: Significantly decreased or worsened, Decreased or worsened, Remained about the same, Increased or improved, Significantly increased or improved

- employee commitment to the profession of public librarianship has
- employee performance has
- the ability to mobilize people to support a change agenda has
- levels of collaboration have
- communication within the library has
- communication outside the library has
- innovation has
- attitude toward customer service has
- staff ability to work with community stakeholders has
- staff ability to identify the community it serves and make appropriate decisions in how it serves has
- staff ability to promote a culture of inclusiveness and diverse participation has
- staff ability to communicate the library's public value has

Would you consider the leadership project to have been a successful leadership learning experience?

Describe the effect of the leadership project on your library.

Describe the effect of your leadership project on your community.

How did your leadership project result in new ways of working inside the library?

Did the leadership project result in new ways of connecting with your community stakeholders?

If yes, why? It not, why not?

Have you remained in contact with any of your peers from the ELI program?

With how many of your ELI peers do you remain in contact?

Please rate the following statements regarding the peer network you developed as a result of the ELI program:

Rating scale: Strongly Disagree, Disagree, Neither Disagree nor Agree, Agree, Strongly Agree

My ELI fellows provide me with valuable personal support.
My ELI fellows provide me with valuable professional support.
I exchange career advice with my ELI fellows.
I exchange library service-related advice with my ELI fellows.
I exchange leadership advice with my ELI fellows.

(continued on next page)

Figure 24-1. Example from Participant Survey (continued)

How would you rate the value of the following program components to your development as a leader?

Rating scale: Not valuable, Somewhat valuable, Very valuable, Exceptionally valuable

Sponsor
Coaching
Leadership project
Situational assessments
Leadership interviews
Peer learning circles
Audio conferences/conference calls
Virtual community (community zero)
Director-in-residence
CEO/sponsor interview questions

Please rate your use of the content you learned during the ELI program.

	Applied the content— very effective/ helpful	Applied the content— not very effective/ helpful	Have not applied the content but plan to	Have no plans to apply the content	Content is not applicable to my situation
Change management					
Political skills					
FIRO-B					
MBTI					
360 assessment					
Project management					
Reflection					
Priority and time management					
Action learning					

CEO/sponsor interview questions

- How, if at all, do you think the fellow's leadership capacity has increased as a result of participating in the ELI program overall?
- To what extent, if at all, and in what ways has the program affected the fellow's understanding of the larger context of public libraries in communities?

- To what extent, if at all, and in what ways has the program affected the fellow's ability to work effectively as a change agent in complex initiatives?
- To what extent and in what ways has the program affected the fellow's vision about the future of the public library?
- To what extent, if at all, and in what ways has the ELI program affected the fellow's political relations skills?
- To what extent, if at all, and in what ways has the ELI program affected the fellow's community planning skills?
- To what extent, if at all, and in what ways has the ELI program affected the fellow's skills in managing organizational change initiatives?
- To what extent, if at all, and in what ways has the ELI program affected the fellow's problem-solving skills?
- To what extent, if at all, and in what ways has the ELI program affected the fellow's collaboration skills?
- To what extent, if at all, and in what ways has the ELI program affected the fellow's negotiation skills?
- What extent, if at all, has participation in the ELI program helped change or revitalize your library's organizational structure? What do the new structures look like? What realignments have been made, if any?
- To what extent, if at all, has participation in the ELI program helped change or revitalize your library's strategic direction? (New priorities? Shift in priorities?)
- To what extent, if at all, has participation in the ELI program helped change or revitalize your library's ways of conducting business? (Customer service? Service strategy changes?)
- What impact, if any, has the ELI experience had on ways your organization works with community partners?
- What impact, if any, did the leadership initiative have on community relations and/or the ways the library connects with the community?
- What impact, if any, has the change initiative had on your constituencies?
- To what extent, if at all, did the leadership lab *project* raise the library's visibility or credibility in the community?
- To what extent, if at all, has participation in the ELI program changed the ways in which your organization supports leadership development?
- What, if any, new strategies or resources have you put in place to support leadership development?
- How were fellows supported? Have you continued to support their development with new strategies or resources?
- To what extent, if at all, did the leadership lab project assignments contribute to changes in the way that you support leadership?
- To what extent, if at all, has the ELI program affected you, personally, as a leader?
- From your perspective, what are the most effective elements and approaches of ELI?
- Do you have any suggestions for how the ELI program can be improved to increase efficiency of its delivery and implementation? To increase its impact?

Using Technology

We used technology throughout the evaluation process from data collection to analysis. As a primary data collection method, we used online surveys, along with telephone interviews. We recorded the interviews and transcribed them for analysis. Because the quantitative analyses required for this report were not complex, we used a spreadsheet calculator rather than a statistical program.

Guideline 3: Benchmark Against Best Practices

Benchmarking a program against evidenced-based best practices can identify areas of strength and weaknesses for purposes of program improvement and replication.

A key purpose of the evaluation was to compare the ELI program to best practices in leadership development. To what degree does ELI use processes, methodologies, and approaches that are considered best practice and/or are supported by research on formal leader development programs?

To address this question, we first identified 10 elements associated with effective leader development programs. We drew these elements from accumulated knowledge from research and practice at CCL (Center for Creative Leadership, 2008; McCauley and Van Velsor, 2004) and from recent studies examining best practices in leadership development in organizations (American Management Association, 2005; APQC, 1998, 2006; Bersin Associates, 2008; Hewitt Associates, 2005). Next, we sought evidence that these best practice elements were presented in ELI, relying on documents describing the initiative and on interviews with the ELI program director and ULC staff.

The 10 best practice elements we identified are

- clearly articulated program goals linked to business needs
- extra developmental attention and resources for high-potential leaders
- careful selection of participants based on criteria to ensure that the program is a good fit for the participants
- program design that integrates general principles of adult learning and the particular needs of the target audience
- frameworks that provide participants with an understanding of the components of effective leadership (for example, competency models, leadership behaviors)
- reliance on challenging experiences and relationships as major drivers of learning, supported by opportunities for feedback and reflection

- strategies to transfer learning to the back-home context
- accountability for development
- evaluation and continuous improvement of the initiative
- an organizational context that supports the program.

We reviewed ELI's use of best practices within each element and then discussed in the final report. Figure 24-2 presents an example from the final report.

The evaluation determined that the ELI program represents exemplary best practices in five out of the 10 elements, is on par with best practices in three additional elements, and uses some best practices in two elements. The areas in which ELI does not currently represent exemplary best practices use represent opportunities for future improvement in designing or reimagining leadership development for future interventions.

Figure 24-2. Example from ELI's Use of Best Practices Final Report

Element 3: Careful selection of participants based on criteria to ensure that the program is a good fit for the participants.

ULC has articulated the characteristics of an appropriate fellow in its program descriptions and application materials:

- has the potential (within five years) to be part of the library's senior leadership team
- understands challenges faced by today's public libraries
- indicates an interest in learning, personal change, and institutional change
- has experience in/knowledge of basic managerial skills (supervising, budget, planning, etc.)
- has credibility in the institution and enthusiastic backing of the library director
- is willing and able to commit at least two days a week (cumulative over 10 months to work on the leadership challenge).

These characteristics are used by the program advisory team (which is made up of current and retired urban library directors). However, libraries do not just nominate individuals to attend the program; their application includes the project the individual will work on and an internal sponsor for the individual and project. Thus, applications are also judged in terms of the appropriateness of the project and sponsor. Although this can make the selection process more complicated (including the need to coach libraries as they are submitting applications), it does have the potential for creating more organizational support for the program.

Although applications are rated on the fellow characteristics above and on the appropriateness of project and sponsor, there is not a strict reliance on quantitative assessments. Lengthy discussions among advisory team members make use of the in-depth knowledge contained within the group in arriving at a decision through sense-making (rather than strictly analytic) processes.

Guideline 4: Present Results to Key Stakeholders in a Way That Is Aligned to Their Needs

When reporting evaluation results, it is critical to know the audience and their preferences in terms of the type and level of information shared, report format, report length, and so forth. During the needs assessment process, we determined that two audiences for the evaluation results would need different levels of information in their reports. Thus, two written reports were created—a comprehensive report for staff, program designers, and others for lessons learned and program improvement and an executive summary on the results of the program to share with a wider stakeholder group and the general public. Figure 24-3 presents an example of a pie chart that illustrates CEO and sponsor perceptions of the increases they have seen in fellows' abilities since participating in the ELI. It is followed by a brief paragraph noting some of the overall takeaways from this particular set of questions, and then by a series of tables illustrating the open-ended comments relative to the quantitative data.

The report also broke out the data by cohort to understand the different perspectives of each participant group and how their program experience was shaped by the design of the program. This is shown in figure 24-4.

The ELI III cohort found the peer learning circle component of the program more valuable than the ELI IV cohort, who rated the virtual community much higher in terms of value. This outcome can be explained by the way the peer circles were organized in each cohort group and the significant enhancements made to the virtual community prior to ELI IV. Analyzing and presenting the data in this way made it apparent that for all participants the leadership project and coaching were critical program components.

By using various pie charts, bar charts, tables, and text, the report addressed multiple learning needs of the target audience for the evaluation.

How the Results Were Used to Make Decisions about the Program

The results of the evaluation were used to shape what ULC hoped would be the next generation design for library transformation. The ELI program was effective at individual level change for participants and for facilitating increased connection between the library and community through new or improved services and involvement, but it did not have the effect on organizational transformation that ULC believed to be necessary for libraries in the 21st century. The next generation design has a greater organizational focus involving a larger group of individuals for development in transformational efforts.

Figure 24-3. CEO and Sponsor Perceptions of Increases in Fellows' Abilities

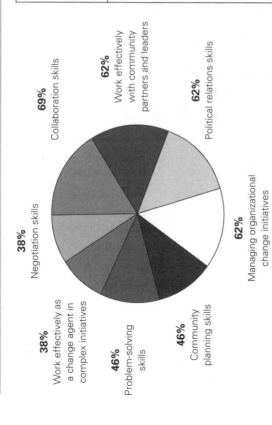

38%
Negotiation skills

69%
Collaboration skills

62%
Work effectively with community partners and leaders

38%
Work effectively as a change agent in complex initiatives

46%
Problem-solving skills

62%
Political relations skills

46%
Community planning skills

62%
Managing organizational change initiatives

The graph above represents the percentage of CEOs/sponsors interviewed who indicated that a skill had increased in the area indicated for one or more fellows as a result of the program.

All of the categories represented in the pie chart are key areas targeted by the program, and fellows and CEOs/sponsors were asked how the program affected the fellow. From the interview data, the areas of greatest skill increases were

• collaboration skills
• working effectively with community partners and leaders
• political relations skills
• managing organizational change initiatives.

Interview Data on the Key Program Outcomes
(21 Fellows, 13 CEOs/Sponsors)

Collaboration Skills

To what extent, if at all, and in what ways has the ELI program affected the fellows/your collaboration skills?

Fellows	CEOs/Sponsors
Increased Skills (16 comments): "Definitely one of the strongest areas that has been worked on both inside and outside the organization. I am not only working outside the organization and with nonprofits, I also started collaborating with other city departments. As a result, I now feel very comfortable calling on the assistance of other departments." **Reinforced Skills** (2 comments): "I've always been pretty good at this, but I learned to collaborate and still move forward on the agenda to be addressed." **No Change** (3 comments): "I've always been a strong collaborator."	**Increased Skills** (9 comments): "Definitely improved. Both were required to work with units outside their regular day work and had to work across departments. What was amazing was that they were able to manage the projects in a way they never had to do before." **Other** (4 comments): "Already very collaborative and her skills may have been enhanced but I think it was always a part of her makeup."

Figure 24-4. Participant Perspective

Value of Program Components: Very Valuable/Exceptionally Valuable

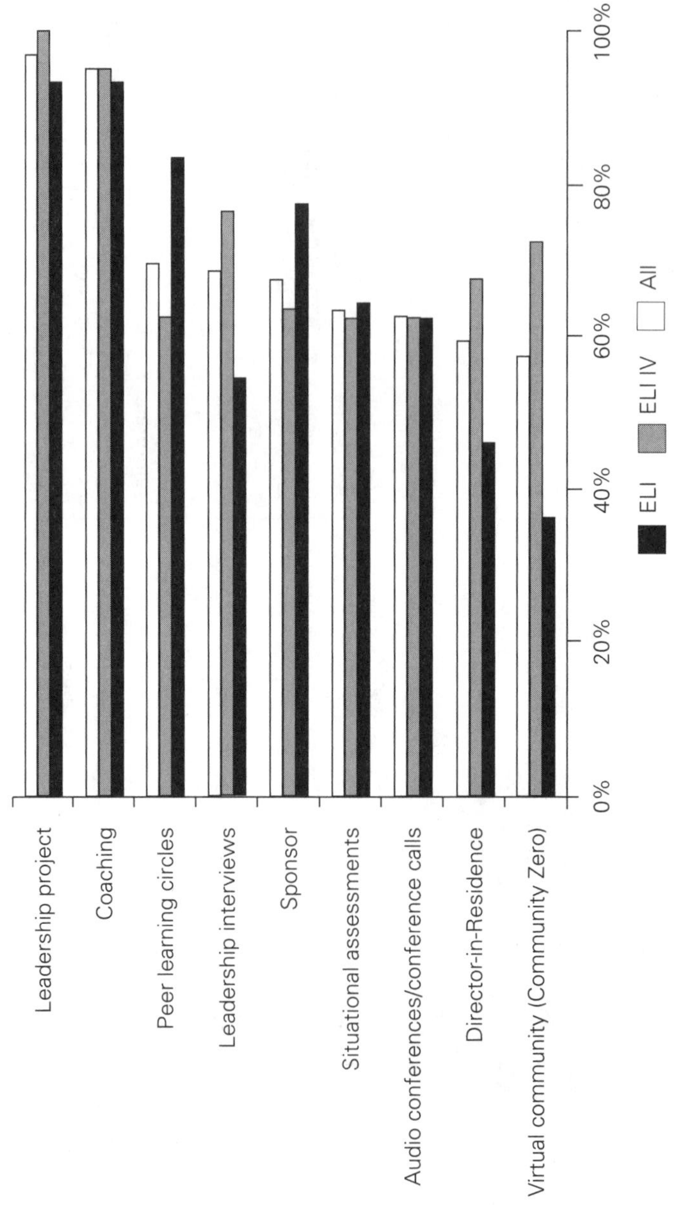

Legend: ■ ELI ▨ ELI IV ☐ All

Knowledge Check

You have been contracted to design and conduct an evaluation of a leadership development program that is in the early stages of needs assessment and planning. This is a program that is being designed by a regional telecommunications company for approximately 50 "critical leaders" in seven different functions. The commonality between them is that they are all responsible for helping the organization expand its product offerings to meet market demand, and none of the leaders are the heads of their function—they all have a vice president to whom they report. There are several key groups of stakeholders: the leaders themselves; the functional vice presidents who are supporting the initiative; the executive team of the company, which includes the president, the seven functional vice presidents, and several executive vice presidents; the talent office, which is responsible for designing and conducting the program; and ultimately the company's board of directors.

What steps would you take to plan the evaluation, including its design, implementation, and reporting phases? What questions do you need to ask of the stakeholders? Check your answers in the appendix.

About the Authors

Emily Hoole, PhD, is the director of the Evaluation Center at the Center of Creative Leadership (CCL). She works on client initiatives, new product development groups, and with internal CCL teams on identifying organizational and leaders' needs, clearly articulating program goals, objectives, and outcomes and evaluating the initiatives for improvement and individual and organizational impact. Prior to CCL, she was the director of evaluation at the Rapides Foundation in central Louisiana. Hoole also served as the executive director of the United Way of Harrisonburg and Rockingham County in Virginia. She holds a doctorate in assessment and measurement from James Madison University. She can be reached at hoolee@ccl.org.

Jennifer Martineau, PhD, is the group director of Global Research, Innovation, and Evaluation at the Center of Creative Leadership (CCL). She is responsible for setting CCL's strategy for these functions in coordination with the current and future needs of clients. She played a foundational role in establishing CCL's Evaluation Center through creating a 360-degree evaluation assessment, designing and launching an evaluation framework used to guide evaluation studies, serving as lead evaluator on many leadership evaluation projects, and hiring talented evaluators. In her evaluation work, her clients include international for-profit and nonprofit organizations, school systems, and governmental agencies. She can be reached at martineauj@ccl.org.

References

American Management Association. (2005). *Leading into the Future: A Global Study to Leadership 2005–2015*. New York: Authors.

APQC. (1998). *Leadership Development: Building Executive Talent*. Houston, TX: Authors.

APQC. (2006). *Leadership Development Strategy: Linking Strategy, Collaborative Learning, and Individual Leaders*. Houston, TX: Authors.

Bersin Associates. (2008). *High-Impact Leadership Development*. Oakland, CA: Authors.

Brinkerhoff, R. O. (2003). *The Success Case Method: Find Out Quickly What's Working and What's Not*. San Francisco: Berrett-Koehler.

Center for Creative Leadership. (2008). *Leadership Development Framework.* Unpublished intranet knowledge asset.

Hewitt Associates. (2005). *Research Highlights: How the Top 20 Companies Grow Leaders*. Lincolnshire, IL: Authors.

Kirkpatrick, D. L. (1998). *Evaluating Training Programs,* 2nd ed. San Francisco: Berrett-Koehler.

McCauley, C. D. and E. Van Velsor. eds. (2004). *The Center for Creative Leadership Handbook of Leadership Development,* 2nd ed. San Francisco: Jossey-Bass.

Additional Resources

Hannum, K. M. and J. W. Martineau. (2008). *Evaluating the Impact of Leadership Development*. San Francisco: Pfeiffer.

Hannum, K. M., J. W. Martineau, and C. Reinelt eds. (2007). *The Handbook of Leadership Development Evaluation*. San Francisco: Jossey-Bass.

Russ-Eft, D. and H. Preskill. (2009). *Evaluation in Organizations: A Systematic Approach to Enhancing Learning, Performance, and Change*. Philadelphia: Perseus.

Chapter 25

Evaluating a Global Sales Training Program

Frank C. Schirmer

In This Chapter

This chapter describes the process and evaluation of a global sales training initiative. After reading this chapter, you will be able to

- describe how one organization measured the impact of a program on declining sales margins

- calculate the ROI in sales training, given the improvement in sales, the profit margin, and the program costs

- summarize results on a simple training scorecard.

Background

The company is a global leader in the field of specialty chemicals. Strong business relationships, a commitment to outstanding service, and wide-ranging application know-how make it a preferred partner to its customers. The company, which is located on five continents, employs more than 20,000 people and in 2006 generated sales of more than $5 billion.

Its innovative products play a key role in its customers' manufacturing and treatment processes or add value to their end products. The company's success is based on the know-how of its employees and their ability to identify new customer needs at an early stage and to work together with customers to develop innovative, efficient solutions.

The margin of this company fell dramatically in the last quarters of 2005 and early 2006. Analysis showed that many of its customers had merged and achieved higher purchasing power (more volume for lower prices). This, however, reflected the whole industry. A margin benchmark in the industry showed a clear weakness in achieving the right margin compared to its key competitor. Therefore, the company launched a training program to turn around its margin erosion. The program included two key elements:

- global pricing software to reflect the cost to serve in the pricing as well as to react to raw material increases more effectively
- initiate an Academy with skill development for value-based selling (VBS) and dealing with negotiations by involving all levels (from CEO to all sales professionals) in all countries.

A German-based consulting organization, LearnVision, conducted the evaluation to control and manage the global development program. It was designed to develop all necessary skills and tools for all levels, as well as to identify barriers and enablers and to demonstrate the success and necessity of a sales effectiveness program. The main focus was to find out whether the program had a positive effect on the organizational margin.

Program Description

This training initiative was developed to establish skills and tools in the work field to link performance improvements with business measures (margin). Value-based selling (VBS) and negotiation was the initial program launched for the newly created Academy. Overall, more than 2,000 participants were trained in modular training sessions across all regions, all divisions, and all sales levels. Roughly 450 sales managers were trained in two- and three-day sales coaching programs, and about 1,700 marketing and sales professionals were trained in two-day VBS and effective negotiation programs. In addition, managers and team leaders received additional coaching tools and specially designed reinforcement tools to enable them to provide their staff with effective support after the training.

The strategy was to train the leaders first and then, about four weeks later, the sales professionals to allow the leaders to position the seminar in advance of the training and use their newly learned coaching tools to improve the commitment and skill application of their staff. The time gap between the two different modules was planned as eight to 10 weeks. Figure 25-1 provides an overview of the concept of value-based selling and pricing—a combination of attitude, communication, tools, and strategic pricing.

Figure 25-1. Value-Based Selling and Pricing

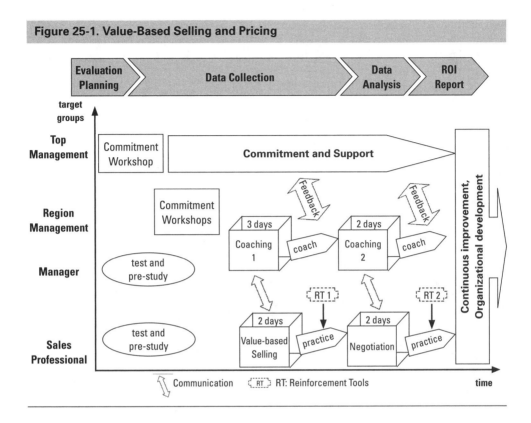

Prior to the training, all participants completed a skill gap test (online questionnaire) to ascertain individual skill gaps concerning VBS and negotiation. All managers gave additional information on their coaching skills. The summary of the analyzed skill gaps for each group, country, and region provided good information for the regional and country-specific implementation. Furthermore, those gaps were included in the global commitment workshop with the CEO and all business leaders and in each regional commitment workshop to enhance support at all management levels globally and locally.

After a pilot training, the global rollout began in January 2007 and continued until March 2008 in more than 28 countries in Europe, North America, Latin America, Asia, and Near East/India, and in seven languages. One success factor was the design of special tools, which are useable in the work field right after the seminar, for the technically minded sales professionals. Figure 25-2 overviews the global rollout timeline.

Parallel to this initiative, the company implemented pricing software to provide consolidated margin data to each sales professional and changed the incentive system from revenue to margin improvements.

Figure 25-2. Global Rollout Timeline

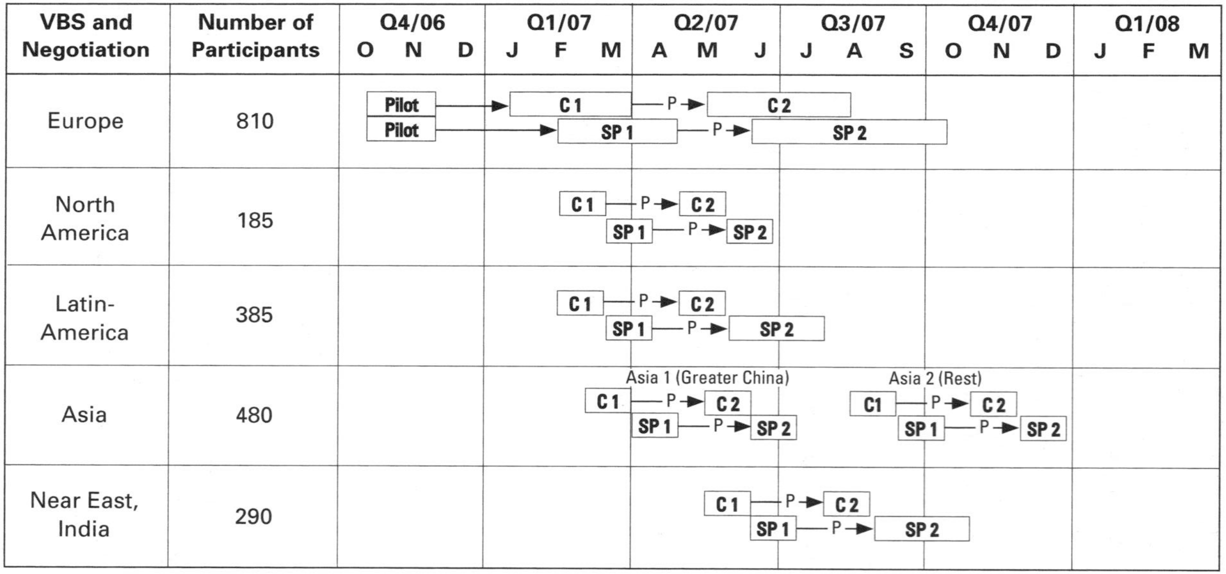

VBS and Negotiation	Number of Participants	Q4/06 O N D	Q1/07 J F M	Q2/07 A M J	Q3/07 J A S	Q4/07 O N D	Q1/08 J F M
Europe	810	Pilot / Pilot	C1 → SP1	P →	C2 → SP2		
North America	185			C1 → P → C2 / SP1 → P → SP2			
Latin-America	385			C1 → P → C2 / SP1 → P → SP2			
Asia	480			Asia 1 (Greater China) C1 → P → C2 / SP1 → P → SP2	Asia 2 (Rest) C1 → P → C2 / SP1 → P → SP2		
Near East, India	290			C1 → P → C2 / SP1 → P →	SP2		

Legend: C 1: Coaching 1; C 2: Coaching 2; SP: Sales Professional; P: Practice Phase

Project Team and Steering Committee

Creating a project team was one key success factor. Members came from each division, human resources, and LearnVision, with the objective to plan and implement the global program effectively to support the marketing and sales strategy. The project team monitored developments using the following phases: evaluation planning, data collection, data analysis, and ROI reporting. They met monthly with management and the steering committee (CEO and major leaders) and issued a monthly progress report to the steering committee so it could monitor barriers and enablers and make decisions for continuous improvement. To be able to support successful implementation, the CEO and his team participated in all seminars.

Content and Design of the Program

The designers initiated a pilot program with a practice phase before the global rollout to save costs and pinpoint program focus. A global team comprised participants from multiple businesses who participated in the pilot session. The outcome was specific tools for the workplace to implement training as a global "living" system. The Bridgetool from the ROI process helped define the exact results-based content and design of the program. The result was that the content was focused and specialized into five days for managers and four days for sales professionals.

The program developers designed a comprehensive prestudy with self-tests and checklists to save seminar time and costs. A cost analysis showed that web-based training sessions were too extensive and provided no extra benefit.

Table 25-1 describes the key content areas and key tools.

A similar practice phase with a measurement system was established after the second module commenced.

One success factor was that all managers received the same key content, tools, and specialized reinforcement tools as the sales professionals, as well as the situational coaching skills to use in the work field. The tools were placed on the intranet for professional use. Another success factor was concentrating on developing the necessary skills for the highest business impact and understanding the whole learning process (before, during, and after) on a global and individual basis.

Business Tools for Highest Impact

Designers created tools to support the implementation of the acquired knowledge in the work field. First the key situation was identified, then special tools for managers, the organization, and sales professionals were designed. The project team set objectives

Table 25-1. Key Content

Target Group	Module 1	Practice	Module 2
Manager, Coach	**Coaching 1: 3 days** • Prestudy upfront as learning tool • Business positioning with commitment tools and test results • Value-Based Selling (VBS) content with profiles to become a solution provider • Coaching content related to VBS with reinforcement tools to be able to develop and challenge the imple-mentation by the sales professionals for the new "coaching culture" • Individual action plan	Learning Transfer, Situational Coaching, Tools, Reinforcement, PAS, DIGL	**Coaching 2: 2 days** • Prestudy upfront as learning tool • Business positioning • Identify the individual and organizational barriers and enablers in the work field and find solutions to overcome the barriers and strengthen the enablers • Negotiation content with 16 negotiation tactics from purchasers and specially designed methodology • Coaching content related to negotiation with reinforce-ment tools to be able to develop and challenge the implementation by the sales professionals • Individual action plan
Sales Professionals, Marketing	**Value-Based Selling: 2 days** • Prestudy upfront as learn-ing tool • Business positioning with commitment tools and test results • Value-Based Selling (VBS) content with profiles to become a solution provider, extended version • Awareness of coaching to understand the managers perspective and develop an effective coaching culture • Individual action plan in conjunction with managers	Learning Transfer, Situational Coaching, PAS, DIGL	**Negotiation: 2 days** • Prestudy upfront as learn-ing tool • Business positioning • Identify the individual and organizational barriers and enablers in the work field and find solutions to overcome the barriers and strengthen the enablers in conjunction with their managers • Negotiation content with 16 negotiation tactics from purchasers and specially designed methodology, extended version • Individual action plan in conjunction with managers

indicating which tool would help under which situation and added them to the intranet. The following tools were designed, positioned, and learned in the seminar and then applied in the work field:

- tools for managers
  - reinforcement using short exercises based on the seminar content for the actual work environment of the employees for better impact in the work place
  - coaching to support the situational applications
  - observer sheets for the skills to be able to change behavior
- tools for the organization, participants, and managers
  - PAS (planning-analysis-strategy) to be used for preparing individual or sales calls/negotiation dialogues
  - DIGL (dialogue guidelines) to be used in front of customers to guide an effective and professional sales call/negotiation dialogue
- product profiles (sales and marketing tool) to be used for quick wins in sales
- action plan with preset objectives related to the key challenges to build the bridge between the training and higher margins (business measures).

ROI Methodology Overview

Building a comprehensive measurement and evaluation process is like a puzzle where the pieces are developed and put in place over time. The ROI model is a step-by-step approach to develop the ROI calculation and the other measures important to stakeholders. Learn-Vision is the only consulting company in Germany with rights to apply this trademarked evaluation process.

Evaluation Levels, Data Types

Various measures report elements of success of a program. The measures are categorized as levels and serve as the framework for evaluation. Measures taken for this evaluation project are categorized as follows:

Level 0: Preprogram test data. To involve all participants and to focus on each individual seminar, a needs analysis tool was provided. The answers from the online questionnaires were sent to the trainers in advance to help them to focus on each individual seminar.

Level 1: Reaction, satisfaction, and planned action. This level measures satisfaction of program participants, along with their intention to apply what they have learned. Almost all organizations evaluate at Level 1, usually with a generic, end-of-program questionnaire.

Although this level of evaluation is important as a participant satisfaction measure, a favorable reaction does not ensure that participants have learned new skills or knowledge.

Level 2: Learning, knowledge. Level 2 focuses on what participants learned (competencies) during the program. A learning test is helpful to ensure that participants have absorbed the content and know how to use it properly. However, a positive result at this level is no guarantee that what has been learned will be applied on the job.

Level 3: Application and implementation. Various follow-up methods are used to determine whether participants apply what they learned on the job. The frequency and use of skills are important measures at Level 3. Although Level 3 evaluation is important to gauge the success of the application of a program, it still does not guarantee that there will be a positive business impact in the organization.

Level 4: Business impact. Focuses on the actual results achieved by program participants as they successfully apply what they have learned. Typical Level 4 measures include output, quality, costs, time, and customer satisfaction. Although the program may produce a measurable business impact, there is still a concern that the program may cost too much.

Level 5: Return-on–investment. The ultimate level of evaluation compares the monetary benefits of the program in relation to the program costs. Although the ROI can be expressed in several ways, it is usually presented as a percentage or benefit-cost ratio. The evaluation chain of impact is not complete until Level 5, ROI evaluation, is developed.

Intangible measures. Although not a different level, intangible measures are the benefits (business impact) directly linked to the training program that cannot or should not be converted to monetary values. These measures are still important in the evaluation process.

Table 25-2 shows the evaluation methods for the program.

ROI Process for Quality Implementation and CIP

The company chose the ROI process as a quality and continuous improvement process (CIP) to be able to monitor implementation and react in time. The ROI process helps to strengthen the result-based approach in the human resources development (HRD) program from the planning stage to the ROI report. It involves all important target groups and gives the necessary information to monitor and steer the implementation for success. Figure 25-3 shows the key steps within the ROI process.

Table 25-2. Evaluation Methods at Each Level

PERFORMANCE	Level of Effectiveness	Aspects to be Evaluated/Controlled	How to Evaluate/Control	QUALITY
	Level 5	ROI (return-on-investment)	Monetary training value to full loaded costs intangibles	
	Level 4	Business impact	Isolate the training effects, convert data to monetary value	
	Level 3	Skill development in the work field, learning transfer	Performance observation from the leaders/trainers, follow-up questionnaire (especially usage of business tools)	
	Level 2	Skill development in the seminar	Competence test: pre- and posttest	
	Level 1	Seminar and trainer acceptance, supposed barriers/enablers	Questionnaires, planned action from the participants	
	Level 0	Involvement and learning gaps	Questionnaire online	

Before the actual content was established, the objectives were defined on all five levels to effectively build the bridge between learning content and business impact. The project team and the chief controller determined a data collection plan and an ROI analysis plan, and the steering committee agreed. These planning documents detail the approach to evaluating the program and are shown in tables 25-3 and 25-4.

To capture all the data from the evaluation levels during implementation, the project team and businesses monitored (mostly online) the specially designed evaluation tools to be able to react accordingly in time on a local and global basis.

Results

The evaluation showed results on the different levels and in different regions and countries. The evaluation tools, their implementation (time and form), and the respective data collection provided early indications to enable instant decisions on improvements.

Figure 25-3. ROI Methodology

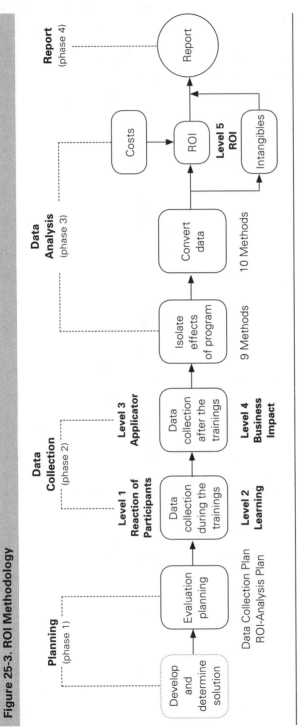

© The ROI Institute, 2009. Used with permission.

Table 25-3. Data Collection Plan

Program: Sales Academy: VBS **Responsibility:** Mr. X, from company **Date:** September 2006

Level	Broad Program Objective(s)	Measures	Data Collection Method/ Instruments	Data Sources	Timing	Responsibilities
1	REACTION/ SATISFACTION • Positive reaction • Action items	**Manager/Sales** • On a scale from 1-6 the average should be greater than 4.6 • 90% of all sales people will fill out the action plans	Online questionnaire	Participants	End of each seminar (time slot 1–7 days)	Trainer ⟶ LearnVision
2	LEARNING • Acquisition of skills • Selection of skills	**Manager/Sales** 90% of the participants have an average of 4.6 (posttraining, scale 1 to 6)	Competence test (pre- and posttest)	Participants	End of each seminar	Trainer ⟶ LearnVision
3	APPLICATION/ IMPLEMENTATION • Use of skills • Frequency of skill use • Identify barriers	**Manager** • 80% of the managers are using the reinforcement tool • All have to identify possible barriers for the sales people	**Manager** • Review	**Manager** • Manager	**Manager** • Next seminar	**Manager** • Trainer ⟶ LearnVision • Top management

(continued on next page)

Table 25-3. Data Collection Plan (continued)

Level	Broad Program Objective(s)	Measures	Data Collection Method/ Instruments	Data Sources	Timing	Responsibilities
3	APPLICATION/ IMPLEMENTATION (continued)	**Sales** • 80% of the sales people use the skills at an average of 4 (scale 1 to 6) • 80% of the sales people use the PAS and DIGL tool	**Sales** • Observer sheet • Action plan review • Online questionnaire	**Sales** • Participants • Participants • Participants	**Sales** • 2 months after seminar during the practice phase 1 and 2 • Next seminar • 10 weeks after seminar 2	**Sales** • Manager → LearnVision • Trainer → LearnVision • LearnVision
4	BUSINESS IMPACT • Margin increase	Delta gross margin per quarter	CPI data from controlling	Business warehouse, SAP	Monthly	Controlling
5	ROI • Gross training margin and fully loaded cost	**Baseline data** Controlling will deliver the baseline data for 2006 (monthly) by end of 2006 and the margin per quarter from Q2/2006 till Q2/2008				

Table 25-4. ROI Analysis Plan

Program: Sales Academy: VBS   **Responsibility:** Mr. X, from company   **Date:** September 2006

Data Items (Usually Level 4)	Method for Isolating the Effects of the Program/ Process	Method of Converting Data to Monetary Values	Cost Categories	Intangible Benefits	Communication Targets for Final Report	Other Influences/ Issues During Application	Comments
Gross margin	Control groups and estimates from experts (benchmark other ROI studies)	Historical data	Fully loaded costs, see separate cost table, for example: • Cost of project team and training costs (external) • Costs of time from participants • Evaluation costs	Will be clarified: job satisfaction, networking, one culture	Communication plan will be set up for continuous communication during the whole process, see separate plan	CPR, organizational effectiveness (new processes) downsizing, STF (strategic task force),including Asia strategy, Reach	Check for baseline data (controlling)

A communication plan for general information and alarm messages listed how to convey intermediate results to the responsible target group. The key information derived from the evaluation and a key driver for initiating the evaluation is the effect of the program on margin.

Business Impact (Level 4)

The business measures were defined and had to be controlled to reflect the ROI analysis plan: average gross margin per month/quarter. The development of the average gross margin was measured 12 months before the training (module 1) and then six months after the training to have comparable data. Figure 25-4 shows the trend-line analysis.

Due to the nature of the business the margin was calculated quarterly, meaning that business development is reflected more precisely. To compare the data, the quarterly gross margin was set in relation to the quarter one year ago. The delta margin was thus given per quarter.

The bold line indicates the trend up until second quarter 2007. The turnaround happened in the third quarter 2007. The gray line indicates the new trend line up until the second quarter 2008. The dotted line indicates the turnaround factor and is set at a conservative level. The delta improvement reflecting the period of the program is 2.8 percent (−2.6 to +0.2).

Isolation Methods for the Program/Training Effects

The original plan to use a country as a control group could not be realized due to the lack of data per participant for a reliable comparison. Although the data from the control group signalled a good training impact (more than 30 percent), it was decided to use another method to isolate the effect for even more conservative data.

Another usually reliable source is to isolate the effect of the program with estimates from experts. The isolation effect was estimated at 35 percent; 65 percent of the impact was estimated to come from other factors (top three: new incentive system, better processes, and increased management attention). The confidence level of 78 percent and the isolation of 35 percent results in a total isolation training effect of 27 percent. In addition, other ROI studies used as a benchmark showed around 30 percent, which confirm the estimates from the experts.

Convert Data to Monetary Value

The data used to convert the isolated program benefit into monetary value came from the controlling department: 1 percent margin improvement equals a benefit of $23 million.

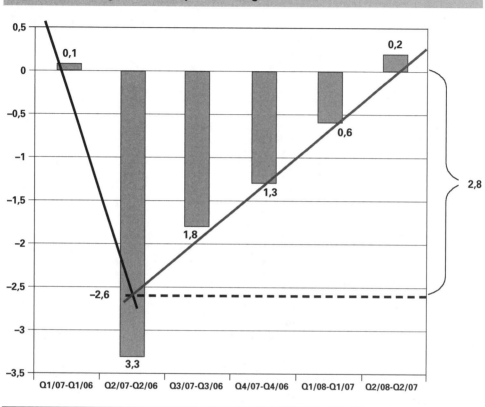

Figure 25-4. Change in Quarterly Gross Margin

Fully Loaded Costs

The fully loaded total costs for the value-based selling project were calculated as $6,672,928.

ROI Calculation

The total training benefits can be calculated as follows:

Total training benefit = 2.8 percent Delta Margin × 0.27 (isolation effect) × $23 million (per Delta percent, converting data) = $17,388 thousand

ROI calculation in percent: [(Total Benefits – Fully loaded costs) ÷ Fully loaded costs] × 100

ROI (VBS) = [($17,388 thousand minus $6,673 thousand) ÷ $6,673 thousand] × 100

ROI (VBS) = 160.6 = 161 percent

Table 25-5. Training Scorecard

Program	Value-based selling (2 days) and negotiation skills (2 days) and coaching (3+2 days), globally (organization development)
Target group	1,700 sales professionals (4 days) and 450 coaches (5 days), global and regional approach
Duration	January 2007 to April 2008
Methods to isolate the training effects	Control group, estimates from experts and benchmark from other ROI studies
Methods to convert the data to monetary value	Historical data from controlling, direct link to delta margin
Program costs (fully loaded)	$6,672,928.00

Results

Level 1: Reaction	Level 2: Learning	Level 3: Application	Level 4: Impact	Level 5: ROI	Intangible Benefits
90 percent of participants planned actions for application in their personal work. The objective "positive reaction" of 4.6 was exceeded by an average of 4.8.	The objective of 4.6 for the competence level was exceeded by reaching almost 5.0.	**Coaches** • Using the Reinforcement Tool: objective 80 percent, result only 30 percent • All have identified barriers **Sales Professionals** • Use of the VBS and negotiation skills: objective 80 percent, result 68 percent	Margin improvement through training: $17,388 thousand	161%	Significant Impact (in percent): • Coaching practice: 73 percent • Sales efficiency: 70 percent • Employee satisfaction: 70 percent

Training Scorecard

The training scorecard shown in table 25-5 provides an overview of the used methods, the defined objectives, and results. This was presented to the management board.

The specially designed content was accepted, and the tools were used in all countries. The Level 1 and 2 implementation were relatively smooth. Some small disturbances were monitored in time and could be solved effectively.

The organization accepted the application of the VBS and negotiation tools for Level 3. This was critical in creating a system based on a result-based approach versus being only a training program. The coaching tools for the manager were not well implemented. The sales professionals stated that their manager only gave situational coaching in 30 percent of cases. The managers said they have given situational coaching but did not get any coaching themselves from their manager (middle manager). The coaching aspect is a critical success factor in every case.

Conclusion and Recommendation

Although the performance of coaching is too low on all levels and in most of the regions, the ROI of 161 percent is still impressive. Looking back from the middle to end of 2008, the major potential tasks for the company are to

- improve the use of coaching during the program (from lip service to unintentional coaching) among all managers, because an organization development initiative would have increased the effectiveness of the program
- enhance the use of the product profiles and link them with the marketing strategy to increase the competence selling solutions more effectively.

It was a pleasure to see how the organization went through this learning process. Managers used the comprehensive data resulting from the training to steer the business more effectively. The first step to develop a global sales behavior system had been taken successfully. The proven connection between training and business impact will help support similar human resources initiatives in the future.

Knowledge Check: Calculate the ROI in Sales Training

Now that you have read this chapter, try your hand at calculating the ROI for a sales training program, given the following data. Check your answer in the appendix.

If

- sales increase an average of $1,750 per week per employee
- profit margin is 2 percent
- 46 employees are involved in the program and the evaluation
- employees work 48 weeks per year
- the cost of the program for all 46 employees is $38,500

What is the ROI?

About the Author

Frank C. Schirmer, Dipl.-Ing., holds a civil engineering degree and is a certified coach and consultant for leadership, team development, sales, service, and quality. For more than 15 years he has supported companies in implementing training solutions including evaluation and ROI, resulting in the application of ROI evaluation to a variety of projects.

Schirmer is managing director of LearnVision and the ROI-Institut, the exclusive implementer of the ROI Methodology in Germany, Austria, and Switzerland. He has published several articles in major magazines around ROI and together with Jack J. Phillips authored the first German ROI book. You can reach him at F.Schirmer@LearnVision.de

~~ **Chapter 26**

Evaluating Technical Training

Toni Hodges DeTuncq

In This Chapter

This case study describes how a basic maintenance course was developed and evaluated. Upon completion of this chapter, you will be able to

▓ develop a plan for conducting an impact study for a technical program

▓ develop an objective map that links learning objectives to performance objectives and performance objectives to business objectives

▓ logically develop conclusions based on the results from an impact study and develop recommendations based on those conclusions.

Background

A large telecommunications company created a basic maintenance course to meet key organizational goals. They developed a task force to flesh out the business, performance, and learning objectives for the design of the course. Representatives from operations, the maintenance field group, the training organization, and an evaluator formed the task force. The goal was to determine what the training organization could do to meet the business and performance objectives and determine what other solutions would be necessary to assist in meeting the goals.

Business Objectives

The operations representative explained that two business areas needed improvement: customer satisfaction and the number of times a residential telephone service call must be repeated due to troubles not being taken care of the first time. In addition, operations wanted to be prepared for an internal audit occurring within the next year. The evaluator asked the operations representative to attach a metric to each of these objectives and record them on an objective map (Hodges, 2002). The evaluator also asked if they expected any barriers within the business, financial, or customer arena, and if enablers could be put into place to mitigate or eliminate the barriers. These were also documented on the map.

Performance Objectives

The field organization looked at the business objectives and brainstormed with the maintainers' supervisors and several successful maintenance personnel for whom the course would be targeted. They listed performance objectives, linked directly to the business objectives, on the objective map. The evaluator asked the field personnel if they expected any barriers within the field operations to interfere with meeting the performance objectives, and if there were enablers that currently existed or could be put into place to mitigate or eliminate the barriers. These also were recorded on the objective map.

Learning Objectives

The training organization then reviewed the performance objectives to begin developing their learning objectives directly linked to each performance objective. They recorded these on the objective map. They also listed any barriers and/or enablers within the training environment and added those to the objective map.

Evaluation

Next up was the evaluation planning. The evaluator worked with the operations representative to determine how to collect the business objective data. This required the operations representative to decide on acceptable standards and delta measures, that is, how much improvement was required or wanted (Levels 4 and 5; Phillips, 2003). They discussed to whom the study reports would be targeted within operations. They worked with the field representative to determine the best approach for gathering performance data (Level 3). The evaluator asked the field representative to whom the communication of the evaluation results would be targeted within the field operations. At this point, they planned the method for isolation and conversion. The evaluator then worked with the training organization to determine how to measure the extent to which the learning objectives were met (Level 2). This completed the objective map for this program; it can be found in figure 26-1. There were some minor revisions made to the map as the design, implementation, and evaluation were conducted, particularly as more enablers were established to mitigate or remove the barriers.

Evaluation Methodology

The evaluators used the organization's standard postcourse satisfaction questionnaire to measure satisfaction (Level 1). The program included a pre-post knowledge-based test to measure most of the learning objectives (Level 2). The test used true/false, multiple-choice, and short-answer questions; as well, the test underwent a content validation to ensure that each of the learning objectives had been addressed in the test (Hodges, 2003). The test was administered as soon as the course began, and an identical test was given after the course was complete. Evaluators reviewed test scores after the posttest completion to reinforce the learning objectives, and then they compared test scores and conducted a t-test to see if there was a statistically significant difference between the pre- and posttest averages. They also analyzed the test questions to determine if certain parts of the course provided lower scores than other parts.

Evaluators also constructed a performance-based test to measure the other learning objectives, which would be used during the in-class scenarios (Level 2). They designed a performance-based checklist and validated its content. In addition, they tested it for inter-rater reliability. This reliability testing is important to ensure that the test would not yield different scores based on the scorer (Shrock and Coscarelli, 2000). Participants reviewed the test before they took it, so they were completely aware of what they would be rated on. This helped them prepare and learn prior to the test and also helped reduce their test anxiety.

Evaluators designed a participant and supervisor online follow-up questionnaire to measure on-the-job performance (Level 3). They piloted the questionnaires and then administered it three months after the course was completed. Participants received a list of the performance objectives and asked to rate on an 11-point scale (0 to 100 percent) the extent to which they believe they or their direct report had been able to successfully complete each behavior. To isolate the effects of the program, they were asked the extent (0 to 100 percent) they believed the result was due to the basic maintenance course. After they completed each of these questions, they were asked how confident they were of these estimates on a 0- to 100-percent scale. They were asked to list barriers that they believed interfered with their ability to use their new skills and the enablers they believed assisted them to use their new skills.

Figure 26-1. Basic Maintenance Course Objective Map

Business Objectives	Metric	Enablers/ Barriers	Performance Objectives	Measurement Methodology	Enablers/ Barriers	Learning Objectives (partial listing)	Measurement Methodology	Enablers/ Barriers
1. Improve customer satisfaction by 50 percent	Customer service index scores	**Barrier:** Service charges increased **Enabler:** Products improved	**1a.** Record customer needs using the customer contact tools	Participant follow-up questionnaire	**Barrier:** Customer contact tools not complete	**1.a.1.** Identify the four main reasons for customer dissatisfaction	Pre-post knowledge-based test	**Barrier:** Not enough classroom time
			1b. Identify intervention during customer calls	Supervisor follow-up questionnaire	**Barrier:** New procedures	**1.a.2.** Identify the eight customer contact tools		
			1c. Check for understanding on each call ensuring the trouble is cleared	**Methods to isolate:** Participant and supervisor estimates and control versus experimental group design	**Enabler:** Job aids to be created	**1.a.3.** Select and apply the appropriate customer contact tools for various customer contact scenarios		
			1d. Suggest products to customers to meet their needs on each call			**1.b.1.** Using the company's troubleshooting process to identify a strategy to locate the fault in a customer's line		
			1d. Close calls using the maintenance field procedures					
			1e. Determine callback procedures					

Business Objectives	Metric	Enablers/ Barriers	Performance Objectives	Measurement Methodology	Enablers/ Barriers	Learning Objectives (partial listing)	Measurement Methodology	Enablers/ Barriers
1. Improve customer satisfaction by 50 percent (continued)						**1.b.2.** Identify the symptoms of residential troubles and common tests required locating these troubles		
						1.c.1. Identify the steps required to communicate with the customer during the process of clearing the trouble		
						1.d.1. Define the classes of service		
						1.d.2. Describe the various optional services (customer calling features)		
						1.d.3. Provide information on maintenance service plans		

(continued on next page)

Figure 26-1. Basic Maintenance Course Objective Map (continued)

Business Objectives	Metric	Enablers/ Barriers	Performance Objectives	Measurement Methodology	Enablers/ Barriers	Learning Objectives (partial listing)	Measurement Methodology	Enablers/ Barriers
1. Improve customer satisfaction by 50 percent (continued)						1.e.1. Describe customer contact, closeout, and callback procedures.		
2. Reduce repeat calls by 25 percent	Cost savings of repeat calls	Barrier: None Enabler: Purchase new technology system	2a. Use correct tools for various maintenance work operations 2b. Inspect tools for replacement or repair each week	Participant follow-up questionnaire Supervisor follow-up questionnaire	Barrier: Lack of supervisor coaching Enabler: Job aid to be created	2.a.1. Identify the basic hand/power tools and materials essential to the performance of various maintenance work operations.	Pre-post knowledge-based test	Enabler: Real-life scenarios for performance based test
			2c. Use the correct tools for required procedure(s) 2d. Complete the maintenance procedure using the correct procedure manual			2.a.2. Describe the proper usage and application of basic/ power tools while completing various maintenance work activities.	Performance-based test using performance-based checklist	

Business Objectives	Metric	Enablers/ Barriers	Performance Objectives	Measurement Methodology	Enablers/ Barriers	Learning Objectives (partial listing)	Measurement Methodology	Enablers/ Barriers
2. Reduce repeat calls by 25 percent (continued)			**2e.** Isolate, diagnose, and repair customer troubles given trouble tickets/ maintenance work requests			**2.b.1.** Correctly inspect basic hand/power tools and determine when to replace or request repair of any faulty tools uncovered		
						2.c.1 (see 2.b.1)		
						2.d.1. Identify common meters and their controls		
						2.d.2. Correctly read meter displays		
						2.d.3. Perform a series of simulated tests to identify, isolate, and locate faults, etc.		

(continued on next page)

Figure 26-1. Basic Maintenance Course Objective Map (continued)

Business Objectives	Metric	Enablers/ Barriers	Performance Objectives	Measurement Methodology	Enablers/ Barriers	Learning Objectives (partial listing)	Measurement Methodology	Enablers/ Barriers
2. Reduce repeat calls by 25 percent (continued)						**2.e.1.** Demonstrate their ability to isolate, diagnose, and repair customer troubles given trouble ticket/ maintenance work requests and appropriate tools.		
3. Improve internal audit scores for maintenance department by 40 points or receive honorary mention award	Audit scores/ award	None	**3a.** Complete all trouble reports thoroughly	Review of reports.	**Barrier:** Workload	**3.a.1.** Explain the importance of a properly completed trouble report.	Pre-post knowledge-based test	None
			3b. Properly code time reports	Follow-up questionnaire with supervisors	**Barrier:** Complexity of reports	**3.a.2.** Describe what comprises the different parts of a trouble report	Performance-based test using performance-based checklist	
			3c. Report all customer dissatisfactions and actions taken to resolve them		**Enabler:** None	**3.b.1.** Properly code a trouble report given various scenarios		

Business Objectives	Metric	Enablers/ Barriers	Performance Objectives	Measurement Methodology	Enablers/ Barriers	Learning Objectives (partial listing)	Measurement Methodology	Enablers/ Barriers
3. Improve internal audit scores for maintenance department by 40 points or receive honorary mention award (continued)			**3d.** Conduct all maintenance procedures in accordance with company's quality standards			**3.c.1.** Given a customer dissatisfaction example, list the different parts of a customer dissatisfaction report		
						3.c.2. Complete a customer dissatisfaction report		
						3.d.1. List the different company's quality standards		
						3.d.2. Demonstrate an understanding of the maintenance quality standards.		

Evaluators used the customer satisfaction index to compare the scores before and after the course for the participants. They also compared after scores to those of a control group (maintainers who had similar attributes but who had not attended the class yet), and tracked and compared the difference in the repeat calls before and three months after the course. The repeat calls of the participants were also compared to those of the control group. The values of the repeat calls were easily converted because the company had an amount associated for each call required. Finally, evaluators reviewed the internal audit scores to see if they were deemed good by operations. Naturally, an honorary mention was hoped for because none had been achieved to date.

Results

Level 1. The course satisfaction questionnaire yielded a 4.2 average (on a 5.0 scale). This exceeded the overall average of 3.8 from all courses.

Level 2. There was a significant difference between the pre-test scores (40-percent average) and the posttest scores (85-percent average) on the knowledge-based test. The range between each was 30 percent and 15 percent respectively. The average score on the performance-based test was 72 percent. However, there was one single score that was different than the rest (an outlier)—45 percent—and it was removed so as to more accurately reflect how the class did as a whole. When the outlier was removed, the average was 82 percent.

Level 3. Evaluators conducted the following mathematics for each of the questions regarding the performances on the follow-up participant and supervisor questionnaires.

> The percent the performance was rated × the percent to which they attributed the performance rating on the course × the confidence rating performance.

> Example: Performance rating (80 percent) × the isolation (60 percent) × the confidence rating (65 percent) = 31 percent

This final rating was then averaged among the different performances. Table 26-1 provides the compilation of the average performance ratings.

All but one of the performances had similar ratings, as seen in table 26-1. The analysis of the individual participant ratings did not find any significant differences among the performances or the participants. Table 26-2 provides the average performance ratings provided by the supervisors.

As shown in table 26-2, there were little differences between the participant ratings and those of the supervisors.

Table 26-1. Average Performance Ratings by Participants

Performance	Performance Rating	Isolation Rating	Confidence Rating	Adjusted Rating
Record customer needs using the customer contact tools	85	80	60	**41%**
Identify intervention during customer calls	90	85	45	**34%**
Check for understanding on each call ensuring the trouble is cleared	84	90	80	**60%**
Suggest products to customers to meet their needs on each call	78	90	75	**53%**
Close calls using the maintenance field procedures	88	90	100	**79%**
Determine callback procedures	85	84	80	**57%**
Use correct tools for various maintenance work operations	90	50	80	**36%**
Inspect tools for replacement or repair each week	95	40	50	**19%**
Use the correct tools for required procedure(s)	65	80	75	**39%**
Complete the maintenance procedure using the correct procedure manual	75	88	80	**53%**
Isolate, diagnose, and repair customer troubles given trouble tickets/maintenance work requests	64	95	85	**52%**
Complete all trouble reports thoroughly	82	75	80	**49%**
Properly code time reports	88	90	90	**71%**
Report all customer dissatisfactions and actions taken to resolve them	75	65	100	**49%**
Conduct all maintenance procedures in accordance with company's quality standards	90	90	90	**90%**
Averages	**82%**	**79%**	**78%**	**52%**

Table 26-2. Average Performance Ratings by Supervisors

Performance	Performance Rating	Isolation Rating	Confidence Rating	Adjusted Rating
Record customer needs using the customer contact tools	80	70	75	**42%**
Identify intervention during customer calls	85	85	40	**29%**
Check for understanding on each call ensuring the trouble is cleared	80	80	80	**51%**
Suggest products to customers to meet their needs on each call	75	90	75	**51%**
Close calls using the maintenance field procedures	80	80	90	**58%**
Determine callback procedures	90	85	90	**69%**
Use correct tools for various maintenance work operations	85	40	90	**31%**
Inspect tools for replacement or repair each week	90	30	60	**16%**
Use the correct tools for required procedure(s)	60	75	80	**36%**
Complete the maintenance procedure using the correct procedure manual	75	80	80	**48%**
Isolate, diagnose, and repair customer troubles given trouble tickets/maintenance work requests	75	95	75	**53%**
Complete all trouble reports thoroughly	75	70	80	**42%**
Properly code time reports	85	85	95	**69%**
Report all customer dissatisfactions and actions taken to resolve them	75	50	90	**34%**
Conduct all maintenance procedures in accordance with company's quality standards	85	85	90	**65%**
Averages	**80%**	**73%**	**79%**	**46%**

Barriers and Enablers. The barrier noted most often by the participants was unavailability of tools needed to complete the job. The enablers noted most often by the participants were the training and peer coaching.

Level 4. The two comparisons for the customer service index scores can be found in table 26-3.

Although the difference in the before and after scores for the participant group was not significant, there *was* a difference with their scores where there was no movement in the control group. Although the difference between the participant and control group reviewed after the participants attended the course was not significant, there was a difference.

The internal audit conducted for the maintenance department three months after the training showed a 25-point improvement from the previous audit one year ago. But after reviewing the results of the postcourse questionnaire used for the basic maintenance course impact study (Level 3), the group received its first honorary mention. The maintenance department was cited for "being accountable for performance and taking steps that produced notable improvement in performance."

The customer service improvement and the internal audit scores and honorary mention were benefits that could not be converted to a monetary value and are therefore considered intangible benefits of the basic maintenance course.

The monetary value of each repeat call (the organizations' standard) was $135.60 each, which reflected the combined loaded hourly rate for the maintenance administrator and the technician and the average time it takes to complete the call. The two comparisons for the participant and the control group, as well as the before and after group, can be found in table 26-4.

These results not only show that both the participant and control groups had similar repeat reports before the training (which made them good comparison groups), but that the control group reports before and after were similar. The control versus experimental

Table 26-3. Customer Service Index Score Comparisons

Customer Service Index Scores	Before	After
Participant group average (n=40)	60 points	80 points
Control group average (n=35)	65 points	69 points

Table 26-4. Repeat Call Number Comparisons

Repeat Call Number	Before	After (three months)
Participant total number (n=40)	52	18
Control group number (n=35)	58	50

(participant) group was used for the isolation, so the difference between the participant and control group after (32) was used for the ROI calculation. This showed a cost savings of 32 × \$135.60 or \$4,339.20. Because the organization did not want to wait an entire year to get the results of the study, they wanted to assume the same amount would be seen in each subsequent quarter, or \$4,339.20 × 4 = \$17,356.80, for an annual savings for this group of 40. The control group and an additional 40 maintainers are expected to complete the course before the next year is out, so the savings represents one-third of the total population. The task force believed they can expect to see a \$52,070 annual savings from the entire group. These savings are the tangible benefits of the program and were used for the ROI calculation.

Level 5. Evaluators amortized the needs assessment (the objective mapping), design, and delivery of the course and the evaluation to determine the costs of the program. The time for the 115 participants spent or to be spent in the program with the facility and computer costs was added, totaling \$40,405. The ROI and benefit-cost ratio (BCR) calculations were as follows:

$$\text{ROI} = \frac{\$52,070 - \$40,405}{\$40,405} = .288 \times 100 = 29 \text{ percent}$$

$$\text{BCR} = \frac{\$52,070}{\$40,405} = 1.288{:}1$$

Conclusions and Recommendations

The task force that was put together to develop the objective map was once again convened to look at the results of the study. The evaluator explained the results to the group and answered questions to clarify where needed. Together they developed a logic map to develop conclusions based on the results and recommendations (Hodges, 2002). Table 26-5 provides the logic map for the basic maintenance course impact study.

Table 26-5. Basic Maintenance Course Impact Study Logic Map

Results	Conclusions	Recommendations
1. The course yielded an average 4.2 out of 5.0 satisfaction rating on the Level 1 instrument.	The participants were satisfied with the course.	
2. A significant difference was found between the pre- and posttest scores with an average post test score of 85 percent.	There was a learning gain.	
3. The performance-based test yielded an adjusted rating of 82 percent.	There was an acceptable demonstration of skills during the training.	
4. Participants estimated an overall adjusted rating of 52-percent improvement in performance on the job.	The participants believed their job performance had improved as a result of the course.	
5. Supervisors estimated an overall adjusted rating of 46-percent improvement in performance on the job.	The supervisors believed their direct reports' job performance had improved as a result of the course.	
6. "Inspecting tools for replacement or repair each week" was rated the lowest by each group (19 percent/16 percent).	Lack of available tools was rated at the single largest barrier on the job and could have caused this rating.	
7. "Use correct tools for various maintenance work operations" was rated the second lowest by each group (36 percent by both).	Lack of available tools appears to have had an effect here as well.	An inventory of available tools must be made and shortfalls taken care of.
8. There was a 20 point score difference in the customer service index score for the participants before and after the training, while the control group showed an 8-point drop.	There was approximately a 33-percent improvement in customer satisfaction as a result of the course, falling short of the 50-percent improvement goal.	

(continued on next page)

Table 26-5. Basic Maintenance Course Impact Study Logic Map (continued)

Results	Conclusions	Recommendations
9. The maintenance department received an honorary mention from the internal audit review, which noted the Basic Maintenance course as an example of accountability and improvement.	An honorable mention was achieved despite not achieving the goal of a 40-point improvement in internal audit scores.	
10. There were 34 fewer repeat calls by the participant group after the training, whereas there were eight fewer calls by the control group.	There was a 65-percent reduction in repeat calls, surpassing the 25-percent improvement goal.	
11. A 29-percent ROI and a 1.29:1 BCR were calculated for this course.	A positive ROI and BCR were achieved.	This course as designed and implemented should be continued. The results of this study should be used to advertise the course offering and the course should be used as a model for other course designs and impact studies.

Communication of Findings

An executive briefing was conducted with the organizations' human resource and operations vice presidents, along with representatives from the financial and training organizations. A complete report was distributed to the participants of the impact study and the results were published in the organizations' monthly newsletter.

Summary

This technical training program yielded a 29-percent ROI, based on a reduction in repeat calls, that is, customer service calls that were unnecessary because calls were misdiagnosed by the maintainers. It also improved customer satisfaction. Based on these results and the fact that the program was evaluated for impact, the operations unit responsible for this program received an improved internal audit score, as well as its first honorary mention.

Knowledge Check

Answer the following questions and check your answers in the appendix.

1. Who should be the stakeholders to develop an objective map for a program and when should the map be initially developed?
2. What was the method(s) to isolate the effect of the program in this study?
3. In this study, the participants and the supervisors were asked the extent to which the performance objectives were met, how much of that success was due to the training, and how confident they were of their ratings. Is it important that the ratings from the participants and the supervisors be the same or similar? Why or why not?
4. Do you believe the recommendations made by the task force were warranted?

About the Author

Toni Hodges DeTuncq is principal of THD & Company. For the past 20 years, she has concentrated on measuring and managing human performance and has conducted and managed operational, systems, and group evaluations for corporate, defense contracting, and government organizations. Her work has included developing individual assessment tools, as well as large organizational tracking tools, all aimed at measuring the performance and monetary value of human resource and systems intervention programs. She currently provides consulting services, which help organizations establish accountable and effective training and evaluation programs, and provides skill enhancement workshops. She has conducted more than 50 impact assessments for organizations such as Bell Atlantic, Verizon Communications, BMW Manufacturing, and more. She has developed system-wide evaluation programs for Bank of America, National Aeronautics and Space Administration (NASA) Goddard Space Flight Center, and Scotiabank, Canada.

DeTuncq was selected as one of nine "Training's New Guard–2001" by ASTD, and was featured in the May 2001 issue of the *T+D* magazine. In 2000, the ROI Network named her "Practitioner of the Year." She has published numerous articles, was the editor of the best selling ASTD In Action series *Measuring Learning and Performance,* and is author of *Linking Learning and Performance: A Practical Guide to Measuring Learning and On-the-Job Application,* and coauthor of *Make Training Evaluation Work.* She can be reached at toni@ thdandco.com.

References

Hodges, T. K. (2002). *Linking Learning and Performance*. Amsterdam: Butterworth Heinmann.

Phillips, J. J. (2003). *Return on Investment in Training and Performance Improvement Programs,* 2nd ed. Amsterdam: Butterworth Heinmann.

Shrock, S. A. and W. C. Coscarelli. (2000). *Criterion-Referenced Test Development: Technical and Legal Guidelines for Corporate Training and Certification.* Washington, DC: International Society for Performance Improvement.

 **Chapter 27**

Evaluating Traditional Training versus Computer Simulation Training for Leader Development

Alice C. Stewart and Jacqueline A. Williams

In This Chapter

Traditional training practices may be adequate for acquiring knowledge regarding leadership, but simulation training may be more useful in helping individuals practice skills and receive feedback. Upon completion of this chapter, you will be able to

- explain why computer game-based simulations are powerful learning tools

- describe the leadership model described in the *VLeader2007* computer simulation

- demonstrate how two training approaches can be compared to determine effectiveness

- use a template for analysis of pre- and posttraining evaluation.

Introduction

The increasingly organic and networked organizations of the 21st century have created a pressing need to develop leadership and decision-making skills throughout the organizational structure. In this case we grapple with the challenge of developing leadership skills and demonstrate how to compare traditional case-based training with computer game-based simulation training. This case examines these two training approaches to determine the effect on participant learning. One training approach is grounded in traditional methods. The traditional method uses lecture, self-assessment, case analysis, and facilitated discussion. The second approach used only a computer game-based experiential simulation, the *VL2007*, supplemented by facilitated discussion of the experience.

VL2007: A Computer Game-Based Simulation for Leader Development

Clark Aldrich (2004) describes the development of such a simulation for the business organizational context in his book *Simulations and the Future of Learning: An Innovative (and Perhaps Revolutionary) Approach to e-Learning*. The algorithm underlying *VL2007* was developed inductively through interviews with practicing managers. The resulting model used in *VLeader2007* is based on three dimensions predictive of successful leadership and one outcome variable. The three leadership dimensions are power, tension, and ideas. The outcome variable is task accomplishment or work. The purpose of the simulation is to provide an opportunity for an individual to play the role of manager in the context of a meeting. The player must identify and promote ideas present in the organization that will accomplish the right work and to prevent the wrong work from being done.

The level of sophistication of this simulation allows the participant to have conversations around various ideas that emerge during meetings. The goal of the simulation is for the participant to experience interactions with others in the organization in such a way as to practice conversations (ways of speaking, reacting, and deciding) that are productive in promoting the manager's goals for the meeting. Part of the value of the simulation is its real-life aspect. The simulated workers stand, sit, gesture, and speak while engaged around a table in a conference room. At the end of the meeting the participant finds out how effective he or she was and what these simulated coworkers say about the participant manager subsequent to the meeting. Thus the participant is able to determine the effect of his or her actions and make changes in his or her behavior to become more effective as he or she continues playing the game.

The simulation has five levels. At the lowest level of the game, the participant is in the position of having the highest amount of formal authority among those in a meeting. As the participant engages in conversations at higher levels of the game, his or her formal authority relative to the simulated people in the meeting is reduced, thus requiring even more skill in communication, creative problem solving, and negotiation to achieve support for his or her ideas. At the initial levels of the game, the participant has substantial position power and can require compliance if desired. As the participant obtains skills and goes up levels within the simulation, his or her position power decreases. At the highest level the player has the lowest position power in the room, thus the player must rely on interpersonal skills and a strategic viewpoint to influence the simulated superiors in the room and to obtain desired outcomes. Assessment data are also designed into this simulation. Each meeting at each level is evaluated based on actions, decisions, and dialogue, and leadership potential scores are assigned.

Comparing the Two Training Approaches

Our goal was to test the effect of two training approaches (traditional and simulation) on the participant's cognitive learning about leadership and developing leadership skills. If the conceptual content of both training programs is the same, we would expect that the two participant groups would exhibit similar cognitive learning. We also considered that there may be differences in the magnitude of learning that occurs in the two training approaches. The traditional way of training may result in cognitive understanding that is clearer and more integrated. The trainees using the *VL2007* software may depend on their experiences and reflections in the game and less on guidance from the trainer to draw conclusions about leader behavior. Finally, we wanted to see which training method seemed to have a greater effect on training transfer by examining perceived leader effectiveness of the participants after the training program had concluded.

Training Evaluation Research Method

To determine the effect of the two training approaches, the evaluation of training proceeded in two phases. In the first phase, the participants were trained using either the traditional training or the simulation training. Data were collected before and after the training to determine participants' perceptions of ideal leader behavior. In the second phase, approximately 10 weeks after the completion of the training intervention, participants engaged in a complex role play in-basket exercise where they were encouraged to apply what they had learned from the training. We collected and analyzed data on leader effectiveness. The participants were a sample of 38 undergraduate honors students enrolled in a two-day leadership training program.

The Training

Faculty trainers developed a traditional training program that emphasized the same concepts as the algorithm of the *VL2007*. The traditional program consisted of readings, PowerPoint presentations, case tools, and discussion questions. The *VL2007* training was individual play on computers in a classroom with facilitated discussion at various intervals. Both groups received the same one-hour introductory lecture. Both groups received 12 hours of training.

Evaluating the Impact of the Training: Data Collection

Each participant in both groups completed one assessment instrument prior to the training and three assessment instruments after the training. The pre- and posttraining assessment was the Ideal Leader Behavior Description Questionnaire XII (Stodgill, 1974). We used this instrument because it captures information about the participant's perceptions of how leaders behave. In addition, participants completed a learning assessment at the end of the training to determine the participant's perception of their learning. Finally, all participants completed a program evaluation instrument to determine that both groups' experiences were equally satisfactory. Including the program evaluation assures that the training itself is responsible for measured differences in cognition and behavior rather that differences that are the result of the quality of the training implementation itself.

Measurement of Training Outcomes

A key factor in understanding the impact of a training initiative is measurement of training outcomes. Particularly important is extending measurement beyond participants' experience to include changes in cognition.

Program Evaluation

The program evaluation instrument measured the participants' satisfaction with their training program. It included 14 items and responses used a 5-point scale, in which 5 represented "excellent" and 1 represented "inadequate."

Learning Assessment

Participants in both groups were asked the same questions regarding their perceived learning of the concepts covered in the training. For each of 16 items, participants were asked about the adequacy of coverage using a 3-point scale. Also for each of the 16 items, participants were asked to rate their level of learning on a 5-point scale ranging from 5, which represented "substantial increase in understanding" to 1, which represented "no increase in understanding at all."

Change in Cognitive Understanding of Leadership

The change in the leadership schema of the participants was measured using the LBDQ=XII (Stodgill, 1974). The LBDQ is a 100-item instrument with a 5-point Likert scale that asks the respondent to "describe the behavior of a managerial leader as you think he or she should act, the ideal managerial leader." This measure was calculated using the pre- and posttraining responses to LBDQ. Data from each LBDQ factor on the pretraining questionnaire was subtracted from the response on the posttraining questionnaire. Negative numbers indicated that the respondent was more likely to agree with the item statement after training. Positive numbers indicated that the individual was more likely to disagree with the item statement after training. A result of zero indicated that the respondent had not changed their response to the item statement as a result of the training.

Analysis of Data and Results of Training

We examined the learning assessment and the program evaluation completed by the participants at the end of the training. Scores on the program evaluation were examined to determine if both training groups had a similar experience. Table 27-1 shows the means for each item. There were no statistically significant differences in participant satisfaction across the two groups.

We examined the scores for each item in the learning assessment to determine if both groups had a similar perception of topic coverage and actual learning. Table 27-2 shows the means for each item associated with perception of coverage and perception of learning.

Table 27-1. Program Evaluation Results

	Mean	
	n=17	n=17
Program Evaluation	**Traditional**	**Simulation**
Topics covered	4.53	4.65
Visual aids in the classroom	4.53	4.55
Length of the program	4.53	4.55
Physical facilities	3.41	3.60
Quality of instruction	4.53	4.60
Quality of food and beverages	4.65	4.60
Interaction among participants	3.88	4.10
Materials and handouts	4.06	4.30
Professionalism of the faculty and staff	4.94	4.90
The use of technology in this course	4.88	4.80

Table 27-2. Self-Reported Learning Assessment

Learning Assessment	Coverage Mean		Learning Mean	
	Traditional	Simulation	Traditional	Simulation
	n=17	n=17	n=21	n=21
1. Making tradeoffs between the uses of power, tension, ideas, and work.	2.82	2.81	4.24	4.14
2. Understanding and using tactics to uncover ideas.	2.65	2.71	3.88	4.24
3. Understanding and using tactics for handling tension or conflict.	2.82	2.67	4.29	4.19
4. Understanding the need for listening and sharing power with others.	2.76	2.86	4.24	3.90
5. Importance of matching your specific tasks (work) to organizational goals and priorities.	2.71	2.62	4.06	4.10
6. Understanding and using tactics for gaining power and influence.	2.88	2.90	4.35	4.14
7. Considering the objectives of others to complete your goals.	2.94	2.76	4.18	3.81
8. Understanding the role of creative thinking.	2.76	2.38	4.00	3.52
9. Understanding that basic leadership behaviors are supporting or opposing ideas, and supporting or opposing others.	2.88	2.90	4.24	4.57
10. Understanding that the goal of a leadership situation is getting the right work done.	3.00	2.95	4.27	4.42
11. Understanding that there are ideas out in the open and there are hidden ideas.	2.53*	2.89	3.73*	4.47
12. Understanding the application of the "directing" leadership style.	2.80	2.95	4.20	4.21
13. Understanding the application of "participating" leadership style.	2.80	2.95	4.13	4.42
14. Understanding the application of "delegating" leadership style.	2.87	2.79	4.13	3.89
15. Understanding the differences between "directing, participating, and delegating" leadership styles.	2.73	2.84	4.27	4.26
16. Understanding the role of critical reasoning.	2.40	2.58	3.73	3.79

*Statistically significantly different from experimental condition at $p < .05$

Only item 11 was statistically significantly different. For both coverage and learning, the traditional group had a lower score on this item. This is consistent with the content of the course in that this idea was essential to the characteristics of the *VLeader2007* simulation and was not as greatly emphasized in the traditional training condition.

Were There Differences in Perception of Leadership?

To examine changes in perception of leadership we examined differences between responses on pre– and post–LBDQ-XII questionnaires for the two groups. First, we used an analysis of variance (ANOVA) to determine if there were statistically significant differences across the two samples *prior* to the training. Means for each group prior to training are shown in table 27-3. In analyzing perceptions of the ideal leader behavior prior to training, only factor 5 showed statistically significant differences between the two groups. The traditionally trained group was more likely to agree with the factor "initiating structure," where the leader clearly defines his or her own role rather than the experimental group. With this exception, the two groups were remarkably similar in their perceptions of the ideal leader prior to the training.

To determine if there were differences in cognitive learning about leadership resulting from the training, we conducted a paired-samples t-test on each group. We found differences; results are reported in table 27-4. For the traditional group, factors 5 and 8 showed significant changes. Perceptions of factor 5, initiating structure, showed a trend toward less agreement with the statement after the training (a higher mean). One explanation for this result is that the content of the training emphasized that leadership is not dependent upon position power. Perceptions of factor 8, consideration, showed a movement toward greater agreement with the statement after the training (a lower mean). The emphasis in the traditional training on emotional intelligence and participative management may be responsible for this cognitive result. Thus trainees in the traditional group changed their perceptions about position power and the importance of consideration and participation.

For the experimental group, factors 2 and 7 showed statistically significant changes. Perceptions of factor 2, demand reconciliation, which indicates the extent to which the leader reconciles conflicting demands, showed significant change. Participants in the experimental group were more likely to agree with statements describing this as the role of the leader after the training. This may be explained by the emphasis in the game-based simulation on role of the leader to manage tension and conflict among the work group. Factor 7, role assumption, measures to what degree the manager actively exercises the leadership role rather than surrendering leadership to others. Participants in the simulation group were less likely to think that leadership role should be held only by the leader.

Table 27-3. A Priori Perceptions of Ideal Leader Behaviors

Ideal Leader Behaviors	Traditional Mean Pretraining n=16	Simulation Mean Pretraining n=19	ANOVA F-Value df=35	ANOVA Significance
Factor 1: Representation	2.00	2.02	0.192	0.664
Factor 2: Demand Reconciliation	1.60	1.56	0.024	0.877
Factor 3: Tolerance of Uncertainty	2.33	2.30	0.001	0.979
Factor 4: Persuasiveness	1.80	1.75	0.077	0.783
Factor 5: Initiation of Structure	1.56	1.77	3.126	0.086
Factor 6: Tolerance of Freedom	2.13	2.29	2.039	0.162
Factor 7: Role Assumption	1.86	1.84	0.263	0.611
Factor 8: Consideration	2.09	1.96	0.920	0.344
Factor 9: Production Emphasis	2.06	2.15	0.577	0.452
Factor 10: Predictive Accuracy	1.76	1.83	0.862	0.359
Factor 11: Integration	1.62	1.74	1.010	0.322
Factor 12: Superior Orientation	1.78	1.76	0.014	0.908

Table 27-4. Change in Learning Regarding Leader Behaviors by Training Group

Ideal Leader Behaviors	Traditional Training			Simulation Training		
	Mean			Mean		
	Pretraining	Posttraining	p-value	Pretraining	Posttraining	p-value
	n=16	n=16	df=15	n=19	n=19	df=18
Factor 1: Representation	2.00	1.96	0.727	2.02	1.98	0.815
Factor 2: Demand Reconciliation	1.60	1.57	0.809	1.56	1.74	0.094
Factor 3: Tolerance of Uncertainty	2.33	2.27	0.490	2.30	2.22	0.331
Factor 4: Persuasiveness	1.80	1.76	0.760	1.75	1.76	0.942
Factor 5: Initiation of Structure	1.56	1.75	0.087	1.77	1.67	0.143
Factor 6: Tolerance of Freedom	2.13	2.17	0.486	2.29	2.27	0.837
Factor 7: Role Assumption	1.86	1.91	0.588	1.84	2.04	0.046
Factor 8: Consideration	2.09	1.95	0.083	1.96	1.98	0.669
Factor 9: Production Emphasis	2.06	2.19	0.236	2.15	2.08	0.473
Factor 10: Predictive Accuracy	1.76	1.73	0.812	1.83	1.66	0.111
Factor 11: Integration	1.62	1.61	0.907	1.74	1.74	1.000
Factor 12: Superior Orientation	1.78	1.71	0.362	1.76	1.67	0.161

Although many of the factors associated with leadership did not change as a result of the intervention, four of the 12 factors (one-third) showed statistically significant change and two more in the experimental group were approaching significance. The fact that the change in factor means were different for the two types of training also supports the idea that the magnitude of learning was different for the two groups.

Did The Training Result in Differences in Leader Effectiveness?

Differences in perception of leader effectiveness were examined using multiple regression. Ten weeks after the initial training, participants from each group separately engaged in a complex, six-hour, in-basket role play where they were to act in the role of an upper level manager. Participants were rated on leader effectiveness using a 360 assessment instrument. These data were used to determine which training program had a stronger effect on leader effectiveness. Results of the analysis are shown in table 27-5.

The regression analysis indicated that type of training intervention (group simulation = 1; traditional = 0) significantly affected leader effectiveness. This provides support for the idea that the simulation training resulted in greater training transfer and higher perceptions of leader effectiveness even when controlling for what they cognitively learned.

Table 27-5. Multiple Regression Analysis

Variable	Model 1 Std. Beta	Model 2 Std. Beta	Model 2 Std. Beta	Model 2 Std. Beta	Model 2 Std. Beta
Intercept	10.6[a]	13.3[a]	16.03[a]	13.069[a]	13.029[a]
Group	0.34[b]	.359[b]	.312[c]	.342[b]	
Gender		−0.350[b]	−.356[b]	−.311[c]	
Student Major		−0.247	−.164	−.214	
Factor 5—Post			−.338[b]		−.391[b]
Factor 8—Post			−.039		.045
Factor 2—Post				−.216	−.156
Factor 7—Post				.148	.316
F-Value	4.69	3.32	2.621	1.731	1.603
Significance	0.037	0.032	0.045	0.159	0.199
Adjusted R—Square	0.095	0.166	0.193	0.097	0.065

[a] = $p < .01$, [b] = $p < .05$, [c] = $p < .10$

DV = perceived leadership effectiveness

Conclusion

New technology provides opportunities for new training tools. Traditional training practices, although adequate for acquiring knowledge regarding leadership, may be less useful in helping individuals practice skills and receive feedback. Without this feedback and reflection, properly using skills and training transfer may be problematic. This evaluation of two training approaches is a systematic and purposeful search for the best method of training that will result in sustained development of leadership skills. Our evaluation of the training found that skills learned from the simulation seemed to transfer more readily and resulted in a more effective outcome for the trainees.

Knowledge Check

Answer the following questions and check your answers in the appendix.

1. The model used in *VLeader2007* is based on three dimensions predictive of successful leadership. What are the three dimensions used in the *VLeader2007* model?
2. What is an appropriate statistical test to determine if a change has occurred from the pretest assessment to the posttest assessment?
3. Why is it important that the trainer determine that there are no statistically significant differences in satisfaction with the training experience in the two training groups?

About the Authors

Alice C. Stewart, PhD, is an associate professor of strategic management in the School of Business and Economics at the North Carolina Agricultural and Technical State University. In addition to strategy, Stewart teaches training and development in the HRM master's program. Her current research examines ways to improve organizational capabilities by developing the skill sets of frontline workers and managers. Her work has appeared in *Current Topics in Management, Health Care Management Review,* the *Journal of International Business Studies, Management Learning, Journal of Business Venturing,* and the *Journal of Small Business Strategy.* Stewart received her doctorate from the University of North Carolina-Chapel Hill. You can reach her at acstewa1@ncat.edu.

Jacqueline A. Williams, PhD, is an associate professor of marketing and sales in the School of Business and Economics at the North Carolina Agricultural and Technical State University. Her research focuses on sales and leadership, customer relationship marketing and management, corporate philanthropy, and service creation. Her work has appeared in the *Journal of Business Ethics, Advances in Business Management Forecasting,* and the *Journal of Services Marketing.* Williams received her doctorate from Florida State University. She can be reached at jacq@ncat.edu.

References

Aldrich, C. (2004). *Simulations and the Future of Learning.* San Francisco: Pfeiffer.

Stodgill, R. M. (1974). *Handbook of leadership.* New York: Free Press.

Additional Reading

Aldrich, C. (May 2006). 9 Paradoxes of Educational Simulations. *T + D* 60(5): 49–50, 52–6.

Aldrich, C. (March 2003). The new core of leadership. *T + D* 57(3): 32–7.

❧ **Section V**

Voices

Rebecca Ray

Prologue

"If I have seen further [than others], it is by standing upon the shoulders of giants."

—Sir Isaac Newton

Over the past 60 years, many giants have made important contributions to the field of training measurement and evaluation. They have shaped our profession and given us the philosophies and tools with which to raise our organizations and ourselves to greater levels of proficiency and effectiveness. This work, the *ASTD Handbook of Measuring and Evaluating Training*, is a unique contribution to the area of evaluation, destined to continue ASTD's tradition of codifying and disseminating the distilled wisdom of our profession and continually raising the bar. Its publication could not be timelier. Few can remember in our professional lives a time when we have experienced such a "perfect storm": pressure to do more and more with less and less while continuing to deliver quality programs and initiatives that drive business results against the challenges presented by a global economy in crisis. Without the ability to articulate the impact of our noble efforts in ways that senior leaders understand and value, we are at even greater risk of significant budget and staff reductions.

In a series of recorded interviews conducted over the past few months, these thought leaders shared their histories, theories, and advice for the profession as well as the creative solutions to the challenges they faced. The commentary contained in the transcripts of these interviews represents the voices of those who have contributed the most in terms of conducting research, applying the methods described in this book, and sharing their knowledge and expertise with others around the world. To hear the actual interviews, download the podcasts at www.astd.org/HandbookofMeasuringandEvaluatingTraining.

The goal of each interview was to capture, albeit briefly, the history of involvement in evaluation and measurement, guiding philosophies, innovative ideas, tools, models and frameworks as well as predictions for the future. Generally, these questions formed the nucleus of each interview:

- Tell us about your involvement with training measurement and evaluation, including the history of your involvement leading up to what you are doing today.
- How has training evaluation changed over the years?
- What progress has the training industry made with evaluation? Is the industry embracing it or avoiding it?
- How do executives really view learning and development and the investments made in these processes?
- Has evaluation made a difference in the perception held by executives of training and development?
- Why do we still see such a low investment in training measurement and evaluation within organizations? How can we facilitate more investment in the future?
- What does the future hold for measurement and evaluation?

The complete and unedited transcripts and podcast recordings provide a deeper glimpse into their thinking but, in the meantime, here are the legends in their own (distilled and lightly edited) words...

❧ Robert O. Brinkerhoff

On how it all started...

I was fortunate to get involved in a graduate program whose focus was program evaluation. I had been five years in the Navy through the Vietnam War period and then went to graduate school. It was a heady time. I went to the University of Virginia, where there was a lot of focus on radical thinking and social action programs, and I got very much involved in the social action programs, particularly radical education programs, street academies, and the like. That time period also saw a big explosion of thinking and program evaluation. We had many brilliant theorists who were working at various centers around the United States, which was all a part of President Johnson's Great Society Program. Evaluation became a federal mandate and requirement, so a number of graduate programs started in program evaluation. I was fortunate to be involved in one, so I studied evaluation as an academic discipline. Much of it was sort of an internship-apprenticeship program, so I spent almost five years in Washington, DC, as a part of that graduate program working to evaluate some of the major drug education and social action programs of the time.

I was more committed to the goals of the social programs than I really was to evaluation, technology, and thinking. That started an early focus on thinking that if the evaluation work wasn't being used and wasn't helping people do a better job, then it really wasn't doing its job. So that was sort of a choice point, realizing that evaluation could be a complete waste of time if its sole purpose was to meet federal requirements and put a report in a file cabinet. There was a huge focus on thinking that people had to really use it to do a better job and change things. The other change point came as I happened to get involved in a large evaluation program that focused on training special education professionals. We had to think about whether the programs that were training the educators were making a difference to the pupils in the classroom and their families. As I began to get more involved in the business and industry of evaluation, the idea stayed with me that the real issue was not figuring out whether the program was working, but figuring out whether the program was doing any good in a larger sense. I think that very much shaped my thinking about the Success Case Evaluation Method.

We started going to [businesses] as clients and the Success Case Method just came about as a way of trying to be much more efficient. So, when we looked at a company that might have put a thousand people through an executive development program or some sort of management leadership education program, we tried to find out whether it was working or not. We realized that if we were going to find people using their training to make a difference, it was much better to be more purposive about things, rather than to choose random samples. We would ask "Who is the most likely to be using their training?" and look for them first, because if it is working for anybody, it is working for the people who really learned it and were excited about it and felt like they could use it. So, we would deliberately select those people beforehand and then follow up with them. An early experience we had was thinking that the best way to be efficient was to look at the Level 1 evaluation data and the Level 2 data because if anyone was likely to use the training it was probably the trainees who loved the program and who learned the most from it, that is, those who scored well on a end-of-session test. But when we went and followed up with those people, what we found was that some of them were using it and some of them weren't. We had to change our definition of success. The best way to find out who was probably using this training was to simply ask them first. We would just do a one-item survey of everyone who had been through the training, asking "Are you using your training in a way that you know is making a difference?" Only a small sample of people would say "yes" to that. Then we could focus our evaluation inquiry on those people and just be much more efficient in finding out if the training was making a difference. That really started to shape the way we thought about how and why to do evaluation.

On how training evaluation has changed over the years...

The important issue that people need to recognize is not *how* are we going to do the measurement but *why* are we going to do it? What should we expect from this initiative? What do people need to know about it? And if we can think clearly about it first, the *how* questions solve themselves, but if we are not clear about *why* we need to know and *what* we need to know, then we will always get wrapped around the axle trying to figure out how to proceed. The question I'd like you to ask is this: "What is the first thing we should think about when we struggle with evaluation?" The answer is this: "Why do we need to do it in the first place?"

On the progress the profession has made in embracing evaluation...

Let me start with the good news. A lot of good people are thinking about this and working with it. You've got all of the good work of Jack and Patti Phillips, Josh Bersin, Cal Wick from Fort Hill, Will Thalheimer, and Kent Barnett of Knowledge Advisors who are creating techniques and technologies that people can use. There is a lot more focus on evaluation, and more techniques are available. Electronic survey methods are terrific and make data collection much simpler. A lot of good positive changes are happening, but things are not changing enough. I have been a presenter for ASTD for almost 30 years. I have had students do some research on past ASTD national programs, and evaluation has been one of the hot topics for the ASTD annual program for more than 40 years. You sort of have to ask yourself why this is an enduring problem. For 40 years, people have asked "How are we going to measure this? How are we going to see if this makes a difference?" While a lot more techniques have become available, there has not been that much clear thinking about why we should be doing it. So, I think one thing that has *not* changed is that people may be doing evaluation because they think they *have* to and are not really thinking about *why* they should do it. We don't see enough clear, strategic, actionable thinking about *why* to do it before we start considering *how* to do it.

On how executives view learning and development and investment in it...

People have got to carefully think through *why* they are doing training and development and *what* to expect from it, remembering that the principal goal of the training is to help the organization and the people in it be successful.

I think it would make a difference to expect more from training, to hold people accountable for using training, and to help them see that it is not a benefit, it is not a giveaway program, and it is not something to increase your enjoyment of your employment with us and ensure that we will retain you. We expect that you will increase your skills and use them on a regular basis. What that helps people see is that they are already spending plenty of money on training and development; they are just not expecting enough return on it. By beginning to *expect* more we will *inspect* more, thus creating the expectation that we will measure and follow up every time we train to make sure that people are, in fact, supporting it and using it.

On how evaluation makes a difference in the perception held by executives of training and development...

I have often had the luxury of presenting our success case findings to senior leaders and even to the board of directors of a company. What I tell them is, "I have some good news and some bad news. The good news is that this $40 million that you have spent over the last three years on this management development training is working. Let me give you some examples of the ways in which it is working and the difference it is making." I will tell them a story, I will say, "Look, here is one of your leaders from an office in the Northeast who used the training and has improved sales by $500 million over the last two years. So that's training that's really making a difference. Now, let me tell you the bad news. The bad news is that it is only happening about 15 percent of the time. In other words, 85 percent of this budget that you've been spending on training and development is being wasted. The kinds of changes that I've told you are happening are not happening anywhere near enough. Let me ask you, what would your company have earned if we doubled the number of people who are using the training?" And then I tell them what difference that would make. You really have their attention when you start telling them about the money and the value they are leaving on the table by failing to hold people accountable for using the training. When I present the data in that way and show them a few simple actions they could take to hold their direct reports accountable for holding *their* people accountable for using the training and when they begin to see how they play a key role in doubling, tripling, and quadrupling the ROI they're getting from the training, they begin to take action. We have seen it happen many times. Not often enough, but still many times.

On why we still see such a low investment in training measurement and evaluation within organizations and how can we facilitate more investment in the future...

If we think of training and development as a staff benefit, then what we mostly care about is whether people participate in it and whether they appreciate and value it. But if you think of it as a business driver, then the critical questions are not did they participate or even did they learn, the critical question is are they *using* it? So, I think what learning and development executives need to do is be thoughtful and strategic in communicating with the senior executive leadership of the organization and helping them shape the right expectations for training and development. Yes, part of it will be staff benefit. It will help the organization to recruit and retain people. So, we should expect it to be valued and we should expect to do it well. But then we also have to help them see that you should demand more from training and development. You should expect it to improve business performance. We should hold people accountable for using their training, not just participating in it. I think if we can get training and development leaders to go out on a limb and raise expectations, then we will see much more demand for providing evidence that it really is making a difference to the business.

On what the future holds for measurement and evaluation...

As I look forward, I think we are seeing more professionalization of the learning and development function. We are seeing leaders who have not only come up through the business ranks, but who are also academically trained in learning and development. I think this is a positive trend. And one of the things we will also see is the downside of professionalization, where people see themselves as learning and development leaders. What is more important is that they see themselves as *business* leaders who happen to be working in the learning and development function. Their principal responsibility is to their customers and clients and to make sure that their organizations are doing the right things and are doing them well. I think the combination of better academic training of these leaders, more professionalization, and higher expectations for them as business leaders will combine to help everyone raise expectations about the value that learning and development can, and should, produce in organizations.

About Robert O. Brinkerhoff

Robert O. Brinkerhoff, EdD, is professor emeritus at Western Michigan University and a senior consultant for the Advantage Performance Group. He is an internationally recognized expert in training evaluation and effectiveness and has been a consultant to dozens of major companies and organizations in the United States, South Africa, and Europe. Brinkerhoff is the inventor of the Success Case Evaluation Method, an innovative technique for evaluating learning programs that relies on qualitative feedback to help understand an organization's training effectiveness.

✀ Mary L. Broad

On how it all started...

My whole professional career has been around training and then moved into the general performance improvement field. My main work employment has been with various federal agencies. The last 10 years or so before I retired in 1993, I was the director of training and then human resource development at the Defense Information Systems Agency—a fascinating place to work. Since my retirement, I have done a variety of consulting, and the theme of evaluation has always been important. We need to know the outcomes and the results of the work that we do. I went back and looked at my first publication with John Newstrom, *Transfer of Training*, back in 1992 and found that, yes, we *were* paying attention to evaluation back then, but sort of as a pro forma thing that everyone needs to do. We did not focus too much on it in terms of what we were urging managers to do, which was really to enrich the workplace to help people apply what they have learned. I think that my real focus on evaluation, as a really high priority, probably occurred not too long after 1992. I was elected to the Board of Governors of ASTD in 1993. Gary Rummler was also on the board—a guy who has been extremely important in the International Society for Performance Improvement, the other professional association with a huge focus on performance. Performance is not so much what people *learn* to do, but it is what they *actually* do. We can help them with that performance—often through training—but also by helping managers to enrich the workplace. That has been my focus ever since. Evaluation is a strong partner with performance because managers need to know how things have worked out—what the results have been. Since that time, the whole process of evaluation has just loomed larger and larger in my mind, and I think it is more and more important that anyone who is in any organization begin to get a feeling for what people need to do to be able to perform well and how we can measure that. So that has been my trajectory in terms of appreciating evaluation.

On how training evaluation has changed over the years...

I grew up, as so many of us have, with the Kirkpatrick framework as the foundation of things. As training and performance improvement get integrated with the way organizations work, we are going to come up with a whole roster of evaluation focuses related to timeliness, accomplishments, savings, satisfaction, and all kinds of measures that will be available and just built in as the particular situation requires so that we won't have to do the same kinds of analysis to get evaluations done. There will be some patterns, approaches, and ways of thinking about it that are way beyond me right now, but certainly the way people are inventing and making inroads into extremely fruitful new ways of doing business, I am sure things will change dramatically. The whole principle of evaluation—of measuring where we are, where we are going, did we get it done, what's still missing—all of those kind of questions are *never* going to go away, and I think we are going to be able to build them in to the way people do their work in a much more smooth and integrated way.

On the progress the profession has made in embracing evaluation...

People in our field have some work to do to help organizations recognize the value of looking at people through a performance lens. Performance refers to the outcomes, the results, the payoff. Managers usually care a whole lot more about these things than they care about whether somebody actually attended a particular training program. So, the outcomes and how we can support the organization in achieving its strategic outcomes are where we can get managers' attention and become better at partnering with them in meeting their goals.

On how evaluation makes a difference in the perception held by executives of training and development...

It is up to us to educate organizations that we can be more than trainers. We can really help them with other aspects of performance. People in our business are probably the few who really pay attention to how well people can do their work. If we show that we really can tune it up and help managers who have a challenge on their hands get something done through improved performance, if we can begin to find those instances where it really paid off, those managers will be some of our best advocates for getting support for dealing with their performance problems. So I think it comes back in a way to people in our field beginning to see themselves differently, beginning to present themselves as partners with management, trying to find instances in the organization where someone can really use their help and working with that person to get some sort of success and then publicizing it. I think we have a lot to do on our own behalf, to market ourselves—perhaps in a different way—as not just presenting training, even very good training, but as helping managers get the performance they want out of the people who work for them. That can get managers' attention and real interest.

We talk about Level 3 evaluations frequently in our line of business, meaning how much people are actually using what they have learned on the job. One point I wanted to make is that Level 3 evaluations are so often considered another aspect of evaluating the training program, the effectiveness of the training program. I think that is totally wrong. Level 2 evaluation, that is, what did people learn in the course of the training event, that is where we learn about the effectiveness of the training. Level 3 actually measures how much the workplace has changed to support the use of that training; it is much more a measure of what the stakeholders in the workplace have done than it is an evaluation of the training.

On what the future holds for measurement and evaluation...

Well, the future is a real challenge, but now may be a good time for people in the field to lay the groundwork for partnerships. In general, I think evaluation has got to become more recognized as an absolutely essential tool. Now, we have some good tools, like the works of good people like Jack Phillips, to help show the payoff—even to show in monetary terms that if we do these kinds of things in these ways then the outcome is really going to be valuable. Now that we can make those kinds of outcomes clear, I think we have some tools to show managers how they can save money, how they can make money, how they can make things work much better, and how they can get where they need to go. I think that the more training becomes on the job and on demand, the more evaluation needs to be embedded in the way the training is designed so we don't have a separate set of decisions such as: "We're going to do this training, should we evaluate it?" Training design and evaluation should be absolutely integrated together. Evaluation is built into the way that the training is presented, is dealt with, and the data are collected.

About Mary L. Broad

Mary L. Broad, PhD, is a certified performance technologist who has served on the ASTD Board of Directors. She is the author and editor of several books, including *Transfer of Training: Action-Packed Strategies to Ensure High Payoff from Training Investments* (1992, with John W. Newstrom); *Beyond Transfer of Training: Engaging Systems to Improve Performance* (2005); and *In Action: Transferring Learning to the Workplace* (1997). As leader of her company, Performance Excellence, she helps organizations improve human performance systems through strategic planning, performance technology, and the transfer of learning for high-priority performance improvement intervention. She is an experienced future-search facilitator for public and private sector clients.

Jac Fitz-enz

On how it all started...

In 1969, I went to work for Wells Fargo Bank in the training department, and that is what got me into the profession. I worked at the bank for several years. Then I went to a computer company as head of human resources and, eventually, in 1980 started and ran the Saratoga Institute until 2002. My involvement with training has always been personal because that is where I started.

I got into the predictive side about two years ago: I had just finished about a third of a series of reports called the *Workforce Intelligence Report*, which is basically a best practices report, and I looked at this thing and I said, OK, what else is there? We can't just keep reporting what other people are doing—whether good or bad—and really advance the profession. We've got to evolve from reporting the basic transactional metrics of 30 years ago and benchmarking and reciting best practices to something else. What is that? To me that was predictability. That pushed me to ask, how do we become predictive? Whether we are talking about making an investment in training or making an investment in something else, all resources are limited, and there is competition for them. So, if we can get into predictability and begin to show that an investment in this or that will give us the kind of return we want, we will run our organizations much more effectively, we will be less frustrated, employees will be more motivated, and so forth. That is my mental model. To do that you cannot just take a given isolated function like training or any other function and say we ought to do *this*. I think you really have to understand the environment in which you are working, which means you have to do a major, comprehensive, in-depth scan of the external and the internal world in which you live. And then look at that and ask, "How does that affect the human structural and relational capital of our organization and how do those things interact?" All I am trying to say here is that human and structural issues interrelate, and you can't just go out and run a training program or any other intervention around the human side without asking yourself: "What about the structural side of the organization? What about the relational capital of people outside the organization, such as competitors, customers, and vendors?" It is a much more complex world than I think most people want to spend time thinking about. If you do not have this understanding as a foundation, then anything you do—whether a staffing strategy, a compensation strategy, or a development strategy—has got to have limited success. And that's what brought me into predictability. We built this model called "Human Capital Management 21."

On how training evaluation has changed over the years...

In 1969, the words *measurement* and *value* were not even in the training lexicon. There has been considerable movement in a relatively small number of people or functions or departments, and some of them are doing wonderful work. I was just with a retailer a week ago that has done some terrific work in showing the value added by the training and development function to the organization, tracing it all the way from improvement in skill and knowledge to a business result, a financial result. So, some people are doing tremendous work, there are just not enough of them. Overall I would guess 25 to 30 percent are doing something significant in the training and evaluation field, but that leaves out 70 percent. You can look at the situation as a glass half full or half empty, but that is my view. There has been about a 25- to 30-percent build-up in evaluation in the last 30 years.

On how executives view learning and development and investment in it...

You can take people who have had practical experience working in a line job, and you can teach them the fundamentals of adult learning. They do not have to be experts in adult learning to run a training function, they simply have to understand a little of the theory behind it so they know when to champion one approach over another. I think it is much easier for them to learn those kinds of fundamentals and then rely on a professional to actually design, develop, and deliver the product and use their line experience to provide guidance.

On why we still see such a low investment in training measurement and evaluation within organizations and how can we facilitate more investment in the future...

If I were running a training function today, I would insist that the people who are playing professional roles—the designers and deliverers of training—go out and spend at least six months in a line job someplace so they understand the day-to-day pressures of people in those kinds of jobs and that the world is *not* driven by a training program. In fact, a training program can be seen as an intrusion to getting the job done. I think they would then come back with a different kind of attitude, and we could begin to build around a more realistic attitude of why we develop people. We do not do it because we like to train. If it does not show value, then we should get rid of it.

As I see it, as a profession, most trainers really don't like measurement. They love to design, develop, and deliver courses and they like to get some positive feedback at Level 1 or 2, but they really don't care to measure and evaluate their work. It is not in their DNA I guess. This is unfortunate because, as a result of that, training and development usually is one of the first functions out the door during a downturn, which makes perfect sense if you look at it from the standpoint of someone outside, such as an investor in the company or management. If we don't explain to people in terms that they can understand and appreciate (creating value by improving skills, knowledge, and attitudes of the workforce), then it really makes sense to get rid of the function or at least downplay it for a while. This is the fundamental thing: We've got to accept the fact that we are in a business—whether for-profit or not-for-profit does not make any difference—we are spending money and there has got to be a return on that money, otherwise it is waste. Unfortunately, so many people in training functions, for a variety of reasons, do not want to do that. As a group and as a profession we have got to turn things around, and we have to get a much greater percentage of people doing some level of quantitative analysis and evaluation.

On what the future holds for measurement and evaluation...

When I finished this thing on predictability I thought, OK, I have done it now, I have made my mark, this is as far as you can go, predictability is the end of the trail. And if you learn how to be predictive in the investment in training or any other function, that's great. That's as far as you can go. I had no sooner finished than people started talking to me about the next step. I now realize there is another evolutionary step, which is what we are calling data integration. All this means is that you look at data at any level and ask yourself "How does this relate to other data in the organization?" If you had the balanced scorecard in mind as a model, you know learning is at the first level, process at the second level, customers at the third level, and finance at the fourth level.

Data integration is the next step, and where it applies to development is, of course, if you do something at the learning level, you should be able to track it through and directly say it is going to touch this kind of human behavior at the process level, which is then going to lead to customer reactions and so on. We are starting to develop algorithms to do that. That, to me, is the next phase.

About Jac Fitz-enz

Jac Fitz-enz, PhD, is a pioneer in human capital strategic analysis and measurement. After holding senior corporate human resource positions, he founded the Saratoga Institute and developed the first international human resource benchmarking service. He later launched the Human Capital Source and the Workforce Intelligence Institute to take human capital valuation to the next level. Named by the Society for Human Resource Management as one of the 50 most influential people in human capital management, two of his books were selected by SHRM for the "Book of the Year" Award: *Human Value Management: The Value-Adding Human Resource Management Strategy for the 1990s* (1990) and *The ROI of Human Capital: Measuring the Economic Value of Employee Performance* (2009). He was honored in ASTD's "Legends" series at the International Conference in 2005.

✍ **Roger Kaufman**

On how it all started...

There is a story about how I came up with my model of strategic planning and needs assessment and the Organizational Elements Model. It started one day with our then five-year old son who kept on asking me "why?," and I, being a full professor, tried to answer him. Between the second and third answer, I ran out of good explanations and I was tempted to say, "Because I said so." That led me to the idea that we really don't push far enough to determine what impact we have. When I was with companies like Boeing and Douglass, we used to have a lot of training, but we were never quite sure (a) whether that training was worth the money, or (b), and more important, whether it had any impact on safety and efficiency. I started thinking about the questions we leave unanswered in our work. We spend so much money, as ASTD has documented, on training. Wouldn't it be nice if we knew what "bang for the buck" we were getting? For instance, the work of the Phillipses in this area has been very important, refocusing us not only on the processes of training, the costs of training, the efficiency of training, but the results and impact. I have been involved with training for a long time and increasingly look forward to answering the question, "So what?"

The Organizational Elements Model links the value chain of what we use (*inputs*), what we do (*processes*), what results we get (*products*), what we can deliver outside the organization (*outputs*), and the external client societal impact (*outcomes*). There is an alignment among the five organizational elements: inputs, processes, products, outputs, and outcomes. It is interesting in our field because just about every result gets called an outcome, which blurs the important distinction among three different kinds of results: two internal, *products* and *outputs*, and the external one called *outcomes*. I came up with the Organizational Elements Model in 1979, and the response to it has been underwhelming. I call those three different levels of results (product, output, and outcome) macro, micro, and mega; mega—the impact on external society—being the one that we should always start with.

Mega thinking is just the idea that every organization is a means to societal end. As my colleague at the Sonora Institute of Technology says, "If you are not adding societal value, you are subtracting societal value." We can go back a few years to the old 1970s and 1980s model of zero-based budgeting. What would happen if we did not fund any training? What do you get from the training dollar and, more important, how do you prove it?

Ian Davis wrote an article in *The Economist* called "The Biggest Contract," where he said societal value is not an add-on to strategic thinking and planning, but is at its core. I hope that we are getting to the tipping point, and I hope this conversation and this handbook will encourage people to not throw away everything they are doing but just add societal value, and I think they will soon find out that they are in good company.

On how training evaluation has changed over the years...

Training evaluation has changed dramatically from not too long ago when people said you can't measure training; it is an intangible. I think what has happened is that more and more professionals, and a lot of them are in this book, have started to show the way that evaluation is not only possible but is vital. Money gets tighter, and we have to show value for it. Training is a pretty big part of the budget. Wouldn't it be nice if you could show managers, supervisors, and executives what they got for their money? When you look at the work of Richard E. Clark and Fred Estes on the effectiveness of training, it is pretty scary stuff. They have some convincing data that indicates that less than 10 percent of what is provided in training ever shows up in the job. That is a 90-percent failure rate—that's expensive! As we get into critical things like airplane security, aircraft maintenance, design and construction of automobiles, food safety, and health safety, the cost of a breakdown or failure can be astronomical, not only in terms of money but also in terms of human life and suffering.

One of the biggest obstacles I see now is people saying, well, this is a bridge too far; we can't do this or we can't talk people into doing this. A lot of consultants and a lot of professionals say that they dare not talk to their boss about the impact of training. So, I think we have to encourage and help people who are on the line to understand that training is a process and it's only valid to the extent that it yields useful results—ideally useful results with the macro, micro, and mega levels aligned. Then and only then can they can prove the value of what they have done and the money they have spent. There is a fear or apprehension that the boss isn't ready for this.

I think that now we have to show value for money. I think one theme of this book is that training has to be about results, and, I would like to add that it's not only about results but about the three levels of results: the building block results, what the organization can deliver, and the societal impact of external clients. When we get this alignment, we can generate numbers and show how to get measurable criteria for all these three levels. If we provide the tools and ideas and indeed the encouragement and support, we will reach the tipping point in not only evaluating for results but in linking the three levels of results.

On the progress the profession has made in embracing evaluation...

People coming out of universities understand and are competent in designing evaluation, which links up with the Organizational Elements Model. The people who are in decision-making positions increasingly understand that this is the safest thing for them to do. I see it moving in that direction. I used to have a period where I was alone in thinking about the societal value and the Organizational Elements Model, then companies like McKinsey & Co. came to the table and said this is at the core. Now I think we are getting to the point that ASTD is aiming for, which is that this is the way to do it. It is not only professional but it is the safest thing to do. I think this book and this series of interviews are good indicators that we are moving in this direction.

On why we still see such a low investment in training measurement and evaluation within organizations and how can we facilitate more investment in the future...

In the past measurement and evaluation has been used primarily for blaming instead of for fixing and improving. I think people ought to be clear about the purposes of the evaluation and what will be done with the data. Instead of coming in and saying that you have done a terrible job and what are you going to do about it, come in and say here are some opportunities for improvement, let's look at this data together and see how we can use this for continual improvement. The culture that should be encouraged is that we use data to make improvements, not to cast blame.

The other thing is the myth that evaluation is expensive. I like to point out that if you worry about evaluation expenses, then what about the costs of failure? It is about cost and consequences and about overcoming the fear about what is going to be done with evaluation data.

I think people don't take on training evaluation because they fear that their boss will not understand it, they will look like fools, and they do not know how to do it. I think the whole idea behind this book is to give people the skills, knowledge, attitudes, abilities, and support to ask and answer the right questions and work with people in the management chain to say, "Yes, this is important."

One of the tools I use in helping them is called the "Yes AND" approach. When somebody says, "OK, I want you to run a three-day training course on sales," you say, "Help me understand how you would measure success?" Without threatening people, you walk people up the value chain to show them their evaluation is going to be based on their success and their boss's success and the boss's boss's success. It's attitude, support, skills, and knowledge that they have the ability to do it—in fact, they might be the only person in the organization who can do it and achieve success.

On what the future holds for measurement and evaluation...

It just plain makes sense, and most of the people in our field not only want, as Peter Drucker said, to do things right, they want to do the right thing. I think it is an ethical issue of external and internal impact, and I think it is a professional issue. The way in which people will get hired and maintained in the future will be based on these questions: "What *results* did you deliver to us?" and "How *valuable* were they?"

About Roger Kaufman

Roger Kaufman, PhD, is professor emeritus of Educational Psychology Learning Systems at Florida State University and a recipient of the Professional Excellence Award. He is also a distinguished research professor at the Institute of Technology in Mexico. A Certified Performance Technologist, he spent years in human resources, training, and engineering positions and served two terms for the U.S. Secretary of the Navy's Advisory Board on Education and Training. He is past president and member for life of the International Society for Performance Improvement and was the recipient of the society's Thomas S. Gilbert Professional Achievement Award. Recognized by ASTD for distinguished contribution to workplace learning and development, he is the creator of the Organizational Elements Model and consults worldwide. He has written more than 265 articles and 39 books on strategic planning, management, performance improvement, needs assessment, and evaluation.

✎ Donald L. Kirkpatrick

On how it all started...

I was at the Management Institute at the University of Wisconsin in Madison, teaching a course on Human Relations for Supervisors. I had my MBA, and I decided I was going on for a PhD at the the School of Education there. I decided that as long as I am teaching in that program, I am going to evaluate it. So I was concerned about two things: the reaction of the people attending our program and learning effectiveness. To evaluate reaction, we used comment sheets and were conscious that participants better go back to their companies saying good things about the programs because they are our customers. I called that a measure of customer satisfaction. We did those every time, and we were sure that people went back and said good things about the program. Sometimes we even had an individual in higher management come and attend a seminar just to see what this was and then he would go back and make decisions about whether to send the supervisors. So it was important to measure that, and I called it *reaction*. We wanted to measure reaction to the program, and we did that regularly. We did not do much learning evaluation, obviously we were trying to teach knowledge and skills and change some attitudes, but we had not done anything in terms of evaluating it. As a part of my dissertation, I did some pre- and posttests to measure the learning effectiveness of the program and did quite a bit to find out that the tests were significant and valid. The dissertation was basically about those two things: reaction and learning.

After my dissertation, I decided I'd better do a little more evaluation and so I decided I'd better go back on the job and see whether the people are using what we have taught them. I would typically ask the supervisors what happened when they got back to their companies: "What is your boss going to say?" Most of them had never even given it a thought. Most of them said, "I don't know." One guy said, "I think I know what my boss is going to say: 'You have been gone and now your work has piled up. I hope you had a good time, but let's get back to work.'" I asked, "Did any of you talk to your bosses before you came?" And a few of them had, but most of them were sent there because the personnel department had signed them up to attend the program. At that time, I thought, well it is important that when they go back, they do something about the training and I was beginning to look at behavior. So I wrote a little booklet and sent it to the superintendents and department heads who were sending their supervisors. And I said, before anyone attends a program, sit down with the people who are attending and say, "Here is an opportunity to learn, I'm all for it, I've approved it, and have a good time in Madison. But, when you come back, I am going to ask you, 'What did you learn and how can I help you apply it?'" I think that made all the difference in the world, in terms of supervisors' motivation. So I started to get into behavior. Then I did some research between my dissertation and the time the articles were published in the ASTD journal five years later. I went into companies and measured behavior change, and I also got into in the area of results and I never gave it much thought. Five years later, the editor of the ASTD journal at that time, Bob, called me and said, "Don, I understand you've done some research on evaluation. Would you write an article for us?" I said, "Bob, I'll tell you what I'll do. I'll write four articles." So at that particular time, when I wrote those articles, I called it reaction, learning, behavior, and results. That was 50 years ago that these articles were printed. I am telling you it is unbelievable what happened after that. People started calling it the "Kirkpatrick Model." I never called it the "Kirkpatrick Model." They started calling it the "Four Levels." I never called it the "Four Levels."

I hoped that they would learn them. That was my only hope. I hoped that I had given them something that would help them evaluate their programs effectively. I had no idea it was going to be translated into foreign languages and used all over the world.

---

50 Years of Evaluation

In 1959, Donald L. Kirkpatrick was asked to write an article on his research into evaluation for the *Journal of the American Society of Training Directors* (now *T+D* magazine). Instead, he offered to write four articles, one for each level, and from them the Kirkpatrick Four Levels of Evaluation was born. The first article was published in the November 1959 issue. From these articles came a series of books, including *Evaluating Training Programs: The Four Levels* (1993), *Transferring Learning to Behavior* (2005, with James D. Kirkpatrick), and *Implementing the Four Levels* (2007, with James D. Kirkpatrick).

On how training evaluation has changed over the years...

At the time, almost every company was using reaction; that was about it. Some were measuring training in terms of learning. But if they got good reactions from the people, if the people went back satisfied and said good things about the training, then the trainers felt good because the participants said great things about them—that was pretty much the way it was when I was at the Management Institute at the University of Wisconsin, back when I started in 1949.

On the progress the profession has made in embracing evaluation...

On *LinkedIn,* I put up a discussion question a few months ago and said, "The four levels are 50 years old now. What do you think? Are they still viable? Are they still in good order or does something need to be changed about them?" Nearly everyone who replied said they are just as good now as they were then. The problem is that people are concentrating on Levels 1 and 2, and there's not enough activity at Levels 3 and 4. I think that's true, and it's going to be true in many companies until training people begin to get the pressure from the jury up above that says that's what we are going to base your budget on. I think that is why James and Wendy's forthcoming book *Training on Trial* is going to have a real impact. They are going to realize that the jury up there is going to look at other things and here's what you can do to be ready for that. How can you be sure that when the jury makes the budget decision that they are going to approve the budget? Because we have proved to them, through examples and through other kinds of things, that we have done the things that should have been done.

The whole idea of a corporate university has taken the training department out of human resources, leaving it by itself. It's finally gotten the status that reports directly to top management. Chief learning officers are very conscious of what is going on. Training has received a lot more prestige in organizations and in the country, and I think the people up there are concerned with not only Levels 1 and 2, but also with Levels 3 and 4.

On how executives view learning and development and investment in it...

What about the executives in those years, way back in the 1950s, 60s, 70s, 80s, and 90s, what kind of evaluation was taking place? Most companies were telling their top people to justify their budget by reporting this is how many programs we ran, this is how many people attended, this is the reaction we got, and we have measured some learning. So, we have done this for the company, and the executives were pretty happy with that. They thought, "Gee, that's great." But then, I wrote something in my dissertation that I will never forget, "By the way, at this particular point most companies are concerned with just reaction and learning but the day of reckoning is coming." This was in the 1959 articles; the day of reckoning is coming when top management will look for more than that. They are going to look for whether people applied training on the job and whether they got better results.

The whole idea now is that the jury up above is looking at not only Levels 1 and 2 but also at Levels 3 and 4. Before, maybe they were satisfied; they'd heard good things about the program. People said, "Yeah, I enjoyed the program; I got a lot from it and so on." And that was good enough. But it's not good enough any more, I can assure you that's the case in practically every company I've run across.

On how evaluation makes a difference in the perception held by executives of training and development...

In this era of "return on expectations," what we're talking about is that we start with the end. We're encouraging companies to go to top management ahead of time and say, "OK, you want a leadership program; now what do you expect to accomplish in a leadership program? How are you going to measure success so we know what to do, what to look for, and what to concentrate on?" What we need to do is to start with them and ask, "What do you expect? You want the leadership program; that was not our idea. Therefore, what do you want? Do you want less turnover? Do you want more productivity? Do you want higher morale? Do you want better customer service? Do you want more customers? What do you think a leadership program can accomplish?" With that kind of thing and maybe a little negotiation between training and top management, we'll get to a point where we'd better be sure that people behave in ways to accomplish these goals. So ahead of time, we have a pretty good idea of what we are trying to accomplish.

On what the future holds for measurement and evaluation...

I think it is pretty well set now that the four levels are still going to remain the basics all over the world. But the emphasis now is going to be the implementation of Level 3 and Level 4 because of the jury up there and because of the kind of pressure on training departments not only to have programs that people like that they learn from, but also to have programs that people will use when they go back and thus have an impact on the business and the organization. We still have to get good reactions and tell people about how good the program was. We still have to measure learning. We who are going to implement effective training in an organization have to partner with top management starting from the beginning, talking to them about what to expect, and concentrating on them helping us. One of the chapters I added to the book *Implementing the Four Levels* was on how to get managers on board. This is key. They have got to get managers on board right from the beginning.

About Donald L. Kirkpatrick

Donald L. Kirkpatrick is professor emeritus at the University of Wisconsin and honorary chairman of Kirkpatrick Partners. In 1959, the publication of his seminal articles on training evaluation created the foundation for the Kirkpatrick Four Level Evaluation Model. He is the author of seven books on training evaluation and human resource topics. He has been a volunteer president of ASTD, and he was honored with the 2003 ASTD Lifetime Achievement in Workplace Learning and Performance Award.

✎ Jack J. Phillips

On how it all started...

It all started in about 1970. I was on the training staff of Lockheed Aircraft, which is now Lockheed Martin, and I was disappointed with what we were doing with evaluation. So I complained about it, and our training director at that time asked me to chair a task force to make it better. And that is what often happens when you complain. I started looking around at what was being done, and we were doing some evaluation at the reaction and learning levels at that point—testing as we called it—and we started looking at what others were doing. At that time, I contacted Don Kirkpatrick who had published some articles about 10 years before then that described those four steps that are now called levels, and I tried to get more updates to see how do you do it, give me some systems, give me something that goes beyond those articles. And Don told me that he was not really working on evaluation at that time. He was a professor at a university teaching management courses, and he said I'm looking forward to other people taking those four levels and doing something with them. And that's what I did. So we started working with this in a more systematic way, trying to understand how to collect data beyond the classroom and how to deal with it. I had the fortune to have a request to conduct a study. It was a study of a cooperative education program, in which engineering students alternated work and school, and when they graduated, we often hired them. We had 350 co-op students. That was a very large budget, and it was on my budget at that time as the co-op director. And I had a request from the chief engineer to show the value of that program. Though it had lots of discussion around it, basically he wanted to see the value it was bringing to the company, yes up to "show me the ROI." That was in 1972 if you can imagine. So, even as early as those days we were getting some requests for that kind of data. So I worked on that as part of a master's thesis, and the statistics were taken at that time and I finished the study. I thought it was a marvelous study, and it was published in the *Journal of Cooperative Education*. We were able to show the actual monetary value of the program using a classic experimental versus control group. But what I noticed wasn't that I had a nice study with some "gee whiz" approaches, what I noticed was the impact it had. I got to keep the program. We actually got funding, so we were able to secure funding. But I think more important is that I got more support for the program. We had problems getting management to support it, and they stepped up and started doing that because when I presented my study not only was the chief engineer in the audience so were the division's engineers. So they became my supporters, improving my relationship with that group which was so critical to what I was doing at that time. And so from that, the journey began. I went to another company as the head of learning and development and continued to work on this. I had a CEO who was interested in seeing the value up to and including ROI. And then in 1983, I published the first book in the United States on training evaluation titled *Handbook of Training Evaluation and Measurement Methods*. It became widespread in terms of adoption and use all over the world. We measured and evaluated not only training and development while I was there, I moved into human resource functions as well. And then went into senior executive roles that still required and conducted evaluation.

In 1992, we founded the ROI Institute to help others with this. Our mission is to help organizations around the world evaluate their programs—all types of programs. So now we are in 52 countries, and we've got about 30 books that support the ROI Methodology. Our books are in 38 languages and are moving the methodology to new applications, to new cultures, and to new countries. We have worked hard to refine a process that can deliver bottom-line results that is executive, professor, researcher and user friendly. We now count about 4,000 organizations using this, and that number is growing. And it is going into all types of organizations, so I'd say it is so pleasing to see the use and acceptance of what we have created over a period of time.

On how training evaluation has changed over the years...

It certainly has mushroomed as an important part of learning and development. It is more evidenced based today than it was before. It is also more quantitative; we started off basically evaluating or collecting a lot of qualitative data. And in the last decade it became more financial. It is identifying the value to an organization in financial terms and getting more data about the contribution of learning. We have come a long way from just using "happiness sheets" many, many years ago as our only evaluation to tremendous focus on evaluation of learning and development functions, and we have had a lot of success. So I am pleased to see the evolution and change over the last three or four decades.

On the progress the profession has made in embracing evaluation...

When we have a large expenditure, it comes naturally these days to see the contributions that expenditure is making. That is the return-on-investment. We have two clients now, for example, that have more than $1 billion of annual expenditures in learning and development. As you can imagine, with that level of expenditure, you have to think about the return. So I think the executives have driven this, of course, they push this same accountability in other functions as well. Now, I also think that it is driven in part by business-minded learning and development managers who have looked at what *value* we are delivering. I remember a comment made by a large package delivery company about 10 years ago; at that time the organization had a greater than $600 million budget in learning and development. And the head of that budget said to the group, as they embarked on this ROI journey, he said, "To this point, the executives have not asked us to show the value of this $600 million expenditure. But I can't imagine them not asking that, and I think it is important for us to do it because we really need to see the value delivered."

On how executives view learning and development and investment in it...

So many of our clients tell us that they earn respect by showing the value. I remember the training manager from Guinness Brewery sending me a note telling me he conducted an ROI study for one of the major programs and presented it to the CEO. He said the CEO probably knew who he was in the organization but had never had a conversation with him directly. And the training manager had a meeting with him to present these data, and it was very positive. The CEO got excited about the data and actually took them to the holding company's quarterly CEO meeting. And the training manager said that since then, the CEO had contacted him and dropped in to see him and began to ask him his opinion on things. He said that it broke the ice of communicating with and getting support from that top group. I think that is an important lesson that we see repeated over and over. This allows us to connect to the business, make improvements in the business, and gain friends at high levels. These executives are not so concerned about reaction data and learning data, in fact they normally don't even want to see that. But they do like to see if there are changes in the way we approach our jobs, so that is what we call application data or if it made an impact in the organization in some business measure, that is impact as we call it. And then a few, in growing number, want to see the actual ROI for major programs.

So, if you can do that, if you can provide these data, they change their perception of the function, of the people involved in that function, and certainly their perception of the funding you may or may not need in the future.

On how evaluation makes a difference in the perception held by executives of training and development...

We have a chapter in this handbook that gets right to that issue. Let me cover what I think is probably some of the key findings of that particular research piece. We had heard from 96 CEOs at the top of very large organizations on the *Fortune* 500 list, and what we saw was a tremendous gap in terms of what we report to them and what they really want to see. If we take the three levels that I mentioned before, I was showing the executives the data that suggest we are making a difference in the organization, that people are operating differently, and that they are improving their work processes—the *application* data. Eleven percent of those CEOs said that they are getting this now, and 61 percent said they would like to have it in the future. But the biggest gap occurs at the next level—*impact*—8 percent of the CEOs said they have data that shows the connection to the business, but 96 percent said they wanted to see these data. That's a huge gap. And third, in terms of *ROI*, 4 percent said they get this now but 74 percent said they wanted to see this. So those gaps really highlight some challenges for us. Now on the positive side, we are making progress in that we have those percentages at Levels 3, 4, and 5: 11 percent, 8 percent, and 4 percent. A decade ago not even that would have been there. But the challenge is that they want to see more at these levels. So we have to keep working on this and pushing our evaluation to those levels in our data collection and analysis and particularly in our reporting.

On why we still see such a low investment in training measurement and evaluation within organizations and how can we facilitate more investment in the future...

I think I would say the number one reason people avoid training measurement and evaluation is a fear of the results—a fear of this level of accountability. After all, if you show the executives who fund these projects that a particular program is not delivering enough value or money to overcome the cost that results in a negative ROI, there's a fear this may reflect on them or their staff or their team. So there is a reluctance to go down that path sometimes. Of course we know it is a mistake to wait on the request, but nevertheless, it's a huge impediment that we see. Also, some people just don't understand how we connect learning to business impact. Particularly with soft skills, we get this question so much: how do we do it? They just can't see it, and they don't know the techniques; it appears complex and consumes too many resources; they don't understand it, and they fear the results.

If you could look across any other function in an organization, you would see a much larger investment in measurement and evaluation than in the learning area. Measurement is basically collecting data, and evaluation is making some sense out of the data. Our best guess is that about 1 percent of the learning and development budget is spent on measurement and evaluation. In our best-practice benchmarking that number ought to be in the 3- to 4-percent level. So we've got to really increase our investment three-fold. And what it will take, I think, is for the chief learning officer to start pushing the evaluation envelope to this level.

On what the future holds for measurement and evaluation...

I think that we will keep pushing the envelope and making progress in probably five areas. First, we will show more connection to the business, showing data to our executives that they appreciate and can relate to. That often includes the business impact data being driven by our programs. And occasionally ROI, showing how the money was wisely invested. Second, I think technology is going to help, and we have technology that can make this less painful and also keep the cost down because it addresses the complexity and the cost of doing some impact studies. Third, I think we are going to build more of it in. I would like to see evaluation positioned as an application tool. For example, we may have an action plan in a program that is there to show the participants how this applies and the impact it will have, but obviously it is evaluation data for us. Action plans need to be built into programs so they don't appear to be add-ons, because an add-on process is always resisted. Fourth, I think we will see more preparation for people coming into this field. Historically, they had little, if any, training in the measurement and evaluation area, but we are seeing a lot of degree programs are putting some serious evaluation and measurement processes into the curriculum. So, people are coming in more prepared for this, and that knowledge often cuts down on resistance to doing it. They come in with the expectation of doing it, and I think that is going to help. And last but not least, I think we have to change the ADDIE model: analysis, design, development, implementation, and evaluation. When the instructional design steps are listed in that sequence, we think about evaluation only after it is all over.

About Jack J. Phillips

Jack Phillips, PhD, is chairman and co-founder of the ROI Institute and developer of the ROI Methodology. Phillips' work spans more than 50 books and 200 articles. Former bank president, *Fortune* 500 human resource director, and management professor, he provides consulting services in more than 50 countries. His research and publications have won numerous awards, including the Society for Human Resource Management's Book of the Year and the Yoder-Heneman Personnel Creative Application Award. Phillips is a former member of ASTD's Board of Directors and the recipient of ASTD's highest honor, the Distinguished Contribution Award for Workplace Learning and Performance.

✎ Dana Gaines Robinson

On how it all started...

When I was a training director at a bank on the East Coast, I was asked to bring supervisory training into the organization. I was actually the first training director they had ever hired; this was in the 70s. And I went out to find a program that I thought would work for us and I did. I found a program provided through a supplier. And doing the cost analysis on that with my management team, it became apparent that this was a much heavier investment than they had anticipated. So they asked me to prove that it would make a difference and if I could, they would support bringing it into the organization. I said, "Oh I can do that!" Then I went back to my office and said, "How the heck do I do that?" and went out to find help. That help came in the form of Jim Robinson so, in a sidebar to this story, that is how I met the man I eventually married. We measured the impact of the program in three ways: attitudinal change, behavioral change, and operational impact. I used a control experimental design—because I was only being funded to train 50 people and there were 300 in the group, it was easy to do. In other words, just by default or by accident we did a lot of things right, and we were able to validate a huge impact in all three of those areas that resulted in my budget doubling for the next year, increasing my staff by two people, and away we went! So the many insights I had out of that have lasted my entire professional life. One of those insights is that the development of skill, while important, is not the same thing as changing performance. Performance change requires a holistic approach in which skill enablement is a piece. Another insight was that when you can validate and affirm to managers that there is a business case for a program, that there is an investment to be made, but there is also a return to be realized, you get support. And so we carried those two learnings forward, and they became part of the work we did in building the models of performance consulting that we now teach people to use.

I was moved into the training and development field in 1976 and was lucky enough and fortunate enough to very early in my career learn the difference between *building skill* and *changing performance.* That is actually one of the key insights I had through a measurement effort. In learning that difference, I took it forward and realized, along with Jim, that there is a lot to be done to help people who work in the learning and development field develop a systemic approach that can be replicated, that moves beyond acquiring skill only, and that looks at changing performance. That really became the basis for our book *Performance Consulting*, which was published in 1995. We take great pride in thinking that we've helped to bring that into the field in a more robust manner, and it has been our life's work to help people become more strategic in their work, focus beyond the solution of learning, and think about what they are doing to actually change performance that will be sustained over time.

On how training evaluation has changed over the years...

I think it's a mixed bag, and I don't think we are where we need to be, but we are better than we used to be. First of all, it is a much more discussed topic than it was in the 1970s when I was doing the work I did. And there is a lot more available to people to teach them how to do this. There are also many more systems that you can adopt and replicate and read about. There is software and technology that supports doing it. So, there are a lot of available enablers that make it easier to do. But it is still "OK," and I am going to use that in quotes, that people in our field don't do this. It is something we accept; in fact it is almost as though people are still surprised if they find out that you are consistently working to measure the impact of at least some of your work every year. If I am a professional and I mention that I deliver training but I don't form learning objectives before I build a program, most people would look askance at that; but if I indicate that I deliver training but no, we haven't been able to measure impact because we didn't do that, people just accept it. And that is a disappointment to me because I would hope by now that it would be much more of a thing that people typically do on those programs for which it is appropriate. I do want to stress that not every learning intervention can or should be measured for impact, but unfortunately too few of them are.

On the progress the profession has made in embracing evaluation...

I am always an optimist, that is my nature, so what I see is movement in a positive type of direction, just much slower than I would have predicted a couple of decades ago. But I do have a lot of hope because of the various enablers that we have through technology and software, through the capability development opportunities that exist, and through the awareness of the criticality of this. And I do believe more and more people who come into our field appreciate and value the need to be business people, to think like business people, and to look at things in terms of investments and returns. With that mental model becoming more embedded in the profession, it bodes well for more of this to be done. Once again there is still the caveat that not everything that is done under a learning umbrella can or should be measured for impact, but we still need to do more of it because many things that could be measured this way are not.

On how executives view learning and development and investment in it...

I think that we need to build both a "push" and "pull" strategy on three levels in the profession, in our organizations and functions, and then within ourselves as professionals. Let me explain. There are times we need to push and be the initiator and build a want for this, and there are times when we can be pulled in when someone is seeking it, and I think we need *both* strategies to be operative.

On how evaluation makes a difference in the perception held by executives of training and development...

Here is a very valuable thing we can do: Would a manager want to know if results are not occurring so we can take additional actions to get results moving in the right direction? If we frame it as, "We are going to help you know you are getting the type of performance that you need from people and the type of results you need from business and, if not, why not?" a lot of managers would see a lot of value in that.

That is the definition of being strategic: you are aligned to a business and you are benefiting the business. And so if we are going to be aligned to the business, then we need to think like business people: What are the business needs here, what is the way in which I can support those, what would be the cost for doing that, what is the return? And, of course, in the learning field there is a very critical insight that took me a few years to get that I hope people are more familiar with now and that is there is only *one* way, *one* way, in which building skills affects the business result and that is through the performance of people. The business styles of an organization don't move in a positive direction because of what I know; they move in a positive direction because of what I do with what I know and therefore, of course, why we feel performance consulting is such a critical, critical part of the equation.

I really feel people that are leading and doing learning and development work in organizations, they are *absolutely* business people. Now their focus or their area of expertise is on learning or human performance improvement. We are business people and we need to approach what we do from a business perspective, and a classic business perspective is here's the investment and this is the return we should anticipate and how do we know if that happens. We owe it to ourselves and to our organizations to do some validation of that.

On why we still see such a low investment in training measurement and evaluation within organizations and how we can facilitate more investment in the future...

As we go into organizations, we often ask people to assess various criteria, the things that are most characteristic of these criteria, and those that are least characteristic of these criteria, and these are the criteria for operating as performance consultants. There are eight of these criteria; one of the criteria that *always* shows up at the bottom of the list is measuring the results of what we do. And so we ask these groups why that is and here is what they share with us. One category of answers is all about how we don't get asked to do this; our managers don't ask us do this, they're busy people, they are moving on to the next thing, and so are we. So it is the lack of focus, the lack of being pulled into doing it. I would say also then the lack of expectation that it will be done. We have many people tell us that they don't do it because they don't know how. And of course that is an overcome-able thing in our field; we know about learning and skill development, and as I mentioned there are many ways to learn this. So that is something we can overcome. And another reason we get is that some people are very wary of what you really learn from doing it because they say you can't isolate training as the variable that made the difference and, if you can't isolate it, why would you bother measuring it? But I believe that many people in our field still do not truly understand that there is a difference between building skill and changing performance. And it is as though people go and acquire the skill and the knowledge that is being provided and then say, "We are OK, the rest will happen." Of course we know it doesn't. There are people in our field who don't feel they are accountable for ensuring people *apply* skill, it is their job to help them learn it but it is management's job to make sure they use it. But of course in performance consulting, we are about a partnership with management and *together* we should share the accountability for getting the impact from what we do. Another reason that I believe it's done infrequently is that measurement is really a front-end process, and, if you haven't identified the performance and business outcomes that you expect from the learning, it's pretty hard to measure whether you got them. It's the old "we have to have our destination in mind." So unfortunately a lot of people don't do enough front-end work to know what those destinations might be. And then I think some people are concerned that they might measure and find limited results. In today's business world that puts us in a vulnerable place. So I think there are a lot of reasons why it isn't done.

On what the future holds for measurement and evaluation...

Performance consulting is really a process in which clients and consultants partner to optimize workplace performance in support of business goals. That is what it is. It is a solution-neutral process. It's not just about learning; it is about optimizing workplace performance and doing whatever is needed to make that happen both in terms of changing performance of people but also in terms of building a workplace infrastructure that allows them to work effectively. So performance consulting is a four-phase process, and one of those phases is measurement; it is the last of the four phases. So measurement has always been an integral part of performance consulting in our minds. Performance consulting is a process that yields results: performance change, workplace change, and business impact. It is about results. And we tend to measure what we produce so if we are producing results, we want to measure those at the levels that are commonly thought of as 3, 4, and 5 in our levels of evaluation. And measurement also helps to determine if results are not occurring as we hoped. So what else might be needed to achieve those results? Measurement is an integral part of performance consulting. It is one of the four phases, and it's affirming that the results we set out to achieve through our performance consulting process and work have, in fact, occurred. I don't see that changing; they are completely integral to each other.

About Dana Gaines Robinson

Dana Gaines Robinson, former founder and president of Partners in Change (a consulting practice founded with her husband, Jim Robinson), developed and advanced the concepts of performance consulting. Exemplary Performance is now the sole distributor of their workshops and consulting services, and Robinson is semi-retired, working on selected projects through the Exemplary Performance organization. She is the coauthor of *Performance Consulting* and *Training for Impact*. A past member of ASTD's Board of Directors, she is the co-recipient, along with her husband Jim, of ASTD's Distinguished Contribution Award for Workplace Learning and Performance.

✎ William J. Rothwell

On how it all started...

I started my career 30 years ago, and I started as a practitioner, not as an academic. I was first a training director and was delivering many training programs in state government in Illinois. After that, I was widely involved in the insurance industry and my company and in setting up a training department from scratch, looking at everything from executive development to hourly workers and skill and technical training in an insurance environment. I have also done a number of consulting projects on training evaluation. I won't drop names, but one state government's entire system of community colleges came to me and asked for consulting assistance in setting up a uniform approach to training evaluation for community colleges that are training to support local businesses and their economic and workforce development efforts. Of course, some years ago I published a book with ASTD, *The Role of the Evaluator*, which talked about the field of learning and performance and the role of the evaluator, among many other roles, in terms of establishing a framework for properly measuring and evaluating the impact of training and other kinds of interventions related to learning or performance improvement purposes. I guess I have had quite a lot of involvement with training evaluation over the years, both in teaching graduate courses, teaching public workshops on training evaluation, and conducting training workshops on other kinds of evaluation such as organization development evaluation or evaluating performance improvement efforts.

On how training evaluation has changed over the years...

Generally speaking, practitioners in our field, learning and performance, have become more sensitized over the years to demonstrate the results of what they do. That is particularly difficult in our field because when we teach people new things, many factors back on the job can affect whether they applied what they learned. Of course we know that people say that only about 8 percent of off-the-job training transfers back to the job in changed behavior.

When we look at some of the reasons for that, we see that short-term memory theory plays a part. We forget about 80 percent of what we have heard within 48 hours. Co-workers or supervisors who were not in attendance in the training that the trainee attended are not positioned well to support what the trainee has learned back on the job. Over the years, I have come to some conclusions about training evaluation. I think one of those is that we have become more sensitized to the relationship between evaluation and needs assessment. And we tend to think of needs assessment as something that is to specify the needs to be met by training. When needs assessment is not done properly, or management mandates training be done without being totally sure that training is the best way to solve the problem, the training doesn't work. And so, this is one of the things that I have come to realize over the years: that training needs assessment and training evaluation go hand in hand and that, many times, requests for return-on-investment information or other things are merely a symptom that the needs assessment was not done properly.

On the progress the profession has made in embracing evaluation...

One of the dilemmas we always face in our field is that we really have two groups of people. One consists of professionals in the field who get a degree, or they become ASTD certified through the Certified Professional in Learning and Performance, or both. Those people tend to regard the training, learning, and performance field as their career, and they stick with it, perhaps for their entire lives. There is another group of people, usually a larger group, who are promoted from within the organization, hold short-term stints in the training function, and then go back out into the line organization or into other capacities. Generally speaking, I think the professionals in this field have become much more sensitized to the need to demonstrate the value of what they do, but that some of the "promoted from within people," that's the very large number who come into the field and leave the field every year, those people tend to drag down the average in terms of awareness about how to do training evaluation, how to collect data, how to convince decision makers that those data are accurate, and how to eventually demonstrate results.

What I do not see is the commitment of or the willingness to commit the staff or the resources necessary to collect those data. Some years ago, in the mid 1990s, I did a small-scale survey of practitioners, and I asked them several questions about evaluation. One of questions was this: "When do the decision makers most often ask you for evaluation information: Before you deliver a training effort, during the delivery of the training effort, or following the delivery of the training effort?" Which would you guess they said most often? The last of course—after the training was delivered. I believe that is too late. We are much better advised to gather the metrics before we make the investment in the training and get agreement with our decision makers about what metrics we will use to measure the success or relative success of the venture. We get them to buy in, and we do that as part of the needs assessment or performance analysis process. And if we can get the "jury" in agreement on the metrics to use, then it will be very difficult for them to change their minds later, not impossible, but more difficult. So then at least we have a target to shoot for. So we know what the grading criteria are by which our efforts are going to be evaluated.

I believe that canny practitioners probably figured this out themselves, and many of them have been doing this already, routinely. They have been trying to collect those metrics, even during the initial interviews and during initial needs assessment so they have got a basis by which to track achievements, during and after, the training is delivered.

On how executives view learning and development and investment in it...

We should never forget that the word *evaluate* contains within it the word *value,* and values, I believe, are what this is all about. Why is it that decision makers always question the return-on-investment or the impact of training, but we *rarely* hear the same issues come up for accounting ventures or for large computer systems? Sometimes those are taken at face value as being worth it. So, I think at the base, one of the issues we are talking about is this: What does management really value? Does the human side of the enterprise command the same level of management support that technology does, or that financial services does, or that marketing does? I really wonder about that. Over the years, I have often wondered why we rarely hear people ask, "What is the impact of our executive bonus plan on achieving business results?" Lately we have heard that question come up after the financial crisis. But before that, people rarely questioned the need for bonuses. So, you see what I am saying— what do we really believe is important? What is worth measuring, and why do we hold one type of activity, like training, to one standard, but sometimes other activities are not held to the same standard?

I worry that people think that evaluation information alone is all they need without realizing that there is a political element to evaluation. Political not in a sense of political parties, but political in the sense of organizational politics where it is one thing to collect data and it's another thing to convince decision makers. And I think focusing on how to convince decision makers and getting their involvement are really key, very important in the whole evaluation arena. If we can pinpoint what a problem is costing us *before* we make an investment in training, one of many kinds of solutions, then I think we are headed in the right direction. So, forecasting benefits means getting clear on the metrics, getting buy-in from the decision makers, getting them to agree those are appropriate metrics, and then tracking accordingly.

On how evaluation makes a difference in the perception held by executives of training and development...

A better way is to think of training evaluation as akin to a legal problem in terms of the way lawyers think of convincing a jury. Now, there is a difference between evidence and proof. Evidence is something we give people to sway them to believe something. And so, a trial attorney would place convincing evidence in front of a jury. The jury is the "try-er of fact." They decide whether the evidence has made the case or not and whether someone is guilty or not guilty. The same is true in our field. Regard the jury as all of the key stakeholders, senior managers, middle managers, even learners who are participating in the effort, other trainers in the training divisions, and even customers and other stakeholders. If we ask the question, "What evidence would it take to convince them that our training had an impact?" I think we are thinking along the right lines. Remembering that no matter what level of evidence we give them, if they have already made up their mind, we will never change it. We could have a fool-proof mathematical formula and a fool-proof research design to show business results, but if the decision makers didn't accept it, the point is not proven. And we have a luxury that trial attorneys do not have, which is that we can ask the jury in advance of the intervention what evidence it will take to convince them that there *was* an impact.

On why we still see such a low investment in training measurement and evaluation within organizations and how can we facilitate more investment in the future...

It goes back to a topic that I discussed in one of my books, *Beyond Training and Development*. Like "Murphy's Law"—you have heard of that, if something can go wrong it will go wrong—you have something called "Rothwell's Theory of Visible Activity," which states that management only values what they see us do directly. They see us perform things like classroom delivery or online instruction, and they equate that activity with meaningful results. But "back-office" activities like needs assessment, which is very important to scope the training, like performance analysis to determine whether training is even a suitable solution to the problem, evaluation efforts which may take place following the training, during the training or before the training, tend not to be *highly* visible instructional delivery efforts.

I believe we have to overcome one issue. We have heard the term used in the quality movement: "the cost of quality." There is also a cost of evaluation. If we are an understaffed training function or learning and performance function, what are we likely to get the greatest payoff in doing? Presenting visible activity or evaluating the results of what we have done? This goes back to the cost of the evaluation, until we feel it is important enough to make the investment in collecting the data and learning what the decision makers want to know. The first question to ask in evaluation is always "Who wants to know?" The second question is "What are they going to do with the information once we find it out. What decisions will they make?" Different groups are going to make different decisions. If we hand evaluation data back to our training instructors, which is often a group that does receive them, the expectation is that they will improve the next delivery. But if we present those data to senior executives, what do we expect them to do? I would guess either continue to fund or increase the funding for the training function as a result of being satisfied with the results achieved.

Some years ago, I wrote a book, *What CEOs Expect from Corporate Training*. In that book, we published quotations from more than 80 CEOs we interviewed about the competencies of the training professional. And when we asked them about evaluation, a number of CEOs expressed some skepticism about trusting evaluation information that is gathered by the same people who were responsible for making the change. In other words, one CEO said that makes about as much sense as trusting an accountant to do his or her own audit. In short, they were saying that they found data collected by training and development professionals about interventions that they themselves had done or had been involved with to be suspect. And it came across to some senior leaders as looking like a "cover your butt" activity. I think we have to be sensitive that not all stakeholders look at us with complete trust.

On what the future holds for measurement and evaluation...

I have seen the field moving increasingly to the "gee-whiz gizmos." I did a literature study recently in the last year, and I found the biggest number of articles about the unveiling and use of new technology and delivery: Second Life and wikis and all of that. So there seems to be great interest in all of these exciting new delivery modalities. But I believe that unless we stay focused on how the training helps us achieve business objectives and get very clear at every step about taking it back to that, it will be a problem for the field longer term.

I just think people are excited about new delivery options that may increase the interest and the motivation level of current or future generations in the workplace—who may be better attuned to certain delivery options than other generations might be. But I am just pleading for people to keep their eye on the ball. The "eye on the ball" means this: How do we get our efforts aligned with business results? How do we make our contributions more visible and make decision makers more aware of those effects? I have nothing against new media; I think that they are exciting. I am simply saying they can distract us from keeping our eyes on the real ball, which is helping the people in the organization get results.

I would like to say that the roles of the business manager, the learning professional, the organization development professional, and the performance consultant are to some extent converging. I think it would be a desirable thing if they were able to do so. Unfortunately, many educational institutions and other places that teach future business leaders still do not adequately emphasize the human side of the business, and this is all the more surprising because every business observer and pundit says that the future rests with innovation: the ability to think creatively and outsmart competitors. And yet, if all we can think of is meeting today's balance sheet numbers without thinking about other things that may not be as easily made tangible, like investments in people, if people and their innovation is what is key to the business then, I think, we face a problem long term.

The organization teaches newcomers what the organization has learned from its experience to preserve institutional memory. But that is past oriented, and I believe what we are starting to see is more use of face-to-face opportunities, few though they may be, particularly in industries that do not have an R&D function like service firms, which, as you know, is so important in this economy. We use group settings for what they should be used for, to generate new ideas. If we understand that training is simply a way to get people to overcome deficiencies and get them up to some standard, then that is kind of past oriented. If we look at group venues as something different from an online venue, where it is fairly easy to convey information, some of that information may well have come from our organizations' past experience. If we look at group settings as an opportunity to generate new knowledge and to make the training—which may now be misnamed—essentially an R&D function for service firms where we can pull people together and generate new ideas, then I think it is dead on to this future of helping to facilitate innovation and creative thinking. So I would like to say that I see training splitting, with a lot of the online and other virtual forms taking over the old, traditional role of training as helping people overcome deficiencies, helping people meet requirements, helping get people up to a standard for their current level and keep them there as technology changes, and helping people prepare for the next level, but then see group settings more frequently used to generate new knowledge.

About William J. Rothwell

William J. Rothwell, PhD, professor of Human Resource Development at Pennsylvania State University, oversees a graduate program in Human Resource Development and Employee Training; teaches graduate courses on the full range of performance technology issues; directs research projects; and consults with organizations in business, industry, government, and nonprofit sectors. He has consulted widely on succession planning and management. A prolific writer, he is author or coauthor of numerous books devoted to training and performance management issues.

$\backsim$ Epilogue

What, then, are the "learnings" from these interviews? What forecast for the future of training evaluation and measurement can we derive from the comments of these legends?

- Standing on the shoulders of those who came before, the history of measurement and evaluation is evolutionary, not revolutionary.
- Many of the innovations came from examining what had been done and simply asking, "why" and "what if?"
- Donald Kirkpatrick, Jack Phillips, and William Rothwell use the same analogy about proof and evidence before a "jury" that increasingly holds our fate in its hands.
- A great consensus exists that there is (and will continue to be) an emphasis on evaluation data at the higher levels, moving beyond reaction and learning (although still important) to behavior change and business/financial impact.
- Dana Gaines Robinson articulated the belief that behavior change that drives results is the only real determinate of value.
- We need to make evaluation a critical element of the front-end work, never an afterthought.
- There is no lack of tools, methodologies, case studies, and now technology to assist us, but they are not a substitute for clear thinking about what we are trying to measure and why. Evaluation is less about the methodology chosen but more about the rationale behind the selection.
- The field of evaluation is not without differing views on key issues. For example, William Rothwell says his executives suggest training professionals not evaluate their own programs; yet, Jack Phillips' research states that executives want the evaluation data. So what should training professionals do? They need to approach evaluation methodically and systematically and ensure they make conservative

assumptions. They need quantitative and qualitative data along with financial and nonfinancial data. Augmenting data with quotes, examples, and specific case examples from highly-regarded executives and stakeholders can not only help drive home the impact, but can help mitigate executive concerns about objectivity. This is what gives results credibility and helps senior leaders trust the evaluation data.

- Partnership with and communication to senior leaders is at the heart of long-term success.
- Both Robert Brinkerhoff and Roger Kaufman look to a future when evaluation also encompasses the impact on society and "the greater good."
- William Rothwell's "Theory of Visible Activity" explains a lot about executive perceptions.
- Dana Gaines Robinson's experience notwithstanding, evaluation work does not always lead to finding your soul mate.
- Among all those interviewed, there was a sense of appreciation for the journey so far, for the many who have embraced the methodologies and practices that shape their evaluation and measurement work, but there was also concern for the relatively small percentage of members of our profession who do this along with a frank assessment of how much further we need to go.

There is no way to capture the depth and breadth of the contribution to the profession, in particular to the field of training evaluation and measurement, of these legends—these giants—in a book chapter or in brief interviews. To be fully appreciated, the richness and complexity of their thought leadership must be experienced through reading their works, studying with them if you are so fortunate, and then applying the concepts and tools to the work we do for our organizations and clients. Perhaps this chapter offers a roadmap for your own continued exploration or a blueprint for the next iteration of innovative thinking about evaluation so that, 20 years from now, the next series of interviews with "legends" will include your voice.

It was my privilege to serve as the interviewer. I have been a beneficiary of their thought leadership and practical frameworks for many years, and, if I have been able to effectively serve the clients and corporations for whom I have worked, it was due in large part to the pioneering work of these legends. I remain deeply grateful to Patti Phillips for the opportunity to be involved with this definitive work and to stand on her shoulders as well for many years to come.

✆ About the Editor of "Voices"

 **Rebecca Ray, PhD,** is a seasoned professional with more than 20 years of academic, corporate, and consulting experience and a track record of success and recognition for excellence and innovation in talent management. In 2008, Ray was selected as the "Chief Learning Officer of the Year" by *Chief Learning Officer* magazine and named to the first-ever list of "Top 100 People in Leadership Development" by *Leadership Excellence* magazine.

Ray has held senior leadership positions at MasterCard Worldwide, Comcast Cable Communications, American Skandia, Prudential Securities, and Merrill Lynch. Prior to her corporate experience, she led a consulting practice that offered leadership assessment and development programs to *Fortune* 500 companies. Her areas of expertise include assessment and selection, employee training and development/corporate universities, management and leadership development, diversity, executive coaching and mentoring, executive education, organization development, employee engagement, performance management, and succession management.

Ray and her various teams have been honored with "Learning In Practice Awards" from *Chief Learning Officer* magazine; Corporate University Xchange's awards for "Excellence and Innovation in Corporate Learning"; and International Quality & Productivity Center's "Best in Class" (CUBIC) awards as well as selection to *Leadership Excellence* magazine's list of "Top Leadership Development Programs" for the "Leadership Excellence" program for senior executives. Her various teams were named to *Training* magazine's elite global list, the Top 100/125, six separate times. Her approach to leadership development and the use of competencies at the executive level formed the basis of a case study response in the *Harvard Business Review;* her accomplishments have also been profiled in *Chief Executive Officer, CIO, Fortune, BusinessWeek, Human Resources, The Financial Times, Workforce Management, Training, Training & Development,* and *Chief Learning Officer* magazines.

Ray serves on the editorial advisory boards for *Training* and *Chief Learning Officer* magazines and on the advisory board for the University of Pennsylvania's Executive Program in Work-Based Learning Leadership. The author of two textbooks and several plays, she holds a doctorate from New York University where she taught as an adjunct professor for many years.

✒ **Appendix**

Answers to Exercises

Chapter 1—Identifying Stakeholder Needs

Needs Assessment for Customer Service Representatives

1. This case presents a clear example of the problems and expense that occur when needs assessment is not done. Not only did the customer service refresher course represent an expense, but there was also the cost of the problem that continued to increase as the correct solution was not applied, including the loss of customers.

2. Recommended solutions are twofold:
   a. new products training
   b. information technology to determine what is needed, whether it is hardware or software, upgrade to the system or new system.

3. At minimum, the following data points should be tracked and reported: customer satisfaction scores, call handle time, number of call escalations, and customer service representatives satisfaction.

Chapter 2—Developing Powerful Program Objectives

Identify the Level of Objective

Objective	Evaluation Level
1. Decrease time spent on completing scheduled machinery maintenance from two days to one.	Level 4
2. Complete all 10 steps on the teller checklist before noon each day.	Level 3
3. Calculate a 1:4 cost-benefit ratio for the leadership development program two years after implementation.	Level 5
4. Increase posttest scores by 10 points over pretest scores.	Level 2
5. Increase customer satisfaction scores on annual stakeholder survey.	Level 4

Chapter 3—Planning Your Evaluation Project

Planning Evaluation

1. **Why has evaluation planning become so important to effective evaluation?**

   The scope and complexity of evaluation projects today requires better planning to avoid running into trouble.

2. **What is a technique to ensure alignment among stakeholder needs, program objectives, and evaluation outcomes?**

   Create evaluation questions that include the solution, the data to measure it, and the standard to judge effectiveness.

3. **List seven ways to collect data.**

   Surveys and questionnaires, tests and assessments, interviews, focus groups, action plans, case studies, and performance records.

4. **What are the key questions to ask when planning data collection?**

   What objectives are being evaluated? What measures are being used to evaluate the objectives? Where are the sources of data? How should data be collected? When should data be collected? Who should be responsible for collecting the data?

5. **List three ways to analyze data.**

   Statistics, qualitative, financial analyses.

6. **What are the key questions to ask in planning data analysis?**

What are the needs of key stakeholders who will receive the final report? What data items have been collected? What data types are there? How can you isolate the effects of the program or solution? How can you best summarize and describe the data? How can you best find relationships and differences among the data? What data can be converted to monetary value? What data should be reported as intangible benefits? Who will be responsible for conducting the data analysis and reporting the results?

7. **What are the four phases of evaluation planning?**

Establish the evaluation baseline, create the evaluation design, create the evaluation schedule, and create the evaluation budget.

Chapter 4—Using Surveys and Questionnaires

Answers to Question Comparisons Exercise

Practice 1:

Option B is correct; Option A was a double-barreled question that asked the respondent to address two different topics in the same question. Additionally it provided limited choices on how to answer.

Practice 2:

Option A is correct; Option B is a loaded question because it includes language saying how good it is (top of the line).

Practice 3:

Option B is correct; Option A is not descriptive—what does effective mean? Effective can mean something different to each respondent.

Practice 4:

Option A is correct; Option B does not provide enough details and answer options to understand the ability to use the skills (what does success look like), and it has limited answer options; question A is also anchored—by including "as a result of participating in the program," the respondent is able to associate his or her behavior to the learning event.

Practice 5:

Option B is correct; Option A includes potentially uncommon language—what is silo thinking? By explaining the specific behaviors, the respondent is able to accurately rate agreement with the statement.

Chapter 5—Designing a Criterion-Referenced Test

A Microtest to Practice Setting a Cut-Off Score

Possible Probability Estimates: Angoff Method of Setting a Cut-Off Score

There is no one correct numerical answer to the exercise because different opinions of the probabilities will result in different cut-off scores. Using the Angoff process correctly, however, means that all of your probability estimates should be between .25 and 1.00 and your cut-off score should be the sum of your five probability estimates. Below are possible probabilities and their total, the cut-off score:

Item	Probability
1	1.00
2	.50
3	.33
4	1.00
5	.65
Sum of Estimates	**3.48**

Cut-Off Score Estimate = 3.48 or 3, when rounded to the nearest whole number

Chapter 6—Conducting Interviews

Developing an Interview Protocol

Answers will vary but the sample below shows all the elements that should be included in the protocol.

Interview for the New Employee On-Boarding Program Evaluation

Interviewer Name: _____

Interviewee Name:_____   Phone Number:_____

Circle one: Male   Female   Job Title: _____

Work Unit: _____   Date Hired: _____

Date and Time of Interview: _____

Instructions to Interviewer are in italics:

Opening Statement

Read the following statement to the interviewee:

Hello, [name of interviewee]. My name is [your name], and I work in [name of your work unit]. *[Spend a moment here in small talk to put the interviewee at ease.*] Thank you for participating in our interviews. We are interviewing the employees who completed our corporate on-boarding program for new employees within the last six months. We want to find out if you think it was valuable to you. All the information you provide will be kept strictly confidential and will be seen only by the program manager. We will use the interview information to improve the program. This interview should take about 20 minutes.

Questions

Ask the interviewee the following questions and note the responses below each question.

1. How valuable do you think the on-boarding program was to you overall?

2. What part of the program did you find to be most valuable?

3. Why was this part of the program most valuable to you?

4. What part of the program did you find to be least valuable?

5. Why was this part of the program least valuable to you?

6. What additions or changes would you suggest making to the program?

7. Are there any other comments or suggestions you would like to make about the on-boarding program?

Closing Statement

Read the following statement to the interviewee:

Thank you so much for participating in the interview. Your input will help us enhance the program for future new employees. We plan to revise the program by the end of the year.

Chapter 7—Conducting Focus Groups

Focus Groups

1. The best candidates for a focus group are the people who are performing well at the performance issue at hand. True or False?

False. Individuals who have the performance issue are the most credible source for gaining insight into the actual cause of the performance issue.

2. **How many participants should be selected to represent a sample of the population under consideration?**

A sample size of 10 percent of the total population being studied is most likely to be an accurate representation of the population.

3. **An internal facilitator is the best person to conduct a focus group. True or False?**

False. Internal facilitators are more likely to be biased and less likely to be trusted than an external facilitator.

4. **What focus group format is the best method to obtain accurate results?**

The Ishikawa and nominal group techniques are useful when a single problem is under consideration. When multiple issues are at hand, a group interview may be more effective.

5. **After organizing all the data and identifying a solution, it is not necessary to review the solution with the focus group. True or False?**

False. Reviewing the proposed solution with the focus groups that provided input on the causes of the problem can provide valuable input as to whether the solution is on target and a comprehensive solution. They can also ensure that problems that existed during the time of the focus group are still relevant at the time of solution development and implementation.

Chapter 8—Action Planning as a Performance Support and Transfer Strategy

Using Action Plans to Calculate ROI

1. Using the formula provided, calculate the total adjusted monthly benefit (Column E) and the annualized program benefit (Column F) for the remaining two action plans collected from the coaching program.

Action Plan #	Unit of Measure	Monthly Improvement Value (A) x	Confidence Level (B) x	Percent Change Due to Program (C) x	Percent Time Applied to Productive Tasks* (D)	Total *Adjusted* Monthly Benefit = (E)	Annualized Program Benefit (use 12) (F)
19	Productivity	$12,000	50%	70%	60%	$2,520	$30,240
20	Time	$8,500	40%	60%	70%	$1,428	$17,136

2. **Instructions:** Now that the performance improvement data have been analyzed from all available action plans, calculate the ROI of the coaching program.

Coaching Program	Your Answer	Actual Answer
Action plan #19	$	$30,240
Action plan #20	$	$17,136
Data from 18 other action plans, isolated and annualized	$84,109	$84,109
10 other participants who did not supply data	-0-	-0-
Total annualized benefits from the coaching program	$	$131,485
Total costs of the program	$65,000	$65,000
Your ROI calculation: Benefits ($131,485) – Program Costs ($65,000) = ($66,485) Program Costs ($65,000) x 100 = ROI %	ROI = ____ %	ROI = 102 %

Chapter 9—The Success Case Method: Using Evaluation to Improve Training Value and Impact

Questions to Assess Understanding of Content

1. According to the Success Case Evaluation Method, why is it often misleading to try to isolate the impact of the training program in an evaluation study?
   a. often it is too difficult to do
   b. other contextual factors are always operating and affect the business impact
      Correct Answer
   c. employee motivation is the biggest determinant of business impact, so it will make the training look ineffective
   d. only some training is expected to produce measurable business results

   In virtually all training initiatives many more variables beyond the learning event will affect the use of the new skills and knowledge back on the job and the impact they will have. In field research it is generally impossible to control for these variables (specific job responsibilities, amount of coaching received, economic conditions, and so forth) as in a scientific experiment. These contextual factors aren't "artificial" or "contaminants" to the learning that should be corrected for. They are real and part of the natural environment. Success Case encourages human resource development professionals to acknowledge that those factors are operating and try to address them. Leverage those factors that help business impact and try to get them to occur all the time; work with senior management to begin to remove those factors that get in the way of performance.

Trying to isolate the impact of training by trying to "correct" for these other factors, can be misleading. It is potentially misleading because it buries the bigger and more important issue: how can the organization structure these factors so the good things happen more often and the bad (hindering) things are removed?

2. The Success Case Method looks at both the *value* obtained from the training and the *unrealized value*. Why are both concepts important? What fundamental questions do each of these two concepts address?

Correct Answer

All training evaluation strategies that focus on Level 4 or 5 examine the value that is produced by the intervention. Success Case Method is no different in this regard. It is a process for determining if participants were able to produce positive business impact (value) by using the skills/knowledge they acquired from the learning intervention. If participants applied the learning back on the job and their efforts produced only minimal (or no) business value, then the organization should seriously consider whether they should stop doing that training.

In most learning interventions some number of participants use their new skills and knowledge quite well and in ways that add value. Unfortunately, many participants do not. This represents the unrealized value or the lost opportunity; often it is larger than the amount of value that was obtained. By estimating both the actual *value* and *unrealized value*, human resource development professionals can build a more compelling case to senior management about the necessity for addressing those factors that reduce the amount of new skill application or pay-off the organization receives from the training.

3. What is the best way to significantly increase the ROI of training?
   a. turn classroom training into e-learning programs which will significantly reduce the costs per training hour
   b. shorten the length of time of any training program to make it more efficient
   c. improve the amount of information/skill people acquire in the training; the more they learn they better they will be able to produce results
   d. get more people to use the training in ways that make a difference to the business

Correct Answer

Although the other options will most likely reduce the cost of the training, this option will directly increase the value (return) of the training. Because ROI=Return / Cost, the ROI number will increase when the numerator (return or value) gets bigger or the denominator (cost) gets smaller, assuming the other stays the same. Reducing the cost (denominator), while keeping the return (numerator) the same, will increase the ROI. However, these reductions in cost are likely to be relatively small compared with the potential large increases in return that could be achieved by getting just a few more people to use the new skills more often or more effectively. We have routinely seen the value produced by a single participant after attending a leadership development program or sales skills program to be greater than $100,000. Helping one or two more people get this kind of return will far outweigh the savings achieved by saving an extra night at a hotel or even eliminating the airfare to travel to a workshop. In other words, the upside on the return (numerator) far outdistances the benefits of reducing the costs.

Chapter 10—Using Performance Records

Case Study

1. **Which type of data does the senior management team desire?**

   The senior management team is more interested in Level 4 (business impact) data, which in this case is the sales growth subsequent to the program implementation

2. **What performance records should be utilized to look for business impact measurement?**

   Sales records reporting average weekly sales per employee

3. **If the only performance record available to measure the impact of the training program is the average weekly sales per employee, do you find the need to convert these numbers into a more usable data?**

   Yes if you want to show the actual contribution of a sale. The average weekly sales per employee must be multiplied by the profit contribution (percent). This conversion is necessary to exclude the contribution of cost of goods sold in the sales increase.

Chapter 11—Using Statistics in Evaluation

Statistical Analysis

Following the steps described in this chapter, what are the general statistics and the interpretation of the statistics?

1. **Using MS Excel, calculate the mean, median, mode, standard deviation, sample variance, kurtosis, skewness, and range.**

Knowledge Prior to Training	
Mean	4.8
Median	5
Mode	5
Standard Deviation	1.61
Sample Variance	2.59
Kurtosis	−0.61
Skewness	0.11
Range	6

Knowledge After Training	
Mean	8.4
Median	8.5
Mode	9
Standard Deviation	0.681
Sample Variance	0.463
Kurtosis	−0.446
Skewness	−0.712
Range	2

2. Create a histogram of the data.

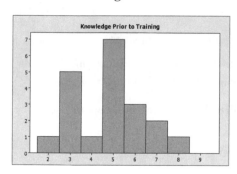
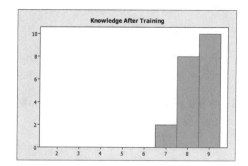

3. Fit a curve to the data.

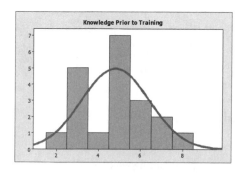
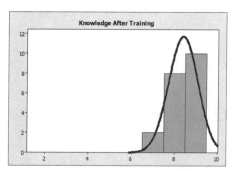

4. Determine if the data are symmetrical or skewed (if they are skewed, are the data left or right skewed).

The data from prior to the training are slightly skewed to the right while the data from after the training are skewed to the left.

Chapter 12—Analyzing Qualitative Data

Analyzing Qualitative Data

1. **Why are qualitative data important to training measurement and evaluation?**

    Quantitative data "show" results; qualitative data "tell" the story. Qualitative data describe the details surrounding the quantitative data.

2. **List three types of validity you need to be concerned with in qualitative analysis. What does each type of validity address?**

    - Descriptive validity answers the question, how accurate is the information.
    - Interpretive validity answers the question, has this information been accurately understood and reported?
    - Theoretical validity answers the question, have we adequately considered all possible explanations for the results we are reporting and not just fit out bias over the data?

3. **List four steps for analyzing qualitative data.**

    - observing and searching
    - sorting and coding
    - discovering and coding
    - re-observe and re-read

Chapter 13—Isolating the Effects of the Program

Isolating Program Effects Using Trend Line Analysis

The improvement in reject rates due to the program is .75 percent. The trend line picks up the routine noise that occurs as reject rates go down. Six months prior to the program reject rates were at 1.85 percent. Had the training not occurred, the reject rate probably would have been at 1.45 percent six months after the timing of the program.

Given that a program did occur, however, the actual reject rate was tracked six months after the program. The actual six months average was .7 percent. Had a comparison been made between the pre-program average (1.85 percent) and the actual post-program average (.7 percent), the amount would have reflected the pre-post difference only, not the contribution of the program.

Because a trend existed, the reject rate would have been at 1.45 percent. So to determine the contribution of the program, the projected reject rate six months after the program (1.45 percent) is compared with the actual six month reject rate (.7 percent), resulting in a different of .75 percent. This is the amount of change attributable to the program.

Chapter 14—Converting Measures to Monetary Value

Converting Program Benefits to Money

Following the five steps to convert improvement in a measure to money described in this chapter, what is the annual monetary benefit to Wines-by-the-Glass for increasing new wine club memberships through training?

1. **Identify the unit of measure.**

   One new membership

2. **Determine the value of the measure (V).**

   $45 × .60 profit margin (standard value) = $27 profit per membership

3. **Determine the change in performance in the measure due to the program ($\triangle$P).**

   Seven new memberships per month per store × .40 due to program = 2.8 new memberships per month per store

4. **Determine the annual change in performance (A$\triangle$P).**

   2.8 per month per store × 12 months = 33.6 per year per store
   33.6 × 30 stores reporting results = 1,008 total new memberships per year

5. **Calculate the annual monetary benefit (A$\triangle$P × V).**

   1,008 memberships × $27 profit per membership = $27,216 annual monetary benefit due to the training.

Chapter 15—Identifying Program Costs

Prorating Development Costs

A large financial institution plans to evaluate a major leadership development program. They are interested in prorating the development program costs over the life of the program. The leadership program will last approximately 18 months. The intent is to run 200 supervisors and team leaders through the program. The development costs were $250,000. This is a very high-profile project and the senior leaders are interested in seeing an ROI for at least one group of 25 participants. The data are summarized as follows:

- Development costs = $250,000
- Program life = 18 months
- Number of participants = 200
- Number of participants included in ROI study = 25

1. **What is the per person cost of developing the leadership development program?**

   $250,000 development costs / 200 participants over the life of the program = $1,250 per person over the life of the program

2. **How much in development cost will be included in the ROI study?**

   $1,250 per person development cost × 25 participants in ROI study = $31,250 in development cost to be included in the ROI study.

Chapter 16—Calculating the Return-on-Investment

Calculating ROI

Now that you have read this chapter, try your hand at calculating the BCR, ROI, and PP.

- The annual monetary benefit of an absenteeism reduction program is $237,800.
- The cost of the program is $175,000.

1. **What is the BCR? What does this tell you?**

   BCR = 1.36:1

   This tells us that for every $1 invested in a program, there are $1.36 in benefits.

2. **What is the ROI? What does this tell you?**

   ROI = 36%

   This tells us that for every $1 invested in a program, the dollar investment is returned and there is a gain of 36 cents ($0.36) over and beyond that investment.

3. **What is the PP? What does this tell you?**

   PP = .74 of one year or .74 x 12 = 8.8 months

   This tells us that the investment will be returned in approximately nine months.

Chapter 17—Estimating the Future Value of Training Investments

Estimating the Future Value of Training Investments

1. **At what point in time can an estimate of the future value of a training and development intervention be developed?**

   Forecasting the future value of a training and development intervention can take place at multiple points in time. Analysis can take place during planning, that is, before a program has been developed. Analysis can take place during development and delivery, that is, while costs are being incurred and benefits observed. At each point in time additional data can be incorporated into the analysis to increase the accuracy of the forecast.

2. **There are many reasons to assess the future value of a training and development investment. In your opinion, what reason do you find most compelling?**

There is no single correct answer to this question; the answer depends on your particular circumstances. However, multiple authors have pointed out that economic analysis applied to training and development puts investments in human capital on the same level as other investments in organizations or as Cascio and Boudreau (2008) point out that "…by the use of cost-benefit models [HRD programs], join with the other function of business in justifying the allocation of scarce organizational resources on the basis of evidence rather than on beliefs (p. 267)."

3. **A key stakeholder wishes to substantially decrease the length of participant time in the delivery program from the current eight hours to four hours. This change would increase the ROI by decreasing the cost. Develop a sensitivity analysis assuming that the value of the benefits is unaffected and the value of the benefits decrease by 0.5 transactions to 6.5 transactions. Use the following data to calculate the ROI. What recommendations could you make to this stakeholder?**

- Scenario 1: The cost of participant time is reduced by 50% resulting in a total cost of $118,000 and the value of benefits remains the same @ $214,285 and

- Scenario 2: The cost of participant time is reduced by 50% resulting in a total cost of $118,000 and benefits are likewise reduced by reduced by 50% and the resulting value is $115,384.

In scenario 1, the ROI will increase substantially because costs are significantly reduced and benefits are estimated to remain the same.

- Net Benefit = Benefit – Cost = 214,285 – 118,000 = 96,285.
- ROI = Net Benefit/Cost = 96,285/118,000 = 82%

In scenario 2, the calculations portray a different picture since the benefits are reduced along with the costs.

- Net Benefit = Benefit – Cost = 115,384 – 118,000 = –2,616.
- ROI = Net Benefit/Cost = –2,615/118,000 = –2.2%

It is not uncommon for stakeholders to be concerned by the costs of a program and to seek ways to reduce those costs and, in this case, participant time is an obvious choice. An evaluator in this situation might probe stakeholder beliefs for expectations about the effect of changes to the cost structure on the expected benefits and then recommend additional analyses. In this case, the best case scenario, a decrease in costs and no change to the benefits shows a substantial increase in the ROI but this scenario may not be reasonable. An alternative scenario, equating the decrease in benefits with the decrease in participant cost results in a slightly negative ROI. The evaluator in this situation might also use other values, such as reducing cost by 50 percent but reducing benefits by a lesser amount. The evaluator might also recommend testing the sensitivity of the ROI in these scenarios to other changes, such as, what would happen if the expectations about the number of sessions and the number of trainees were also changed along with the changes to the cost structure. The key point is that the evaluator is in a position to engage stakeholders in a discussion based on an analysis of the best available evidence and, as a result, the discussion is more likely to be based in evidence rather than beliefs and opinions.

4. **There is a need to develop an economic forecast for multiple training programs. Additionally, stakeholders wish to explore how various levels of funding might affect noneconomic variables such as participant learning and customer service quality to name a few. What method might complement an ROI analysis and include these other noneconomic variables and allow stakeholders to explore these issues?**

A systems model might be a useful solution in this case. A systems model could in this situation incorporate the economics of multiple training programs and incorporate the other variables, including "soft" variables into the model. Furthermore, a systems model built in the appropriate software would also allow evaluators and stakeholder to quickly simulate multiple scenarios and explore the implication of various decisions.

Chapter 18—Reporting Evaluation Results

Reporting Evaluation Results

1. **As someone involved in this training and study would you consider the reporting of the evaluation results acceptable? If not, why?**

The communications violated many basic principles for disseminating results:

- Reports were not generated in an immediate fashion to allow enhancements to be implemented.
- Communications were not tailored to the interest and needs of the unique stakeholders.
- No consideration was given to customize the type of media used for senior management versus the participants.

This is a classic example of designing a valuable training program but misusing time and resources by failing to deliver on the communication plan.

2. **If *you* were on the team designing the measurement study how would you have designed the communication plan?**

Below is a suggested communication plan for the Green Goods marketing strategy project.

Communication Plan for Green Goods Strategy Team

Green Goods Communication Document	Communication Target	Distribution Method
Complete report with appendices	• Program sponsor WLP staff • Selling team manager	• Distribute and discuss in a special meeting
Executive summary	• Senior management in the marketing units • Senior corporate management	• Distribute and discuss in regularly scheduled meeting
General interest overview and summary without the actual calculation (5-8 pages)	• Sales reps involved in training	• Mail with letter
General interest article (one page)	• Sales reps from all sales teams and company employees	• Publish in company publication
Brochure highlighting program, objectives, and specific results	• Team leaders with an interest in the program • Prospective sponsors including all marketing teams	• Include with other marketing materials

Chapter 19—Giving CEOs the Data They Want

Knowledge Check

1. **What is the gap between what learning and development professionals provide to executives and what they want to see in terms of results? Be precise.**

The first gap is with application results. Eleven percent of executives say they are receiving Level 3 data; however, 61 percent say they want it. We must show how people are applying the knowledge, skill, and information they gain through programs in terms that resonate with leaders.

The second gap is with business impact results where 8 percent of executives say they receive it and 96 percent say they want it. This is our biggest challenge and we must try to show the connection of our programs to the business. The third gap is with ROI where 4 percent of executives say they receive it and 74 percent said they would like to have it. This is second most important area where we need to place our focus next to showing the business impact of programs. Providing executives results in economic terms places learning programs at the same level of accountability as other investments. These are terms senior leaders understand and appreciate.

2. **What are the implications of the gaps for business impact and ROI?**

This is our biggest challenge. If we don't step up to the issue, we could easily lose budget, support, and influence. We can no longer wait for executives to ask for this information. We must be proactive in providing it routinely and consistently. It can be done and it is being done by hundreds of learning and development organizations.

3. **What are the implications of 18 percent of executives setting the investment level based on the pay off they see from the investment?**

This is important because almost one-fifth of executives are basing funding on perceived payoff of the learning function. This may drastically alter the funding that is provided in the future. If a higher percentage of executives require this type of data, learning and development may be moving to a zero-based budgeting process. This will require showing the value of each program before the program is even funded.

Chapter 20—Using Evaluation Results

Knowledge Check: Measuring the Value of a New Hire On-Boarding Program

1. **For each of the following groups, what level of targeted results will you gather and share and what targeted decisions can be made from the results provided to each group?**

The Chain of Evidence is shared with everyone involved in the project in a summarized form so everyone knows the scope and intent of the project.

Below, the results from levels that each group will focus on and study are listed:

1. **Instructional designers and trainers**
   Level of results: Levels 1 and 2
   Targeted decisions:
   - Improving program development and delivery
   - Ensuring training is targeted to strategic goals

2. Training leaders and consultants

Level of results: Levels 3 and 4

Targeted decisions:

- Improving follow-up and reinforcement in to increase on-the-job application
- Improving business partnerships
- Reducing costs by trimming non-strategic training

3. Business supervisors and managers

Level of results: Levels 3 and 4

Targeted decisions:

- Improving decisions about training choices for direct reports
- Enhancing engagement of direct reports through support and accountability
- Improving performance of direct reports
- Improving department/division KPI metrics

4. Business executives

Level of results: Level 4

Targeted decisions:

- Communicating strategic objectives to focus training and reinforcement efforts
- Modeling and communicating the business partnership approach to training, performance, and strategy execution

Chapter 21—Implementing and Sustaining a Measurement and Evaluation Practice

Knowledge Check

2	Secure senior leader involvement and engagement.
5	Create and support a measurement community.
3	Develop measurement and evaluation processes.
1	Develop goals.
2	Select a subject matter expert to partner with.
4	Identify technology required to support data collection and communication.
5	Develop and implement required learning.
3	Integrate new processes with existing program design and development processes.
1	Develop specific and measurable outcomes.
4	Determine the impact on organizational structures.
2	Develop individual and organizational experience.
1	Identify what you want to avoid.
5	Develop roll-out plans and measurement criteria for each business unit.
3	Develop assessment processes.
4	Identify human resources required to support your strategy.
2	Follow through with concise and targeted communication.

Chapter 22—Selecting Technology to Support Evaluation

Musts and Wants

An objective is a must if you can answer yes to all three of these questions:

1. Is it mandatory (required)?
2. It is measurable (set limit)?
3. It is realistic (can be met)?

All other objectives are wants.

Chapter 23—Evaluating mLearning

Designing an mLearning Evaluation Strategy

Following the steps described in this chapter, how would you evaluate the mlearning taken by the nursery workers? How would you attempt to measure success of each of the business objectives?

Level 1

You want to know the participants' reaction to the training. Consider asking how helpful the mlearning was to understanding their job requirements and whether they would recommend using the same training next spring or developing comparable training for the fall season.

Level 2

Consider including "test your knowledge" questions throughout the mlearning units. Include questions regarding the consequences of violating the plant care schedule.

Level 3

Monitor the daily checklist as a measure of application of knowledge. Consider sending a brief survey that can be accessed on mobile devices to supervisors and employees. Focus the majority of the questions on evidence indicating employees have applied what they learned in the mlearning units. Be sure to include questions to supervisors regarding any midcourse corrections they deemed necessary. Corrections may be an indicator of barriers to application of learning. If corrections included customizing real time updates to daily checklists or other performance support tools, note the changes and application of the updated information. Monitor the supervisors' interim report to determine whether application data are reported. Also consider a follow-up survey to supervisors at the end of the spring season to identify how barriers were mitigated. These lessons learned may be incorporated in the fall training.

Level 4

Review the standard data collected regarding sales of perennials and fertilizers, annuals discarded due to poor condition, repeat customers, and customer satisfaction. Calculate the difference scores between the current spring season in each zone and the previous spring season in the same zone to determine whether the business objectives were met. Consider requiring supervisors to provide an estimate regarding how much changes in the key metrics can be attributed to the mlearning program.

Level 5

Calculate the cost of developing, delivering, and evaluating training—including any real time updates or customizations for individual employees throughout the spring season.

Calculate the cost of benefits (for example, increased sales, decreased waste).

Calculate the Benefits/Cost Ratio (BCR) by dividing the program benefits by the program costs.

Calculate the return-on-investment (ROI) by dividing the net program benefits by program costs and multiplying the result by 100.

Chapter 24—Evaluating Leadership Development: A Case Study

Knowledge Check

1. Work closely with the talent office to understand the program's design and intended outcomes and design the evaluation to align with them.
2. Understand the way in which the development of the 50 critical leaders is expected to result in the anticipated outcomes.
3. Identify the role of the leader's managers in the success of the initiative.
4. Ask the key stakeholders for their preferences regarding the type of data collected, timing, format of the results, type of reporting, and so forth.
5. Design an evaluation that addresses the intended outcomes as expressed by the talent office or other key stakeholders through the use of multiple methods (for example, interviews, retrospective 360-degree evaluations, and ROI studies) and multiple sources (for example, participants, managers, peers, direct reports, and customers).
6. Collect data at the time(s) when the outcomes are anticipated to become visible or detectable.
7. Build in ongoing communication opportunities for key stakeholders and plan specific sessions to discuss program implementation and progress to identify learning and understand the impact of the program.

Chapter 25—Evaluating a Global Sales Training Program

Calculate the ROI in Sales Training

Now that you have read the chapter, try your hand at calculating the ROI for a sales training program, given the following data. If:

- Sales increase an average of $1750 per week per employee.
- Profit margin is 2%.
- 46 employees are involved in the program and the evaluation
- Employees work 48 weeks per year
- The cost of the program for all 46 employees is $38,500

What is the ROI?

- $1750 \times .02 = \$35$ profit per week
- $35 (average profit increase) $\times$ 46 (number of employees) $\times$ 48 (number of weeks worked in one year) = \$77,280 in profit for one year
- ROI = [($77,280 – \$38,500)/\$38,500] $\times$ 100 = 100.7%

Chapter 26—Evaluating Technical Training—Basic Maintenance Course

Knowledge Check

1. **Who should be the stakeholders to develop an objective map for a program and when should the map be initially developed?**

   The stakeholders should include representatives from operations, the expected field group, the training organization, and an evaluator. An initial objective map should ideally be developed as soon as a business need is identified and then updated as the program design evolves.

2. **What was the method(s) to isolate the impact of the program in this study?**

   At least one method to isolate should be used in an impact study. In this case, two methods were used: participant and supervisor estimates and control versus experimental groups.

3. **In this study, the participants and the supervisors were asked the extent to which the performance objectives were met, how much of that success was due to the training and how confident they were of their ratings. Is it important that the ratings from the participants and the supervisors be the same or similar? Why or why not?**

   They should be similar because the similarity indicates true performance. If they vary a great deal it would indicate that the respondents are having a difficult time understanding what the performance is, or that there is some type of prejudice going on. Either way, the analyst does not know which set of metrics to use. Most often, the supervisor ratings are somewhat lower than the participants. The decision was made to use 15 percent as the maximum variance, meaning, if the difference in the scores was 15 percent or less, they were accepted as a measure of true performance.

4. **Do you believe the recommendations made by the task force were warranted?**

In this case, the results led to clear conclusions and the conclusions led to the recommendations. In some cases, the connections are not so clear and recommendations may be left to decision makers, such as the financial stakeholders. The Logic Map used here, helps the analysts (the representative task force) not jump to conclusions and draw unwarranted recommendations.

Chapter 27—Evaluating Traditional Training versus Computer Simulation Training for Leader Development

Knowledge Check

1. **The model used in *VLeader2007* is based on three dimensions predictive of successful leadership. What are the three dimensions used in the *VLeader2007* model?**

The three dimensions used in the *VLeader2007* model are power, tension, and ideas.

2. **What is an appropriate statistical test to determine if a change has occurred from the pretest assessment to the posttest assessment?**

The appropriate statistical test to determine if a change has occurred is to compare the means of the pre and post tests using a paired-sample t-test.

3. **Why is it important that the trainer determine that there are no statistically significant differences in satisfaction with the training experience in the two training groups?**

You do not want statistically significant differences in satisfaction because you do not want the learning results to be contaminated by a poor training experience. Because you want to determine the impact of the training program, bad implementation of the training could explain differences in training outcomes. Thus you must check to determine that all training groups were equally well satisfied with their experience.

✎ About the Editor

Patricia Pulliam Phillips is president and CEO of the ROI Institute, the leading source of ROI competency building, implementation support, networking, and research. A renowned expert in measurement and evaluation, she helps organizations implement the ROI methodology in countries around the world. Phillips teaches others to implement the ROI methodology through the ROI certification process as a facilitator for ASTD's ROI and Measuring and Evaluating Learning Workshops and as adjunct professor for graduate-level evaluation courses. She serves on numerous doctoral dissertation committees, assisting students as they develop their own research on measurement, evaluation, and ROI. In addition to editing this book, she authored Chapter 14, Converting Measures to Money, and Chapter 16, Calculating the ROI. She is author and co-author of a variety of books on the topics of measurement, evaluation, and ROI, including *Beyond Learning Objectives* (ASTD, 2008), *Show Me the Money* (Berrett-Koehler, 2007), and *The Value of Learning* (Pfeiffer, 2007). Phillips can be reached at patti@roiinstitute.net.

Index

A

Aaron, B. C., 38, 40, 173–187

accountability, 30

action planning

applications, 113

benefits, identifying intangible, 120

communicating, 112

data collection using, 31, 34

defined, 108–109

effectiveness of, 117

follow-up, 118, 119

how it works, 109, 110

integrate into ADDIE, 109, 111–112

knowledge check, 122–123

managers/supervisors, role of, 112

monetary value, determining, 114–117

objectives, identifying, 109, 111

participants, 112

peer/facilitator review of, 117–118

reporting results, 120–122

return-on-investment, calculating, 119–120, 121

role of, 113

teaching, 114

time needed for, 114

why use, 107–108

ADDIE, 1, 109, 111–112

Aldrich, C., 374

Angoff method, 80–81

Annulis, H. M., 15–28

application objectives, 22, 23

Ask.com, 193

ASTD Competency Model: Mapping the Future, 266

B

Balanced Scorecard, The (Kaplan and Norton), 247

basic maintenance course

background, 355–356

evaluation planning and methodology, 356–357, 364

knowledge check, 371

objectives, 356, 358–363

recommendations, 368, 370

results, 364–368, 369–370

benefit-cost ratio (BCR), 214–215

Block, P., 249

briefings, executive, 254

Brinkerhoff, R. O., 125–134, 298, 387–391, 323

Broad, M. L., 392–395

Broslawsky, T., 239–251

Burkett, H., 31, 34, 107–124

business requirement, defining, 6

C

Cardenas, J., 201–211

case studies, 32, 34–35, 241

central tendency measures, 150–152

Chain of Evidence, 273–274

Chi-square, 162

communication/reporting
audience, 245
case studies, value of, 241
Chain of Evidence, 273–274
credibility of program team, role of, 242
feedback, 248–249
format, 246, 247
implementation and, 288–289
importance of, 239–240
knowledge check, 250–251
media selection, 241, 246
plan, 242–244
reactions to, 250
reasons for, 244–245
results to management, 249
scorecards, 246–248
targeted, 241
testimonials, 242
timely, 240
unbiased, 242

competency skill assessments
benefits and pitfalls of, 12
needs assessment and, 13

condition, 19

conduct, 19

content validity, 76

control groups, 174, 175, 176–178

converting measures to monetary value
benefits to, 228
databases, 193, 196
estimating, 194, 195, 196
experts, 193, 196
guidelines, 198
historical costs, 193, 196
importance of, 189–191
intangible measures, 196, 197
knowledge check, 198–199
standard values, 191–193, 196

statistics, 193, 196
steps for, 194–195, 197
techniques for, 191–195, 196

Cornell University, School of Hospitality Management, 193

Coscarelli, W. C., 73–84

costs, 7, 8
analysis, 38–39, 41
categories, 203–207
estimating, 207, 208–209
estimating implementation, 226–227
estimating planning, 226
fully loaded, 202
identifying, 201–211
importance of, 201–202
knowledge check, 210
pressure to disclose, 202
prorated versus direct, 203
sources of, 203
without benefits, 202

Crane, K., 165–171

criterion, 18

criterion-referenced tests (CRTs)
cut-off scores, 79–81
designing, 73–74
guidelines for creating, 82–83
knowledge check, 81–82
length of, 77–79
model for, 74, 75
validity, 76–77
value of, 74
weighting items, 78–79

current state, identifying, 7

cut-off scores, 79–81

D

data, hard and soft, 23

data analysis
advantages and disadvantages of, 39, 40–41
converting measures to monetary value, 189–199

data analysis *(continued)*
    costs, identifying, 201–211
    costs/financial, 38–39, 41
    isolating effects, 38, 40, 173–187
    key questions, 39, 41
    planning, 35, 42–43
    qualitative, 38, 40, 165–171
    return-on-investment, calculating, 38–39,
        40–41, 213–222
    statistics, 38, 40, 149–164
    type to use, 147
databases, 193, 196
data collection
    action planning, 31, 34, 107–124
    advantages and disadvantages of, 32, 33–35
    case studies, 32, 34–35
    criterion-referenced tests, 73–84
    focus groups, 31, 34, 97–106
    interviews, 31, 33–34, 85–95
    key questions, 32
    multiple methods, using, 89
    performance records, 32, 35, 135–145
    planning, 30
    planning template, 32, 36–37
    success case method, 125–134
    surveys and questionnaires, 31, 33, 55–72
    tests, 31, 33
Davis, W. R., 21
decision making, 30
de Rosairo, N., 35
descriptive statistics, 150
DeTuncq, T. H., 355–372
Dugas, S., 18

E
Ebscohost, 193
Edwards, L. A., 97–106
estimating, 181–184
    converting measures to monetary value,
        194–195, 196
    forecast analysis, 174, 175, 180–181

estimating future value
    implementation costs and benefits, 226–227
    knowledge check, 234
    planning costs and benefits, 226
    rationale for, 224
    return-on-investment, 226–232
    statistical analysis, 232
    systems modeling, 232–233
    timing (continuum), 224–227
    tips, 233–234
    utility analysis, 233
evaluation. *See* measurement and evaluation
evaluation planning. *See* planning
executive briefings, 254
executive interviews, 254
Executive Leadership Institute (ELI) program.
    See leadership development case example
executive surveys, 254
executive viewpoints
    application measures, 259–260
    impact and return-on-investment measures,
        260–262
    importance of, 253, 254
    influencing, 262–263
    investment level, 255
    knowledge check, 263
    learning measures, 258
    methods for obtaining, 254
    metrics and, 255–256
    reaction data, 257

F
feedback, 248–249
financial analysis, 38–39, 40–41
Fischer, D. H., 53
Fitz-enz, J., 396–399
Flawless Consulting (Block), 249
focus groups
    assessment of, 105
    benefits and pitfalls of, 12
    conducting the session, 104

focus groups *(continued)*
    data collection using, 31, 34
    facilitator, selecting, 98, 99
    group interview questions, 99–100
    importance of, 97–98
    Ishikawa diagrams, 100–101, 102
    knowledge checks, 105
    needs assessment and, 12
    nominal group technique, 101–104
    participants, selecting, 98
    session format, 98–99
    solutions, identifying, 105
Ford, D. J., 29–51
forecast analysis, 174, 175, 180–181
    See also estimating future value

G
Gadd, R., 307–319
Galwey, 298
gap analysis, 6
    between current state and business
        requirements, 7
Gaudet, C. H., 15–28
global programs
    background, 337–338
    business impact, 350
    business tools, 341, 343
    content and design of, 341, 342
    converting measures to monetary value,
        350–351
    isolation methods, 350
    knowledge check, 353
    project team and steering committee, 341
    recommendations, 353
    results, 345, 350
    return-on-investment methodology, 343–353
    scorecard, 352–353
    value-based selling and pricing, 338–339
Google, 193
Grabowski, J., 159
Greenberg, I., 151, 157

H
Historians' Fallacies (Fischer), 53
Hoole, E., 321–336
Hubble, C., 55–72
human resources, implementation and, 290–291

I
Iannetta, J., 150
impact objectives, 22–23
impact studies, 254
implementation
    advocacy and support, 285
    checklist, 292
    communication, 288–289
    experience, use of individual, 285–286
    experts, use of subject matter, 286–287
    goals, 284
    human resources and, 290–291
    identifying what to avoid, 284
    knowledge check, 293
    outcomes, developing, 285
    performance improvement, 289–290
    plan, 292
    senior leadership, role of, 287–288
    technology and, 291
inferential statistics, 150
input objectives, 19–20
interviewers, selecting and training, 92–93
interviews
    advantages and disadvantages of, 11, 88
    assessment of, 93–94
    data collection using, 31, 33–34
    evaluation of training using, 87
    executive, 254
    focus group, 99–100
    guidelines for planning and conducting,
        89–94
    knowledge check, 94
    needs assessment and, 10–11
    objectives, 89
    pilot testing, 92

interviews *(continued)*
    protocol, sample, 91–92
    questions, writing, 90
    schedules, 92
    structured versus unstructured, 86–87
Ishikawa diagrams, 100–101, 102
isolating effects
    chain of impact, 175–176
    control groups, 174, 175, 176–178
    data analysis and, 38, 40
    estimating, 181–184
    forecast analysis, 174, 175, 180–181
    importance of, 173–174
    knowledge check, 185
    techniques for, 174–175
    trend line analysis, 174, 175, 179–180

J
job relatedness, 76–77

K
Kaplan, R., 247
Kaufman, R., 400–403
Kirkpatrick, D. L., 404–408
Kirkpatrick, J. D., 265–282
Kirkpatrick, W. K., 265–282
Kirkpatrick four levels, 266–267, 309–310, 323
KnowledgeAdvisors, 298
knowledge checks
    action planning and, 122–123
    basic maintenance course and, 371
    communication/reporting and, 250–251
    converting measures to monetary value and, 198–199
    costs, identifying, 210
    criterion-referenced tests and, 81–82
    estimating future value and, 234
    executive viewpoints and, 263
    focus groups and, 105
    global program and, 353
    implementation and, 293

    interviews and, 94
    isolating effects and, 185
    leadership development and, 335
    mLearning and, 318
    objectives and, 27
    performance records and, 143–144
    planning evaluations and, 50
    qualitative analysis and, 170
    questionnaires and surveys and, 70–71
    results and, 280–281
    return-on-investment, calculating and, 221
    simulation training and, 383
    statistical analysis and, 163–164
    Success Case Method and, 133
    technology and, 304
kurtosis (skewed data), 159–161

L
leadership development case example
    background, 322–323
    benchmarking/best practices, 330–331
    knowledge check, 335
    multiple methods, 324–329
    outcomes defined, 323–324
    participant survey, 326–329
    results, presenting, 332–334
Learn.com, 299–300
learning and development
    See also mLearning
    objectives, 20–21
    opportunities for, viii–viv
legal defensibility of tests, 76–77

M
Manalu, R. H., 135–145
Mankin, D., 30
Marrelli, A. F., 85–95
Martineau, J., 321–336
McLinden, D., 223–236
mean, 150–152

measurement and evaluation
    benefits, xiv–xv
    challenges, vii–viii, xii–xiv
    need for, xi
    steps, xv–xvii
    trends, viii
median, 150–152
mLearning
    defined, 307–308
    Kirkpatrick levels, 309–310
    knowledge check, 318
    role of, 308–309
    traditional training versus, 310–316
Metrics That Matter, 298
Microsoft Excel, 153, 154, 157, 161
Minitab, 153
mode, 150–152
monetary value. *See* converting measures to
    monetary value
Mooney, T. P., 125–134
Mussoline, G. R., 149–164

N

needs assessment
    business requirement, defining, 6
    costs, 7, 8
    current state, identifying, 7
    gap analysis, 6
    gaps between current state and business
    requirements, 7
    importance of, 3
    key questions, 4–5
    methods for, 10–13
    order taker versus the consultant, 4–5
    solutions, identifying, 7–8
    steps, list of, 6
    training, value of, 8–10
net present value (NPV), 217–218
nominal group technique, 101–104
norm-referenced tests (NRTs), 73–74
Norton, D., 247

O

objectives
    application, 22, 23
    constructing, 16, 18–19
    impact, 22–23
    importance of, 15
    input, 19–20
    interview, 89
    knowledge check, 27
    learning, 20–21
    levels of, 16, 17, 19–27
    meaning and value of, 16
    reaction, 20, 21
    return-on-investment, 23–24
    SMART, 16, 18
    summary of, 25
    V-model, 26

P

payback period (PP), 216–217
performance improvement, 289–290
performance records
    converting measures to usable data, 142–143
    data collection and, 32, 35
    data sources, 141
    importance of, 135–136
    knowledge check, 143–144
    linking with business measures, 136–140
    records, identifying appropriate, 140–141
Phillips, J. J., 253–264, 409–414
Phillips, P. P., 189–199, 213–222
Pierre, C., 63
planning
    See also action planning
    evaluation project, 29–51
    importance of, 29–30
    needs assessment, 3–14
    objectives, developing, 15–28
    tool, comprehensive, 44–48
Provencher, D., 192

Q

qualitative analysis
  data analysis and, 38, 40
  importance of, 165–166
  knowledge check, 170
  quantitative versus, 166
  steps, 168–169
  techniques, 167–168
  validity and, 167, 168
quantitative analysis, 166
questionnaires and surveys
  accuracy, 64–65
  assessment of, 65
  benefits and pitfalls of, 11
  body of, 60–61
  conclusion of, 61
  content, creating, 57, 60–63
  data collection using, 31, 33
  distribution of, 65–70
  drafting, 63–64
  effectiveness, optimizing, 63–65
  executive, 254
  feedback, 64
  follow-up, 68–69
  functionality, 64
  introduction to, 57, 60
  knowledge check, 70–71
  needs assessment and, 10
  planning, 56–57, 58–60
  purpose of, 55
  response rates, 65–66, 67
  sample size, 65, 66
  scope of, 56–57
  steps in developing, 55–56
  structure of, 57
  testing of, 64–65
questions
  close-ended, 62, 86
  finalizing, 61, 63
  intent, 61
  open-ended, 62, 86–87
  rank or order, 62
  rating, 63
  types of, 61, 62–63
  writing interview, 90

R

Ray, R., 385–386
reaction objectives, 20, 21
reporting. *See* communication/reporting
results
  for business executives, 271–272, 273,
    276–277
  for business supervisors and managers, 271,
    273, 275–276
  Chain of Evidence, 273–274
  communicating, 273–274
  example of, 278–280
  for instructional designers and trainers, 269,
    273, 275
  Kirkpatrick levels, 266–267, 309–310
  knowledge check, 280–281
  purpose of, 266
  for training leaders and consultants,
    269–271, 273
  for training participants, 268–269, 273, 274
  types of, 267–268
return-on-investment (ROI), 23–24
  benefit-cost ratio, 214–215
  benefits, defining, 228–229
  calculating, 38–39, 40–41, 119–120, 121,
    213–222
  chain of impact, 220
  converting benefits to monetary values, 228
  costs, defining, 227
  defined, 215–216
  example of forecasting, 230–232
  forecasting, 226–232
  importance of, 213–214
  knowledge check, 222
  net present value, 217–218
  payback period, 216–217

return-on-investment (ROI) *(continued)*
programs suitable for, 220–221
sensitivity analysis, 230
targets, 218
Robinson, D. G., 415–419
Rothwell, W. J., 420–426

S

sample variance, 153
Scherwinski, M., 70
Schirmer, F. C., 337–354
scorecards, 246–248
Sensei/ROI, 298–299
sensitivity analysis, 230
7-Eleven, Field Consultant Certification
Training, 278–280
Shrock, S. A., 73–84
Simulations and the Future of Learning
(Aldrich), 374
simulation training. *See* training, simulation
versus traditional
SMART objectives, 16, 18
Smith, K., 295–305
solutions, identifying, 7–8
SPSS, 153
standard variation, 153
statistical analysis
central tendency measures, 150–152
Chi-square, 162
converting measures to monetary value, 193,
196
data analysis and, 38, 40
descriptive, 150
estimating future value, 232
importance of, 149–150
inferential, 150
interpreting and understanding data,
153–158
knowledge check, 163–164
kurtosis (skewed data), 159–161

t-test, 162
variation measures, 152–153
Stawarski, C. A., 307–319
Stewart, A. C., 373–384
structured versus unstructured interviews,
86–87
Success Case Method (SCM), 298, 323
applications, 125–126
business case, 127–128
knowledge check, 133
mean or average effect, 128
training realities, 127–133
SurveyGizmo, 325
SurveyMonkey, 297, 325
surveys. *See* questionnaires and surveys
systems modeling, 232–233

T

technology
decision-making tips, 296–297, 300–304
examples, 300
implementation and, 291
KnowledgeAdvisors, 298
knowledge check, 304
Learn.com, 299–300
objectives, classifying, 301
Sensei/ROI, 298–299
SurveyMonkey, 297
tests, data collection using, 31, 33
training
effective versus effectiveness, 267–268
realities, 127–133
success, 126–127
value of, 8–10
training, comparison of simulation versus
traditional
data collection, 376
differences in leader effectiveness, 382
differences in perception of leadership,
379–381

training, comparison of simulation versus (*continued*)

    knowledge check, 383

    outcomes, 376–377

    research method use, 375

    results, 377–378

    VL2007, 374–375

trend line analysis, 174, 175, 179–180

t-test, 162

U

unstructured versus structured interviews, 86–87

utility analysis, 233

V

validity

    approaches to managing, 168

    qualitative analysis and, 167

    test, 76–77

Vance, D., 22

variation measures, 152–153

VL2007, 374–375

V-model, 26

W

Wallace, D., 283–294

Williams, J. A., 373–384

Willmore, J., 41

Y

Yahoo!, 193

Z

Zoomerang, 325

Zuniga, L., 3–14

THE *ASTD* MISSION:

Through exceptional learning and performance, we create a world that works better.

The American Society for Training & Development provides world-class professional development opportunities, content, networking, and resources for workplace learning and performance professionals.

Dedicated to helping members increase their relevance, enhance their skills, and align learning to business results, ASTD sets the standard for best practices within the profession.

The society is recognized for shaping global discussions on workforce development and providing the tools to demonstrate the impact of learning on the organizational bottom line. ASTD represents the profession's interests to corporate executives, policy makers, academic leaders, small business owners, and consultants through world-class content, convening opportunities, professional development, and awards and recognition.

Resources
- *T+D (Training + Development)* Magazine
- ASTD Press
- Industry Newsletters
- Research and Benchmarking
- Representation to Policy Makers

Professional Development
- Certificate Programs
- Conferences and Workshops
- Online Learning
- CPLP™ Certification through the ASTD Certification Institute
- Career Center and Job Bank

Networking
- Local Chapters
- Online Communities
- ASTD Connect
- Benchmarking Forum
- Learning Executives Network

Awards and Best Practices
- ASTD Best Awards
- Excellence in Practice Awards
- E-Learning Courseware Certification (ECC) through the ASTD Certification Institute

Learn more about ASTD at www.astd.org.
1.800.628.2783 (U.S.) or 1.703.683.8100
customercare@astd.org

080615.31410